STATES, SCARCITY, AND CIVIL STRIFE
IN THE DEVELOPING WORLD

STATES, SCARCITY, AND CIVIL STRIFE IN THE DEVELOPING WORLD

Colin H. Kahl

PRINCETON UNIVERSITY PRESS   PRINCETON AND OXFORD

Second printing, and first paperback printing, 2008
Paperback ISBN: 978-0-691-13835-0

The Library of Congress has cataloged the cloth edition of this book as follows

Kahl, Colin H., 1971–
States, scarcity, and civil strife in the developing world / Colin H. Kahl.
p.   cm.
Originally presented as the author's thesis (Ph.D.—Columbia University, 2000).
Includes bibliographical references and index.
ISBN 0-691-12406-X (cloth : alk. paper)
1. Political violence—Developing countries. 2. Political violence—Philippines.
3. Political violence—Kenya. 4. Developing countries—Economic conditions.
5. Developing countries—Social conditions. 6. Developing countries—
Population—Environmental aspects. I. Title.
JC328.65.D48K34   2006
303.6'09172'4—dc22   2005047653

British Library Cataloging-in-Publication Data is available

This book has been composed in Palatino

Printed on acid-free paper. ∞

press.princeton.edu

Printed in the United States of America

10   9   8   7   6   5   4   3   2

To my mother, Margaret Hackett ————————————

Contents

Illustrations

Figures

Maps

Tables

Acknowledgments

THERE ARE MANY people and institutions I would like to thank. First and foremost, I express my gratitude to my advisers at Columbia University, Robert Jervis and Jack Snyder. Their critical insights helped guide the early stages of this project, and their mentoring was central to my preparation as a political scientist. I also thank Thomas Homer-Dixon of the University of Toronto and Jack Goldstone of George Mason University. Their scholarly work provides the foundation for much of my thinking on population and environmental matters, and they have both been kind enough to offer me substantial amounts of advice and constructive criticism over the years. Some of the ideas presented in chapter 1 appear in my article "Demographic Change, Natural Resources, and Violence," *Journal of International Affairs* 56, no. 1 (fall 2002): 257–82; and chapter 4 draws, in part, on my article "Population Growth, Environmental Degradation, and State-Sponsored Violence: The Case of Kenya, 1991–93," *International Security* 23, no.2 (fall 1998): 80–119. I am indebted to the reviewers and editors at *Journal of International Affairs* and *International Security* for their helpful comments and suggestions. A host of others also read and commented on my work, including Richard Betts, Nazli Choucri, Tim Crawford, Geoff Dabelko, Mike Desch, David Dessler, David Downie, Bud Duvall, Page Fortna, Frank Gavin, Peter Gleick, Eugene Gholz, Sam Huntington, Robert Keohane, Marc Levy, Ronnie Lipschutz, Daryl Press, Dick Price, Aaron Seeskin, Kathryn Sikkink, Jon Western, Leslie Vinjamuri, and Marcia Wright. Thank you all. Finally, I thank all my colleagues and students at the University of Minnesota for their patience and encouragement.

For assisting my research, I am indebted to the helpful librarians at Columbia University, Harvard University, the University of Michigan, the University of Minnesota, the World Resources Institute, the United States Agency for International Development, and the Library of Congress. I also thank Chip Barber of the World Resources Institute for his help in acquiring important documents on the Philippines.

This book could not have been completed without financial assistance from a number of institutions. For their generous financial support, I thank the United States Institute of Peace, Harvard's John M. Olin Institute for Strategic Studies, the Political Science Department, Institute of War and Peace Studies, and Center for International Earth Science Information Network at Columbia University, and the Department of Political Science at the University of Minnesota.

Last but not least, I would like to thank Biza Repko, my mother Margaret Hackett, and my brother Ian Kahl. Without their love, friendship, and support, this project would not have been possible.

Abbreviations

AFP   Armed Forces of the Philippines
ASALs   arid and semiarid lands
ASEAN   Association of Southeast Asian Nations
CBR   crude birth rate
CCCC   Citizens Coalition for Constitutional Change
CDR   crude death rate
CHDF   Civilian Home Defense Forces
CPP   Communist Party of the Philippines
DENR   Department of Environment and Natural Resources
DES   demographic and environmental stress
DP   Democratic Party of Kenya
DRC   Democratic Republic of Congo
ECK   Electoral Commission of Kenya
EZLN   Ejército Zapatista de Liberación Nacional
FAR   Forces Armées Rwandaise
FAO   Food and Agriculture Organization
FORD   Forum for the Restoration of Democracy
IMF   International Monetary Fund
IPCC   Intergovernmental Panel on Climate Change
IPPG   Inter-Parties Parliamentary Group
KADU   Kenya African Democratic Union
KANU   Kenya African National Union
KBC   Kenya Broadcasting Company
KHRC   Kenya Human Rights Commission
KPU   Kenya People's Union
LDP   Liberal Democratic Party
MRND   Mouvement Republicain National pour le Developpement
NARC   National Alliance Rainbow Coalition
NAK   National Alliance of Kenya
NCCK   National Council of Churches of Kenya
NCA   National Convention Assembly
NCEC   National Convention Executive Committee
NDF   National Democratic Front
NDP   National Development Party
NEDA   National Economic and Development Authority
NEMU   National Election Monitoring Unit
NPA   New People's Army

PNG   Papua New Guinea
PRI   Partido Revolucionario Institucional
RAM   Reform the Armed Forces Movement
RPF   Rwandan Patriotic Front
RUF   Revolutionary United Front
RTZ   Rio Tinto Zinc
SNM   Somali National Movement
SPM   Somali Patriotic Movement
TFR   total fertility rate
UNDP   United Nations Development Programme
UNPD   United Nations Population Division
USAID   United States Agency for International Development
USC   United Somali Congress
WWF   World Wildlife Fund

STATES, SCARCITY, AND CIVIL STRIFE
IN THE DEVELOPING WORLD

1

Plight, Plunder, and Political Ecology

CIVIL STRIFE in the developing world represents perhaps the greatest
international security challenge of the early twenty-first century.[1]
Three-quarters of all wars since 1945 have been within countries rather
than between them, and the vast majority of these conflicts have occurred in the world's poorest nations.[2] Wars and other violent conflicts
have killed some 40 million people since 1945, and as many people
may have died as a result of civil strife since 1980 as were killed in the
First World War.[3] Although the number of internal wars peaked in the
early 1990s and has been declining slowly ever since, they remain a
scourge on humanity. Armed conflicts have crippled the prospect for
a better life in many developing countries, especially in sub-Saharan
Africa and parts of Asia, by destroying essential infrastructure, deci-
mating social trust, encouraging human and capital flight, exacerbating food shortages, spreading disease, and diverting precious financial
resources toward military spending.[4]

Compounding matters further, the damaging effects of civil strife
rarely remain confined within the afflicted countries. In the past decade alone tens of millions of refugees have spilled across borders, producing significant socioeconomic and health problems in neighboring
areas. Instability has also rippled outward as a consequence of cross-
border incursions by rebel groups, trafficking in arms and persons, dis-
ruptions in trade, and damage done to the reputation of entire regions
in the eyes of investors. Globally, war-torn countries have become ha-
vens and recruiting grounds for international terrorist networks, organized crime, and drug traffickers.[5] Indeed, the events of September 11,
2001, illustrate how small the world has become and how vulnerable
even superpowers are to rising grievances and instabilities in the developing world.

Although there is no single cause of civil strife, a growing number
of scholars and practitioners suggest that rapid population growth,
environmental degradation, and competition over natural resources
play important causal roles in many of these conflicts. Several high-
profile theoretical works and case studies suggest that demographic
and environmental pressures can, under certain conditions, contribute
to civil strife.[6] Moreover, an emergent body of cross-national research

supports this conclusion. Recent quantitative studies analyzing the correlates of internal wars from the 1950s to the present indicate that population size and population density are significant risk factors.[7] Another important study points out that countries at earlier stages of the demographic transition (when birth rates and death rates are both high), as well as those with large numbers of young adults and rapid rates of urbanization, have been much more prone to civil strife over the past three decades.[8] In terms of environmental factors, recent statistical work indicates that countries highly dependent on natural resources,[9] as well as those experiencing high rates of deforestation and soil degradation, and low per capita availability of arable land and freshwater, have higher-than-average risks of falling into turmoil.[10] In short, many researchers now conclude that it is impossible to fully understand the patterns and dynamics of contemporary civil strife without considering the demographic and environmental dimensions of these conflicts.

Outside the ivory tower, numerous policy makers and commentators have reached similar conclusions. In 1991, for example, the then NATO secretary general Manfred Worner argued that "the immense conflict potential building up in the Third World, characterized by growing wealth differentials, an exploding demography, climate shifts and the prospect for environmental disaster, combined with the resource conflicts of the future, cannot be left out of our security calculations."[11] Three years later, in an infamous *Atlantic Monthly* article entitled "The Coming Anarchy," the influential journalist Robert Kaplan went so far as to suggest that the environment was "*the* national security issue of the early twenty-first century. The political and strategic impact of surging population, spreading disease, deforestation and soil erosion, water depletion, air pollution, and, possibly, rising sea levels in critical, overcrowded regions . . . will be the core foreign policy challenge from which most others will ultimately emanate."[12] Echoing these sentiments, Nafis Sadik, the former executive director of the United Nations Population Fund, wrote in 1998:

> Many features of today's or very recent conflicts—whether in the Balkans, Afghanistan, the Caucasus, Rwanda, Somalia, Zaire, or elsewhere—are all-too-familiar . . . namely ethnic, religious, and economic. However, there are other features and signs which are much less familiar . . . Most alarming among these is the rapid growth of the world's human population and the implications this may have for global stability and security. . . .
>
> Social and environmental change . . . is taking place on a scale that has never been witnessed before . . . To cope with these changes, governments

need resources and capabilities which, in all too many cases, fall seriously short of what are available . . . If support for the most disadvantaged developing countries (and there are many in or near that position) is not forthcoming in the years ahead, it seems likely that instability and disorder will be experienced on a much larger scale than they have even today.[13]

This view has gained traction in Washington as well. Throughout much of the 1990s the National Security Strategy (NSS) of the United States referred to demographic and environmental pressures as threats to both the stability of developing countries and, ultimately, America's national interests. In the 1996 NSS, for example, the Clinton administration stated:

America's security imperatives . . . have fundamentally changed. The central security challenge of the past half century—the threat of communist expansion—is gone. The dangers we face today are more diverse. . . . [L]arge-scale environmental degradation, exacerbated by rapid population growth, threatens to undermine political stability in many countries and regions.[14]

In 2000 the U.S. National Intelligence Council's *Global Trends 2015* report included an analysis of demographic and environmental trends as part of its discussion of the possible causes of internal conflict. Commenting on the report, the *New York Times* suggested that it was indicative of a growing awareness in Washington that "issues like the availability of water and food, changes in population and the spread of information and disease will increasingly affect the security of the United States."[15]

In many ways, of course, all this changed after 9/11. Indeed, the Bush administration's 2002 NSS is illustrative of the fact that the security focus of the U.S. government has shifted almost entirely to the twin menaces posed by terrorism and weapons of mass destruction.[16] Yet even in the Bush administration, demographic and environmental challenges have not completely fallen off the radar screen. In a July 2002 speech, for example, Secretary of State Colin Powell declared:

Sustainable development is a compelling moral and humanitarian issue. But sustainable development is also a security imperative. Poverty, destruction of the environment and despair are destroyers of people, of societies, of nations, a cause of instability as an unholy trinity than can destabilize countries and destabilize entire regions.[17]

More recently an October 2003 report commissioned by the Pentagon's Office of Net Assessment to study the security implications of future climate change concluded:

There is substantial evidence that significant global warming will occur during the 21st century . . . [and] the result could be a significant drop in the
human carrying capacity of the Earth's environment. . . .

   As global and local carrying capacities are reduced, tensions could mount
around the world. . . .

   . . . Because of the potentially dire consequences, the risk of abrupt climate
change . . . should be elevated beyond a scientific debate to a U.S. national
security concern.[18]

Do population and environmental pressures actually put countries
at higher risk of experiencing civil strife? Although current research
suggests a possible correlation, and many scholars and policy makers
assert a causal relationship, the causal mechanisms linking demographic and environmental pressures to civil strife are still poorly understood. Existing studies on the subject point to a number of important dynamics, but several crucial causal pathways and interactions
with social and political variables are ignored. This book seeks to fill
the explanatory gap and thereby enhance our understanding of the
population–environment–civil strife connection. Toward this end it examines both the degree to which demographic and environmental
pressures can be said to cause civil strife in developing countries, and
the underlying dynamics and processes involved in this relationship.
Moreover, in a significant departure from much of the existing literature, the book takes a careful look at the social and political factors that
exacerbate, or mitigate, the potential for violent conflict.

The goal of this chapter is to lay the foundation for the theoretical
and empirical core of the book by taking stock of the current state of
our knowledge. The following sections outline arguments advanced
by three distinct schools of thought—neo-Malthusianism, neoclassical
economics, and political ecology—and point to their limitations.

The Neo-Malthusian Perspective

Neo-Malthusians work broadly within the intellectual tradition of the
Reverend Thomas Malthus, whose famous 1798 treatise, *An Essay on
the Principles of Population*, argued that exponential population growth
would eventually outpace the ability of the planet to provide for
human needs.[19] In the contemporary period neo-Malthusians argue
that enormous demographic and economic changes have combined to
place severe pressures on both the natural environment and the
world's poor, lowering the quality of life for millions and threatening
the political stability of many developing countries.

Pressures on the Planet, Pressures on the Poor

The past century witnessed unprecedented population growth, economic development, and environmental stress, changes that continue to this day. From 1900 to 2000 world population grew from 1.6 billion to 6.1 billion. Since 1950 alone 3.5 billion people have been added to the planet, with 85 percent of this increase occurring in developing and transition countries.[20] Worldwide population growth rates peaked in the late 1960s at around 2 percent a year, but the current rate of 1.2 percent still represents a net addition of 77 million people per year. The differential population growth rates of rich and poor countries have also become more pronounced. The current annual rate in high-income countries is 0.25 percent compared to 1.46 percent for developing countries as a whole. Moreover, within the subset of the forty-nine *least* developed countries the annual rate is currently 2.4 percent.[21]

The global economy has also experienced tremendous growth over the past century. Estimates vary, but the global economy most likely increased twenty to forty times its 1900 level by 2000. The tempo of change has been especially pronounced since the end of the Second World War; between 1950 and 2002 the global economy grew from 6.7 trillion to 48 trillion.[22] This incredible economic expansion occurred during a time of accelerating globalization and, especially since the 1980s, rising faith in the power of markets and privatization. Economic growth, globalization, and the harnessing of market forces have allowed for average living standards to advance faster than world population growth, improving the quality of life for billions. Nevertheless, the benefits of economic growth and globalization have been unevenly distributed within and across countries and regions.[23]

In the 1990s, for example, average economic growth per capita was less than 3 percent (the threshold needed to double incomes in a generation given constant rates of inequality) in 125 developing and transition economies, and 54 of these countries were actually poorer in 2000 than in 1990.[24] More than 1.2 billion people currently live in extreme poverty, defined as an income of less than $1 a day, and a total of 2.8 billion (more than half the population of the developing world) live on less than $2 a day. Although the proportion of people suffering from extreme poverty fell from 30 percent to 23 percent during the 1990s, the absolute number only fell by 123 million because of a 15 percent increase in the population of low- and middle-income countries. Driving most of this progress was China; excluding China, the total number of extremely poor people worldwide *increased* by 28 million, and thirty-seven of sixty-seven countries with data saw poverty rates increase in the 1990s. Worst off was sub-Saharan Africa, where per capita income fell by 5 percent and 74 million additional people descended into extreme poverty (producing a regional total of 404 million living on less than $1 a day in 1999). Other key indexes of human welfare also reveal a similar pattern: overall progress but also numerous countries falling further behind. Over the past decade thirty-four countries had lower life expectancy, twenty-one had a larger portion of people hungry, and fourteen had more children dying before age five.[25]

This pattern is further reflected in widening gaps between rich and poor. In 1960 the ratio between the GDP per capita in the twenty richest and twenty poorest countries was 18 to 1; in 1995 the ratio was 37 to 1.[26] Between 1980 and the late 1990s inequality also increased *within* 33 of 66 countries for which adequate data are available. All told, the richest 5 percent of the world's people now receive 114 times the income of the poorest 5 percent, and the richest 1 percent receive as much as the poorest 57 percent. Non-income measures tell a similar story. A decade ago children under five were nineteen times more likely to die in sub-Saharan Africa than in rich countries, but they are now twenty-six times more likely. Indeed, Latin America and the Carribbean were the only parts of the developing world where disparities in infant mortality compared to rich countries did not widen in the 1990s.[27]

Rapid demographic and economic change over the past century have placed severe and accelerating pressures on natural resources and planetary life-support systems. The traditional Malthusian notion that exponential population growth alone drives strains on the environment has long been refuted; no serious thinkers, including neo-Malthusians, now maintain that human-induced environmental changes are a mere function of numbers. Rather, neo-Malthusians argue that the relationship between population growth and the environment is mediated by consumption habits, and by the technologies used to extract natural resources and provide goods and services.

Neo-Malthusians contend that resource depletion and environmental degradation result from the interaction between population growth, extreme wealth, and extreme poverty. The material intensive and pollution-laden consumption habits and production activities of high-income countries are responsible for most of the world's greenhouse gases, solid and hazardous waste, and other environmental pollution. High-income countries also generate a disproportionate amount of the global demand for both nonrenewable resources (e.g., fossil fuels and non-fuel minerals) and certain products from renewable resources (e.g., grain, meat, fish, tropical hardwoods, and products from endangered species).[28]

Although consumption and production activities by rich countries may be the primary drivers of global environmental challenges, poverty and inequality within developing countries with fast-growing populations have placed significant burdens on local environments, especially on arable land, freshwater, forests, and fisheries. Impoverished individuals in developing countries frequently live in the most fragile ecological areas and are often driven to overexploit croplands, pastures, water resources, forests, and fisheries in order to eke out a living. Many have been forced to migrate to marginal areas because of overcrowding on better land. In the past fifty years the number of people living on fragile lands in developing countries doubled to 1.3 billion,[29] and rural population growth remains higher than average in countries with 30 percent or more of their population on fragile land. Fragile ecological areas, which represent 73 percent of the Earth's land surface, have very limited ability to sustain high population densities and are particularly vulnerable to degradation, erosion, flooding, fires, landslides, and climatic change.[30]

Numerous signs suggest that the combined effects of unsustainable consumption, population growth, and extreme poverty are taking their toll on the environment. More natural resources have been consumed since the end of the Second World War than in all human history to that point.[31] The consumption of nonrenewable resources has significantly increased, although it has risen at a slower rate than population and economic growth as a result of changes in technology. The global consumption of fossil fuels (which account for 77 percent of all energy use) in 2003 was 4.7 times the level it was in 1950.[32] High-income countries consume more than half of all commercial energy, and per capita energy consumption is five times greater than in developing countries.[33] In terms of non-fuel minerals, 9.6 billion tons of marketable minerals (e.g., copper, diamonds, gold) were extracted in 1999, almost twice as much as in 1970. And, once again, high-income countries account for the majority of mineral demand.[34]

In terms of renewable resources, the World Wildlife Fund (WWF) has recently calculated humanity's "ecological footprint" by comparing renewable resource consumption to an estimate of nature's biological productive capacity. A country's ecological footprint represents the total area—measured in standardized global hectares (ha) of biologically productive land and water—required to produce the renewable resources consumed and to assimilate the wastes generated by human activities. In 1999 each person on the planet demanded an average of 2.3 global ha, but countries varied widely in their footprint. On average, high-income countries demanded 6.5 biologically productive ha per person compared to 2 ha for middle-income countries and 0.8 ha for low-income countries. All told, the global footprint in 1999 amounted to 13.7 billion biologically productive ha, exceeding the 11.4

billion ha estimated to exist by about 20 percent. While the ecological footprint approach is only a partial measure of the impact humanity is placing on nature, it does suggest an unsustainable rate of consumption of renewable resources over the long run. Indeed, the WWF calculates that humanity has been running an ecological deficit with the Earth since the 1980s.[35]

This conclusion is reinforced by signs of growing depletion and degradation of renewable resources. Worldwide, 23 percent of all cropland, pasture, forest, and woodland (totaling 2 billion ha) have been affected by soil degradation since the 1950s, impacting the livelihoods of perhaps 1 billion people. Of these lands, about 16 percent are so severely degraded that the change is too costly to reduce, 46 percent are moderately degraded, and 39 percent are lightly degraded.[36] Deforestation has also been rapid over the past century. There were 5 billion ha of forested area worldwide at the beginning of the twentieth century; now there are less than 4 billion ha. One-fifth of all tropical forests have been cleared since 1960, with the bulk of this deforestation occurring in developing countries. In the 1990s alone low-income countries lost 8 percent of their forested area as a result of global and local demand for timber, the conversion of forests into large-scale ranching and plantations, and the expansion of subsistence agriculture.[37]

Land resources are not the only resources under siege. Freshwater, which is critical for both human survival and economic development, is becoming increasingly scarce in many areas. Over the past quarter century global per capita water supplies have declined by one-third, and 1.7 billion people in developing regions are currently experiencing water stress (defined as countries that consume more than 20 percent of their renewable water supply each year). If current trends persist, as many as 5 billion people could face such conditions by 2025.[38] The world's fisheries are also being stressed. Around 70 percent of commercial fisheries are either fully exploited or overexploited and experiencing declining yields, and about 34 percent of all fish species are at risk from human activities. This is not only troubling from a biodiversity perspective; millions of individuals depend on fisheries for employment and 1 billion people worldwide rely on fish as their primary protein source.[39]

The Deprivation Hypothesis

For more than a decade neo-Malthusians have argued that these demographic and environmental pressures can, under certain conditions, lead to violent conflict between and within countries. Four major hypotheses have been advanced linking demographic and environmental change to political instability and violent conflict: *simple scarcity, transboundary migration, deprivation, and state failure.*[40] The simple scarcity[41] and transboundary migration[42] hypotheses link population growth, environmental degradation, and scarcity to military competition and violent conflict *between* countries. However, there are both empirical and theoretical reasons to doubt that these factors are significant causes of international wars.[43] Consequently, the discussion here focuses on the neo-Malthusian arguments linking demographic and environmental factors to violent conflict *within* countries.

According to the deprivation hypothesis, population growth, environmental degradation, and maldistributions of natural resources often conspire to produce absolute and relative deprivation among the poor in developing countries, thereby increasing the risks of political turmoil.[44] In many of the world's least-developed countries, rapid population growth contributes to downward pressure on wages, un- and underemployment, and rising levels of landlessness, all of which exacerbate poverty and income inequality. Rapid population growth, environmental degradation, and unequal resource distributions can also produce acute scarcities of natural resources. Of particular concern for contemporary neo-Malthusians are renewable resources that can become scarce if they are consumed or degraded at unsustainable rates or distributed in ways that deny access to subsets of the population.[45] Because large numbers of individuals in developing countries continue to reside in rural areas where they are directly dependent on renewable resources for their livelihood, emerging scarcity can create substantial hardships.

As deprived individuals and social groups engage in increasingly fierce competition for dwindling natural and economic resources, the deprivation hypothesis suggests that intergroup violence becomes more likely. Deprivation also increases the risk of rebellion against the state by encouraging individuals to support insurgents and other challenger groups seeking to overthrow the status quo.[46] Norman Myers, for example, has argued that individuals impoverished by population growth and environmental degradation "become desperate people, all too ready to challenge governments through ... guerrilla groups." And Jessica Tuchman Mathews has posited that the demographic and environmental impact on a country's security is generally "felt in the downward pull on economic performance and, therefore, political stability. ... [E]conomic decline leads to frustration, resentment, domestic unrest or even civil war."[47]

The State Failure Hypothesis

Proponents of the state failure hypothesis, most notably Jack Goldstone and Thomas Homer-Dixon, agree that population and environmental pressures in developing countries often generate intense hardship among agricultural laborers and the urban poor. They contend, however, that strong and capable states are typically able to prevent such deprivation from coalescing into organized violence through a mix of relief for aggrieved individuals, co-optation of opposition leaders, and outright coercion. Therefore, large-scale violence is only likely to occur when social grievances emanating from rapid population growth, environmental degradation, and natural resource scarcity combine with eroding state authority and escalating intra-elite competition.[48]

Severe demographic and environmental stress can threaten the capacity, legitimacy, and cohesion of the state in developing countries by simultaneously increasing demands for government expenditures, exacerbating intra-elite competition, and decreasing government revenues. Rapid population growth, environmental degradation, and natural resource scarcity typically generate demands from suffering individuals and social groups for costly investments in rural and urban infrastructure, public sector employment, expansion of social services, farm and industrial subsidies, and development projects. Demographic and environmental pressures also produce both winners and losers among the elite, sparking intra-elite conflicts—either between state and social elites or among elites within the ruling party and military—that pose their own challenges to the state. Some segments of the elite may benefit from their ability to capture windfall profits arising from scarcity-induced increases in resource value, for example, whereas those unable to capture these resource rents, as well as those left to compete for shrinking government largesse and public-sector jobs, may suffer. As rifts among elites inside and outside the government grow, these can jeopardize state cohesion and legitimacy, and produce a growing pool of political entrepreneurs willing to mobilize social groups to challenge the regime.[49]

Finally, at the very moment that demands on the state are increasing and elite feuds are escalating, the state's ability to address these problems may decline. Studies suggest that demographic and environmental pressures can reduce revenue flows to the state, especially in countries with imperfect markets and slow-growing or highly skewed economies. Rapid population growth can lower per capita economic productivity, contribute to higher dependency ratios, and cut into domestic savings rates, and environmental degradation and emerging resource scarcities can erode the natural resource base that the economies of many poor countries ultimately depend on.[50] Under these conditions states may find themselves in an impossible situation, since they cannot raise revenue through taxation without worsening grievances among struggling individuals or alienating regime supporters. The remaining alternatives are to increase government debt, print money (causing inflation), rely more heavily on corruption to maintain loyalty among regime allies, or some combination of all these options, further weakening state capacity and legitimacy.[51]

In sum, according to the state failure hypothesis, demographic and environmental pressures place strains on states in developing countries. As the state weakens, its ability to manage social conflict becomes more limited at the precise time that mass grievances and elite conflicts are on the rise, elevating the risk of violent turmoil.

Criticisms

Neo-Malthusian accounts of civil strife are vulnerable to several criticisms. Many neoclassical economists, for example, challenge the posited linkages between population growth, environmental degradation, resource scarcity, and economic decline (and therefore deprivation and state failure). Recently this work has been supplemented by studies which suggest that resource abundance, rather than scarcity, is more likely to produce underdevelopment, political instability, and violence. These arguments are discussed at length in the next section.

It can also be argued that neo-Malthusian hypotheses suffer from an excess of demographic and environmental determinism. Some neo-Malthusians advance models that describe automatic and simplistic causal linkages between population and environmental pressures, on the one hand, and civil strife, on the other. This type of determinism exaggerates the causal importance of demographic and environmental factors, and ignores or downplays crucial intervening factors and processes.

The charge of determinism clearly applies to the deprivation hypothesis, which significantly overpredicts incidents of civil strife. After all, if poverty and a sense of injustice were sufficient to lead people to rebel against their governments or fight one another, the world's poor would constantly be engaged in organized violence. This, of course, is not the case. The deprivation hypothesis fails to acknowledge that individuals contemplating organized violence face significant collective action problems. At the individual level, the risks to one's life and property inherent in antistate or intergroup violence generate high potential costs, and the choice to forgo wages and peaceful exchange with others creates large opportunity costs. On the benefit side of the equation, each individual's contribution, in and of itself, has very little impact on the prospects for success, and the benefits to be accrued from joining a violent social movement are frequently "public," or collective, in nature (i.e., they are non-rival and non-excludable). This can create powerful incentives for individuals to "free-ride" on the efforts of others, which, in the aggregate, works against the formation of organized conflict groups.[52] Given these challenges to collective action, it is essential to understand how certain intervening variables, especially patterns of social organization, affect the ability of aggrieved individuals to overcome these problems and mobilize.

Moreover, although the deprivation hypothesis seeks to explain a political outcome, it is curiously apolitical. In particular, it fails to recognize that the prospects for violence are substantially shaped and shoved by the strength of the state and the ability of political institutions to offer peaceful avenues for addressing grievances.[53]

The state failure hypothesis seeks to correct some of these shortcomings by "bringing the state back in," and, in doing so, it points to a number of fundamental causal dynamics. Indeed, the arguments advanced by Goldstone and Homer-Dixon provide the building blocks upon which much of the theoretical account provided in chapter 2 is built. Yet, as currently articulated, the state failure hypothesis is incomplete in two important respects. First, despite its state-centric focus, the causal role of the state remains under-theorized. Existing accounts largely envision state weakness as a "permissive" factor contributing to conflict; that is, given mounting social grievances and disputes among elites, state weakness provides structural opportunities that permit these conflicts to escalate to violence. This is true, but it is not the whole story. As I describe in chapter 2, state failure also brings about an internal security dilemma that produces powerful incentives—not simply opportunities—for antistate and intergroup violence. Furthermore, the current state failure hypothesis focuses largely on "bottom-up" dynamics, in the sense that state weakness opens political space for social groups to direct violence upward toward the state or sideways toward one another. But as the discussion of state exploitation dynamics in chapter 2 demonstrates, civil strife can also emerge through a "top-down" process whereby state elites themselves engineer and direct violence downward toward social groups.

Second, while proponents of the state failure hypothesis recognize that a number of intervening variables mediate the relationship between population growth, environmental stress, and civil strife, more work needs to be done to systematically incorporate these intervening

not explained well

variables into an explanation for violence. Goldstone, for example, notes that "neither environmental degradation nor population growth *by themselves* act as motors of regional political crises."[54] Similarly Günther Baechler contends that "passing the threshold of violence definitely depends on *sociopolitical* factors and not on the degree of environmental degradation as such."[55] And Homer-Dixon argues that,

> environmental scarcity produces its effects within extremely complex ecological-political systems. . . . [W]hen it does contribute to violence . . . it always interacts with other political, economic, and social factors. Environmental scarcity's causal role can never be separated from these contextual factors, which are often unique to the society in question.[56]

Unfortunately, most of the scholars who have acknowledged the importance of intervening variables have tended to overcorrect for the determinism of the deprivation hypothesis by constructing "kitchen sink" accounts that remain too underspecified or indeterminate. The laundry list of important intervening variables identified by the literature includes, among other factors, cultural conceptions of the environment and social justice; the level of social ingenuity; the degree and type of social cleavages; the nature of civil society and the quality of trust, norms, and networks between social groups; the nature of political institutions; system legitimacy; the autonomy of the state; and the leadership skills, ideology, and organizational resources of challenger groups and governing elites.[57] Of these, the presence of corrupt and authoritarian political institutions and deep social cleavages appear to matter most, but additional clarification is needed to identify precisely how these intervening variables interact with demographic and environmental pressures to produce violent conflict.[58] This challenge is taken up in chapter 2.

intervening variables

The Challenge from Neoclassical Economics

The neo-Malthusian view has long been criticized by scholars working within the tradition of neoclassical economics. The neoclassical rebuttal to neo-Malthusianism starts by challenging the notion that population growth and environmental degradation inevitably lead to resource scarcity and economic decline, calling into question the causal connection to civil strife. More recently a small but influential cadre of scholars has also advanced a set of claims that inverts the causal relationship between scarcity and violent conflict; resource abundance, rather than scarcity, is argued to be the source of political instability and armed struggle.[59]

Adaptation and the Positive Effects of Population Growth

Neoclassical economics believe that neo-Malthusians are overly pessimistic about the negative consequences of rapid population growth
and environmental degradation. Neoclassical economists argue that
markets, governments, and other social institutions usually adjust to
population and environmental pressures, heading off significant resource scarcities before they emerge or lead to violent conflict.[60] Sum-
marizing this position, Bjørn Lomborg argues:

> There is often a general tendency throughout this discussion [of scarcity-
> induced] conflict to *presume* that environmental scarcity indeed sets in more
> and more often. . . .
>   As should be abundantly clear [from the evidence], we are far from ex-
> hausting our raw material resources. . . . We continuously find new re-
> sources, use them more efficiently, recycle them, and substitute them. . . .
>   Consequently, although the discussion of environmental stresses and their
> connection to conflict is clearly an important area of research, it is important
> to realize that, on the main issue areas, resources have not been becoming
> increasingly scarce but rather more abundant.[61]

The basic economic logic underlying this claim is straightforward: rising prices stemming from increased demand for, or decreased supply
of, natural resources force individuals, firms, and governments to
adapt by developing cheaper substitutes, conservation methods, and
more efficient means of extraction.

Neoclassical economists also contest the connection between population growth and economic decline (and hence state failure). Here it
is argued that population growth generates positive effects, including
economies of scale, larger labor forces, and induced innovation and
technological change, that tend to balance out the negative effects emphasized by neo-Malthusians. Neoclassical economists contend that
government policies are much more important than population
growth in determining prospects for economic development.[62]

The Honey Pot Hypothesis

The adaptation argument seeks to undermine the neo-Malthusian
claim that population growth and environmental degradation necessarily create unbearable strains on societies and states. Other neoclassical arguments directly address the relationship between natural resources and civil strife. One claim centers on so-called honey pot
effects. According to the *honey pot hypothesis*, abundant supplies of val-

uable natural resources create incentives for conflict groups to form and fight to capture them.[63] This may spawn attempts by regional warlords and rebel organizations to cleave off resource-rich territories or violently hijack the state. Once seized, control over valuable natural resources fuels conflict escalation by allowing the parties to purchase weaponry and mobilize potential recruits.[64] In short, profit seeking motivates and empowers insurgents in resource-rich countries. As Paul Collier argues,

> Rebellions either have the objective of natural resource predation, or are critically dependent upon natural resource predation in order to pursue other objectives. These, rather than objective grievances, are the risk factors which conflict prevention must reduce if is to be successful.[65]

Echoing these sentiments, de Soysa contends that "greed rather than grievance (at least in terms of the availability of natural resources is concerned) is likelier to generate armed violence."[66]

The Resource Curse Hypothesis

Some neoclassical economists argue that natural resource abundance increases risks of civil strife by producing weak states via a set of developmental pathologies known collectively as the resource curse. Proponents of the *resource curse hypothesis* provide both economic and political foundations for this claim.[67]

Resource abundance is argued to contribute to economic stagnation over the long run through a number of crowd-out effects sometimes referred to as "Dutch Disease." As the economists Jeffrey Sachs and Andrew Warner note, "the core of the Dutch Disease story is that resource abundance in general or resource booms in particular shift resources away from sectors of the economy that have positive externalities for growth."[68] When capital and labor focuses on booming natural resource sectors, they are drawn away from other sectors of the economy, increasing their production costs. These economic distortions slow the maturity of non-resource tradable sectors, harm their competitiveness, and thereby inhibit the kinds of economic diversification, especially an early period of labor-intensive manufacturing, that many neoclassical economists suggest is vital for long-term growth.[69]

An over-reliance on exports of minimally processed natural resources is also argued to make countries vulnerable to declining terms of trade and the highly volatile nature of international commodities markets. In the absence of a diverse array of exports, especially manufactured goods that tend to have more stable prices, resource-rich countries are prone to dramatic economic shocks when prices for primary commodities inevitably crash.[70]

Beyond the economic distortions created by local resource abundance, there is also a political dimension to the resource curse. The most common political argument focuses on problems associated with "rentier states." States that accrue a significant amount of revenue from natural resource exports that they directly control are prone to developing corrupt, narrowly based authoritarian or quasi-democratic governing institutions. When states capture enormous rents from natural resources, they face far fewer incentives to bargain away greater economic and political accountability to the populace in exchange for broader rights of taxation.[71] Instead, natural resource wealth can be used to maintain rule through patronage networks and outright coercion. The institutional makeup of rentier states therefore reduces the prospects for broad-based, benevolent economic and political reform, weakening the state over the long term and generating substantial societal grievances. These conditions are ripe for violent revolt.[72]

Criticisms

Neoclassical arguments related to the adaptive capacities of markets and societies have substantial merit. After centuries of debate it is clear that doomsaying claims about the inevitable relationship between population growth, environmental degradation, and resource scarcity have proven false. Indeed, as noted by Nancy Birdsall and Steven Sinding, two scholars sympathetic with the neo-Malthusian view: "The effects of markets and institutions—sometimes good, sometimes bad—can easily swamp the effect of population change on resource use, degradation, and depletion."[73] Nevertheless, neoclassical economists tend to be overly optimistic about the prospects for adaptation. While markets and institutions have frequently adapted to population and environmental pressures at the global level and within wealthy industrialized countries, serious local scarcities continue to emerge within developing countries. Moreover, adaptation has been much more successful in heading off shortages of nonrenewable resources than renewable ones. This is somewhat ironic since nonrenewable resources are, by definition, finite, whereas renewable resources are capable of naturally regenerating themselves if they are not consumed or degraded too rapidly.

Several related hurdles appear to undermine the operation of neoclassical logic, especially as it relates to local scarcities of renewable resources throughout much of the developing world. First, in many developing countries the markets, property rights, government policies, judicial (contract-enforcing) institutions, basic infrastructure, research facilities, extension services, and human capital required to transform price signals into adaptation are imperfect, absent altogether, or distorted in ways that actually compound resource problems. Second, critical renewable resources such as arable land and freshwater often lack cheap substitutes or easy, short-term tech-fixes. This leaves conservation as the major adaptation mechanism. Unfortunately, the economic policies and poverty that drive many environmental pressures in the first place often undermine the capacity of individuals and governments to make timely and expensive investments in conservation. Finally, neoclassical economists tend to underrate the degree to which environmental systems become stressed in nonlinear, rapid, and irreversible ways, producing sudden surprises and scarcities that are difficult to respond to, at least in the short term. Therefore, adaptation, even if it eventually occurs, may be too late to head off significant transitional difficulties and conflicts.[74]

What about the neoclassical claim that population growth does not retard economic progress? For decades, studies failed to find a strong statistical correlation between population growth and per capita economic output, appearing to give credence to the neoclassical position. Nevertheless, recent models that disaggregate population growth into several components (i.e., population size and density, as well as changes in mortality and fertility, labor force size, and youth dependency ratios) suggest that the net effect of rapid population growth on economic progress in developing countries has been negative, at least since the 1980s.[75] In the most prominent study, population size and density alone do not appear to undermine economic growth (and may, over the long term, have a positive effect) but, "the positive impacts of population density, size, and labor force growth are more than offset by the costs of rearing children and maintaining an enlarged youth-dependency age structure."[76]

Furthermore, although economic growth is certainly possible in the context of rapid population expansion, the prospects for such growth hinge on the initial level of economic development and the adoption of appropriate economic strategies. Unfortunately, in many poor countries, government policies have encouraged capital-intensive industries that underutilize abundant supplies of labor. Governments have also adopted other policies ill-suited for labor-intensive agricultural sectors, such as high taxes on farm inputs and outputs. Compounding matters, economic policies have tended to overemphasize urban areas at the expense of investments in rural development. Development strategies have thus often been incompatible with the promotion of

What neo-Malthusian?

economic growth in an environment of rapid population growth.[77] And, "while it can be demonstrated that 'population problems' are largely due to inappropriate government policies, it is also clear that, *given* these policies, population growth can exert a stronger adverse impact."[78] This all suggests that the effects of population growth are likely to vary from context to context. In some cases, the effects may be negligible or even positive. But, in other cases, the effects are likely to be negative, sometimes profoundly so.

Turning to neoclassical conflict hypotheses, the honey pot hypothesis also suffers from a number of problems. First, the greed-based logic of the honey pot applies much more to nonrenewable mineral resources than to renewable ones, with the partial exception of timber. Nonrenewable resources are especially likely to be implicated in violent conflicts in which valuable resources themselves are the main prize to be captured, as opposed to conflicts emanating from the more diffuse social and economic effects of environmental degradation and renewable resource scarcity. The incentive and capability to capture nonrenewable resources is especially high, because mineral resources tend to be much more valuable per unit of volume, geographically concentrated, and easily tradable than most renewable resources. These features make nonrenewable resources considerably more "lootable."[79] It should come as no surprise, therefore, that the vast majority of examples of honey pot–driven conflicts revolve around oil, precious metals, diamonds, and other valuable minerals; quantitative research suggests that there is no statistically significant relationship between an abundance of legal agricultural commodities or other renewable resources and the onset or duration of civil strife.[80] Instead, renewable resources are much more likely to be sources of grievance-based struggles. Agriculture, forestry, and fishing contribute much more to employment than do capital-intensive nonrenewable resource sectors, and access to arable land (or inexpensive food) and freshwater is vital to extremely poor individuals throughout the developing world. Degradation, depletion, or maldistributions of these resources can therefore directly implicate the survival of much larger numbers of people in rural areas than nonrenewables can.[81] Under these conditions, grievance rather than greed is likely to be the primary motivation for armed struggle.

Second, natural resource scarcity and abundance as conceptualized by neo-Malthusians and neoclassical economists are not opposites; they both can, and often do, exist at the same time at different levels of analysis. Oil, precious metals, gemstones, and the other troublesome resources discussed by the honey pot hypothesis may be abundant locally *but they are scarce globally.*[82] Indeed, it is the global scarcity of these resources that makes them so valuable and thus such huge prizes to seize through violence. Moreover, the logic of the honey pot clearly applies *more* to situations in which initially abundant resources become increasingly scarce over time. After all, if natural resources were truly abundant, they would be of little value and thus not worth fighting over. As natural resources are consumed or degraded at unsustainable rates, their value increases and rival social groups confront greater incentives to seize them. For example, Michael Klare's research on contemporary resource clashes in Angola, the Indonesian and Malaysian regions of Borneo, the Democratic Republic of Congo, Sierra Leone, and elsewhere finds that rising global demand and scarcity-driven price increases provide additional incentives for contending social groups and elites to capture control of valuable mines, oil fields, and timber stands, by force if necessary.[83]

Finally, like the deprivation claims advanced by neo-Malthusians, honey pot arguments locate the origin of violence in the incentives of societal actors. By themselves, however, these incentives are not enough to explain violence; strong states should be able to deter or otherwise frustrate these groups before they form or become capable of seizing valuable natural resources to finance their activities.[84] In other words, like grievance-based clashes, greed-based ones are only likely to occur when states are weak. *Reason of our control US polity*

The resource curse hypothesis makes up for this last deficiency by endogenizing the state into its explanation for civil strife, but resource curse arguments confront their own set of shortcomings. First, like the honey pot hypothesis, economic and political components of the resource curse apply much more to countries dependent on the export of nonrenewable resources than renewable resources. Here several characteristics distinguish mineral-dependent economies and polities from countries dependent on renewables (again, with the partial exception of timber). Mineral countries frequently depend on a highly capital-intensive industrial enclave characterized by low employment and skewed wage structures, making the economic distortions particularly acute. These countries also tend to be economically dependent on a single resource, making them more sensitive to price volatility.[85]

Furthermore, the rents generated by mineral exports are extraordinary, with the bulk of these rents captured by the state. This is especially true of oil but is also the case with other minerals. As Sachs and Warner note, "we should distinguish minerals (which generally have high rents) from agriculture (which generally has low rents). In the same vein, perhaps processed agriculture should be distinguished from primary agriculture."[86] States in the developing world also exercise sole ownership rights over subsoil assets and, often, public forestlands. This means that export revenue from these resources is not mediated through domestic private actors but instead accrues directly to the state and allied firms. This differs dramatically from the situation in most countries dependent on exports of agriculture, since these resources tend to be privately owned (even if sometimes highly concentrated). Thus, since government officials have the ability to extract and control unusually high income from nonrenewables, the pathologies of rentier state politics are likely to be much more acute than in countries dependent on most renewable resources.[87]

Second, even if the logic of the resource curse provides some insight into the challenges confronting late-developing economies and polities with initially abundant renewable resources, this position does not necessarily compete with, or negate, the basic causal claims advanced by neo-Malthusians. If development is viewed as a hypothetical sequence of temporal stages, a good case can be made that the developmental pathologies of the resource curse and those emerging from rapid population growth, environmental degradation, and resource scarcity can all occur and interact with one another within the same country over time. During stage 1, when resources are abundant, a country may become highly dependent on these resources, and elements of Dutch Disease and rentier state politics may take hold. Then, during stage 2, demographic and environmental pressures may produce growing scarcities, undermine the economy, and contribute to political crises in the way described by neo-Malthusians *precisely because* the country developed such a strong dependence on exporting natural resources in the first place. Lastly, at stage 3, scarcity and economic crisis may eventually force the government and the private sector to promote diversification as a means of resuscitating growth. This hypothetical sequence suggests that neoclassical theorists tend to focus on the logic involved in the leaps between these temporal stages without sufficiently recognizing the risks of transitional violence during the middle stage emphasized by neo-Malthusians.

By ignoring transitional dangers, neoclassical economists miss important contributors to civil strife. The experience of the world's poorest countries suggests that many are currently stuck in stage 2, where high dependence on natural resources, rapid population growth, environmental degradation, and emerging scarcities conspire to threaten political stability. Recent reports by both the UN Development Programme (UNDP) and the World Bank, for example, suggest that the least developed countries tend to be those that are most dependent on minerals, agriculture, forestry, fish, and other natural resources.[88] Unfortunately, as the UNDP notes,

> Slow world market growth, unchanging technologies and often volatile and declining world prices for these commodities offer much too narrow a base

for economic advance. Continued heavy dependence on a handful of primary commodity exports provides no chance of long-term success. This unfortunate situation afflicts much of Sub-Saharan Africa, the Andean region and Central Asia.

Exacerbating these structural problems is rapid population growth, which tends to be fastest in countries with the lowest human development. These challenges can seriously hinder the availability of farmland and increase environmental degradation (deforestation, soil degradation, fisheries depletion, reduced freshwater).[89]

This potential compatibility between the supposedly rival claims made by neo-Malthusians and neoclassical economists may actually be supported by the quantitative findings provided by some resource curse proponents. Most notably, Collier and his associates in the World Bank Development Research Group use the percentage of a country's GDP made up of primary commodity exports as a measure of resource abundance/scarcity. However, as Indra de Soysa notes,

> The finding that the ratio of primary exports to total exports is strongly related to conflict can very well be interpreted to mean that poor countries, which are dependent on primary goods exports, are facing Malthusian crises and are unable therefore to meet the demands of society, leading to subsistence crises, which is in fact the argument put forth by the proponents of "eco-violence."[90]

Moreover, the same studies which suggest that natural resource dependence makes countries conflict-prone also indicate that population size and population density, especially in the context of poor economic conditions, place countries at higher risk of civil strife.[91]

Finally, like the neo-Malthusian state failure argument, the resource curse hypothesis discusses the state without fully theorizing its role in conflict. Resource curse accounts fail to include a broader discussion of the ways in which social and political intervening variables affect the relationship between resource endowments and violence.

Political Ecology

Political ecology represents a third major approach to the population–environment–civil strife connection that draws extensively on the Marxian tradition in political economy and the Foucaultian tradition in cultural theory. Political ecology concerns itself chiefly with the various ways in which global and local political economies parcelize the natural world, assign value to these parcels, distribute them in particular ways, and thereby contribute to patterns of exploitation and violence.[92]

The Centrality of Resource Distribution

As Nancy Peluso and Michael Watts note, political ecology emphasizes "the entitlements by which differentiated individuals, households, and communities possess or gain access to resources within a structured political economy. It grants priority to how these entitlements are distributed, reproduced, and fought over in the course of shaping, and being shaped by, patterns of accumulation."[93] Colonialism, the expansion of capitalism, and the integration of markets via globalization have historically meant that the value of natural resources has been largely constituted by the power, policies, and consumption habits of wealthy industrial countries and their allies among the elite in developing countries. Moreover, the structure of both the contemporary international trading system and most domestic economies is such that the distribution of these resources is skewed in favor of these powerful actors.[94] Consequently, many poor, subsistence, and indigenous communities in developing countries experience so-called scarcities of vital natural resources for distributional reasons, even under objective conditions of global or local abundance. As such, for political ecologists, scarcity is an artifact of social interactions within certain international political and economic structures, not a result of demographic pressures and natural limits. As Nicholas Hildyard argues:

> Resource shortages and ecological degradation are primarily the result of the uneven social measures that "manufacture scarcity all over the world for the economic and political gain of powerful interests." The systematic inequalities that block peoples' access to income, health, education and democratic rights, for example, are primarily responsible for the geographical and sociological "profile" of ecological degradation. Even in those instances where ecological scarcity appears unconnected to social scarcity, its character is nonetheless "defined by economic forces, which are . . . fundamentally linked to the social and cultural tendencies that fuel pro-scarcity politics."[95]

Political ecologists thus believe that population growth and environmental degradation, in and of themselves, are not very important sources of either scarcity or violence. Indeed, political ecologists contend that accounts which privilege these "natural" sources of scarcity and violence mask the historical and structural origins of both phenomena.[96] Although environmental degradation may play some role, it is only insofar as *both* environmental degradation and violence are produced by systems of inequality.

Political ecologists also deride neo-Malthusians such as Homer-Dixon who attempt to bridge the gap between the two approaches by including "structural scarcity" (unequal resource access) in their models alongside "demand-induced scarcity" (from population growth) and "supply-induced scarcity" (from environmental degradation). Political ecologists believe that this move amounts to "analytical obfuscation."[97] They insist that "differentiating between socially generated scarcity and absolute [natural] scarcity is a *sine qua non* for any sensible discussion of the causes of ecological degradation, deprivation, food scarcity and other problems often attributed to 'overpopulation'—and hence the social upheaval, including violence, that they can help trigger."[98]

Conflict Hypotheses

Although political ecologists are clearly interested in the politics of violence,[99] they offer "no single [causal] theory of violence as such."[100] Nevertheless, it is still possible to extract some basic causal claims regarding the sources of civil strife. Placing the politics of resource control and distribution at the center of their analyses leads political ecologists to posit, at least implicitly, three ways in which conflicts over natural resources can lead to violent conflict within countries. Ironically, despite their rejection of mainstream perspectives, elements of each mirrors a number of the arguments advanced by neo-Malthusians and neoclassical economists. First, civil strife may erupt as local communities rise up to challenge unequal resource distributions and the state responds by using violent means to crush resistance movements. I call this the *distribution hypothesis*. This claim has much in common with the neo-Malthusian deprivation hypothesis, although it obviously identifies a different source of deprivation. For political ecologists, these resource-related conflicts are driven primarily by structural inequalities rather than population growth or "natural" scarcity.[101] Second, political ecologists argue that powerful state actors, corporations, and rebel groups may use violence against one another or against disadvantaged communities in their efforts to seize control of valuable natural resources, paralleling the logic of the neoclassical honey pot hypothesis.[102] Finally, some political ecologists have argued that a local abundance of valuable natural resources distorts economic and political development, employing the same reasoning as the neoclassical resource curse hypothesis.[103]

Criticisms

A central cleavage between neo-Malthusians and political ecologists is their apparent disagreement regarding the importance of natural ver-

sus social sources of scarcity. Neo-Malthusians discuss both, but political ecologists are right that natural sources appear to trump social ones in many neo-Malthusian accounts. Unfortunately, political ecologists make the opposite error when they claim that natural and social sources of scarcity are "wholly unrelated processes"[104] or suggest that distributional concerns are *always* more important.[105]

A more sophisticated approach would take seriously each contributor to scarcity—local population growth, environmental depletion and degradation stemming from international demand and local economic practices, and resource inequality—and closely analyze the ways that they interact. It is certainly true that population growth, environmental degradation, and resource inequality are different types of natural and social processes, and that these processes do not always produce resource scarcity. Indeed, as neoclassical economists point out, demographic and environmental pressures sometimes encourage conservation, rehabilitation, substitution, and other adaptation efforts. Still, none of this negates the fact that under many circumstances the synergy of population growth, environmental degradation, and resource inequality *does* produce scarcity.

A simple hypothetical demonstrates why an approach that downplays or ignores this possible interaction is a poor way to think about questions of resource scarcity. Imagine two forty-hectare areas of arable land, each with ten farmers. In one of these areas land is distributed equally across the population (4 ha each), while in the second area 20 percent of the population controls 60 percent of the land (leaving eight farmers with only 2 ha each). Now imagine that each farmer requires at least 1 ha to support his or her family. Under conditions of zero population growth and zero environmental degradation, there will be sufficient land to support each farmer's family *even in the area with a highly skewed distribution of land*. In contrast, if both areas are experiencing an annual population growth rate of 3 percent, the populations of each will double every twenty-three years. In less than fifty years land will become scarce (relative to the survival needs of farmers) *even in the egalitarian area*, while poor farmers in the skewed area will experience scarcity in half that time. Now imagine that the supply of arable land in each area is not constant but instead is in gradual decline because of soil erosion. In this situation poor farmers will experience scarcity even sooner under *both* scenarios. Explaining or understanding the timing and magnitude of scarcity experienced by poor farmers in these two hypothetical areas obviously requires a thoughtful consideration of the origins and implications of inequality. But a singular focus on inequality is insufficient. A full account *also* requires a consideration of the effects of, and interactions with, population growth, environmental degradation, and the adaptive capacities of local communities and institutions.

Beyond the issue of resource distribution, the specific conflict hypotheses advanced by political ecologists parallel the general logic of the deprivation, honey pot, and resource hypotheses discussed by their rivals. As such, the criticisms already examined apply to them as well. More generally, the theoretical claims made by political ecologists suffer from a high degree of indeterminacy and underspecification. There is very little conceptual elaboration or theoretical operationalization of most of the approach's central features and posited causal connections. For example, although Peluso and Watts argue that "the contours of the broad political economy (under which complex class and social forces operate) and how the rhythms of environmental change and accumulation shape the processes of exclusion, disenfranchisement, and displacement must be specified," neither they nor others working in this vein do so satisfactorily.[106] Crucial concepts such as capitalism, regimes of accumulation, production, labor, culture, and discourse typically go undefined; the causal relationships between these factors and key actors such as the state, firms, middle and upper classes, peasants, and urban workers (not to mention indigenous cultural communities, religious organizations, nongovernmental organizations, and other subsets of local and transnational civil society) are left vague; the causal logic whereby political, economic, and discursive practices and structures constitute particular environments and patterns of violence is underspecified; and, perhaps most important, the complex relationship *between* material processes and discursive ones is simply asserted rather than carefully theorized. This underspecification makes the various arguments advanced by political ecologists very difficult to evaluate relative to their competitors.

Understanding the Population–Environment–
Civil Strife Connection

This book seeks to improve our understanding of the population–environment–civil strife connection in several important respects. First, it examines the degree to which demographic and environmental factors cause civil strife, and goes to great lengths to elaborate upon, and empirically demonstrate the nature of, the causal relationship. In doing so, the theoretical argument I put forth draws on a broad array of insights from the general study of internal wars. Second, my analysis focuses intensively on the intervening variables that exacerbate, or potentially mitigate, the risks of civil strife. In other words, my theoretical and empirical analysis places as much emphasis on social and political variables as on demographic and environmental ones.

Focusing on these causal processes and intervening variables also provides an opportunity to address a number of methodological limitations plaguing current research in this area. Existing quantitative studies suggest a possible correlation between population and environmental factors, on the one hand, and civil strife, on the other. However, these studies are not very helpful in identifying and empirically tracing the nature of the causal relationship.[107] Previous qualitative case study research has helped to address this issue, but these studies have tended to select cases where violence occurred and then to search for demographic and environmental connections. The lack of variation in the dependent variable (the degree of civil strife) is problematic. After all, without looking at cases where demographic and environmental pressures were acute yet violence did not erupt, we are unable to discern the conditions that make conflict more or less likely.[108] Indeed, Homer-Dixon, the target of much criticism in this regard, has himself argued that future research should focus on cases that "exhibit all the precursor conditions hypothesized to produce violence . . . but that do not exhibit violence. Such cases, if found, will further our understanding of the many contextual factors that can influence the strength of the relationship between environmental scarcity and violence."[109] In this book I take up the methodological and empirical challenge by analyzing instances where violent conflict occurred as well as those where it was muted or avoided altogether.

The Argument in Brief

The independent variable in my analysis is *demographic and environmental stress* (DES), a composite variable representing the interaction of rapid population growth, environmental degradation, and unequal distribution of renewable resources. I contend that there are two causal pathways whereby DES causes violence: *state failure* and *state exploitation*. The modified version of the state failure hypothesis presented in chapter 2 suggests that violent conflicts occur when DES puts pressure on both society and the state, simultaneously increasing the incentives and opportunities for social groups to engage in violence via the logic of the security dilemma. State exploitation represents a second pathway to bloodshed. These conflicts occur when population and environmental pressures provide state elites and their allies with incentives and opportunities to instigate violence that serves their narrow self-interests.

I further argue that two key intervening variables, *groupness* and *institutional inclusivity*, play decisive roles in determining which countries are most prone to DES-induced state failure and state exploitation conflicts. Countries with high degrees of groupness are deeply cleaved along ethno-cultural, religious, or class lines. These conditions encourage violence by helping to overcome the collective action problems inherent in the formation of conflict groups, whereas low degrees of groupness frustrate such mobilization. The second important intervening variable, institutional inclusivity, refers to the degree to which a wide array of societal actors have the ability to influence the government and, in particular, constrain the executive. I contend that inclusive institutions check violence by facilitating societal cooperation in the face of a weakened state and by making state exploitation more difficult, whereas exclusive institutions short-circuit cooperation and leave state elites free to instigate violence.

I evaluate the empirical plausibility of these claims through a careful examination of the communist insurgency in the Philippines and ethnic land clashes in Kenya. These cases were chosen for both theoretical and pragmatic reasons. Theoretically the cases exhibit variation in all three causal variables—DES, groupness, and institutional inclusivity—over time and space, providing excellent opportunities to test the specific effects of each. Pragmatically both countries have good demographic and environmental data going back for several decades, which cannot be said of many developing countries. This should increase our confidence in the empirical findings.

The remainder of the book is organized as follows. Chapter 2 presents my theoretical argument. Chapters 3–5 evaluate my theoretical claims empirically by examining civil strife in the Philippines and Kenya. Chapter 3 tests the plausibility of the state failure argument by analyzing the demographic and environmental roots of the communist insurgency in the Philippines. Chapter 4 tests the plausibility of the state exploitation argument by exploring state-sponsored ethnic clashes over land in Kenya. Chapter 5 revisits both conflicts and discusses the ways in which different levels of groupness and institutional inclusivity account for variations in the degree of violence over time and space within each country. Chapter 6 summarizes the theoretical and empirical claims, applies them to a number of other recent cases of conflict and nonconflict, and draws lessons for the future.

2

States, Scarcity, and Civil Strife:
A Theoretical Framework

> Since my youth I have lived under the threat
> and insecurity of fighting. The first problems I
> remember were tribal . . . it must have been a
> dispute over rights either for water or for land.
> These are the only things that neighboring
> tribes argue about.
> —Nizela Idriss, pastoralist, Chad

ALTHOUGH several major studies have successfully demonstrated that
links exist between population growth, environmental degradation,
natural resource scarcity, and violence within countries, a more systematic theoretical framework is required.[1] Without such a theory, existing
causal claims are difficult to evaluate empirically and offer inadequate
guidance for those interested in preventing or limiting the humanitarian, social, and strategic costs of civil strife in the decades ahead. In this
chapter I seek to move the theoretical debate forward by providing a
framework that places the state at the center of the analysis and focuses
as much on the social and political processes involved in producing
conflict as the demographic and environmental ones. The theory I outline draws extensively on arguments advanced by neo-Malthusians regarding the demographic and environmental sources of violence. To
this foundation I add other insights from long-standing theories of revolution and rebellion, as well as more recent theories of civil and ethnic
conflict from the field of international relations. In doing so, I strive to
build a theoretical bridge between the study of demographic and environmental conflicts and the broader study of internal wars.

My argument begins with the claim that demographic and environmental stress can produce significant pressures on societies and states
in the developing world. By way of various ecological, economic, and
social effects, population and environmental pressures reverberate
into politics and produce two potential pathways to civil strife: *state*

The epigraph is quoted from *Greenwar: Environment and Conflict* edited by Olivia
Bennett (Washington, D.C.: The Panos Institute, 1991), p. 7.

failure and *state exploitation*. State failure conflicts occur when DES substantially weakens state authority, thereby reducing the government's ability to maintain order and increasing the opportunities and incentives for antistate and intergroup violence via the logic of the security dilemma. State exploitation conflicts, in contrast, occur when threatened state elites seize on natural resource scarcities and related social grievances to instigate conflicts that advance their parochial interests. The final part of my argument contends that two key intervening variables, *groupness* and *institutional inclusivity*, play decisive roles in determining which countries are most prone to state failure and state exploitation conflicts. I argue that violence is particularly likely in the context of high degrees of groupness (i.e., societies that are sharply cleaved along ethno-cultural, religious, or class-based lines) and low degrees of institutional inclusivity (i.e., countries with highly discriminatory and repressive political systems).

The chapter begins with definitions of a number of key concepts. I then outline my state-centric theory of demographically and environmentally induced civil strife. Concluding the chapter is a discussion of methods, procedures, and case selection. This sets the stage for the empirical tests of the theory in chapters 3–5.

Key Concepts

Before detailing my theoretical argument, three key concepts employed throughout must be clearly defined: *demographic and environmental stress, civil strife,* and *the state.*

I define *demographic and environmental stress* as a composite variable encompassing (1) rapid population growth; (2) the degradation of renewable resources; and (3) the maldistribution of renewable resources.[2] The justification for analyzing population growth, environmental degradation, and unequal resource distribution together stems from the high degree of causal interaction between them. Because of this interaction, it would be difficult, and probably fruitless, to study the components of DES in isolation. Guatemala provides an excellent example. In Guatemala a heavily skewed distribution of land—3 percent of farmers controlled 65 percent of the country's best farmland during the 1990s—directly deprives small farmers of an essential resource. This problem is greatly compounded by Guatemala's rapid rate of population growth, which was approximately 2.7 percent a year between 1990 and 2000 and as much as 9 percent in some rural areas. Together, poor land distribution and population growth have contributed to environmental degradation by encouraging small farmers to migrate to steep hillsides and forests, converting these poorly suited areas into crop-

and pastureland. The Guatemalan government has further encouraged this migration and degradation by choosing to open up marginal lands for cultivation instead of redistributing land.[3]

As this example makes clear, I do *not* conceive of demographic and environmental stress as a purely "natural" variable standing outside social, political, and developmental systems. On the contrary, DES is a "natural-social" variable; DES is always embedded in, and at least partially the result of, the social, political, and developmental context within a given country. These contextual factors influence the extent and severity of population growth and environmental degradation by affecting the choices people make about family size and resource use, and they also determine the distribution of resources. Nevertheless, attempts to treat social, political, and developmental variables as wholly determinative of DES (i.e., the claim advanced by some economists and political ecologists that DES is completely endogenous and not "independent" in any strict social science sense) are shortsighted for at least two reasons. First, some aspects of DES *are* independent of social, political, and developmental variables (e.g., ecological vulnerability) or become independent once processes are set in motion (e.g., population momentum or irreversible environmental degradation). Second, the causal connection between DES, on the one hand, and society, politics, and development, on the other, runs both ways. As we will see below, population growth, environmental degradation, and resource inequality clearly affect and place constraints on social, political, and economic outcomes. Thus, while we should not artificially separate DES as a variable from its context, it would also be a mistake to treat DES as wholly endogenous to other variables. Instead, it is more productive to employ a balanced conceptualization that incorporates and discusses the interconnections between natural and social factors.[4]

A second important concept employed throughout this work is *civil strife*, which I define as large-scale, sustained, and organized violent conflict within a country. This includes revolution, rebellion, insurgency, civil and ethnic war, and sustained campaigns of terrorism. It does not include smaller-scale or less-organized forms of internal violence, such as riots and crime, or international conflicts.

Finally, I seek to construct a state-centric theory of demographically and environmentally induced conflict. I define *the state* along Weberian lines as a set of governing institutions and organizations led and coordinated by individuals occupying offices that authorize them to make and implement binding rules for all people within a territorially demarcated area.[5] This definition points to the dual role the state plays in my causal story: the state as an actor, in the sense of representing a set of individuals and organizations that act according to their preferences;[6] and the state as a set of institutions that enable and constrain the behavior of both state elites and social groups seeking to influence state policy.[7] This definition conceptualizes the state in terms of the broadest and most unique function it is *authorized* to carry out: binding rule making. It resists the temptation to include in the definition the specific functions states have traditionally carried out, such as guaranteeing internal order by monopolizing violence, or the empirical existence of the state's capacity to *actually* make and enforce binding rules upon society. The specific functions and empirical capacities of states are incredibly important for determining a state's strength or weakness but not its existence.

A State-Centric Theory of Demographically and Environmentally Induced Civil Strife

The causal connections between population growth, environmental degradation, resource inequality, and civil strife are rarely direct and obvious. Rather, DES can generate several ecological, economic, and social effects that, when refracted through certain forms of social organization and types of political institutions, make deadly conflict more likely. The challenge for any systematic theory is to clearly identify the connections and logics involved in this complex causal story.

Pressures on Society

DES produces myriad pressures on society. These pressures include renewable resource scarcity, economic marginalization, and shifts in demographic characteristics, the interaction of which can produce significant deprivation and rising social grievances.

RENEWABLE RESOURCE SCARCITY

Rapid population growth, in conjunction with the degradation and maldistribution of renewable resources, can lead to a scarcity of these resources in countries lacking the technological, social, and political ingenuity to adapt.[8] Renewable resources are natural resources, such as arable land, fresh water, forests, and fisheries that *theoretically* regenerate themselves indefinitely through normal ecological processes.[9] Renewable resource scarcity emerges when the stock or flow of a renewable resource is quantitatively depleted or qualitatively degraded at a rate faster than the rate of regeneration, or distributed in such a way as to artificially deprive individuals of the resource.[10]

Both rapid population growth and voracious consumption habits can lead to scarcity by increasing the demand for natural resources, while environmental degradation—stemming from these factors or from unsustainable production and extraction activities—can generate scarcity by decreasing resource supply. Environmental degradation can also generate scarcity indirectly if the rising price of a resource makes it more difficult for some individuals to obtain it, or if the purchasing power of individuals dependent on a degraded or depleted resource for employment declines, thereby reducing their ability to obtain *other* vital resources.[11] Finally, as Thomas Homer-Dixon has argued, a skewed distribution of resources can produce a condition of "structural scarcity" for large segments of a country's population by concentrating a resource "in the hands of a few and subject[ing] the rest to greater scarcity."[12]

Population growth and environmental pressures are already putting incredible strains on the Earth's renewable resource base and promise to place even greater strains on the planet's ability to provide for human needs in the future. World population grew from 1.6 billion to 6.1 billion during the twentieth century. More than three-quarters of this increase occurred after the Second World War, with 85 percent occurring in developing countries. Although global population growth has slowed appreciably in recent years, the forty-nine least developed countries in the world are still growing at a rate of 2.4 percent per year (representing a doubling rate of less than thirty years). Indeed, by 2050, the United Nations medium projection estimates that the world population will grow from its current level of 6.3 billion to 8.9 billion, with 97 percent of this increase occurring in developing countries.[13]

Global demand for natural resources has also been driven by the runaway consumption habits of high-income countries. Indeed, some have estimated that it would require the resources of five Earths if everyone currently alive in the world consumed resources at the level of the average American.[14] Taken together, local population growth, international demand, and unsustainable economic practices have created a situation in which many renewable resources in developing countries are being depleted or degraded faster than the rate of natural replenishment. Consequently, many countries are experiencing shortages of cropland and water, as well as declining forests and fishstocks.[15] Indeed, after a careful analysis of every major estimate of human carrying capacity made in recent decades, the renowned demographer Joel Cohen concludes:

> The human population of the Earth now travels in the zone where a substantial fraction of scholars have estimated upper limits on human population

size. These estimates are no better than present understanding of humankind's cultural, economic and environmental choices and constraints. Nevertheless, the possibility must by considered seriously that the number of people on the Earth has reached, or will reach within half a century, the maximum number the Earth can support in modes of life that we and our children and their children will choose to want.[16]

Before moving on, two caveats must be kept in mind regarding renewable resource scarcity. First, scarcity is always relative and subjective, not absolute and objective. Scarcity is experienced by human beings. As such, the degree of scarcity is determined by what individuals or groups need, or feel they need, to survive or maintain their standard of living. There is no absolute and objective level below which a reduction of the stock or flow of renewable resources or their maldistribution will cause all individuals to experience "scarcity." Second, measurements of scarcity need to be disaggregated. Because aggregate national measurements of the quantity and quality of renewable resources often mask the degree of scarcity experienced by individuals and groups at lower levels of analysis, scarcity must be analyzed at the regional, local, and group level.

ECONOMIC MARGINALIZATION

In developing countries with stagnant or slowly growing economies, DES contributes to economic marginalization. Labor intensive sectors of the economy remain much larger than capital-intensive ones in many developing countries. Unfortunately, individuals engaged in labor intensive activities, especially agriculture and other endeavors in which people are directly dependent on natural resources for subsistence and employment, are particularly vulnerable to DES-induced marginalization.[17]

In rural areas of the developing world population growth, environmental degradation, and maldistributions of critical resources often work in tandem to produce lower wages, chronic poverty, landlessness, and income inequality. This economic marginalization, in turn, contributes to greater damage to the environment, and the vicious cycle continues. The population of many developing countries, especially in Africa and Asia, is still predominately rural, with 3.2 billion residing in the countryside in 2000. According to some estimates, about 900 million poor people living in rural areas depend directly on nature's bounty for their livelihoods. For these individuals, the subdivision of land or downward pressure on wages as a result of population growth, environmental stress (e.g., soil degradation, deforestation, overfishing, freshwater scarcity, and natural disasters such as droughts and floods), and unequal resource distribution conspire to pose significant threats to their survival.[18] An increasing number of rural residents lack access to productive employment or land. Without jobs or land to subsist on, the poor are forced to migrate to marginal lands or cities to survive. Those who choose to stay in the agricultural sector must eke out a living by creating and cultivating plots on arid or semi-arid lands, hillsides and mountainsides, tropical forests, and other ecologically fragile areas, or by grazing livestock herds where vegetation is sparse or soils and shrubs are easily degraded. A viscious cycle often emerges under these conditions. As economic activities on marginal lands have increased, so have deforestation, soil erosion, desertification, pollution and depletion of groundwater, and overhunting and overfishing. This environmental degradation, in turn, reduces the carrying capacity of the natural resource base, exacerbating poverty and inequality for those who depend on these resources, placing additional pressure on the environment.[19]

Population growth can also contribute to economic marginalization by swelling the ranks of the urban and rural un- and underemployed. Bulging labor forces have combined with stagnant economies to produce record numbers of jobless in recent years. In the Middle East and North Africa, for example, the labor force grew by an average of 3.3 percent per year between 1993 and 2003, meaning that labor markets had to absorb 3.6 million new people every year. The economies of the region were unable to keep pace, and, in 2003, the unemployment rate throughout the Middle East and North Africa was 12.2 percent, the highest in the world. All told, between 1993 and 2003 the total number of unemployed individuals in the world increased from 140.5 million to 185.9 million.[20]

The problem of economic marginalization is magnified in a stagnant economy by its nonlinear nature. For example, if country A with a population of 150 can provide 100 jobs, 50 people are marginalized. If the population doubles to 300 people while the job market fails to expand, there will be 200 marginalized individuals. In this hypothetical example, the population has only doubled, but the number of marginalized individuals has increased by a factor of four.[21] In addition, as evidenced above, economic marginalization and DES often feed off each other, creating a positive feedback loop in which population and environmental pressures contribute to marginalization, which, in turn, encourages the poor to overexploit the environment to survive, and so on.

Finally, economic marginalization stemming from DES can be further aggravated by state and societal elites who capitalize on scarcities of cropland, timber, or other resources to enrich themselves at the expense of others. When population and environmental pressures lead to renewable resource scarcity, the value of the resource in question increases. As Homer-Dixon notes, this "can open up opportunities for fast profits from speculation on resources. It also becomes easier to corner the market on key resources—that is, to capture such a significant fraction of the resource pool that monopolistic profits can be extracted."[22] Consequently, at the very time that DES impoverishes the many it can fill the coffers of the few. And as elites seize control over critical resources and engage in rent-seeking behavior, those marginalized by the direct effects of scarcity are hurt further still.[23]

DEMOGRAPHIC SHIFTS

Population growth and environmental pressures frequently lead to important shifts in the demographic composition of countries, including changes in age structure and rates of urbanization. Countries with consistently high fertility rates and gradually declining infant mortality typically experience "youth bulges," that is, a demographic structure in which younger cohorts make up a large proportion of the total population.[24] This describes the situation in many developing countries. In the Occupied Palestinian Territories, for example, 65.1 percent of the population was under the age of twenty-five in 2000, and 46.4 percent was under the age of fifteen. In the developing world as a whole, 51.5 percent was under the age of twenty-five, and 33 percent was under the age of fifteen in 2000; excluding China, the total was 55.4 and 35.9 percent, respectively.[25]

Demographic and environmental stress can also increase rates of urbanization. Population growth in urban areas can contribute directly to the "natural" growth of cities.[26] Urbanization is also fostered by rural-to-urban migration, which appears to account for 40 to 60 percent of annual city growth in developing countries. "Pull" incentives for migration include greater perceived opportunities for education, employment, health care, and other social services in cities compared to rural areas. Other forces "push" rural residents into cities. Here DES can lead to migration, as increasing poverty, degradation and maldistributions of land, water, forest, and fishery resources, and reduced agricultural employment all encourage people to move to urban areas in search of a better life.[27]

Natural growth and rural-to-urban migration are currently leading to an explosion of cities in developing countries. Although the absolute number of individuals living in rural areas in developing countries is expected to remain about the same over the next several decades, both the number and the proportion of people living in urban areas are expected to increase substantially. In 1950 only 18 percent of people in developing countries lived in urban areas compared to 40 percent in 2000; by 2030 the proportion living in urban areas is predicted to rise to 56 percent. The total urban population in developing countries may grow from its 2000 level of 2 billion to nearly 4 billion by 2030, representing an average annual increase of 2.4 percent. In contrast, the rural population in developing countries is projected to increase by only 0.2 percent per year in the period from 2000 to 2030 (although the rate is expected to be much higher in Africa, where, despite high rates of urbanization, the rural population may triple by 2030). The predicted increase in the number of very large cities will also take place predominantly in developing countries. Out of forty cities with at least 5 million inhabitants in 2001, thirty-one were in developing countries (including thirteen of seventeen megacities with 10 million or more inhabitants); by 2015 forty-eight of the fifty-eight projected large cities will be in developing countries (including seventeen of twenty-one megacities).[28]

DEPRIVATION AND INCREASED SOCIAL GRIEVANCES

DES can increase the level of grievances within societies. The primary sources of such grievances are absolute and relative deprivation brought on by population and environmental pressures on the poor. Absolute deprivation occurs when there is a discrepancy between what people get and what they need. Relative deprivation occurs when there is a discrepancy between what people get and what they feel they are entitled to. Relative deprivation frequently goes hand in hand with increasing hardship but can be present even when individuals' living standards are improving if others' are improving even more.[29]

Demographically and environmentally induced resource scarcity and economic marginalization can lead to both types of deprivation. As absolute levels of hardship increase and the supply of economic and natural resources shift away from poorer segments of society, resentment will grow among those receiving the short end of the stick. Once again, the Occupied Palestinian Territories demonstrate these dynamics. A combination of rapid population growth (nearly 4 percent a year from 1990 to 2000), intensive agricultural practices, and fragile water ecosystems have resulted in a scarcity of freshwater in the West Bank and Gaza Strip. However, Palestinians experience this scarcity to a much greater degree than Israeli settlers do. This stems from a conscious decision by the Israeli state to use its control over scarce water resources to curry favor with Jewish settlers while increasing its social control over Palestinians. The end result is a profound sense of relative deprivation among Palestinians.[30]

Demographic shifts can also lead to a sense of deprivation. Youth bulges can result in large numbers of uneducated, unemployed, and otherwise frustrated young people who feel both absolutely and relatively deprived.[31] In the Middle East and North Africa, for example, 25.6 percent of those between the ages of fifteen and twenty-four were unemployed in 2003; in sub-Saharan Africa 21 percent of those in this age range had no job. History suggests that such youths are prone to radicalization. In Sri Lanka, for example, both the Sinhalese national insurgency in 1970 and the Tamil rebellion in the 1980s reached their peak levels of support when the numbers of fifteen to twenty-four year olds exceeded 20 percent of the total population of their respective groups.[32] Cross-national data point to similar dynamics at work elsewhere as well.[33]

In some cases urbanization can also contribute to deprivation and ratchet up the level of social grievances. While it is true that the standard of living and quality of life of urban dwellers in developing countries is, on average, better than it is in rural areas, the benefits of urban life frequently do not extend to the poorest groups within cities. Many city residents face appalling conditions. Presently hundreds of millions of urban residents in developing countries lack access to clean drinking water and latrines, sewage is often released into waterways untreated, and one- to two-thirds of urban solid waste is not collected. An excess of 1 billion people live in cities where air pollution is greater than healthful levels. Furthermore, poor urban migrants tend to cluster in squatter settlements, where they are frequently exposed to extreme environmental hazards, such as industrial emissions, and can easily become trapped in chronic poverty. At the same time rising expectations generated by the promise of government services, coupled with greater access to diverse media information on the "good life" enjoyed by wealthier city residents at home and abroad, can significantly increase the sense of relative deprivation. While the majority of urbanites will believe that their lives have improved, this is much less likely among the poor and dispossessed. Indeed, income inequality, and thus the potential for relative deprivation, is much wider in urban areas than in rural ones.[34]

These problems resulting from urbanization can be seen throughout the developing world. Even before the recent economic troubles in the rapidly industrializing cities of Southeast Asia and Latin America, the infrastructure lagged far behind their growing needs. And in poorer regions absolute deprivation is extensive. Across Africa, for example, urban dwellers in Abidjan (Côte d'Ivore), Dakar (Senegal), Kinshasa (Democratic Republic of Congo), Lusaka (Zambia), Nairobi (Kenya), and other cities "are confronting rampant urban population growth, a breakdown in urban services such as water and sanitation, a deterioration in urban environmental quality, the AIDS epidemic, and growing social tensions—problems rendered all the more intractable by the extensive poverty of the region."[35]

A sense of deprivation will likely be translated into grievances if individuals or social groups come to blame or resent others for their predicament. Grievances may be directed against the state, other groups, or both. Antistate grievances will emerge when the state is seen as passive in the face of, or an active participant in, significant deprivation, whether it is absolute or relative. These grievances will often manifest themselves, at least initially, in rising demands for better government-provided goods and services, in addition to growing calls for political and economic reforms, such as land reform, reductions in corruption, and greater political participation. More violent manifestations are also possible. Rapid population growth, soil erosion, deforestation, and unequal land distribution in El Salvador, for example, significantly increased antistate grievances and support for communist rebels during the 1980s.[36] Iran provides another illustration. Prior to the 1978 Iranian revolution, demographic pressure on the agricultural sector of the economy contributed substantially to mass opposition against the Shah. The Iranian population nearly doubled from almost 17 million to 32 million between 1950 and 1976. Despite the Shah's efforts at land reform in the early 1960s, only 22 percent of Iran's peasants in the 1970s acquired sufficient land for subsistence. Significant rural-to-urban migration contributed to unemployment, a profound sense of relative deprivation (as new urbanites quickly became aware of disparities in national income and lifestyles), and added fuel to the revolutionary fire.[37]

In other situations grievances will emerge among different social groups themselves as a result of population and environmental pressures. This is likely when a sense of relative deprivation makes losers resentful and covetous of the gains of others. Intense resource competition can also increase intergroup grievances by creating zero-sum conflicts of interest between groups. In Xinjiang Province in western China, for example, Muslim poverty, feelings of absolute and relative deprivation, and intergroup competition result from a combination of high rates of Muslim population growth and state investment funds for irrigation and agricultural improvements that are heavily biased in favor of areas settled by Han Chinese immigrants.[38] Intergroup grievances typically manifest themselves in such activities as increased legal disputes, protests, sporadic violence, and calls for the state to intervene. Finally, in some cases antistate and intergroup grievances will increase simultaneously. This is likely when disadvantaged groups attribute their plight to state collusion with societal rivals.

Pressures on the State

DES can also produce severe strains on states, contributing in extreme circumstances to collapse of state authority.

STATE STRENGTH AND STATE WEAKNESS

A state's strength represents its ability to actually realize, in the empirical sense, its binding rule-making authority. Two key factors determine the degree of state strength or weakness: a state's functional capacity and its cohesion.[39] A state's functional capacity for binding rule making depends on a combination of coercive power, administrative capacity, and legitimacy of authority.[40] In the context of explaining demographically and environmentally induced conflict, these aspects of functional capacity should be evaluated in terms of their impact on the state's ability to provide individuals and groups with economic and physical security, and deter or repress collective violence.

A second key determinant of strength or weakness is a state's cohesion. Cohesion represents the degree to which state elites are unified or divided, both in terms of their interests and their strategies for advancing these interests. While functional capacity determines the theoretical capacity of the state to make and implement binding rules, the degree of state cohesion determines the ability and willingness of disparate state elites to act as a unified actor when such collective action is necessary to carry out governmental functions. In terms of maintaining domestic order, the ability and desire of state elites to unify behind policies designed to address societal demands or otherwise head off organized antistate or intergroup violence is especially important.

State strength can be mapped along a continuum, with "very strong" and "very weak" states representing opposite ends. As the functional capacity or cohesion of the state decreases, the state becomes weaker (see Figure 2.1). States "low" in *both* functional capacity and cohesion are prime candidates for failure.[41] Such situations are likely to be characterized by what Charles Tilly calls "multiple sovereignty": a situation in which members of a previously subordinate segment of the polity assert sovereignty, nonruling contenders mobilize into blocs successfully exerting control over some portion of the state, and/or the ruling coalition fragments into two or more competing factions contending for power.[42]

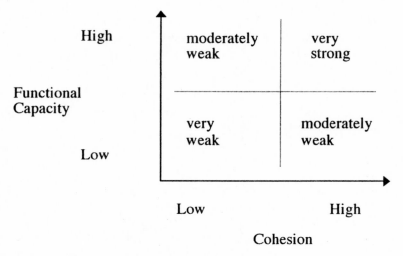

Figure 2.1. State Strength

DES AND STATE WEAKNESS

DES can weaken a state's functional capacity in several interrelated ways. First, the pressures that drive increased social grievances can also weaken the state. As we saw above, the demands placed on the state from suffering segments of the economy and marginalized individuals are likely to grow as population and environmental pressures mount. Demands may include calls for costly development projects, such as hydroelectric dams, canals, and irrigation systems, subsidies for fertilizer and other agricultural inputs, and urban demands for employment, housing, schools, sanitation, energy, and lower food prices. Demands by key societal elites, regime supporters, and urbanites are likely to be given top priority by the state. DES may produce some winners among the elite, especially among those capable of capturing windfall profits from increasingly scarce natural resources, but others will suffer as economic activities are undermined by environmental degradation or as population growth increases competition for employment. Demands from elites and regime supporters for compensations for economic losses, often in the form of subsidies or public-sector jobs, obviously must be taken seriously if the state wishes to preserve its foundation of support.[43] Rising urban needs also require governmental attention, because even the strongest states have to be wary of urban unrest. Overall, rising societal demands stemming from DES increase fiscal strains and thus risk eroding a state's administrative capacity by requiring budgetary trade-offs. A state's legitimacy may also be cast in doubt if individuals and groups blame the government for their plight.[44] The state's legitimacy may decline, for example, if the government fails to implement land reform in the face of significant rural population growth or if state corruption and patronage appear widespread in a context of swelling urban unemployment rates.

To make matters worse, state interventions to meet rising demands can have unanticipated consequences that further reduce the administrative capacity and legitimacy of the state. Meeting urban demands, for example, often generates a positive feedback loop whereby improved access to goods and services increases "pull" incentives for rural-to-urban migration, which, in turn, increases urban demands and the threats perceived by central authorities.[45] Furthermore, as Homer-Dixon notes, many of the interventions and development schemes that state elites see as necessary to meet rising urban and rural demands in the short term end up seriously distorting prices, encouraging corruption, accelerating debt, and aggravating the kinds of economic inefficiencies that undermine administrative capacity in the medium and long term.[46]

Second, DES can undermine overall economic productivity, thereby reducing the revenue available to local and central governments at the very time that rising demands require greater expenditures.[47] Population growth is not universally detrimental to the economy. Nevertheless, in countries with stagnant economies, scarce or costly natural resources, poorly defined property rights or otherwise dysfunctional markets incapable of efficiently allocating critical natural resources, and government policies biased against labor (the most abundant factor of production in most developing countries), rapid population growth can undermine economic productivity.[48] Some economists suggest that population growth may lower the ratio of capital to labor and that the resulting "capital shallowing" can reduce the per capita economic productivity of a society.[49] More substantially, rapid population expansion tends to increase dependency ratios and make it more difficult for households to educate and pass on capital to children. By creating large numbers of young people who cannot be educated or productively employed, population growth can undermine the productivity of workers and reduce a country's ability to compete in the global economy.[50] Higher dependency ratios, in addition to other forms of economic marginalization stemming from DES, also force households to shift a greater proportion of financial resources toward basic consumption, limiting their ability to save. In the aggregate, lower domestic savings rates can undermine investments necessary for long-term economic growth or force public and private actors to borrow from abroad, thereby increasing foreign debt.[51] Lastly, as we saw above, rapid population growth can force the state to shift government spending toward meeting short-term societal demands, thereby limiting the funds available for more productive, growth-oriented investments.[52]

Environmental stresses, including the loss of valuable agricultural land and reductions in crop yields as a result of soil erosion or pollution, water shortages, the loss of timber and fuelwood owing to unsustainable forestry practices, and the loss of hydroelectric power and transportation because of the siltation of rivers and reservoirs, can also lead to economic decline and reduce the flow of revenue to the state.[53] Environmental depletion and degradation will obviously have the most serious adverse effects on countries whose economies depend on natural resources. In Central America, for example, renewable resources accounted for more than half of all economic production, half of all employment, and most exports during the 1980s. Over the course of the decade rapid population growth, deforestation, soil erosion, sedimentation of dams, waterways, and coastal fishing grounds, and grossly unequal land tenure systems all contributed to a precipitous decline in per capita income, aggravating serious fiscal crises throughout the region.[54] In the current period the World Bank's estimate of "net national savings" provides a window into the drag that environmental stress is having on the economic prospects of many low-income countries dependent on natural resources. This measure is meant to capture not only a country's economic surplus but also its depletion of natural resources, accumulation of pollutants, and investments in human capital. According to these calculations, many developing countries currently have low or negative adjusted net savings.[55]

Economic decline and a reduction in administrative capacity can set in motion feedback loops and other negative consequences that confront states with additional challenges. As the economy declines states may face greater incentives to exploit their country's natural resources rapidly and unsustainably in order to generate revenue. Even when this strategy is successful in providing a short-term economic boost, it may undermine the very natural resource base on which medium- and long-term economic development depends.[56] A reduction in a state's administrative capacity can also encourage environmental degradation. In China, for example, a decline in the capacity of the central government to exert its authority over localities has hindered the state's ability to prevent degradation of water resources.[57]

Third, DES can undermine a state's coercive power. Obviously revenue shortfalls can limit the funds available for police and armed forces. Population growth and internal migration can also reduce a state's relative coercive power by creating large concentrations of individuals in

urban areas or outlying rural areas that are increasingly costly to control.[58] Moreover, renewable resource scarcities sometimes contribute to
growing concentrations of wealth and power among societal elites capable of capturing the profits from the increased value of these resources. This, in turn, can reduce a state's coercive power. As local and
regional elites increase their wealth and power, they may create competing loci of authority, thereby reducing the state's relative coercive
capacity and legitimacy over subnational units. Population pressures
and control over land and water resources in the KwaZulu-Natal region of South Africa, for example, helped to solidify the political control of quasi-autonomous warlords during the Apartheid era.[59]

In addition to weakening the functional capacity of states, demographic and environmental stress can also undermine state cohesion
by generating acute competition and disagreements among elites inside the state. This can occur in at least three ways. First, cohesion will
erode if environmental degradation and resource scarcity creates intra-
governmental competition over those resources. In China, for example,
provinces have engaged in fierce competition over scarce water resources necessary for agriculture, industry, residential use, and hydropower.[60] Second, if population and environmental pressures undermine a country's economy, state elites will be forced to compete for
shrinking budgets. This can encourage increased factionalism and bureaucratic infighting, thereby frustrating the state's ability to take decisive, unified action to address socioeconomic problems. Finally, cohesion will be undermined if state elites disagree among themselves
about the appropriate strategy for responding to demands and grievances arising from marginalized segments of the populace. In extreme
cases disputes can paralyze governments by dividing state elites into
rival factions of reformers, moderates, and reactionaries incapable of
working together to meet growing societal needs.

It should be noted that state weakness resulting from DES will not
necessarily occur in a linear fashion. Instead, the process whereby state
authority erodes will likely exhibit nonlinear "threshold effects": states
will first become stressed, then brittle, and then vulnerable to a rapid
collapse. In addition, state weakness may not occur to the same degree
in all parts of a country at the same time. It is more likely that state
authority will wane unevenly across the regional landscape of a country. A state in decline will be forced to cede authority bit by bit. Eventually the state may control little more than the capital city and its immediate surroundings.[61] Consequently, the scenarios discussed below for
the outbreak of violent conflict as a result of state weakness could conceivably occur at the local, regional, or national levels as state authority
declines at these different levels of governance.

Finally, the "straw that breaks the camel's back" need not be demographic or environmental in character. Population and environmental pressures are frequently medium- and long-term sources of state weakness, whereas the proximate cause in any given case may be a set of short-term policy decisions or exogenous shocks. Such proximate causes include economic mismanagement, significant changes in a country's terms of trade, a global economic crisis, a short-term climatic shock, externally imposed structural adjustment or pressure for political reform, foreign military involvement, or other similar events. Nevertheless, the rate and magnitude of DES can significantly condition the vulnerability of a state (i.e., the government's ability to accommodate such poor policies or shocks). All told, states made brittle by DES are more prone to failure brought on by any number of non-DES factors.

Two Pathways to Civil Strife

Scholarly work on the general causes of internal wars suggests that state weakness makes countries particularly prone to civil strife. A substantial weakening of state capacity and cohesion can lead to violent "bottom-up" conflicts initiated by societal actors, including both antistate and intergroup conflicts, if the state loses its ability to maintain order and a security dilemma emerges among social groups. Alternatively state weakness can lead to "top-down" conflicts initiated by threatened state elites who instigate violence in a desperate bid to perpetuate their rule.[62] Using these arguments as building blocks, I contend that pressures on societies and the states emanating from DES create two potential pathways to civil strife: *state failure* and *state exploitation*.

THE STATE FAILURE HYPOTHESIS

State failure conflicts occur when the state is substantially weakened, thereby increasing the opportunities and incentives for antistate and intergroup violence. As we saw in chapter 1, the neo-Malthusian scholars who employ a state-centric approach to demographic and environmental conflict tend to focus on this pathway. Specifically, these authors contend that the erosion of state authority expands the structural opportunities (or "political space") for antistate challengers.[63] The view that state weakness is a permissive cause of strife follows the line of argument advanced by many contemporary students of revolution and rebellion in sociology and comparative politics.[64]

Strong states prevent organized antistate and intergroup strife by altering the cost-benefit calculations of individuals and groups contemplating violence as a possible means of advancing their interests. States possessing powerful coercive apparatuses—police, armed forces, and intelligence organizations—can dramatically increase the costs of intergroup and antistate violence, and thus deter or repress such strife before it threatens the status quo political order. This suggests that a state's overall coercive power, commonly measured in terms of its monopoly on the means of physical force, is an essential determinant of a state's ability to prevent organized violence. Nevertheless, coercive power is rarely enough, in and of itself, to maintain order in the face of substantial antistate grievances. And, paradoxically, an over-reliance on the *actual* application of force may be both a sign of weakness and *increase* the risks of turmoil by enhancing insecurity among affected groups (see the discussion of the security dilemma below).

A comprehensive assessment of the relationship between state strength and the maintenance of order must therefore acknowledge the importance of the state's administrative capacity, legitimacy, and cohesion. States with a strong and capable administrative apparatus can limit incentives for violence by helping individuals and groups satisfy their basic needs for education, housing, social services, food, water, sanitation, energy, and so on.[65] Furthermore, high levels of legitimacy may substantially compensate for low levels of coercive power. A state's legitimacy, or "right to rule," is determined by the degree of confidence and trust among key social groups in the state's intention to protect their fundamental interests and values. High levels of legitimacy ratchet up the normative inhibitions and perceived costs associated with collective violence. On the other hand, a state whose authority is deemed completely illegitimate will find it much more difficult to maintain domestic order indefinitely regardless of its coercive power. The absence of legitimacy means that individuals have little confidence in the ability of the status quo to preserve their basic interests and values. This lowers the threshold required for individuals and groups to switch their allegiance to antistate challengers promising a better life.[66] Finally, a state's cohesion matters too. Cohesive states that maintain the loyalty of key factions and regime supporters are much less vulnerable to challenges from within and are also better equipped to respond effectively to social grievances.

Organized antistate and intergroup violence becomes a real possibility when individuals and groups calculate that the benefits to be accrued from violence outweigh the costs. State weakness makes it more likely that individuals and groups will choose violence as a means of advancing their interests by lowering the costs of such action. Exactly *how* weak the state must be to permit organized violence undoubtedly varies depending on the context. If the costs associated with the status quo order are sufficiently intolerable, for example, desperate individuals and groups may take a risky gamble and engage in violence even in a political context where we might normally expect the state to be strong enough to deter such violence. Nevertheless, while the exact threshold of state failure may vary, it is surely the case that as the state weakens, the opportunities, and therefore the prospects, for violence increase.

This conceptualization provides an essential corrective to analyses that focus solely on societal sources of violence and ignore the state. But current state failure accounts miss a number of important dynamics linking demographically and environmentally induced state weakness to conflict. Not all instances of state failure result in conflict; there are many more weak states in the world than there are antistate and intergroup conflicts. In other words, existing state failure accounts overpredict conflict in the context of a weakened state. State strength is an extremely important factor shaping the cost-benefit calculations of potential combatants, but it is not the only one. Organized antistate and intergroup violence are very costly enterprises. As I discussed in chapter 1, at the individual level, the cost-benefit calculation confronting potential participants in collective violence provides powerful reasons for them to sit on the sidelines and let others do the fighting. Furthermore, at the group level, there are high potential costs to communal violence, as well as benefits to be gained by continuing to cooperate peacefully and engage in exchange with other social groups.[67] We would therefore not expect every instance of state failure to lead to civil strife. The key questions, then, become (1) Under what conditions is the erosion of state authority most likely to result in civil strife? and (2) What role do demographic and environmental forces potentially play?

Like the boys deserted on the uninhabited island in William Golding's *Lord of the Flies*, individuals and groups interacting in a social environment that lacks a strong central authority are prone to violent conflict when they come to fear that others will victimize them if they fail to fight. In other words, state failure conflicts are most likely when DES and state weakness produce a "security dilemma." International relations scholars, especially those in the Realist tradition, have long argued that the anarchic nature of the international system not only permits conflict but actually encourages violent clashes between countries via preventive and preemptive acts.[68] These scholars argue that violent conflict arises not only from incompatible interests and greed but also from tragedy. At the center of this argument is the notion of the security dilemma. The logic of the security dilemma can also help us understand why violent conflicts sometimes occur *within* countries.[69]

First, as the state weakens, it generates a great deal of insecurity. An emerging anarchy within countries creates a situation in which no neutral central authority is capable of providing the collective goods of economic and physical security to the populace. Social groups—including ethno-cultural, religious, and class-based groups, as well as remnants of the state and its organizations—will be left to fend for themselves. Because groups want to remain independent and economically and physically secure, they must be wary of any actions taken by other groups that might threaten their security. Unfortunately, as each group attempts to protect its core interests and values, its actions and preparations, even if ostensibly taken for defensive purposes, can incite fear in others. An anarchic political context can thus create a situation in which even steps taken by groups with no interest other than maintaining their security can set off an action-reaction spiral that leaves all parties worse off and less secure. This is the security dilemma.[70]

It should be noted that the total absence of state authority (i.e., anarchy) is not required for an internal security dilemma to operate. The logic of the security dilemma only requires (1) the absence of a *neutral* central authority capable and willing to resolve societal conflicts before they escalate; and (2) a significant threat to a vulnerable group's prospects for survival. The security dilemma may thus operate at levels of state failure short of complete collapse. As the state weakens, for example, it often tilts toward a particular segment of the population in an effort to solidify its key supporters, leaving others to fend for themselves. Moreover, in the face of rising antistate grievances, weakened and increasingly desperate states typically begin to rely more heavily on repression, which, in turn, magnifies insecurity among targeted groups. Ultimately, if the state cannot protect the survival of some groups or becomes a potential danger to them, then abandoned and threatened groups face incentives to engage in self-help behavior, potentially threatening others—including the weakened state itself—and setting in motion the action-reaction dynamics of the security dilemma.[71]

Second, the general dynamics linking state failure to the emergence of a security dilemma will be compounded in countries plagued by high levels of DES, because groups will face other direct threats to their security emanating from renewable resource scarcity, economic marginalization, demographic shifts, rising social grievances, and intergroup competition. These threats produce additional incentives for individuals and groups to restructure the political order to meet their needs, by force if necessary. Furthermore, scarcity and resource competition often create conditions under which membership in conflict groups is essential for securing access to these resources. DES thereby makes it easier for political entrepreneurs to use access to scarce natural resources as selective incentives to encourage individuals to mobilize around potentially violent causes. Thus, even when state failure alone may be insufficient to create a security dilemma, the *combination* of state failure and the various pressures placed on individuals and social groups by DES produce a particularly volatile social context.

The security dilemma stems from two fundamental problems facing social groups as the state weakens. One problem is uncertainty regarding the intentions and motivations of others. As John Herz once observed: "whether man is 'by nature' peaceful and cooperative, or aggressive and domineering, is not the question. . . . It is his uncertainty and anxiety as to his neighbors' intentions that places man in this basic dilemma, and makes the 'homo homini lupus' a primary fact of the social life of man."[72] Strong and neutral states are capable of substantially mitigating the problem of uncertainty. By serving as third-party facilitators of communication and arbitration between social groups, strong states reduce uncertainty by increasing the flow, reliability, and impartiality of information.[73] Additionally, by providing physical security for groups against the potential attacks of others, strong and neutral states reduce the importance of any remaining uncertainty. Not surprisingly a significant erosion of state authority creates a complex and confusing situation in which groups are likely to be much more uncertain regarding the intentions and motivations of others, including the motivations of the weakened state itself. Uncertainty is enhanced by the fact that some groups, seeking to exploit the emerging anarchy to advance their interests, have strategic incentives to misrepresent their *own* intentions to obtain bargaining advantages over rivals or misrepresent the intentions of *others* in order to mobilize support.[74] Finally, even if groups are fairly confident that others currently harbor no aggressive designs, there is no guarantee that these intentions will not change.[75] As Russell Hardin notes, "One need not hate members of another group, but one might fear their potential hatred or even merely their threat."[76]

A second problem is the inability of actors to credibly commit not to exploit the cooperative and peaceful positions of others. Even if groups are fairly certain of one another's current intentions and interests, they may still find themselves in a tragic spiral of insecurity and conflict if (1) they value their survival highly (a reasonable assumption); (2) there is some probability that a rival group will threaten this survival; and (3) it is difficult for their opponents to credibly commit to forsake violence.[77] The situation is especially precarious when an imbalance of group power creates opportunities for a stronger group—often elements of the weakening state or its current or former allies—to exploit the weak, or creates fear on behalf of the weak that this will

be the case. Under such circumstances a credible commitment on behalf of stronger groups not to exploit their position is very difficult,
and weaker groups, fearing oppression or destruction, face incentives
to engage in preventive or preemptive violence. Unfortunately this is
exactly the scenario likely to emerge as the state weakens in countries
with high levels of DES.

Even if weaker groups are pessimistic about their chances of victory,
an acute security dilemma raises the perceived costs on inaction and
thus the likelihood of violence. If the costs of doing nothing are high—
because status quo threats to security are severe—and future chances
for success appear even more bleak, weaker groups will be encouraged
to engage in a "now or never" gamble for survival.[78] Under normal
circumstances the inherent collective action problems involved in
forming conflict groups suggest that even a moderately weak state
should be capable of preventing widespread antistate or intergroup violence. Nevertheless, if the combination of DES and declining state authority poses a significant threat to the survival of a disadvantaged
group, the cost-benefit calculus facing individuals will be altered. Most
obviously the benefits to engaging in collective action increase substantially. The costs, relative to doing nothing, also decline. If doing nothing risks annihilation, joining a conflict group may seem rational even
if the probability for group success is only marginally increased by any
one individual's participation. In other words, an individual with little
to lose might as well take a chance. Finally, as noted above, conflicts
over or inspired by natural resource issues, such as access to land or
forest resources, often provide spoils only to those who participate.
This generates significant private gains to be had from joining conflict
groups and facilitates the efforts of political entrepreneurs to overcome
problems associated with free-riding.

Ultimately, in the highly insecure landscape likely to emerge as state
authority wanes and demographic and environmental threats to vulnerable groups mount, it takes very little to start a spiral of violence.
The initial spark could result from a random act of intergroup violence, a preemptive act taken under the assumption (reasonable or
mistaken) that a rival group soon intends to attack, or any other similar event. Whatever its source, the nature of the security dilemma
makes violence especially difficult to contain once it begins.[79] The
quest to guarantee security and independence under conditions of
state weakness and scarcity conditions all groups to adopt worst-case
thinking; they must assume that violence and exploitation is possible
from any other group at any moment. The occurrence of even small
amounts of organized violence makes this fear a reality and forces all
groups to quickly act to secure their positions. Reprisal and counter-

reprisal transform a situation in which all *feel* vulnerable into one in which all *are* vulnerable; apparent, and frequently illusory, conflicts of interest turn into real ones.[80]

THE STATE EXPLOITATION HYPOTHESIS

State exploitation conflicts represent a second pathway whereby DES-induced pressures on society and the state in developing countries can lead to violence. State exploitation is primarily a top-down process and can occur at levels of state weakness far short of total collapse.

Social schisms emanating from demographic and environmental pressures present state elites in the developing world with both incentives and opportunities to instigate violence. On the incentives side of the equation, rising grievances and social conflict, if left unchecked or unchanneled, can potentially threaten the actual or perceived viability of a regime. All regimes, even the most authoritarian ones, require some base of social support to stay in power. In a country experiencing severe DES, state elites are likely to fear an erosion of this support if they are unable to meet rising societal demands.

Threats to a regime encourage state elites to search for strategies that will stabilize their base, mobilize new supporters, and co-opt or crush political opponents.[81] State elites sometimes conclude, tragically, that the instigation of intergroup violence is an effective means of achieving these goals. Obviously, inciting intergroup violence can be a brutally effective way of crushing political opponents. Less obvious, but no less important, is that organized intergroup violence can divert attention away from the regime's failings while also making key social groups dependent on the state for their physical well-being, thereby ensuring their allegiance. The insecurity generated by state-sponsored intergroup violence provides existing and potential allies of the state with powerful incentives to support the regime; after all, if these groups back the regime, both their chances for survival and their share of the spoils from victory increase dramatically.[82]

Incentives for state-sponsored violence are only half the story, however, because state elites cannot create intergroup bloodshed by fiat. Since violence is costly for participants, individuals and groups must have good reasons to attack their neighbors. It is here that DES provides threatened elites with golden opportunities to perpetuate their rule. The natural resource and economic competition engendered by mounting population and environmental pressures can easily result in zero-sum distributional conflicts between social groups, and absolute and relative deprivation stemming from DES can expand the breadth and depth of intergroup animosities. This creates a kind of social tinderbox with ample opportunities for state elites to spark violent con-

flicts by fanning the fears, hatreds, and desires of contending groups.
Elites may indirectly incite violence by capitalizing on propaganda advantages, such as control over newspapers, television, radio, and public appearances, in order to exaggerate the threats posed by certain
groups or the potential gains to be had if one group attacks another.[83]
In other instances elites may actually engineer clashes by supporting
or encouraging attackers and then standing aside while opposing
groups kill one another. This kind of direct encouragement is most
likely to succeed when the state can ensure participants concrete benefits, such as access to coveted natural resources, if they engage in violence.

Because of the inherent threats to the long-term stability of any regime posed by societywide warfare, we would expect state elites to
prefer to keep state-sponsored violence from escalating to civil war.
Nevertheless, even if this is what most state elites ultimately prefer,
they may, like the sorcerer's apprentice, lose control of the forces they
unleash. State exploitation makes it incredibly difficult for ruling elites
to credibly commit to prevent future aggression by the regime or its
allies. Under such circumstances victimized groups concerned with
their security and fearful of future hostilities may feel compelled to
initiate preventive or preemptive violence before the situation wors-
ens, even if their prospects for success are low.[84] As Hardin notes, intergroup violence can lead to the collapse of general expectations of
reasonable behavior, "making preemption seem to be a compelling interest, thereby ensuring future violence."[85] In the spiral of attack and
counterattack that ensues, an entire society can easily be dragged into
the Hobbessian vortex of all-out civil war.

If intergroup violence is inherently difficult to control, why would
state elites ever step on the slippery slope to begin with? There are two
possible reasons. First, immediate needs to reduce DES-induced threats
to the stability of the regime may encourage state elites to adopt short
time horizons. Under such circumstances long-term costs tend to be
heavily discounted, and actions that appear irrational in the long term
may be viewed as rational in the short term. Second, since most of the
potential benefits from such gambles will be accrued by those in power
while the bulk of the potential costs will fall on the citizenry and opposition, state elites may be willing to run the risk of broader conflict.[86]

Intervening Variables

Not all instances of DES-induced state failure or state exploitation lead
to large-scale violence. In this section I suggest that two intervening
variables, *groupness* and *institutional inclusivity*, play crucial roles in de-

high groupness   low groupness

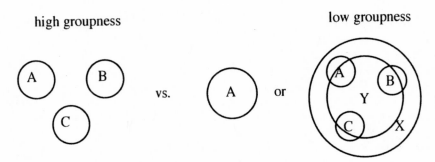

A, B, C, X, and Y represent different identity-groups.

Figure 2.2. Groupness *

termining when state failure or state exploitation dynamics are most likely to spawn civil strife.

GROUPNESS

Demographically and environmentally induced state failure and state exploitation conflicts are more likely in societies characterized by high degrees of groupness. Here groupness is conceptualized in terms of the degree and nature of social cleavages. Individuals always have multiple identities and group affiliations. The degree of groupness in any given society depends on the extent to which clusters of individuals depend on distinct identity groups—whether ethno-cultural, religious, or class-based—for economic and physical security as opposed to a number of overlapping and crosscutting identity groups.[87] Societies characterized by high degrees of groupness tend to be heterogeneous with few overlapping and crosscutting group affiliations and interests. In contrast, both homogeneous societies dominated by a single identity group and heterogeneous societies with significant crosscutting group affiliations and interests manifest low levels of groupness. Figure 2.2 provides an illustration to help clarify the distinction between "high" and "low" degrees of groupness.

   High degrees of groupness increase the prospects for both state failure and state exploitation conflicts by facilitating the formation of conflict groups. Strong group identification can contribute to conflict group formation by encouraging individuals to conceptualize the costs and benefits associated with their personal choices in *collective* rather than individualistic terms. Even when individuals strongly prefer change in the status quo and believe violence to be the best route for achieving such change, an individualistic cost-benefit calculation tends to encourage free-riding; if an individual's contribution to the preferred outcome is slight and violence is costly, then he or she will be inclined to sit on the sidelines and let others take all the risks. However, if costs and benefits are defined in collective terms, individuals realize that their individually rational behavior is collectively irrational, because, in the aggregate, widespread free-riding prevents the advancement of group interests. A collective conceptualization of interests thus makes collective action more likely.[88]

Furthermore, a high degree of groupness increases the prospects for conflict group formation even if individuals fail to define their preferences in collectivist terms. Michael Taylor has argued that the prospects for joining an organized conflict group are higher when individuals are part of a preexisting community of people who share at least some beliefs and values in common, engage in direct and many-sided interactions, and enjoy some form of reciprocity.[89] A strong community allows individual actions to be monitored, and communities frequently have at their disposal a powerful array of positive and negative social sanctions that can be used as selective incentives to encourage participation in conflict groups. The existence of a community also facilitates conditional cooperation (i.e., cooperation based on direct or defuse reciprocity). Participation in organized violence "is conditioned on others continuing to participate, but the experience of conditional cooperation, the knowledge conditions which are necessary for successful conditional cooperation (i.e., knowing that others are cooperating), and the effectiveness of social sanctions used during a rebellion all derive from the fact that the participants in the rebellion are members of a pre-existing community and will continue to be members of the same community after the rebellion."[90] Thus, in game theoretic terms, cases of organized violence are embedded in a larger "iterated" game of social interaction within the community. Consequently, failure to participate in organized violence on behalf of the group might bring about social sanctions and threaten an individual's ability to reap benefits from other aspects of participation in the community. This encourages individual participation in conflict groups even if individuals conceive of costs and benefits solely in individualistic terms.

Finally, a high degree of groupness also lowers the costs for political entrepreneurs seeking to mobilize conflict groups in order to advance their own interests. Since discrete groups already exist, political entrepreneurs do not have to spend as many precious resources overcoming collective action problems to create them. Instead, elites can devote their time, energy, and resources to assuring the support of preexisting groups for their cause. Significant social cleavages and high degrees of group cohesion further facilitate elite-driven mobilization by making it much easier for elites to target discreet groups for propaganda purposes.[91]

While high degrees of groupness make countries more conflict prone, a low degree of groupness has the opposite effect. Significant crosscutting group ties and interests increase the perceived costs for individuals contemplating antistate or intergroup violence. The more individuals see violence as self-defeating, the less likely it is to occur.[92] Moreover, if individuals have several groups to which they can turn in order to meet their basic needs for economic and physical security, as well as psychological benefits from group membership, sanctions arising from a failure to participate in violence on behalf of any particular group will be less likely to overcome collective action problems. Conflict group formation is also less likely because a low degree of groupness dramatically increases the organizational costs for political entrepreneurs.

INSTITUTIONAL INCLUSIVITY

A second important intervening variable is institutional inclusivity. The state, as defined above, is both a set of actors (state elites) and organizations, and a set of institutions that enable and constrain state elites and social actors. As conceptualized here, the inclusivity of state institutions refers to the degree to which key social groups are institutionally empowered to participate in, and potentially influence, decision making by state elites, especially the executive. Inclusive institutions guarantee a broad spectrum of social groups membership in the decision-making tiers of the executive (e.g., cabinets, the civil service, the military, etc.) or representation in a national legislature institutionally empowered to influence and constrain executive policies. Somewhat inclusive states allow structurally disadvantaged groups input into national decision making. Highly inclusive institutions also provide groups with mutual vetoes or require supramajorities for policy decisions impacting significantly on group rights.[93] In exclusive states, on the other hand, a narrow clique of state elites and their allies makes decisions without significant constraints.[94]

Although institutional inclusivity is no panacea, there are powerful reasons to suspect that countries with inclusive institutions will be less prone to demographically and environmentally induced civil strife. Institutional inclusivity makes state failure conflicts less likely by encouraging individuals and groups to opt for nonviolent strategies to voice their grievances and guarantee their economic and physical security. In the late 1960s Samuel Huntington made the bold claim that revolutions do not occur in democratic systems: "The absence of successful revolutions in democratic countries . . . suggests that, on the average, their political systems have more capacity for absorbing new groups into their political systems than do political systems where power is equally small but more concentrated."[95] This prediction has largely been borne out: no revolutionary movement has succeeded in overthrowing a democratically elected government, suggesting that inclusive institutions empirically hamper organized violence.[96]

Why would inclusive institutions help prevent state failure conflicts? In conditions of state weakness, individuals and groups are encouraged to engage in self-help. The self-help strategy they choose, however, depends on their menu of options. In the most basic sense, inclusive institutions create options, or the perception of options, for securing the needs of individuals and groups without resort to violence. And since large-scale organized violence is always an incredibly risky and costly enterprise, even for stronger parties, there is a general presumption toward choosing nonviolent strategies if they are available. As Ernesto "Che" Guevara famously observed: "Where a government has come into power through some form of popular vote . . . and maintains at least an appearance of constitutional legality, the guerrilla outbreak cannot be promoted, since the possibilities of peaceful struggle have not yet been exhausted."[97] We would therefore expect inclusive institutions to significantly complicate the mobilization efforts of political entrepreneurs seeking to build support for organized antistate or intergroup violence. Since the triggers for the spiral dynamics of the security dilemma are the mobilization and countermobilization of conflict groups, as well as the actions they take to advance their interests and preserve their security, and since inclusive institutions are likely to siphon off support for conflict groups by providing peaceful mechanisms for meeting interests, we would expect the security dilemma to be far less acute. In contrast, the security dilemma is likely to be intense in weak states with exclusive institutions. Because the state is decidedly tilted toward a narrow slice of society, excluded individuals and groups will have little faith that the government can or will provide for their security. These groups will thus have little choice but to pursue extra-institutional self-help strategies, including organized violence.[98]

Beyond undermining mobilization efforts, inclusive institutions also facilitate nonviolent compromise between social groups by providing a forum that makes it easier for parties with a basic common interest in peaceful coexistence to resolve residual conflicts of interest, whether these conflicts arise from DES or other security threats generated by state weakness, without taking up arms. In the language of the new institutional economics, the existence of inclusive institutions lowers the "transaction costs" involved in reaching cooperative arrangements relative to the costs of reaching an agreement in the absence of such institutions.[99] Inclusive institutions also provide a forum for repeated conflict resolution, thereby lengthening the "shadow of the future." Compromise is encouraged because groups feel that they can trade concessions now on certain issues for advantageous deals on other issues down the line.[100] The more confident disadvantaged groups are that stronger groups will continue to respect their rights, the less they will fear becoming victims, and the easier it will be for stronger groups to make credible assurances.[101] In countries with exclusive institutions, however, prospects for future cooperation and trust are lower, and intergroup resentment and fear will be greater.

In sum, state failure conflicts are much more likely when the state is weak and institutions are exclusive. In such contexts the rule of law is likely to be replaced by the rule of the jungle; weaker groups will fall prey to their more powerful rivals. If the state is too weak or too biased to impose a just solution, and if political institutions do not empower victims of severe deprivation and insecurity to peacefully influence government practices or, at the very least, check potential exploitation by stronger social groups, disadvantaged groups are faced with the following menu of unpalatable and extra-institutional choices: (1) silent suffering at the hands of more powerful actors; (2) peaceful mobilization with little prospect for success; or (3) support for armed resistance. Given these choices, civil strife is much more likely than in weak states with inclusive institutions.[102]

Finally, inclusive institutions also reduce the likelihood that DES will result in state exploitation conflicts. In exclusionary polities state elites and their allies have both the power and the incentive to exploit resource scarcities and manipulate social schisms in order to advance their narrow self-interests, because the social costs of such policies are spread out across society while the benefits are accrued by the narrow clique at the top. Furthermore, control over the apparatus of the state provides state elites and their allies an enormous potential to harm disadvantaged groups. Under these circumstances disempowered groups are likely to fear for their economic and physical survival, and the state and its allies will find it extremely difficult to credibly commit not to exploit their position of power and privilege. More inclusive institutions, however, put constraints on state exploitation. Because the very actors potentially hurt by state abuses are also empowered to influence government decisions, state exploitation, at least in its most extreme varieties, is less likely to occur or lead to violent conflict.[103] Moreover, because privileged groups know that it will be difficult and costly to exploit weaker groups, they are less likely to try.[104]

INTERACTIONS BETWEEN CAUSAL VARIABLES

To a significant extent, the degree of groupness and institutional inclusivity in any given polity are determined by factors that are prior to, and independent of, demographic and environmental forces. Nevertheless, population growth and environmental pressures, increased social grievances, and the processes of state failure and state exploitation can have some effect on the level of groupness, institutional inclusivity, or both. Interaction effects are especially likely with regard to groupness. Groupness will probably increase as natural resource scarcity, economic marginalization, and demographic shifts increase hardships, as the state weakens, or as the state tilts strongly in favor of some groups while leaving others to fend for themselves. Under such circumstances disadvantaged individuals will increasingly turn to identity groups and local organizations to provide them with economic and physical security.[105] As Michael Ignatieff observes, individuals tend to retreat to their groups "when the only answer to the question 'Who will protect me now?' becomes 'my own people.' "[106] In Egypt, for example, economic marginalization engendered by population pressures has led increasing numbers of individuals in Cairo and elsewhere to turn to radical Islamic groups for basic social services and the hope of a better life. As the Egyptian journalist Mohammed Auda notes, desperate Egyptians are prone to "join people who believe this is a society that must be destroyed because it can't be changed. And population is one of the main causes."[107]

Moreover, threats to the survival of a disadvantaged group create powerful incentives for elites within the group to act as political entrepreneurs and provide selective incentives to encourage mobilization, thereby increasing the degree of groupness. Elites themselves may feel threatened, and if they have sufficient political, organizational, or economic resources to provide selective incentives, their individual action can make a powerful difference in the probable outcome. Following Olsonian logic, we would expect such elites to utilize their resources as selective incentives to facilitate the formation of conflict groups.[108] Alternatively, opportunistic elites may capitalize on threats, real or imagined, to fellow members of their disadvantaged group as a means of gaining political support and power. Under normal circumstances these elites may not have sufficient resources to convince members of their group to mobilize, but threats to group survival lower the threshold of required selective incentives by increasing individual incentives to cooperate.

Under a more limited set of circumstances DES, as well as the state failure and state exploitation DES produces, may also affect the degree of institutional inclusivity. In countries that already have fairly exclusive institutions, government research discrimination may intensify if the threats produced by population growth, environmental degradation, and a significant weakening of the state encourage governmental repression. As Homer-Dixon notes, demographic and environmental pressures "might overwhelm the management capacity of institutions in developing countries" and encourage state elites to adopt policies that are more "extremist, authoritarian, and abusive of human rights" in order to address emerging threats to the regime's survival.[109] Similarly, already exclusive states may become more so if natural resource scarcities and state exploitation increase the concentration of political power in the hands of the few at the top.

Finally, there is likely to be some interaction, or at least an elective affinity, *between* groupness and institutional inclusivity. On the one hand, highly cleaved societies may be more inclined toward exclusive institutions in the first place. On the other hand, if institutions become more exclusive, disadvantaged groups face added incentives to mobilize in opposition.[110] Groupness and institutional inclusivity should therefore be conceptualized as partially endogenous intervening variables. In other words, they influence, and to some degree are influenced by, the effects of DES and each other.

SUMMARY

The general causal logic of my theoretical argument is summarized schematically in Figure 2.3.

Research Methods and Case Selection

The nature of the causal variables and interactions identified by my theoretical framework poses interesting challenges for empirical investigation. In what follows, I describe and defend the research strategy used to evaluate the viability of my theoretical argument in some detail.

The Nature of DES as a Variable and the Need for an Intensive Qualitative Research Design

DES is clearly neither a universally necessary nor wholly sufficient cause of civil strife. Even if DES is a necessary condition for violence in *a particular case* of civil strife, it is certainly not a necessary variable *across the universe of possible cases.* As conflicts in the former Yugoslavia,

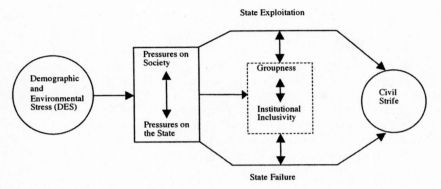

Figure 2.3. Causal Diagram

Northern Ireland, Chechnya, and elsewhere demonstrate, civil strife can occur in the absence of significant population and environmental pressures. Moreover, DES is not a wholly sufficient cause of violent internal conflict since all countries experiencing significant population growth and environmental pressures do not descend into chaos. Instead, DES is a conjunctural variable; even when DES plays a role in conflict, it does so as part of a causal chain that results in organized violence only when other intervening variables are also in play. That said, some conjunctural variables are more important and inherently interesting than others. If a conjunctural variable is not merely an additive component of a causal chain but also interacts with and aggravates other key links in the chain, it is *synergistic* and deserves careful study as a potentially powerful source of violence.

Given the nature of DES as a causal variable, an intensive qualitative research design represents the most appropriate method of testing the theoretical argument put forth in this chapter.[111] First, adequate data and measurements of many important demographic and environmental variables—reliable census data, land distribution data, and measurements of various kinds of environmental degradation and natural resource scarcity—simply do not exist for enough countries over a long enough period to engage in a reliable statistical test of the theory with a large sample size.[112] Therefore, for practical purposes, it is more fruitful to choose a small number of countries with rich data for intensive study.

Second, given the subjective and intersubjective nature of many of the variables in my causal model (e.g., scarcity, deprivation, elite cohesion, state legitimacy, group identity, etc.), the kinds of rigid coding

practices required to conduct a large quantitative study would necessarily compromise the internal validity (accuracy and reliability) of the
test. In general, the larger the number of cases, the less time, on average, analysts can invest coding each case, and the more likely there is
to be significant measurement error. As Stephen Walt notes, when key
variables and effects have to be measured and operationalized with a
high sensitivity to context, "we are often better off with a small number
of *valid* observations, as opposed to a large number of observations
that do not really tap the concept(s) we are trying to explore."[113]

Third, statistical analyses have difficulties with highly interactive
systems involving a conjunction of multiple causes, two-way causality,
causal chains involving a high degree of path dependence, and nonlinear relationships in which specific threshold points (for scarcity or state
collapse, for example) vary from context to context. In-depth case studies utilizing process tracing are much better suited to analyzing these
cause-effect relationships.[114]

Finally, quantitative tests are most appropriate when asking questions about the frequency of a particular correlation between independent and dependent variables, and for inferring the causal weight of
independent variables. This approach is not all that helpful, however,
when analyzing and assessing the causal role of a conjunctural variable
like DES or a theoretical argument like the one presented in this chapter. Statistical models are not well suited to answer "how" questions.
These types of questions, which lie at the heart of my theoretical argument, hone in on causal dynamics and processes. More appropriate
here is an intensive qualitative approach that explicitly analyzes *the
conditions under which* each distinctive type of causal pattern occurs
rather than attempting to address *the frequency to which* each outcome
or causal pattern occurs.[115]

Testing the Theory's Predictions

To set up a qualitative test of my argument, it is imperative to clearly
describe the types of evidence that would support or refute it. The theory outlined in this chapter makes two sorts of predictions: conjunctural and process-based. The conjunctural predictions are the theory's expectations regarding the probability of civil strife (the value of
the dependent variable) given the conjunction and values of DES,
groupness, and institutional inclusivity (the independent and intervening variables). Given that DES is neither necessary nor wholly sufficient, these predictions specify "under what conditions" we would expect DES to lead to civil strife. These predictions are presented in Table

TABLE 2.1
Conjunctural Predictions

Degree of DES	Degree of Groupness	Institutional Inclusivity	Probability of Civil Strife
high	high	exclusive	likely
high	high or low	inclusive	not likely (as a result of DES)
high	low	inclusive or exclusive	not likely (as a result of DES)
low	high or low	inclusive or exclusive	theory indeterminate (likelihood of civil strife determined by variables unspecified by the theory)

2.1. If the empirical record coincides with these conjunctural predictions, the theory is given tentative support, contingent on further testing. However, if the causal variables are aligned in a particular way but the outcome differs from the one predicted, the theory will be called into question.

The theory outlined in this chapter also makes a number of process predictions. These are the predictions regarding "how" the causal dynamics and processes are expected to operate. At the broadest level the theory predicts that DES will lead to civil strife when population growth, environmental degradation, and resource inequality significantly increase pressures on society and the state, thereby setting in motion state failure or state exploitation dynamics. The theory also makes a number of process predictions related to the operation of intervening variables: (1) a high degree of groupness will facilitate conflict group mobilization; (2) a low degree of groupness will frustrate or minimize conflict group mobilization; (3) exclusive institutions limit nonviolent self-help options and facilitate state exploitation; and (4) inclusive institutions increase the menu of nonviolent self-help options and place constraints on state exploitation. If these processes are in evidence in the case studies, the theory is supported; if different processes are involved, the theory is refuted.

My strategy for testing these predictions is to choose cases with sufficient temporal or spatial variation in the causal variables to cover the full range of the theory's conjunctural predictions, and then to engage in process tracing within each case to determine whether the causal dynamics operate as the theory expects.[116]

Within the analysis of each case I also evaluate two types of alternative explanations. I first compare my argument to case-specific alternative explanations that emphasize nondemographic and nonenvironmental variables. If these alternatives are found wanting, it argues for an inclusion of DES into a full understanding of the causes of civil strife. I then evaluate the possibility that demographic and environmental factors are important but that they operate in ways different from the ones specified by my theoretical framework. Specifically I compare the modified version of the state failure hypothesis and the state exploitation hypothesis outlined in this chapter to four rival hypotheses discussed in chapter 1:

1. The neo-Malthusian *deprivation hypothesis*: DES-induced poverty and natural resource competition are sufficient to produce antistate or intergroup violence.

2. The neoclassical (and political ecology) *honey pot hypothesis*: Locally abundant supplies of valuable natural resources encourage rebel groups to form and fight to seize them.

3. The neoclassical (and political ecology) *resource curse hypothesis*: Locally abundant supplies of valuable natural resources retard economic development and entrench corrupt authoritarian regimes, encouraging rebellion.

4. The political ecology *distribution hypothesis*: Resource conflicts are driven primarily by structural inequalities rather than "natural" scarcity emerging from population growth and environmental degradation.

Case Selection

It is commonly recognized that a single case study can yield a large number of relevant observations for testing a theory.[117] Two kinds of case disaggregation are useful for enlarging the number of observations: temporal and spatial. A single case may produce numerous relevant observations if the values of the causal variables vary over time. Temporal variation within a case allows a comparison of the same country at time $t, t + 1, t + 2$, and so on. A case may also be disaggregated spatially based on variation in the values of causal variables across geographic subunits within a single country, thereby allowing a controlled comparison of two or more of these units.[118]

In addition to increasing the number of observations for testing a theory, investigating temporal and spatial variation has two added benefits. First, temporal variation is much more useful than cross-country variation for testing the posited causal effects of DES as a variable. Because DES is not a necessary cause of civil strife across the universe of possible cases, a comparison of countries with varying degrees of DES would not tell us anything not already stipulated at the outset.

A finding that conflict occurred in countries without severe DES would only confirm that there are many different potential causes of civil strife, but it would not speak to the question of whether DES can be one of those causes. In contrast, variation in the degree of DES over time within the same country allows us to answer this question while also providing the variation required to draw credible causal inferences. Second, and more generally, the observations from temporally and spatially disaggregated cases are often much more comparable than those from cross-country analyses. One common criticism of cross-country comparisons is the difficulty of identifying different countries with similar values of key "control variables"—variables outside the model being tested that the analyst wishes to hold constant—but different values of the causal variables. Within-case variation helps to resolve this difficulty. Of course, one potential drawback to this approach is that external validity (i.e., the generalizability of a theory) may be undermined by an exclusive focus on a single country. This problem can be addressed, at least in part, by including an analysis of more than one country.[119]

The two major cases examined in chapters 3–5 are the communist insurgency in the Philippines and ethnic land clashes in Kenya. Each case is broken into two parts. The first part (chapters 3 and 4) analyzes the demographic and environmental roots of conflict, and the second part (chapter 5) examines the importance of intervening variables in explaining variations in levels of violence over time and space.

An analysis of civil strife in the Philippines and Kenya provides an excellent opportunity to test the plausibility of my theoretical argument. Both countries have a rich supply of fairly reliable demographic and environmental data. Taken together, these two cases also have sufficient temporal and spatial variation in the values of the causal variables to cover the full range of the theory's predictions. In both the Philippines and Kenya the level of DES increased over time, ultimately reaching a very high level. Both cases also exhibit variation in the intervening variables posited to mediate the relationship between DES and civil strife. In the Philippines the degree of groupness was low prior to the 1950s and increased afterward. The degree of institutional inclusivity also varied; Filipino political institutions were exclusive prior to 1986 but became more inclusive afterward. In Kenya the degree of groupness was high in rural areas of the country but low in urban areas. Moreover, political institutions remained exclusive prior to the initiation of the democratization process in the early 1990s, and institutions became much more inclusive after 1997.

The Philippines and Kenya cases also manifest interesting variation on the dependent variable side of the equation. The communist-led civil war in the Philippines began in the late 1960s and reached its high point in the mid-1980s during the last years of the Marcos regime, but it then declined substantially in the late 1980s and early 1990s. In Kenya the ethnic bloodshed that occurred in 1991–95 and again in 1997 only affected some parts of the country; large urban areas remained fairly calm, and, as a result, the country did not descend into all-out civil war. Moreover, ethnic clashes became less pronounced over the course of the 1990s, and by 2002 the country peacefully entered a new stage of democratic governance. Consequently, there is temporal variation in the dependent variable in the Philippines, and geographic and temporal variation in Kenya. This variation allows for an analysis of "dogs that didn't bark," that is, instances where high levels of DES were present and yet violent conflict was not. Analyzing such cases provides crucial insights into the "under what circumstances" question. In addition, as noted in chapter 1, existing research has been criticized for only looking at cases of high DES and high violence rather than similarly situated cases of high DES with a low incidence of violence. My analysis of the Philippines and Kenya seeks to overcome this criticism.

Finally, the particular combination of variation in the causal variables and variation in the dependent variable in the Philippines and Kenya cases makes them strong tests of my intervening variables. The existence of some degree of conflict in both countries makes them especially demanding tests of the posited causal effects of groupness and institutional inclusivity. I argue that both low degrees of groupness and inclusive institutions play pacifying roles, short-circuiting the link between DES and large-scale internal violence. However, once civil strife breaks out in a country, it tends to take on a life of its own. The heightened insecurities produced by ongoing hostilities makes *de*escalation of conflict extremely difficult.[120] Consequently, if there were any instances in which we would expect low degrees of groupness and inclusive institutions *not* to tamp down conflict, it would be instances of preexisting or ongoing strife. If variation in the intervening variables can account for the deescalation of violence even under these circumstances, it would provide particularly strong evidence in favor of the theory.[121]

3

Green Crisis, Red Rebels: Communist Insurgency in the Philippines

Land doesn't grow, while families do.
  —Pedro Bologna, Filipino rice farmer, 1987

As recently as World War II, the more than
7,000 Philippine islands were lavishly en-
dowed with rainforests, fish, fertile lowlands,
and extensive mineral deposits. Since then
. . . the plunder of these resources has been
taking place at a rate that is among the
fasted in the world. . . . [T]here are few places
you can go in the Philippines without meeting
some sort of ecological disaster.
  —Robin Broad and John Cavanagh,
    Plandering Paradise, 1993

The Philippines I traveled [in the 1980s]
displayed one more enduring reality, one
which made the country vulnerable to a
communist appeal as much as poverty and
political powerlessness. This was its utter
lawlessness and its remoteness from the
normal workings of government. The rural
Philippines existed in a kind of civic vacuum where the government's writ did not run
and public services were minimal. . . . [I]t
was not into a model democracy blessed with
portents of prosperity that the young communists moved. It was into an impoverished
countryside cursed with an almost anarchic
criminality and regarded indifferently by the
government in Manila.
  —William Chapman, *Inside the Philippine
    Revolution*, 1987

ON DECEMBER 26, 1968, the seventy-fifth anniversary of Mao Zedong's birth, José Maria Sison and ten other radical Filipino students and intellectuals met secretly in a barrio in Pangasinan Province in northern Luzon. Their immediate purpose was to create a new Communist Party of the Philippines–Marxist-Leninist (Mao Zedong Thought) (CPP); their long-term purpose was to overthrow the government of Ferdinand Marcos. In early 1969 Sison joined forces with Bernabe Buscayno, a former field leader of the Huk rebellion against the Japanese who was known as "Commander Dante," to form the New People's Army (NPA). At its inception the CPP-NPA was hardly a force to be reckoned with. By Sison's account, the eleven founders of the CPP represented a total membership of less than one hundred, and the NPA consisted of only sixty guerrillas equipped with perhaps thirty-five World War II vintage rifles. Nevertheless, by the time Marcos was ousted in 1986, the CPP had become the largest nongoverning communist party in Southeast Asia, and the NPA consisted of an estimated thirty thousand fighters supported by a mass base of one million Filipinos fighting the first truly national rebellion in the country's history.

How did such a rag-tag force grow into one of the most enduring insurgencies in the world? I argue that the growth of the communist insurgency in the Philippines had its roots in the tremendous demographic and environmental stress that began to reverberate throughout Filipino society in the late 1960s. Over the course of the 1970s these pressures contributed to escalating poverty and inequality, and placed significant strains on the Philippine state. Coupled with a shortsighted development strategy and changes in the international economy, DES contributed to the economic crisis that gripped the country in the early 1980s and dramatically reduced the state's ability to maintain control over huge swaths of the archipelago. As the state weakened, peasants, landlords, and remnants of the state itself all resorted to self-help strategies to ensure their economic and physical security. And as each group strove to guarantee its own survival, their activities had the paradoxical effect of creating additional insecurity for others via the spiral dynamics familiar to students of the security dilemma. The result was an explosive rise in communist support and an escalation of the simmering insurgency into a nationwide civil war.

This chapter is organized into several sections. The first provides a brief historical background and overview of the communist insurgency. The next section focuses on the various sources of strife: DES, pressures placed on Filipino society and the state, and the security dilemma. The chapter concludes with a comparison of my argument to a number of alternative explanations.

Background and Overview

The Philippines is an archipelago made up of some 7,100 islands stretching over approximately 1,800 kilometers. The country is divided into three broad island groups: Luzon, the Visayas, and Mindanao. Of the country's total area of 300,000 square kilometers (km^2), 94 percent is located on just 13 islands (see map).

In 1521 the Portuguese explorer Ferdinand Magellan discovered the archipelago. Shortly after claiming the islands for Charles I of Spain and naming them after Crown Prince Philip, Magellan was killed by a local chief. Spain returned four decades later and conquered the country. Their first permanent settlement was established in 1565, and Manila was founded six years later. For more than three hundred years Spain ruled the island chain through a mix of civil, military, and ecclesiastical authority. However, toward the end of the nineteenth century, as the last vestiges of Spain's international empire began to slip away, colonial rule over the Philippines became increasingly difficult to maintain. In 1896 Filipino peasant unrest, rooted in landgrabbing by agricultural elites and compounded by rural population growth, bubbled over into active revolution against colonial authorities. When war broke out between Spain and the United States in 1898, Filipino uprisings combined with U.S. military intervention to overturn Spanish rule. The American victory, codified in the Treaty of Paris of 1898, ceded the Philippines to the United States. A guerrilla war ensued, waged by peasants opposed to U.S. occupation. After years of bloody fighting, the United States eventually pacified the rebellion by gaining the support of wealthy, well-educated elites tempted by an American promise of early self-government. In 1934 the U.S. Congress came through with this promise by establishing the Commonwealth of the Philippines and providing for a ten-year transition to full independence.

Japan sidetracked this process on December 7, 1941, by invading the Philippines. The Japanese soon occupied Manila and the Filipino president Manuel Quezon was evacuated to the United States, where a Commonwealth government-in-exile was established. Despite extensive elite collaboration with Japanese authorities, resistance to Japanese control in the Philippines was more widespread than in any other Southeast Asian colony. Communist radicals in Central Luzon formed the Hukbalahap (or Huks, a Tagalog abbreviation for "People's Army against the Japanese") and organized a peasant rebellion against the occupiers and their allies among the landed elite.

On July 4, 1946, following its victory over Japan, the United States transferred sovereignty and the Philippines became an independent re-

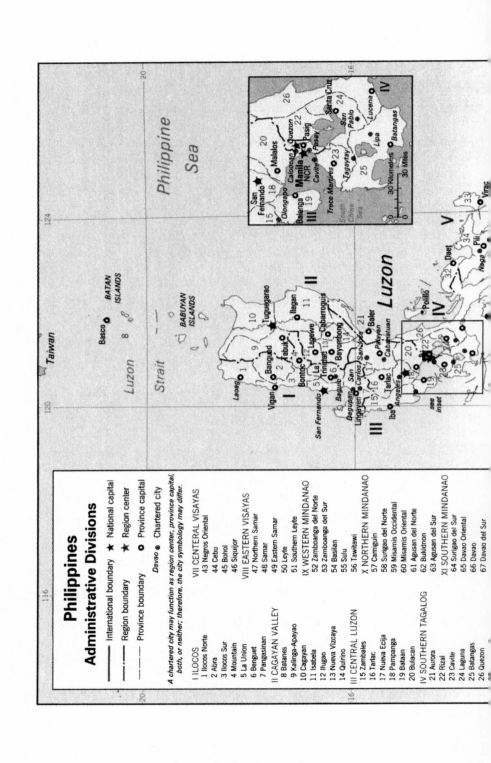

Philippines
Administrative Divisions

International boundary

— · — · — Region boundary

— — — Province boundary

★ National capital

★ Region center

◉ Province capital

Davao ◉ Chartered city

A chartered city may function as region center, province capital, both, or neither; therefore, the city symbology may differ.

I ILOCOS
1 Ilocos Norte
2 Abra
3 Ilocos Sur
4 Mountain
5 La Union
6 Benguet
7 Pangasinan

II CAGAYAN VALLEY
8 Batanes
9 Kalinga-Apayao
10 Cagayan
11 Isabela
12 Ifugao
13 Nueva Vizcaya
14 Quirino

III CENTRAL LUZON
15 Zambales
16 Tarlac
17 Nueva Ecija
18 Pampanga
19 Bataan
20 Bulacan

IV SOUTHERN TAGALOG
21 Aurora
22 Rizal
23 Cavite
24 Laguna
25 Batangas
26 Quezon

VII CENTERAL VISAYAS
43 Negros Oriental
44 Cebu
45 Bohol
46 Siquijor

VIII EASTERN VISAYAS
47 Northern Samar
48 Samar
49 Eastern Samar
50 Leyte
51 Southern Leyte

IX WESTERN MINDANAO
52 Zamboanga del Norte
53 Zamboanga del Sur
54 Basilan
55 Sulu
56 Tawitawi

X NORTHERN MINDANAO
57 Camiguin
58 Surigao del Norte
59 Misamis Occidental
60 Misamis Oriental
61 Agusan del Norte
62 Bukidnon
63 Agusan del Sur

XI SOUTHERN MINDANAO
64 Surigao del Sur
65 Davao Oriental
66 Davao
67 Davao del Sur

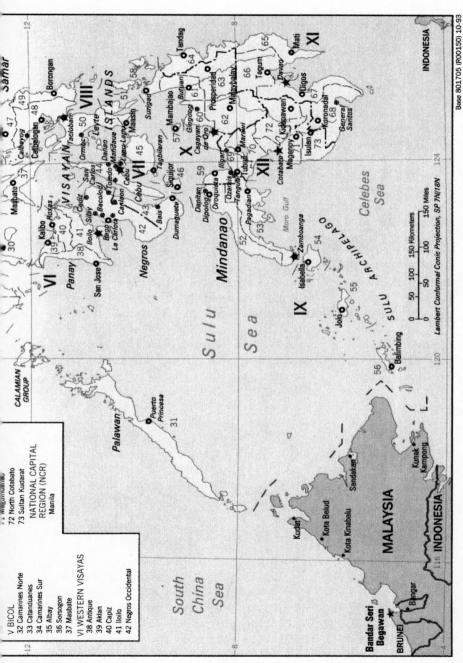

Samar

Borongan

Calbayog
Catbalogan
Tacloban
V I S A Y A N
Maasin
Masbate
Ormoc
Leyte

VIII
ISLANDS
Surigao
Tandag
XI
Mati

Siquijor
Tagbilaran
Dumaguete
Mambajao
Gingoog
Surigao
Prosperidad
Buruan
Tagum
Davao
Digos
Koronadal
General
Santos

Kalibo
Roxas
Iloilo
Silay
Bacolod
Toledo
Cebu
Canlaon
La Carlota
Dapitan
Dipolog
Oroquieta
Ozamis
Tengis
Pagadian
Cagayan
de Oro
Iligan
Marawi
Malaybalay
Midsayap
Cotabato
Midsayap
Isulan
Kidapawan
Magapay

VI
Panay
San Jose
Negros
Mindanao

Zamboanga
Isabela
Jolo
Balimbing

Puerto
Princesa
31

South
China
Sea

Sulu
Sea

Celebes
Sea

Sulu

ARCHIPELAGO

Moro Gulf

CALAMIAN
GROUP

Palawan

INDONESIA

MALAYSIA

Kudat
Kota Belud
Kota Kinabalu

Sandakan
Kunak
Kampong

BRUNEI
Bandar Seri
Begawan
Bangar

INDONESIA

V BICOL
32 Camarines Norte
33 Catanduanes
34 Camarines Sur
35 Albay
36 Sorsogon
37 Masbate
VI WESTERN VISAYAS
38 Antique
39 Aklan
40 Capiz
41 Iloilo
42 Negros Occidental

72 North Cotabato
73 Sultan Kudarat
NATIONAL CAPITAL
REGION (NCR)
Manila

Lambert Conformal Conic Projection, SP 7N/18N

0   50   100   150 Kilometers
0   50   100   150 Miles

Base 801705 (R00150) 10-93

public. Nevertheless, many aspects of Philippine–U.S. relations were unaltered. Economic rehabilitation was largely financed with American aid and many characteristics of the colonial economy were maintained. Free trade between the two countries was prolonged and an agreement was reached fixing the peso/dollar exchange rate. Moreover, as a condition of U.S. aid, the Philippine Constitution was amended to give American investors parity with Filipinos in the realm of natural resource exploitation. Military ties also remained close, with the United States keeping more than two hundred bases across the archipelago.

Postcolonial politics continued to be controlled by the interests of rural elites and characterized by peasant unrest. Since the goal of the Huks went beyond expelling Japanese forces to include more widespread social and agrarian reform, their struggle continued even after Japan was defeated. Fearing that the Huks represented a new Chinese Communist threat, the United States helped the Philippine government intensify efforts to defeat the festering rebellion. American military assistance to the Philippines increased and the Filipino government was pressured, with little initial success, to implement agrarian and labor reforms to bolster regime legitimacy and to undermine support for the Huks. After 1951, in the face of an increasingly effective counterinsurgency campaign led by Philippine defense secretary (and soon to be president) Ramon Magsaysay, Huk activities waned significantly. A combination of Huk atrocities and government concessions toward the peasantry eroded support for the rebels. The U.S.-trained Philippine armed forces gained the upper hand and, by 1955, all but a few of the Huk fighters tired of the struggle.

Communist insurgency in the Philippines remained dormant until the 1965 election of the Nacionalista Party candidate and the then Senate president Ferdinand Marcos to the office of president. In 1969 Marcos became the first Filipino president to be reelected to office. Marcos secured his victory by pouring large sums of government money into the provinces and bribing local officials. His victory was therefore widely viewed as fraudulent and, in the context of growing economic malaise, opposition to his rule began to increase.[1]

In the last week of 1968 Sison formed the CPP. Like many intellectuals of his generation, Sison had come of age in a postwar climate increasingly characterized by anti-American nationalism. Sison had long subscribed to communist ideals but had lost faith in the pro-Soviet Partido Kumistang Pilipinas (PKP), the original Filipino communist party established in 1930. He therefore struck out on his own to build a new party along Maoist doctrinal lines, calling for a "people's war" against the corrupt democratic system, national capitalism, and the accomplices of foreign imperialism. However, for the CPP to prosecute this war, it needed an army. Thus, in early 1969, Sison and the Huk veteran Commander Dante established the CPP–affiliated NPA. From bases in northern and Central Luzon, the NPA began limited activities. Aided by growing poverty among the peasantry and the ineptness of local police authorities, the guerrillas soon experienced gains, especially in Central Luzon. By 1970, according to the American embassy, the NPA contained perhaps four hundred regular armed forces and five hundred armed personnel, in addition to three to four thousand unarmed support personnel and a mass base of between thirty and eighty thousand. Nevertheless, the Philippine military soon began dealing heavy blows to the budding insurgency. A number of NPA units were wiped out and numerous cadres were captured. Having failed to develop a stable base in traditional Huk strongholds in the lowland rice-growing plains of Tarlac and Pampanga (in Central Luzon), the guerrillas were forced to fall back into the mountainous jungles of Isabela Province at the foot of the Cordilleras in northern Luzon.

The fate of the CPP-NPA took a dramatic turn beginning in 1972. Faced with growing opposition and an imminent loss of power because of a constitutional provision limiting presidents to two terms, Marcos declared martial law on September 22, 1972. Congress and habeas corpus were abolished, as were free elections, free speech, and a free press. Within days Marcos erected a full-scale dictatorship and arrested more than sixty thousand political opponents. Among these prisoners was Senator Benigno Aquino, a member of one of the country's most powerful families and a long-time rival from the Liberal Party who was widely expected to win the presidency in 1973. Many commentators believe that Marcos was behind a botched attempt to assassinate Aquino and a number of his Liberal Party colleagues during a bombing incident at the Plaza Miranda in 1971. Although Aquino was not present when the bomb went off, several other politicians were seriously injured or killed. Marcos blamed the bombing on the Communists, despite the fact that no culprits were ever apprehended. This incident took on added importance in 1972, when, after another series of bombings and a staged ambush of Defense Minister Juan Ponce Enrile (also blamed on the CPP-NPA), Marcos justified the imposition of martial law as necessary to combat the mounting communist threat.

The declaration of martial law had a paradoxical effect on the growth of the CPP-NPA. On the one hand, the Communists came under heavy military attack. On the eve of martial law, for example, seven thousand government troops launched a massive offensive against the NPA in Isabela. In total, Marcos's anticommunist campaign in northern Luzon sent a force of nearly ten thousand government troops backed by helicopters, jet fighters, armor, and artillery against fewer than five hundred lightly armed guerrillas. Many cadres were either killed or captured, and the rest were dispersed throughout the archipelago. On the other hand, the upsurge in repression drove hundreds of well-educated youths into the countryside, where they became communist cadres and eventually leaders. The communist leadership scaled down its military activities. Armed with Mao's "Little Red Book" and a renewed focus on building grass-roots support and organization, the CPP-NPA began to recover and grow anew. By the late 1970s the NPA was clashing with government forces much more frequently throughout Mindanao, Negros, Samar, northern and southern Luzon, and Panay.[2]

In 1976 the NPA estimated its troop strength at fifteen hundred. By 1980 the size of NPA forces was estimated to be between thirty-five hundred and eight thousand. By 1985 estimates suggested that the number of NPA fighters had grown to perhaps thirty thousand. This growth was especially startling since it was achieved for the most part without any foreign assistance from China or the Soviet Union. The accuracy of these figures is, of course, difficult to determine. Nevertheless, as Table 3.1 illustrates, there is no doubting the dramatic upward trend evident in both NPA estimates and those made by the U.S. and Filipino governments. Nor is there any doubt that Filipino and American officials came to see the NPA as a serious threat. Until the mid-1980s officials in both governments had viewed the NPA as little more than a nuisance. But as the size and activities of the NPA grew, and the Philippine military was forced to spread itself thin across the archipelago to defend against mobile rebel units, the significance of the communist threat could no longer be ignored. Richard L. Armitage, U.S. Assistant Secretary of Defense for International Security Affairs, warned in 1984 that "the insurgents are building their base and could tip the balance of military power within the next several years."[3] A 1985 report prepared for the U.S. Senate Committee on Foreign Relations was similarly dire: "The CPP-led movement has developed to the point where it seems to have a credible chance of overthrowing the Government within five to ten years if present trends continue. This appears to be the case despite the insurgents' problems in securing arms and their lack of outside support."[4] And a 1985 article in the *New Republic* suggested that, "if current political and economic trends continue, by the end of the decade these Filipino Maoists are likely to pose a serious and perhaps irresistible challenge to the government of the Philippines."[5]

The political influence of the CPP-NPA also grew dramatically over this period. When martial law was announced guerrillas were active in only four of the country's seventy-three provinces. Yet, by the mid-

TABLE 3.1
NPA Troop Strength, 1968-1988

Date of Estimate	U.S. and Filipino Government Estimates	NPA Estimates
1968–69		35
1972	1,000–2,000	350
1976		1,500
1977		1,500
1979	2,000–3,000	
1980	3,500	8,000
1981	3,600	
1982	6,000	10,000
1983	7,500	20,000
1984	8,000–10,000	
1985	10,000–25,000	
1983–85		30,000
1986	20,000–22,000	
1988	24,000–26,000	

Sources: Greg R. Jones, *Red Revolution: Inside the Philippine Guerrilla Movement* (Boulder, Colo.: Westview, 1989), 129–131; Richard J. Kessler, *Rebellion and Repression in the Philippines* (New Haven, Conn.: Yale University Press, 1989), p. 56; Larry A. Niksch, *Insurgency and Counterinsurgency in the Philippines*, prepared for the United States Senate Committee on Foreign Relations (Washington, D.C.: U.S. Government Printing Office, 1985), p. 21; and David Wurfel, *Filipino Politics: Development and Decay* (Ithaca, N.Y.: Cornell University Press, 1988), p. 227.

1970s, the CPP-NPA claimed to be active in more than thirty provinces. This activity included propaganda and organizational work in addition to armed struggle. The insurgency claimed to be active in forty provinces distributed across all regions of the archipelago by 1977, and by 1983 this number had climbed to sixty provinces. Two years later the U.S. government estimated that the communist rebels enjoyed influence (defined as a situation in which at least 50 percent of residents were sympathetic) in 35 percent of the country's *barangays* (the lowest administrative unit, of which there are 41,400), and claimed that the CPP-NPA was in actual control of at least 12 percent. By 1987 CPP-NPA influence had increased to 37 percent, cadres were active in all seventy-three provinces, and Communist Party leaders claimed a nationwide mass base of 1 million people. Throughout its people's war against the government, CPP-NPA strength was greatest in Samar in Eastern Visayas, Negros and Panay in Western Visayas, Northern and Eastern Mindanao, the Bicol Peninsula of southeastern Luzon, the Cordillera Mountains, and Cagayan Valley in northeastern Luzon. The CPP-NPA also had a considerable presence in Davao City, the Philippines' largest southern urban center, where huge slum areas and rural approaches to the city came under communist control before the government finally succeeded in rooting them out in 1986.[6]

After the imposition of martial law the CPP attempted to broaden its urban appeal, with mixed success, by creating the National Democratic Front (NDF). The goal was to mobilize support for a united opposition to Marcos from segments of Philippine society traditionally nervous of direct involvement with the CPP, such as the church and the middle class. The NDF was meant to serve as an avenue for the CPP to pursue a political route to power to supplement, although not supplant, its military struggle in the countryside. In the early 1980s the CPP sought to strengthen the role of the NDF by having the front downplay communism in favor of broader nationalist themes. In 1985 the New Nationalist Alliance, or Bayan (Bagong Alyansang Makabayan), was created with NDF support to serve as a front for a front and to broaden the coalition of forces aligned against Marcos.[7] The CPP was confident in the prospects for success stemming from the combination of people's war and overt political struggle. As early as 1981, in an interview conducted from his prison cell, Sison predicted that "the CPP alone cannot dislodge Marcos from power. But a united front for armed struggle [including the NDF] can, within the near future, not exceeding a decade."[8]

In short, little more than a decade after Marcos used the largely fabricated "communist menace" to justify martial law, the CPP-NPA evolved into a genuine threat. The government found itself fighting the first truly national insurgency in the country's history. The war ultimately cost forty thousand Filipinos their lives and displaced millions of others.[9]

Sources of Strife

Population growth, environmental degradation, and resource inequality created huge strains on both Filipino society and the state during the Marcos years. By the late 1970s Filipino society had reached the breaking point. When a series of exogenous shocks besieged the country in the early 1980s, state authority collapsed and creeping lawlessness swept across the countryside. Surrounded by an increasingly

anarchic and violent world, thousands of poor Filipinos turned to communist insurgents as their last best hope of securing their economic
and physical well-being.

Population Growth, Inequality, and the End of the Land Frontier

Population growth was extremely rapid in the Philippines during the
twentieth century. In 1903 the Philippine population totaled only 7.6
million. By 1948 that number had ballooned to 19.2 million. Only
thirty-two years later, in 1980, the population had more than doubled
to 48 million, and by 1990 the figure that reached 60.6 million. This
represented a threefold increase since 1948 and an eightfold increase
since the beginning of the twentieth century. The annual population
increase in the Philippines was thus very high. Between 1948 and 1960
the population grew at an average annual rate of 3 percent. The annual
rate was 3.1 percent between 1960 and 1970 and 2.7 percent between
1970 and 1980, before declining to 2.3 percent between 1980 and 1990.
As the population expanded, population density also grew dramatically. In the postwar period, population density grew from 64 persons
per km^2 in 1948 to 90 in 1960, 122 in 1970, 160 in 1980, and 202 in 1990.[10]
Consequently, by the 1980s, the Philippines ranked among the most
densely populated countries in the world. Table 3.2 provides a detailed
regional breakdown of population statistics for the 1960–90 period.

This population surge stemmed from very high fertility rates and
declining mortality. During the period under investigation here, the
total fertility rate (or TFR, the average number of children born to a
woman during her childbearing years) in the Philippines was very
high. According to National Demographic Surveys conducted in 1973
and 1983, the TFR was 5.97 and 5.08, respectively, in those years.[11]
Moreover, rates were especially high in rural areas. In 1983, for example, the rural TFR was 7 births per woman, compared to only 3.8 births
for women in urban areas.[12] Although the average number of births
per woman steadily declined, the crude birth rate (or CBR, the total
number of births per 1,000 people in the population) declined less consistently because of an absolute increase in the number of women in
their childbearing years. The CBR of 39.2 in 1970, for example, dropped
to 34.8 in 1975 but then increased to 36.3 in 1980 before falling again
to 31.7 in 1985. The overall mortality rate also declined considerably in
the postwar period, although the decline in deaths slowed after 1960.
Between 1948 and 1960 the crude death rate (or CDR, the number of
deaths per 1,000 people in the population) dropped dramatically from
21.6 to 12.8. In 1970 the CDR was 10.8 per thousand, dropping to 7.9
per thousand in 1985.[13]

TABLE 3.2
Population of the Philippines, 1960–1990

		1960			*1970*		
	Area (km²)	*Population*	*Density*	*Intercensal Population Growth Rate*	*Population*	*Density*	*Intercensal Population Growth Rate*
Philippines	300,000	27,087,685	90	—	36,684,486	122	3.1
Luzon	139,298.2	14,061,448	101	—	19,688,100	141	3.4
National Capital Region	636.5	2,462,488	3,869	—	3,966,695	6,232	4.1
Cordillera Administrative Region*	16,196.4*	—	—	—	—	—	—
Region I: Ilocos Region	21,564.4 12,840.2*	2,427,581	113	—	2,990,561	139	2.1
Region II: Cagayan Valley	36,403.1 26,837.7*	1,202,066	33	—	1,691,459	46	3.5
Region III: Central Luzon	18,230.8	2,525,379	138	—	3,615,496	198	3.7
Region IV: Southern Tagalog	46,924.1	3,081,227	66	—	4,457,008	94	3.8
Region V: Bicol Region	17,632.5	2,362,707	134	—	2,966,881	168	2.3
Visayas	56,606.4	7,642,073	135	—	9,032,454	160	1.7
Region VI: Western Visayas	20,223.2	3,078,305	152	—	3,618,326	178	1.6
Region VII: Central Visayas	14,951.5	2,522,802	169	—	3,032,719	203	1.9
Region VIII: Eastern Visayas	21,431.7	2,040,966	95	—	2,381,409	111	1.6
Mindanao	101,998.8	5,384,264	52	—	7,963,932	78	4.0
Region IX: Western Mindanao	18,685.0	1,350,731	72	—	1,869,014	100	3.3
Region X: Northern Mindanao	28,327.8	1,297,345	46	—	1,952,735	69	4.2
Region XI: Southern Mindanao	31,692.9	1,352,798	42	—	2,200,726	69	5.0
Region XII: Central Mindanao	23,293.1	1,383,390	59	—	1,941,457	83	3.4

Sources: National Economic and Development Authority (NEDA), National Census and Statistics Office, Republic of the Philippines, *1980 Census of Population and Housing: Philippines,* Vol. 2: *National Summary* (Manila, Philippines: NEDA, 1980); and *Factbook Philippines* (Quezon City, Metro Manila, the Philippines: Active Research Center, 1994).
* The Cordillera Administrative Region (CAR) was created out of provinces from the Ilocos Region and Cagayan Valley by Executive Order 220 in July 1987. All 1990 numbers for the CAR, Ilocos, and Cagayan have been adjusted to account for this.

TABLE 3.2
Population of the Philippines, 1960–1990 (*cont'd*)

	Area (km²)	1980			1990		
		Population	Density	Intercensal Population Growth Rate	Population	Density	Intercensal Population Growth Rate
Philippines	300,000	48,098,460	160	2.7	60,648,887	202	2.3
Luzon	139,298.2	26,080,694	187	2.9	33,340,545	239	2.5
National Capital Region	636.5	5,925,884	9,310	3.0	7,928,867	12,467	3.0
Cordillera Administrative Region*	16,196.4*	—	—	—	1,145,880	63	2.3*
Region I: Ilocos Region	21,564.4 12,840.2*	3,540,893	164	1.7	3,550,606*	277*	2.0*
Region II: Cagayan Valley	36,403.1 26,837.7*	2,215,522	61	2.7	2,340,652*	87*	2.0*
Region III: Central Luzon	18,230.8	4,802,793	263	2.9	6,198,957	340	2.6
Region IV: Southern Tagalog	46,924.1	6,118,620	130	3.2	8,265,784	176	3.1
Region V: Bicol Region	17,632.5	3,476,982	197	1.6	3,909,799	222	1.2
Visayas	56,606.4	11,112,523	196	2.1	13,041,668	230	1.6
Region VI: Western Visayas	20,223.2	4,525,615	224	2.3	5,393,333	267	1.8
Region VII: Central Visayas	14,951.5	3,787,374	253	2.2	4,593,151	307	2.0
Region VIII: Eastern Visayas	21,431.7	2,799,534	131	1.6	3,055,184	143	0.9
Mindanao	101,998.8	11,135,722	109	3.4	14,297,462	140	2.5
Region IX: Western Mindanao	18,685.0	2,528,506	135	3.1	3,159,197	169	2.3
Region X: Northern Mindanao	28,327.8	2,758,985	97	3.5	3,509,821	124	2.4
Region XI: Southern Mindanao	31,692.9	3,346,803	106	4.3	4,457,076	141	2.9
Region XII: Central Mindanao	23,293.1	2,270,949	97	1.6	3,171,368	136	3.4

In the late 1960s and early 1970s population growth combined with a highly unequal distribution of land to close the so-called land frontier in the lowland portions of the Philippines. Between 1945 and 1965 agricultural output increased primarily through the expansion of the total amount of land under cultivation in the lowlands. Indeed, until the1960s, the total ratio of cultivated land to population did not decline because new land was brought into cultivation at a faster rate than that of population growth. From the late 1940s to the late 1950s the population grew at an average annual rate of 3.1 percent, while cultivated land grew by 3.8 percent per year. During the 1960s, however, the expansion of cultivated land was only 1.4 percent per year, while the rate of annual population growth remained more than 3 percent. Thus, after 1965, the supply of lowlands that could easily be converted to agriculture was largely exhausted and, for the first time, the average farm size began to decline; between 1960 and 1980 the number of farms increased from 2.17 million to 3.42 million, but the size of the average farm declined from 3.16 hectares (ha) to 2.63 ha. The exhaustion of the frontier is also apparent from data on the average amount of arable land available per person employed in agriculture. In 1960 there was 0.94 ha of arable land per person employed in agriculture. By 1970, however, it had dropped to 0.72 ha per person, and by 1980 there was only 0.53 ha per person, little more than half what the average had been only twenty years earlier.[14]

As dramatic as these statistics seem, they actually understate the severity of the land crisis that emerged in the lowlands, because they say nothing about how the land was distributed. Indeed, at the very time that population growth was placing more pressure on available arable land, that land was becoming more concentrated in the hands of large landowners.

Historically land distribution in the Philippines has been highly unequal. Beginning in the early eighteenth century powerful Spanish friars encouraged a rapid transformation from shifting to sedentary cultivation in the lowlands. In the early nineteenth century commercial crops grown for export took on greater importance in the economy, and land ownership became increasingly concentrated in large estates known as *haciendas*. Many of these haciendas were initially owned by church orders or Chinese or Spanish mestizos (people of mixed ancestry). When control over the Philippines transferred to the United States, friar estates were bought by the government and resold to native elites. Export agriculture was further expanded under American rule as a result of the 1909 Payne-Aldrich Tariff Act, which opened free trade between the Philippines and the United States. The emphasis on export agriculture became even more pronounced after the Second

World War. In 1962 the Philippine government eliminated controls on foreign exchange. The resulting devaluation of the peso brought windfall profits to agricultural exporters and encouraged greater investments in that sector.[15] Wealthy landlords acquired, or illegally seized, vast tracts of land to grow sugar, coconuts, pineapples, and bananas for export. Many farmers lost their land to larger farms and plantations, as small holdings were sold to owners of larger tracts of land or leased to multinational corporations. Other land was taken illegally by elite families who exploited the peasants' ignorance of the law, laid claim on productive land, and then used their political influence to secure proper titles. Indeed, as David Wurfel notes, "the rapid acquisition of huge estates since [the 1950s], particularly in Mindanao and other frontier areas, is hard to quantify because so many transactions have been illegal or unreported."[16] Poor landless farmers were increasingly forced to sign on as day laborers earning incredibly low wages, and others were left both landless and unemployed. Moreover, as large landowners increased their reliance on mechanized farming techniques, ever greater numbers fell into the latter category.[17]

Reliable countrywide data do not exist for land ownership and distribution.[18] It is, nevertheless, possible to get a rough idea of land inequality. In 1960, based on estimates by the Philippine government, farms of 3 ha or less made up 62.4 percent of all farms but only 24.7 percent of the total agricultural land; in contrast, farms of 10 ha or more made up only 5.5 percent of all farms but 33.2 percent of all agricultural land. The situation was little better twenty years later: in 1980 farms of 3 ha or less made up 68.9 percent of all farms and 29.6 percent of all land, and farms of 10 ha or more were 3.4 percent of farms but 26 percent of the total agricultural land. Moreover, the average size of farms in the category of farms under 3 ha actually declined from 1.4 ha in 1960 to 1 ha in 1980, revealing the role that population growth played in aggravating land inequality.[19] All told, during the Marcos years, it was estimated that 20 percent of the Philippine population owned 60 to 80 percent of the land.[20] Furthermore, inequality was even greater than these numbers suggest since many small farmers leased or sharecropped their lands.[21]

The Marcos government ostensibly sought to address growing land pressure by engaging in land reform and encouraging the adoption of new agricultural technologies. After his election in 1965 Marcos took baby steps toward furthering the modest program of land reform initiated a few years earlier by his predecessor, Diosdado Macapagal. Shortly after declaring martial law Marcos announced his intention to accelerate these efforts by transferring all rice and corn farms in excess of 7 ha to tenants.[22] However, government estimates at the time established that 57 percent of tenant farmers worked on land owned by persons with *fewer* than 7 ha. In addition, like all past efforts to redistribute land, this new wave of reform foundered in the face of landed elite opposition. The new law was easy to circumvent. Since it only applied to rice and corn farms that were tenanted, many landlords evaded the law by shifting to other crops. Others circumvented the law by splitting up land holdings among several family members so that the farms fell below the 7 ha ceiling.[23] Population growth also frustrated land reform *even in those very few areas where it was implemented*. Landlords found that population pressure made it easy for them to locate a surplus of new, compliant laborers to work their land. This encouraged landlords to expel their previous tenants and shift their operations to wage labor arrangements, which were exempt from reform.[24] By the time Marcos was ousted only 11 percent of all rice and corn tenants had been put on the road toward ownership as a result of land reform efforts.[25]

Another strategy employed by Marcos to relieve land pressures was the promotion of "green revolution" technologies and techniques. Beginning in the late 1960s the Marcos government began encouraging a shift away from extensive cultivation (the expansion of acreage) to intensive cultivation (getting more out of each portion of land). To increase production the Marcos regime introduced high-yielding varieties of rice into the Philippines and significantly increased investments in irrigation and fertilizer.[26]

The onset of the green revolution succeeded in increasing rice production but failed to solve the land problem in the lowlands for at least two reasons. First, increasing productivity failed to cause a shift in labor out of agriculture, thereby relieving land pressure, because industrial and service-oriented employment grew too slowly.[27] Second, and somewhat perversely, the green revolution actually furthered the trend toward the concentration of land and an emphasis on export crops. As intensive techniques promised increases in rice yields—the staple food crop in the Philippines—on *less* land, the Marcos regime felt free to encourage bringing *more* land under cultivation for export crops. Between 1962 and 1985 the area under cultivation for export crops and corn doubled from 5 million to 10 million ha, while the area devoted to rice held steady at little more than 3 million ha.[28] Land was thus concentrated into the hands of fewer and fewer rich landowners, thereby worsening the land shortage in the lowlands.

In sum, land scarcity in the lowlands became endemic in the Philippines from the late 1960s. It should be emphasized, however, that the closing of the land frontier was not really a breaching of some natural carrying capacity. Rather, it was a social frontier that was crossed as a consequence of the interaction between rapid population growth and government development strategies that perpetuated the historical concentration of land.[29]

As the population swelled, land became more concentrated, and as the green revolution failed to liberate individuals from the land, landlessness became widespread. Between 1980 and 1985 alone the number of landless agricultural households increased from 40 percent to 56 percent. Increasing numbers of landless farmers were forced to work for wages that often fell below the subsistence rural poverty line, while millions of others left the lowlands to search elsewhere for employment and a means of survival.[30] During the 1970s, 60 percent of the total migrant population ended up in cities.[31] This helps to explain why urban areas, where fertility rates consistently fell below the national average, nevertheless experienced significant population increases. In 1948, 73 percent of the Philippine population lived in rural areas. In 1960, 1970, 1980, and 1990 the percentage residing in rural areas declined to 70 percent, 68 percent, 62 percent, and 51 percent, respectively.[32] The majority of urban population growth occurred in Metropolitan Manila (also known as the National Capital Region), where the population more than doubled from 2.5 to 5.9 million between 1960 and 1980. By 1990 the population of Metro Manila approached nearly 8 million (see Table 3.2).

Millions of others migrated to the country's hilly and mountainous upland areas, defined as areas with a slope of 18 percent or higher. Forty-six percent of the uplands in the Philippines have slopes of 18–30 percent (over half of which lie in Mindanao), while the remaining uplands have slopes exceeding 30 percent. The uplands comprise about 16.8 million ha (56 percent of national territory), are home to most of the Philippines' tropical forests, and are, for the most part, ill-suited for agriculture.[33] Population growth in the uplands was relatively low from the 1960s through the mid-1970s but was extremely rapid from 1975 on. In 1960, 8.2 million people resided in upland areas; by 1985, 17.5 million people (32 percent of the Philippine population) lived in upland areas. All told, high rates of upland migration and high fertility rates accounted for an upland population growth rate of 3.2 percent between 1950 and 1985, compared to the national average over that period of 2.8 percent. Between 1980 and 1985 upland population growth reached almost 4 percent a year, well above the national average of 2.3 percent. Population density also increased dramatically. Densities in upland areas were relatively low in the 1960s and 1970s, but by the 1980s upland areas with a slope between 18 and 30 percent had an average density of 260 people per km^2, with several locations reaching densities of greater than 300 people per km^2. Upland growth was

TABLE 3.3
Changes in National Forest Cover in the Philippines, 1950–1987

	Percentage of Total Land Area with Forest Cover
1950	49.1
1957	44.3
1969	33.5
1976	30.0
1980	25.9
1987	22.2

Source: David M. Kummer, *Deforestation in the Postwar Philippines* (Chicago: University of Chicago Press, 1992), p. 56, Table 7.

highest in regions with large remaining areas of semi-cleared forestland. Mindanao experienced the fastest rise in upland population growth, the uplands in Central Luzon grew rapidly, and, despite significant out-migration, highlands in the three Visayas also absorbed large numbers of in-coming residents.[34]

Deforestation, Soil Erosion, and Coastal Degradation

The Philippines experienced severe and extensive degradation of its forests, soils, and coastal regions during the period under investigation here. The country has long been dominated by its lush tropical forests, yet during the twentieth century, and especially in the post–World War II period, the Philippines witnessed some of the most rapid deforestation the world has ever seen. When Spain discovered the Philippines in 1521 various types of forest covered nearly 90 percent of the archipelago (or almost 27 million of the country's 30 million ha of land). In 1900, nearly four hundred years later, 70–80 percent of the total land area was still covered by forest, most of which was situated in the uplands. Sixty percent of the Philippines remained forest-covered in the late 1930s, but logging and farming on forestland increased sharply after the Second World War, placing unprecedented pressure on forest ecosystems.[35]

Tables 3.3, 3.4, and 3.5 demonstrate the accelerating rate of deforestation in the postwar period. In 1950, 49.1 percent of the Philippines' total land area had forest cover. This number plummeted to 33.5 percent by 1969 and to 22.2 percent by 1987. The Philippines thus lost

TABLE 3.4
Deforestation Rates in the Philippines, 1950–1987

	Average Annual km²	Percentage
1950–57	2,210	1.58
1957–69	2,262	1.91
1969–76	2,081	2.14
1976–80	3,048	3.64
1980–87	1,570	2.17

Source: David M. Kummer, *Deforestation in the Postwar Philippines* (Chicago: University of Chicago Press, 1992), p. 57, Table 9.

more than 14 million ha of forest (representing nearly half the country's total land area) between 1900 and 1987, with 8 million ha lost between 1950 and 1987 alone. The average annual deforestation rate also picked up considerably during the postwar period, from a rate of 1.58 percent in 1950 to 3.64 percent in 1980, before slowing to 2.17 percent by 1987. In addition to this dramatic quantitative decline in forestland, there was a substantial qualitative drop as well. By 1987 undisturbed old growth dipterocarp forest made up less than 3 percent of the total remaining forests. This represented a 90 percent decline of old-growth forests in only thirty years. As a result, much of the forests remaining at the end of the twentieth century were mossy forests over 600 meters in elevation with little commercial value.[36]

When forests are decimated to the extent seen in the Philippines, critical ecological services are wiped out, with effects that ripple throughout local environmental and social systems. One of the most significant effects of deforestation was a dramatic rise in soil erosion. The Philippines' ecology is particularly vulnerable to soil erosion owing to its topography, climate, and soil characteristics. The steeply sloping land in upland areas is especially susceptible to erosion, because it has little vegetative cover, tends to be acidic, and is low in organic matter. Heavy and seasonally concentrated rainfall and frequent typhoons compound this vulnerability.[37] The maintenance of forest cover is essential to minimizing soil erosion within forestlands and surrounding catchment areas, because healthy forests act like a sponge that absorbs excess rainfall and slowly releases it in the dry months. The loss of forests disrupts the effective regulation of water flow, causing runoffs to occur in extremes: heavy flows and flooding occur during the rainy seasons, and water shortages and droughts become more common during the dry season.[38]

TABLE 3.5
Superregional Deforestation Rates in the Philippines, 1950–1987

	Annual Deforestation Rates (in km² and percentage)			
	Mindanao	*Palawan*	*Visayas*	*Luzon*
1950–69	1,007 (1.9)	46 (0.5)	350 (2.4)	839 (1.7)
1969–80	1,246 (3.5)	184 (2.1)	435 (4.8)	567 (1.5)
1980–87	448 (1.7)	171 (2.4)	187 (3.1)	781 (2.5)
Total deforested area, 1950–87 (km²)	35,979	4,098	2,743	27,652
Percentage of total forest loss (km²)	44.71	5.09	15.84	34.36

Source: David M. Kummer, *Deforestation in the Postwar Philippines* (Chicago: University of Chicago Press, 1992), p. 58 (Table 10).

During the 1980s it was estimated that the Philippines was losing around 1 billion cubic meters of agricultural topsoil every year. This is the equivalent of 100,000 ha of land 1 meter deep, or 50 tons of soil per hectare per year.[39] Surveys conducted in 1983 identified thirteen of the country's seventy-three provinces as having more than half their areas eroded. In 1985, 50 percent of the Philippines' seasonally cropped areas were believed to be subject to soil erosion, and by the end of the 1980s government estimates concluded that twenty-five provinces, including many of the country's important agricultural regions, had 40 to 87 percent of their surface areas subject to severe erosion.[40] A World Bank study at the time concluded that soil erosion had become "such a widespread and pronounced problem that it is generally ranked as the most serious environmental problem in the Philippines."[41]

Soil erosion results in the loss of soil nutrients, topsoil, and even the entire soil to river channels and the open sea. During the period under investigation here soil erosion in the Philippines generated both upstream (on-site) and downstream (off-site) consequences. Upstream costs included reduced agricultural production, forced abandonment of land, and compensatory conversion of additional forestland for cultivation.[42] Downstream, soil erosion and unchecked rainfall runoff stemming from deforestation resulted in alternating floods and water shortages, leading to the siltation of rivers, lakes, dams, irrigation canals, and other waterways. This substantially reduced the efficiency of water use and undermined crop yields.[43] The sedimentation of rivers and streams, for example, affected the operation of irrigation systems and reduced the water for cultivation in Luzon and Mindanao. The increased sediment load of rivers and streams also greatly increased the frequency and severity of floods throughout the Philippines. Deforestation in Northern Mindanao, for example, contributed to catastrophic floods in 1981 that killed 283 people, injured 14,000, and left tens of thousands of others homeless. Similar flooding occurred, and continues to occur, throughout the Philippines as a result of denuded forests and the erosion of soil.[44]

Deforestation and the soil erosion associated with it resulted from the interaction between unsustainable logging practices and population growth in the context of significant land inequality. Legal and illegal logging led to the conversion of primary forests to secondary forests (i.e., forests with fewer, inferior, and younger trees). As such, logging was a major cause of deforestation in the Philippines. Under Marcos, logging took on an increasingly central role in the country's political economy. In 1960 the total area devoted to forest concessions was 45,000 km^2, or 15 percent of the country's total area. Between 1971 and 1977 this rose to 98,000 km^2 (or nearly one-third of the total area), declining to 56,000 km^2 by 1987. Log production also increased during this period, from 6.3 million cubic meters in 1960 to an average of 10.5 million cubic meters between 1968 and 1975 (peaking at over 15 million cubic meters in 1975), before declining to approximately 4 million cubic meters in 1987. The percentage of log production exported during this period increased from around 50 percent in 1960–61 to an average of 78 percent during the 1967–72 period, although in 1987 only 5 percent were exported. These figures clearly show the rapid increase in officially sanctioned logging in the late 1960s and early 1970s under Marcos, and the high degree of dependence on foreign markets (primarily Japan) for export. Moreover, since these statistics come from the government, and since the government had incentives to underreport, the statistics should be considered minimum figures.[45]

Most forests in the Philippines are public lands, and private investors have historically secured license agreements from the government to log on this land. Prior to martial law, access to natural resources, including timber concessions, was allocated based on the political power of landed elite families. Concessions allowed elite families to secure windfall profits. This, in turn, increased the political influence societal elites had on the state by increasing their ability to finance political campaigns and channel funds to political officials.[46] When Marcos declared martial law in 1972 he abolished parties, elections, and legislative bodies, thereby making local elites much more dependent on the government for access to economic resources. This had the effect of breaking the hold of the landed elite on politics, and made the state apparatus considerably more autonomous from the traditional ruling class. Nevertheless, "although it freed the state from the traditional elite as a class, the martial law regime did not alter the traditional relationship between political power and control over natural resources: Marcos simply centralized control over economic resources in the hands of the fraction of the traditional elite most closely aligned with him and his family."[47] The granting of timber concessions became a way for Marcos to secure the continued loyalty of allies and supporters.[48] Indeed, the martial law regime opened up more forests for exploitation per year than the democratic regime had during the log-export boom of the 1960s.[49] Political leaders were often major stockholders and board members of logging companies, and many of Marcos's cronies received their own timber licenses. Defense Minister Enrile, for example, controlled logging companies with leases totaling hundreds of thousands of hectares, and Herminio Disini, another close Marcos associate, obtained almost 200,000 ha in timber concessions in northern Luzon. In addition, even political leaders without direct ties to timber companies often had financial interests in the timber concessions within their subnational units stemming from the payoffs and royalties they received.[50]

The political economy of forestry contributed to unsustainable logging practices in the Philippines in several ways. First, the concession system was set up in such a way that the government captured very little of the economic rent from the exploitation of forest resources. From the second decade of the twentieth century on the Philippines used a system of fixed forest charges. These charges tended to value timber resources at an artificially low level (only 1 to 3 percent of real market value in log form). As a result, loggers paid very little of the economic rent they earned from exploiting publicly owned lands to the state. Estimates suggest that, prior to 1981, the government only collected between 4 and 30 percent of the rents, depending on the timber product. In the 1970s forestry contributed only 0.5 to 1.3 percent of total government revenues, and from 1970 to 1982 government revenues amounted to only 8.8 percent of total export values. Between 1979 and 1982, including both export tax receipts as well as license fees, total government revenue from the forestry sector was $170 million. This amounted to less than 12 percent of the $1.5 billion potential rent and was not even sufficient to cover the government's administrative and infrastructure costs associated with timber harvesting. The lost rent went to logging companies as windfall profits and robbed the industry of any incentive to use forest resources efficiently or sustainably.[51]

Second, the vast profits earned by loggers facilitated the corruption of forestry officials.[52] Corruption and the disproportionate amount of political connections enjoyed by the logging industry made it extremely difficult for relatively weak regulatory agencies to enforce government requirements concerning reforestation, timber stand improvement, and forest protection.[53] Moreover, because of corruption and poor enforcement of government regulations, a considerable amount of unlicensed (i.e., illegal) logging occurred under Marcos, often with de facto protection from law enforcement and military officials.[54] While figures on illegal logging do not exist, the World Bank estimated in 1989 that the total volume of illegal extraction during the Marcos years might have been equal to legal activities.[55] Export data reinforce the conclusion that illegal logging was widespread. Between 1980 and 1982, for example, Japan, the largest importer of Philippine forestry products, reported total imports that were approximately 250 percent greater than official Philippine log export figures to Japan.[56]

Third, and finally, the market for forest resources was further perverted by the duration of forest concessions. Under the concessions system, timber license agreements were awarded to private investors to log on publicly owned forestland for one to ten years (eventually changed to twenty-five years in the 1970s) on a noncompetitive basis. Since the harvest cycle of many tropical species exceeds these time periods, concessionaires had no incentive to adopt long-term strategies of forest preservation. Instead, they were encouraged to maximize profits through short-term exploitation.[57]

In short, an ideal market with prices that reflected the full economic and social costs of logging did not exist in the Philippines. In the place of a market capable of encouraging the conservation of forest resources, the tight connection between political power and logging interests created a distorted market that provided every incentive to plunder Philippine forests in order to maximize short-term economic and political gain.[58]

Loggers were largely responsible for clearing primary forests, but millions of poor farming families, forced to migrate to new hilly and mountainous upland locations by rapid population growth and the lack of available arable land in the lowlands, destroyed much of the remaining secondary forest by clearing trees and vegetation to make way for subsistence agriculture.[59] Loggers facilitated this migration by building roads into the heart of the forest and by clearing the uplands for potential use by migrants.[60] Logging concessionaires also had a number of powerful incentives to encourage migrant inflows. Migrants provided a secure supply of cheap labor and helped to clear underbrush and other vegetation that inhibited timber hauling. Encroachments by migrants also provided loggers with an excuse to forgo costly forest improvement and reforestation efforts. Furthermore, once the migrants finished clearing the secondary forest, loggers could apply for permits to convert the land to plantations, allowing them to profit a second time from the cleared land. All told, the highest rates of population growth in the uplands tended to occur in those areas with logging concessions. By 1985 more than 62 percent of the total upland population lived in timber concession areas, representing approximately half of all forest lands.[61]

The surge in upland population and agriculture was a major cause of deforestation. Cultivated area in forestland increased from 582,000 ha in 1960 to more than 3.9 million ha in 1987, representing an average annual increase of 7 percent. Consequently, although cultivated upland areas amounted to only 10 percent of lowland cropped areas in the 1960s, it increased to 40 percent of lowland cropped areas in the 1980s. Much of this expansion occurred on forestland. In the 1980s alone 60 percent of the 2.7 million ha of expanded cropland throughout the Philippines came from expansion of agriculture into previously forested land with slopes between 18 and 30 percent.[62]

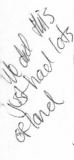

The shifting, slash-and-burn cultivation techniques (known locally as *kaingin*) employed by upland migrant farmers (known as *kaingineros*) were incredibly destructive to the remaining forests.[63] In the decades following the closing of the land frontier the process of migrant-induced deforestation typically occurred in the following manner: migrant farmers first cut down young trees and other vegetation left untouched by loggers when the primary forest was cleared; they then burned the area to convert it to arable land; and lastly they planted it for three or four successive crop years with annual crops (e.g., rice, corn, and root crops). The accumulated humus on the topsoil made the cleared areas initially fertile. However, since excessive soil erosion is unavoidable in areas with a slope of greater than 30 percent, and persistent conservation practices are required in uplands with lower slopes to avoid erosion, this fertility was inevitably short-lived. Indeed, the technique of shifting agriculture has historically been attractive to poor migrant farmers precisely because it allowed them to minimize cash input requirements and conservation efforts by substituting land for labor and fertilizer.[64] The sheer number of people moving to the uplands compounded these destructive practices. When the upland population was thinly dispersed, farmers could simply move on to virgin land when the soil's productivity declined. As the population swelled, however, farmers were forced to remain in the same place longer and engage in more frequent cropping, which shortened the fallow period and resulted in greater soil erosion. Indeed, by 1980, "in many upland municipalities that were once sparsely populated, the population density had exceeded the critical [sustainable] limit for shifting agricultural systems of 200 persons per square kilometer."[65]

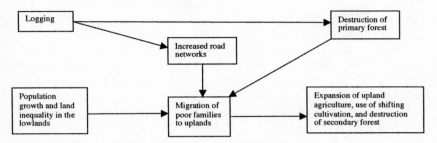

Figure 3.1. Causes of Deforestation in the Philippines

The lack of secure tenure and titling made a bad environmental situation even worse. Upland areas and newly settled lands have traditionally been "open access" with no secure tenure or titling. As a result, migrant farmers had little incentive to invest in land improvements and nutrient maintenance. Lack of secure tenure prevented farmers from using land as collateral to obtain credit for investments in land improvements and biased crop choices against tree crops. Poor farmers were thus encouraged to minimize labor and inputs, and to shift to sites with higher fertility after soil resources were depleted. All told, this process of slash-and-burn clearing and subsistence cultivation prevented the resurgence of forest vegetation and contributed to substantial long-term degradation of forestlands.[66] Moreover, as we saw above, deforestation and related environmental degradation in the uplands contributed to significant environmental degradation in the lowlands. A vicious cycle emerged whereby migration to the uplands created degradation in the lowlands, encouraging further migration to the uplands, and so on.[67]

The historical process of deforestation in the Philippines is summarized in Figure 3.1.[68]

In addition to deforestation and soil erosion, coastal degradation also became a significant problem in the Philippines during the Marcos years. Mangrove forests declined significantly as a result of accelerated cutting for fuelwood and the conversion of mangrove forests to brackish water fishponds. Estimates suggest that the 450,000 ha of mangroves thought to exist in 1918 were reduced to 240,000 ha in 1980 and to 150,000 ha by the end of the decade.[69] Coral reefs were also destroyed at an alarming rate as a consequence of cutting and (illegal) export of coral, destructive fishing techniques (such as the use of dynamite and cyanide fishing), industrial and agricultural pollution, and the destruction of mangrove forests (which left coral reefs more vulnerable to typhoon damage). In the early 1980s it was estimated that only

30 percent of the country's coral reefs were in good or excellent condition; the remaining reefs were severely degraded.[70]

Lastly, while no precise data on nationwide fish stocks exist for the period under investigation here, it appears that fisheries declined substantially as well. Fish production, which increased consistently for decades, leveled off in the 1980s, as did the gross value added from the fishing industry. Many experts attributed this leveling off to overfishing, warning that the total actual catch was approaching the total potential catch.[71] By the mid-1980s it was estimated that eleven of the fifty major fishing grounds for municipal (near-shore) fishermen had been overfished beyond their sustainable yield as a result of increased competition between small fishermen and intrusion by larger commercial ones.[72] Other forms of coastal degradation further exacerbated the decline of fisheries, since coral reefs and mangroves serve as breeding, feeding, and nursery grounds for fish and other marine life.[73]

Population growth, land inequality, and environmental degradation in upland areas were all deeply implicated in the destruction of coastal ecosystems. Thousands of poor Filipinos migrated to coastal areas as a result of population pressures, land inequality, and a general lack of other economic opportunities in adjacent agricultural areas. Between 1970 and 1980 the number of households dependent on fishing increased from 275,865 to 581,670, and the total number of fishermen increased from 375,658 to 1,054,645.[74] Fishing beyond the sustainable yield, the use of destructive fishing techniques, excessive fuelwood cutting, and conversion of mangroves were all a direct consequence of increasing numbers of impoverished people competing for shrinking resources. Moreover, as in upland areas, a vicious cycle emerged: poor individuals degraded the coastal environment, which ultimately made them poorer and more desperate, which encouraged more degradation, and so on.[75] The health of near-shore ecosystems was also damaged by ecological destruction in upland areas. Siltation stemming from deforestation and soil erosion increased water turbidity and reduced light penetration, which damaged, and in some cases completely smothered, many offshore coral reefs and seagrass beds.[76]

Pressures on Society

Acute DES in the Philippines during the Marcos years led to the economic marginalization of millions of Filipinos. This is not immediately apparent from a cursory glance at available economic statistics, which suggest that the Philippine economy performed quite well under Marcos until the early 1980s. Annual GNP growth averaged 6 percent between 1962 and 1974, and 3.6 percent between 1974 and 1986. Over those same two periods of time, the average annual growth in per capita GNP was 3.1 percent and 1 percent, respectively.[77] However, this respectable economic growth is less impressive on closer examination. The economic performance of the Philippines was by far the lowest of all Southeast Asian countries. For example, Indonesia, the second lowest economic performer, had a per capita growth rate of 4 percent a year from 1960 to 1980. In addition, events in the early 1980s demonstrated how fragile the Philippines economy was. In 1983 the Philippines entered its most severe economic crisis of the postwar era (the causes of which are discussed below). In 1983 growth in GNP dropped to 1.3 percent, and in 1984 and 1985 growth rates plummeted to −7.1 percent and −4.1 percent, respectively. Per capita income contracted as well. In 1981 GNP per capita was 65 percent above its level in 1962; by 1986 it was only 36 percent above its 1962 level.[78]

Furthermore, economic growth figures provide a very inaccurate picture of the plight poor Filipino families faced during the Marcos period, *even before the economic crisis of the early 1980s*. In particular, the data mask the fact that the country's poor experienced deepening absolute and relative impoverishment from the late 1960s to the mid-1980s largely as a result of demographic and environmental pressures. Trends in real wages and unemployment clearly demonstrate the growing immiseration of many poor families. Between 1962 and 1986 real agricultural wages declined an average of 1.6 percent per year and, in total, fell by roughly one-third over that same period. Urban wages declined even more significantly. In 1980 the real wages of urban workers were less than half what they were in 1962, and available data suggest that wages continued to decline during the 1980s. Between 1962 and 1986 the real wages of unskilled laborers in Metro Manila declined at an average annual rate of 5.8 percent, with wages for skilled workers falling by 5.2 percent a year.[79] There was also substantial unemployment during this period. Total unemployment declined somewhat in the 1960s and early 1970s but rose in the late 1970s and early 1980s. Between 1976 and 1986, 20 to 25 percent of the labor force was consistently idle.[80]

As a consequence both absolute and relative poverty increased. The percentage of Filipino families living below the poverty line increased from 41 percent in 1965 to 43.8 percent in 1971, 51.5 percent in 1975, and 58.9 percent in 1985. In rural areas the situation became particularly dire. By 1985, 63.2 percent of rural families fell below the poverty line and 35 percent of the rural population fell below the subsistence level.[81] Rural poverty was most prevalent among rice and corn farmers, coconut farmers, sugarcane workers, municipal fishermen, and marginal upland farmers.[82] The gap between rich and poor in the Philippines, which has consistently ranked among the most inequitable countries in the world, also widened from the late 1950s until the early 1980s. In 1956 the richest 20 percent of the population received 55 percent of the total national income, while the poorest 20 percent received 5 percent; by 1983 the richest 20 percent received 59 percent of the total income, while the poorest 20 percent received 3 percent. By 1985 official data suggested that the gap was shrinking, but this conclusion was almost certainly incorrect. The economist James Boyce persuasively argues that this data missed an actual increase in inequality during the 1980s by failing to account for changes in income understatement, relative prices, and differences in family size. After correcting for some of these factors, Boyce estimates that the richest 10 percent of the population had 9.3 times the income of the poorest 30 percent in 1961, 13.9 times their income in 1971, and 15.2 times their income in 1985.[83] In sum, data on real wages, unemployment, and poverty provide strong evidence that many poor families experienced substantial declines in real incomes during the Marcos years. At the same time the incomes of the rich rose so much that average per capita income actually increased, creating the mirage that national welfare was progressing.

DES was a central factor in this growing economic marginalization, evidenced by the fact that landless agricultural workers, new urban migrants, upland farmers, and municipal fishermen made up the poorest of the poor in the Philippines throughout Marcos's tenure.[84] Population growth, the end of the land frontier, and environmental degradation contributed to the growing immiseration of poor Filipinos in several interrelated ways. First, population growth substantially increased the total *number* of individuals living in poverty. If one considers the percentage of families living in poverty, and the fact that the average poor family in the Philippines was larger than the national average, then the total number of impoverished individuals may have increased from 17.4 million in 1971 to 33.5 million in 1985 owing to population growth. This represents a total increase of 16 million people, or almost a doubling in just a decade and a half. Moreover, even if this is an overestimate, more conservative calculations still suggest a net increase of 10–14 million additional impoverished Filipinos over this time period. Whichever estimate is correct, clearly the total number of poor people grew dramatically.[85]

Second, DES reduced the incomes of the poor. Population growth led to unemployment and declining real wages in both rural and urban areas. Rapid population growth combined with the mobility of farm workers to increase the ready supply of (increasingly landless) labor faster than demand. This problem was compounded by three components of the Marcos government's development strategy: the emphasis on capital-intensive, import-substituting industrialization; the preference for export agriculture; and the onset of the green revolution, which increased the mechanization of agriculture. These policies had the effect of undermining labor absorption at the very time that the supply of labor was expanding. The result was high rates of joblessness and lower wages for those who found work.[86] Or, to put it more graphically, "the result of these changes was a Philippine peasantry in debt and often homeless, living marginal lives on the fringes of great estates or clustering in shacks in towns."[87]

Population growth and the increasingly skewed distribution of land in the lowlands also worsened poverty by reducing average farm size and increasing the number of people forced to migrate to, and to rely for their livelihood on, ill-suited upland areas and crowded coastal zones.[88] Large-scale deforestation, soil erosion, and coastal degradation increased the precariousness of life for struggling farmers and fishermen by undermining the already fragile ecosystems they had come to depend on.[89] In the 1980s two-thirds of the Philippine population still depended on agriculture, fisheries, and forests to make a living. Under these circumstances severe environmental degradation could not help but cause economic marginalization.[90] As Robin Broad and John Cavanagh observe: "To live, people [in the Philippines] eat and sell the fish they catch or the crops they grow—and typically these people exist at the margin. For them, the ecological crisis . . . becomes an immediate, and life- and livelihood-threatening, crisis."[91] Upland farmers, for example, were forced to depend on easily eroded soil capable of producing only about half the average yield of lowland rain-fed fields and only about a third the yield of lowland irrigated fields. The farm size threshold necessary to provide adequate incomes was thus much higher in upland areas than in the lowlands. As the uplands became more crowded and degraded, incomes that derived from this fragile land inevitably declined.[92] The degradation of fisheries also contributed to economic marginalization. Even though total production did not stagnate until the 1980s, catch per unit of effort declined steadily since 1949, and fishery rent declined from the 1970s on. As a result, the proportion of fishing households living below the poverty line increased from 53.6 percent in 1971 to 71.5 percent in 1985.[93] Overfishing also contributed to marginalization by putting strains on domestic food supply. Fish and other seafood provide more than half the protein in the average Filipino household, and they are especially important to the poor because fish costs less than meat or fowl. However, because of overfishing, "the supply of fish for domestic food consumption failed to keep pace with population growth, and the poor increasingly found fish too expensive."[94]

Economic Crisis and Pressures on the State

The economic growth experienced by the Philippines prior to the 1980s was deceiving not only because it masked increasing marginalization for a substantial segment of the population but was deceptive in another respect as well: it relied on the shaky foundation of a flawed capital intensive, import-substituting industrialization strategy and the unsustainable exploitation of the country's natural resource base, and was financed by high levels of foreign borrowing.

When Marcos became president in 1965 the external debt of the Philippines was $800 million. By 1970 it had grown threefold to $2.3 billion, equivalent to 36 percent of the country's GNP at the time. In 1981 the debt topped the $20 billion mark, and by the time Marcos was ousted in 1986 the debt stood at $28.3 billion, the equivalent of more than 90 percent of GNP.[95] External funds allowed the government to finance high budget and trade deficits and thus maintain the spending that fueled moderate economic growth. However, accumulating debt and the onerous payments it required also made the economy highly susceptible to external economic changes. The time of reckoning came in the early 1980s. World interest rates climbed to double digits and international commodity prices fell, cutting Philippine export prices by 30 percent from 1980 to 1982. Soon new loans to cover the widening trade deficit were no longer available. The assassination of Benigno Aquino in 1983 also increased the perception both outside and inside the Philippines that the country was coming unglued. Consequently, commercial credit lines to the Philippines dried up and capital flight accelerated, contributing to the shrinking of international reserves. In October 1983 the Marcos government was forced by the exhaustion of its foreign exchange reserves to declare a debt moratorium and undertake a stabilization program backed by the International Monetary Fund (IMF) in order to reschedule debt obligations and secure new funds. The ensuing structural adjustment measures—devaluation and floating of the peso, tight monetary policies, steep interest rate increases, reduction of the budget deficit, and the lifting of price controls—sent the economy careening into its worst crisis in the postwar era. Between 1982 and 1985 the country's GNP fell by 10 percent, and GNP per capita plummeted by 15 percent.[96]

The crisis was triggered by a series of exogenous shocks, but its roots ran much deeper. One fundamental cause was the development strategy adopted by Marcos. This strategy placed the highest priority on capital-intensive, import-substituting industrialization to the disadvantage of the agricultural and export sectors of the economy, and made the economy highly dependent on external funds. From 1962 to 1970 the Philippine government sought to encourage import substitution by devaluing the peso to curtail imports of consumer goods and by raising tariffs. Despite these efforts, imports continued to rise and the Philippines faced a serious balance of payment crisis in 1970 (exacerbated by excessive spending by Marcos during the 1969 presidential campaign). The Marcos government turned to foreign lenders to keep the economy afloat. The oil price shock of 1973–74 accelerated the borrowing trend by increasing both the demand for foreign exchange to pay for more expensive oil imports and the supply of external funds from banks eager to recycle surpluses from oil exporters. (The Philippine economy took a similar hit in 1979–80 following the second round of oil price increases.) The trade deficit, and the need to borrow to finance the deficit, also grew as a result of changes in the value of the peso and declines in international commodity prices. Following further devaluation of the peso in the early 1970s, at the behest of the IMF, the value of the peso again began to appreciate. This was partly because of the influx of foreign exchange from the loans themselves and partly a conscious attempt by the government to keep imports of capital goods cheap. Soon the peso was overvalued relative to other currencies. At the same time international prices for the Philippines' chief agricultural exports fell. Thus, despite the Marcos government's general bias in favor of export crops over other types of agriculture, as well as pressure to export more to generate needed foreign exchange, the overvalued peso and declining commodity prices caused agricultural export earnings to slump. Meanwhile, the industrial sector continued to enjoy high rates of effective protection, relied on imported inputs, and had little export potential. The end result was an escalating need to borrow heavily from abroad to finance imports.[97]

Foreign loans failed to contribute to significant and sustainable growth because the funds were invested inefficiently. The vast majority of foreign borrowing was channeled through the Philippine state either because it was public-sector debt or publicly guaranteed private debt. Control over billions of dollars of borrowed money was used to aggrandize the Marcos regime and underwrite an extensive system of patronage. Much of the money was channeled to investments in capital-intensive technology for the inefficient industrial sector, as well as to large, low-yielding, long-term infrastructural projects. Other funds were lent through government banks to inefficient public corporations or funneled directly to the Marcos-Romualdez family and the regime's political and economic allies. Returns on investments were thus insufficient to cover interest payments and have enough left over to encourage sustainable growth.[98]

DES AND THE ECONOMIC CRISIS

To end the story here, however, would ignore another fundamental cause of the economic crisis, namely, DES. Demographic and environmental pressures were deeply implicated in the economic downturn in several ways. First, DES contributed to the debt crisis by helping to create a significant gap between investment needs, government expenditures, and domestic savings, thereby forcing the government to borrow from abroad. Population pressures and land shortages in the lowlands forced the government to make substantial investments in the green revolution and in agricultural development to enable a shift from extensive to intensive cultivation. These investment needs played a key role in encouraging external borrowing. Immediately after assuming the presidency Marcos staked his reputation on meeting these needs through the provision of a vast array of infrastructural projects, especially in Mindanao. The government borrowed from abroad throughout the late 1960s and 1970s in order to pour funds into dams, a network of irrigation systems, and other rural infrastructure such as farm-to-market roads. Funds were also required to finance subsidies for fertilizer, pesticides, irrigation water, and other inputs, and to pay for a massive supervised credit program with subsidized lending rates and the expansion of the field-based staff of the Ministry of Agriculture.[99] Indeed, "rural development was one of the official reasons why the Marcos administration engaged in heavy borrowing, especially during the martial law years 1972–86. In fact, the Marcos budget ministry declared the 1970s the decade of countryside development."[100]

DES created other demands on the state as well. In particular, as urban populations grew rapidly, demands increased for an array of services including health needs, housing, education, sanitation, energy and utilities, communication, and transportation. A perverse yet predictable feedback process emerged whereby public and private investments in additional services and the concentration of development efforts in cities, especially Metro Manila, "pulled" additional migrants into urban areas, further increasing demands. Consequently, by the 1980s Manila's population had grown rapidly, perhaps 10 percent of the city's residents lived in slums, and service systems had become severely overloaded.[101]

At the same time that DES generated growing demands for investments, population growth and DES-related economic marginalization hurt the ability of the government to finance these investments without borrowing from abroad. Population growth and related poverty helped to keep domestic savings low. Statistical analyses conducted by Dante Canlas suggest that high birth rates in the Philippines throughout the period from 1948 to 1980 had the effect of depressing household savings. Population growth ate into aggregate income, and large families with higher dependency ratios were forced to shift more of their shrinking income away from savings and toward consumption in order to meet the immediate needs of children. In short, since most Filipino families were both large and poor during the Marcos years, very little income was left over for savings.[102] From 1961 to 1970 the domestic savings rate averaged less than 20 percent of GNP. The rate remained below 25 percent during the 1970s and slumped to below 20 percent during the economic crisis of the early 1980s. This low level of domestic savings produced a savings-investment gap that ranged from -2 percent to more than -8 percent of GNP per year from 1971 to 1983.[103] "Increased external indebtedness filled the gap between growing investment and current expenditures and limited domestic resource mobilization."[104] Commentators at the time noted the critical importance of the lack of domestic savings to the economic crisis. Bernardo Villegas, the chief economist at the Center for Research and Communications in Manila, observed in the mid-1980s that, "if the misallocation of resources resulting from flawed economic policies and political interference had been largely financed by domestic savings, the Philippine economy might still have had sufficient flexibility to bounce back within a relatively short period of time. Unfortunately, the Philippines went on a borrowing spree . . . and now has to face the harsh reality of paying back its loans from the resources of an economy that is hardly growing."[105]

Compounding matters further, low levels of demand for industrially produced goods, also a by-product of increasing economic marginalization, combined with low domestic savings rates to guarantee that the flawed development strategy adopted by Marcos would result in massive debt. In order to grow, the capital-intensive, import-substituting industrial sector of the economy relied primarily on increases in domestic demand. Yet, "with low productivity and incomes in both the rural farm sector and the traditional services and informal urban sectors, such rapid growth [in demand] could hardly be forthcoming."[106] Absent such demand growth, the industrial sector continued to rely on costly government support and protection. And, as noted by a 1989 U.S. Agency for International Development (USAID) report, "government support for unsustainable industrial policies was financed increasingly through external borrowings *as private savings levels remained low.*"[107] In sum, to the extent that DES perpetuated the gap between investment needs, government expenditures, and domestic savings, it played an important role in causing and exacerbating the debt crisis.

Second, environmental degradation contributed to the economic downturn by cutting into the Philippines' export earnings and undermining overall economic productivity. Traditionally the Philippines' principal exports have been products from the natural resource sector. As these resources became stressed and degraded, export earnings declined, contributing to problems in the balance of payments and reducing the revenue stream to the state. Nowhere was this more apparent than in forestry. In the late 1940s the Philippines decided to use its forest resources as a source of foreign exchange to finance its development program. In 1949 forest products made up only 1.5 percent of total exports, but this increased to 11 percent by 1955. In the 1960s the export of logs and lumber doubled. Forestry's share of total exports reached 33 percent by 1969, by which time forest products made up the largest single category of Philippine exports. However, as Boyce observes, "when mistreated . . . the tropical rainforest becomes a nonrenewable resource. The constraint of non-renewability began to bind in the 1970s."[108] By 1974 the percentage of total exports made up by forest products fell to 12 percent, and by 1986 it had fallen to 6.6 percent, largely because of deforestation. As of 1986 forestry contributed only 1.6 percent to the country's GNP, compared to almost 4 percent of GNP in the early 1970s.[109] The dropoff in exports combined with declining terms of trade to contribute to growing trade deficits that, in turn, required greater reliance on external borrowing and deepened the debt crisis.[110] Moreover, because the government failed to capture most of the potential rent from logging, it lost a significant source of revenue for rural development and loan repayment. Between 1979 and 1982, for example, the Philippine government captured only 16.5 percent of logging rents. Had the government captured 50 percent, logging rents would have contributed more than $300 million a year to government revenue over this period.[111]

Environmental degradation had other, more diffuse negative effects on the economy as well. These costs are very difficult to quantify accurately, and the data necessary to draw a definitive conclusion do not exist. Nevertheless, since we know that natural resources remained central to the Philippine economy during the period under investigation, employing over 50 percent of the labor force and contributing a third to the total economy and to total exports, it is not surprising that available data suggest that significant costs were imposed on the economy by destructive environmental practices.[112] Deforestation, for example, placed costs on the economy beyond the loss of export revenue.

As noted above, forests in the Philippines are essential to the functioning of watersheds (river systems that flow to the sea) that make agriculture and nearshore fishery production systems viable. Forests hold the topsoil and regulate water flow released into the lowlands for irrigation, industrial uses, and hydroelectric power. Thus, at the very time that deforestation dramatically reduced forestry's direct contribution to the economy, a study by the Philippine Department of Environment and Natural Resources (DENR) concluded that, "its negative impact on the economy [was] amplified through the primary level [of] production."[113] Deforestation-induced soil erosion in the uplands lowered the capacity to grow new forests and crops, and disruption in river and stream flow caused flooding during the rainy season, destroying good agricultural land in the lowlands, and extreme dryness during the dry season, reducing irrigation capacity and making it more expensive. Deforestation also contributed to the siltation of irrigation systems and shortened the life of hydroelectric dams. Finally, siltation of nearshore areas degraded fishery resources.[114]

Good national data on the on-site/upstream and off-site/downstream costs resulting from deforestation and soil erosion do not exist, but local studies indicate substantial costs. A 1988 World Resources Institute study of the Magat watershed in the Philippines suggested that on-site/upstream costs were very high. The costs averaged about $50 (P1,000) annually per hectare of land converted from forests to upland crops, or about 10–20 percent of the expected gross returns.[115] Based on this study, the World Bank estimated total on-site/upstream national erosion costs on the order of $100 million (P2 billion) a year in the 1980s.[116] Downstream costs associated with deforestation and soil erosion were probably much greater, although data on these costs are even less reliable. Estimates made by the Philippine government for 1988 suggest that annual off-site/downstream costs associated with adverse impacts on irrigated agriculture, coastal fishing, and hydropower generation may have been very high throughout the 1980s. The annual cost to irrigated agriculture in 1988 was estimated to be P3.5 billion (15.5 percent of the total value of irrigated rice production); the cost to coastal fishing as a result of declining production was estimated to be worth P935 million; and power losses for hydropower were estimated to be P466 million. All told, these costs totaled P4.9 billion for 1988 alone. Nevertheless, since these off-site/downstream cost estimates are based on assumptions lacking good hard data to support them, they should be seen as merely suggestive not definitive.[117]

Overall, how important were the negative costs of DES to the economic crisis that gripped the Philippines in the 1980s? Arguably, very important. Wilfredo Cruz and Robert Repetto of the World Resources

Institute, for example, estimate that the costs produced by environmental degradation were an important contributor to the economic downturn:

> Growth was maintained during the [1970s] by building up external indebtedness and drawing down important domestic assets, especially natural resources. Like a highly leveraged business, the Philippine economy was increasingly vulnerable to external shocks and internal structural flaws.[118]
>
> Over the 12 years preceding the Philippine's debt crisis, asset loss in just these three resources [forests, soils, and fisheries] together averaged 4 percent of GDP each year. By contrast, the annual current account deficit, indicating the rate at which external liabilities were building, averaged only 3.2 percent of GDP per year. The Philippines' national balance sheet was literally eroding, and at a much faster rate from natural resource deterioration than from the more publicized foreign borrowing. . . . Both contributed to the ensuing economic crisis. The costs of servicing the debt became increasingly heavy. The loss of natural resource assets also cost the economy dearly in output, exports, employment, and income.

The negative effects of population growth and resource inequality magnified the costs associated with environmental degradation, and were thus also thoroughly implicated in the steep economic decline experienced in the 1980s. As another World Resource Institute study concluded in 1988: "The mismanagement of resources has led to environmental degradation; unequal access to resources has contributed to poverty and increased pressure on natural resources; and population pressure has exacerbated both poverty and environmental degradation. This dynamic has precipitated an economic crisis that influences the Philippines' political future both directly and indirectly."[119] In short, although DES was certainly not the only cause of the country's economic woes, it was a major contributing factor and interacted synergistically with other causes.[120]

STATE FAILURE

Beginning in the late 1970s and accelerating in the early 1980s, the confluence of the various trends discussed above caused a dramatic weakening of the Philippine state, undermining its authority and ability to govern. State weakness manifested itself in four ways. First, the administrative capacity of the state declined significantly. The main instruments of local government in the Philippines are administrations in towns and barangays, which vary in size, consisting of thirty-five to two hundred families. In the 1980s the country had more than fifteen thousand towns and more than forty-one thousand barangays. Under Marcos, and especially after the declaration of martial law, local government became more dependent on the national government, but the flow of resources from the center (Metro Manila and Central Luzon) to local governments in the periphery failed to keep pace with both inflation and the expanding population base.[121] The economic downturn of the early 1980s magnified this trend, resulting in a crisis of local governance. In 1982 Major General Delfin Castro, the commander of the Southern Command on Mindanao, noted the need for more resources to address local governing needs but recognized that "the government has no resources to push development sufficiently."[122] Interviews with local officials in the early and mid-1980s pointed to several problems with local administrative capacity that worsened during the economic crisis, and directly or indirectly fueled the growth of the communist insurgency. These included the small size and quality of town administrative staffs and police, poor communication and contacts between local governments and the center and between local governments themselves, the lack of resources to provide needed social services, and the increasing inability and unwillingness of the central government to provide the needed resources in the face of growing economic crisis.[123]

The increased budgetary constraints stemming from economic decline meant, in particular, a significant reduction in the provision of basic social services. In the 1980s it was estimated that the government expenditure on social services per family (after subtracting the salaries of government personnel and maintenance and operating expenses) was only two-thirds of what the average poor family paid in taxes.[124] A 1984 study concluded that, "the poor generally do not have access to social services in health, nutrition, and education. . . . Institutional services in terms of extension services do not as a whole reach most of them because of poor physical infrastructure and limited manpower in the extension agencies."[125] Problems were especially severe in the most economically marginalized regions of the country, such as Mindanao and Negros, where the insurgency enjoyed its greatest success.[126]

Second, the coercive power of the state declined. In the wake of the declaration of martial law Marcos sought to build a powerful coercive apparatus. Military spending increased tenfold between 1972 and 1977 in constant pesos (in constant dollars, the military budget increased threefold over this time), and the percentage of the national budget devoted to the armed forces nearly doubled to 22.6 percent by 1977. The size of the Armed Forces of the Philippines (AFP) grew from 53,000 in 1971 to over 100,000 by the mid-1970s and more than 150,000 by 1979. Marcos used increases in the military budget and changes in personnel to establish himself as both the supreme patron and supreme commander of the armed forces. This centralization was furthered by the integration of local police forces into the national security apparatus under the command of the Philippine Constabulary. Also essential to military reorganization was the formation of the Civilian Home Defense Forces (CHDF). The goal was to organize and train thousands of civilians to provide local security for towns and *barangays* throughout the Philippines. In actuality, CHDF units were comprised of part-time soldiers and vigilantes who were poorly trained, armed, and controlled. Located largely in Mindanao and other hotbeds of rebellion, these units were frequently deployed to protect the interests of the landed elite.[127]

The expansion and reorganization of the military was, according to a statement by Marcos in 1980, necessary in order to address "the continuing challenges of subversion and insurgency."[128] Yet the changes in the military actually hurt the coercive power of the state as corruption increased significantly and training and discipline eroded.[129] These problems were magnified by the economic crisis. Inflation increased and defense spending fell, leading to critical shortages of resources for transportation and communication equipment, food, clothing, medicines and medical care, and pay.[130] As a result of these deficiencies Admiral Robert L. J. Long, commander of American forces in the Pacific, made the following assessment of the AFP to the U.S. Congress in 1983: "I can categorize the Armed Forces of the Philippines today as incapable of performing what I would call organized functions that any armed forces should be able to provide for its own self-defense."[131] By the time Marcos was ousted, the fifty thousand combat troops the government had in the field were simply not sufficient to defeat the NPA. As Richard Kessler notes:

> The economy's deterioration fostered a general malaise that provided a breeding ground for insurgents and a shortage of resources that made it more difficult to strengthen the military. . . .
>
> Pervasive corruption of military procurement procedures had left the military in an extremely weak position to deal with the insurgency precisely at the moment the insurgents adopted a more aggressive strategy. . . . By 1984, it was evident that the AFP would have difficulty in reaching the 10:1 combat ratio considered essential for defeating the NPA.[132]

Third, the combination of DES and economic decline eventually crushed the legitimacy of the Marcos regime. After the declaration of martial law, economic performance became the linchpin of the state's legitimacy. As population pressures mounted, the chasm between rich and poor widened, efforts at land reform fizzled, social services eroded, corruption and government abuses worsened, and the national economy went into a tailspin, poor Filipinos blamed the state and legitimacy plummeted. "Corruption and the plundering of resources destroyed what remained of the government's legitimacy, especially in rural areas, leaving a vacuum to be filled by the CPP's infrastructure."[133] Eventually, in the wake of the economic collapse of the 1980s, the rich also lost faith in the Marcos government, playing an essential role in his downfall. "The elites who watched their business empires being absorbed by Marcos cronies and also watched the decline of the Philippines in relation to its major competitors in Asia experienced the psychological equivalent of the wage rate decline."[134] Elite allegiance to the regime was largely dependent on the government's ability to keep resources flowing through the patronage machine; the debt crisis shut off the flow and thus caused the regime's fragile basis of support to crumble.[135]

Finally, the combination of DES, the economic crisis, and the growing insurgency caused the cohesion of the state to erode, especially within the military and between military leaders and Marcos. During his tenure as president Marcos appointed all the key military commanders so as to guarantee their loyalty. This had the effect of advancing many who had no combat experience, causing a great deal of resentment among junior officers. Marcos's armed forces chief of staff, Fabian Ver, for example, was once Marcos's chauffeur. Not surprisingly Ver was seen by the bulk of the military as a purely "political" general, not a professional. Military resentment increased in the early and mid-1980s as a consequence of decreasing defense budgets as well as inadequate supplies and support in the field. Junior officers became disgruntled over the government's failure to address local development needs, declining popular support for the military, and the growing strength of the CPP-NPA, all of which increased these officers' antipathy toward their ineffective leaders.[136] In early 1985 a military reform group, the Reform the Armed Forces Movement (RAM), began to organize. The group consisted of junior officers affiliated with the defense minister Enrile, whose authority had been undermined by Ver. The group's goal was to form a shadow military command and plot a coup to replace Marcos. In a May 1985 statement RAM declared that they were motivated by the perception "at a very early stage [of] the gradual and insidious isolation of the government and the AFP from the very people it was supposed to serve. There are indications that the military is slowly being destroyed as the whole profession that it used to be."[137] The collapse of military support, especially the defection of Enrile and Lt. Gen. Fidel Ramos, proved decisive in 1986 when Marcos could no longer count on the armed forces to defend his regime in the face of Corazon Aquino's "people power" revolution.[138]

The Security Dilemma and the Growth of Insurgency

By the late 1970s pressures on society and the state arising from severe DES began to generate an acute security dilemma in the Philippines. This situation intensified in the early 1980s as economic chaos created ever more anarchic conditions, especially in the countryside. As the state weakened, groups from all across the social spectrum, including the weakened state itself, resorted to self-help strategies to protect their economic and physical security. Many poor Filipinos threw their support behind the CPP-NPA, the government increased its reliance on poorly trained and equipped paramilitary and military units, criminal activities grew, and landed elites colluded with local military forces or raised private armies. As groups jockeyed to guarantee their economic and physical security, spiraling dynamics took hold: economic exploitation and insecurity drove the poor to support the CPP-NPA, who promised land reform and fundamental changes in the social structure; the threat posed to the state and landed elites by the growing strength of the insurgents increased the military's resort to force and resulted in substantial human rights abuses; this created escalating threats to the physical security of the poor, further encouraging them to support the rebels, who offered protection; this increased the threat to the state and elites; and so on.

Economic and physical insecurity emanating from the combination of DES and state failure was the driving force behind support for the CPP-NPA and the escalation of the civil war. By the late 1970s and early 1980s population pressure, unequal land distribution, environmental degradation, the growing chasm between rich and poor in both rural and urban areas, and the inability and unwillingness of the state to provide essential social services had conspired to make life for the poor more precarious than ever. It was this life-threatening sense of economic insecurity and relative deprivation, rather than ideology, that initially encouraged so many poor farmers, fishermen, indigenous upland communities, and urban squatters to turn to the communist rebels.[139]

The insurgents were keenly aware of the economic insecurity caused by DES, especially the hardships experienced by subsistence farmers and indigenous communities in upland areas. From the beginning, the CPP-NPA understood that this suffering would help their mobilization efforts and lay the foundation for their mass base. As early as 1968 Sison wrote: "The main content of the people's democratic revolution is the struggle for land among the peasants."[140] In his memoirs, reflecting on the origins of the rebellion, Sison echoed these sentiments. He pointed to the exhaustion of the land frontier as an essential cause of rural support for the insurgency.[141]

Sison's predictions turned out to be more than class warfare rhetoric. The CPP-NPA did especially well in newly cultivated upland areas where land title was weak, the environment easily degraded, and migrants and indigenous communities often faced the loss of their farms to corrupt officials and large corporations, "a fact that Sison especially noted."[142] The hunger for land created by DES generated opportunities for the CPP-NPA to use the promise of lower rents, wage increases, debt reduction, and land redistribution as selective incentives to win the support of poor farmers. Unlike Marcos's hollow commitments to land reform, which only served to elevate expectations and frustrations, the CPP pledge to provide "land to the tillers" represented more than empty promises. The Communists supervised land reform in many areas they controlled in exchange for the allegiance of rural residents. This included such efforts as seizing land and issuing titles to the landless, "renegotiating" tenancy arrangements with landlords and lowering rents, providing irrigation, preventing livestock theft, lifting farm production levels, and the like.[143]

As DES and the emerging economic crisis caused real wages and incomes to decline and unemployment and landlessness to rise, CPP-NPA influence expanded. From the late 1970s on, the CPP-NPA had enormous success in the localities hardest hit by demographic and environmental pressures. As one former communist leader recounted, "increasing population in the more hilly and isolated areas[,] as a result of population pressure in the lowlands, provided the NPA with a social base."[144] Support for the Communists in Negros, a province in Western Visayas specializing in sugar grown for export, provides a case in point. Population growth in Negros collided with landgrabbing by elites to produce land scarcity, escalating rates of hunger, poverty, landlessness, and migration to marginal lands. Desperate and dispossessed sugar workers became the poorest of the country's poor—80 percent of the population was estimated to be living in poverty in 1979—and increasingly turned to the guerrillas as their only alternative if they wished to survive.[145] A leading sugar planter in Negros commented in 1986: "The communists are very active here, recruiting members on every farm. The workers are easy prey for the communists. What have they got to lose?"[146]

The story repeated itself in other parts of the Philippines. In the Cordillera Mountains in northern Luzon, for example, the NPA gained substantial support from indigenous upland communities whose livelihoods were threatened by logging operations and the resulting deforestation.[147] "The magnitude of the land problem can be summed up here" one Communist Party official noted in reference to the slash-and-burn farmers forced to survive on the heavily deforested and eroded mountainside. "Look at these people trying to cultivate the rocky hill-side. They have nowhere else to go."[148] This, of course, had two mean-ings: they had nowhere else to go but to upland areas, and they had nowhere else to turn but to the communist rebels.

Both DES and support for the insurgency were also substantial throughout Mindanao. Historically Mindanao attracted migrants be-cause of its fertile land and abundant natural resources. As the land frontier was exhausted, population density in Mindanao increased, as did deforestation, soil erosion, and other forms of environmental deg-radation. In the 1970s and 1980s wages fell, unemployment rose, and many small farmers lost their land to plantations and logging compa-nies.[149] "There is convincing evidence," a 1985 Congressional Research Service report noted, "that the CPP has found fertile ground among the thousands of small farmers on Mindanao who have lost their land and social roots to large agri-businesses and logging firms."[150]

The economic insecurity caused by DES was compounded by the weakness of the state. Although Marcos was still asserting as late as 1984 that the government had "succeeded in attending to the basic needs of our people," this was simply not the case.[151] As the capacity of the state waned, corruption mounted, and social service spending declined, a void was created that the Communists happily filled. An AFP general in northern Mindanao, for example, admitted that the in-surgency "[is] not purely a military problem. It needs social, political and economic solutions. The people in the hinterlands don't feel the presence of the government. They don't get services from the govern-ment. No one is dispensing justice, so they resort to the NPA."[152] Other military officials voiced similar opinions. One AFP colonel observed that "the apathy of government officials [to address development con-cerns] has contributed to the growth of the insurgency," and another commented that the rebels "have told the people many credible things. They ask the people if they've seen any health services, any police, any mayors in the rural areas. . . . There are dozens of solutions our govern-ment can't provide at the moment."[153] Even Defense Minister Enrile ad-mitted in 1983 that the CPP-NPA would remain an "endemic" problem until there were additional efforts to promote rural development.[154]

Commentators outside the Philippine military shared this same view. In 1981 a Western diplomat observed that "it is misleading to look at the NPA as a straight insurgency. . . . [The Communists are] working to displace the government in delivering goods and ser-vices."[155] By the mid-1980s Western diplomats in the Philippines noted that the CPP-NPA was making "advances almost by government de-fault. The government is just not in business in a lot of places . . . [pro-ducing the perception of] an old and atrophied government from which a great number of people are alienated. How can you project this government as providing a better future than the NPA?"[156] The 1985 Congressional Research Service report on the insurgency reached the same conclusion:

> The weakness of government at the grass roots and falling living standards are longstanding ills of the society, though they have become worse recently and therefore have specific impact on the contemporary insurgency situation. . . .
>
> The shrinking financial input from the national government adds to its remoteness from large areas of the country. . . .
>
> The decline in the Philippine economy since 1979, the economic crisis since August 1983, and the imposition of government controls in key sectors of the economy have reduced the capacity of government to finance economic development and deliver basic services, have limited the income received by agricultural producers, and have increased national poverty. People in all areas visited pointed to falling living standards of the people, especially in rural areas; and many linked them to the growing appeal of the CPP-NPA.[157]

Beyond economic insecurity, there was also a potent physical dimension to the security concerns driving the civil war. The weakening of the Philippine state created an emerging anarchy characterized by lawlessness, hydra-headed threats to the physical security of poor Filipinos, and escalating violence.[158] As the Philippine state weakened, military resources were reduced. And as communist mobilization and attacks spread throughout the Philippines, the AFP was forced to spread itself thin.[159] The state's "self-help" strategy for dealing with impending disintegration was to increase reliance on CHDF units. By the mid-1980s the size of CHDF units had grown to sixty-five thousand. However, since these paramilitary groups were poorly trained, controlled, and paid, they represented a significant source of insecurity for many rural residents. Moreover, they often colluded with local landowners to eject farmers lacking land titles. Protection from death, rape, robbery, landgrabbing, and other criminal acts by CHDF units became an additional incentive to support the CPP-NPA.[160]

Treatment by regular military forces was often no better. The decline in the state's coercive power manifested itself in lower levels of training, equipment, and morale, while poor leadership and factionalism within the military undermined AFP effectiveness, and growing populations in the countryside made rural areas increasingly ungovernable.[161] A private report compiled in 1985 as part of the "World Political Risk Forecasts" argued that the Philippine government was incapable of blunting communist penetration into local areas because of "weak police forces and town administrations, growing financial constraints on municipal governments, and the [population] size of many towns." The report noted serious concerns such as the lack of uniform training and inadequate transportation, radios, food, clothing, and medical care for troops in rural areas. "These problems erode morale, contribute to military misconduct and reduce operational capabilities." Growing NPA success, rooted in its mobility, local support, and ability to stretch the AFP thin, increased the sense of desperation within the Philippine military. At the same time poor leadership by Ver also concentrated the military's elite battalions in Manila to protect Marcos, thereby further enfeebling the AFP's counterinsurgency efforts in the countryside. The combination of the state's inability to provide security and the *insecu*rity created by escalating human rights abuses at the hands of an unprofessional and frustrated military increased the pool of recruits from which the CPP-NPA could draw. The "World Political Risk Forecasts" report concluded: "Public fear of the military is the product of the armed forces' bad reputation in military-civilian relationships. Civilians constantly raise the issue of military abuse and corruption. Drunken members of the Philippine Constabulary (national police) have caused difficulty, but the public is also aware of civilian abuse at military checkpoints, and the torture and execution of suspected insurgents and supporters. The problem is severe and has alienated much of the civilian population."[162]

The harsh strategies the military adopted to cut off the guerrillas from their civilian base, including summary executions and forced migrations, disrupted village life in many regions of the Philippines. The perception grew among the poor that the AFP was an army of occupation rather than a neutral provider of law and order. "With few ties to the people they were supposed to defend, little sympathy for them, and few resources to work with, it was inevitable that the military would be viewed as the enemy."[163] The need for protection against rising government abuses caused numerous poor Filipinos to flock to the Communists. Many came to echo the sentiments expressed by one elder from a village located in the rainforests of southern Luzon: "We must learn how to use a gun to protect us from the savage military."[164] Quite simply, as one church official in Negros observed in the mid-1980s, people were "more frightened by the military than [by] the New People's Army."[165] Even an AFP general was forced to concede in 1984 that military abuses represented "one of the causes of the insurgency. This is where we are losing our fight against the NPA."[166]

The NPA also engaged in violence against civilians, but during most of the 1980s the insurgents were much more disciplined than the AFP, and their attacks much less indiscriminant. This bolstered their "Robin

Hood" image and helped maintain the support of the poor farmers, fishermen, indigenous communities, and urban slum dwellers whose interests they claimed to advance. Indeed, many among the poor came to refer to the NPA as "Nice People Around" and viewed them as a much preferred alternative for the provision of physical security. As an American member of the Federation of Asian Bishop's Conference put it: "The people would like the NPA to be sort of a people's militia so they can get on with their basic concerns."[167]

Further threats to the physical well-being of the poor emerged from nonstate actors. Some of these threats were diffuse and criminal in nature: incidents of banditry, cattle rustling, rape, and murder all became more common as a creeping lawlessness spread throughout the Philippines. Other threats to the poor arose from the private armies raised by some large landowners as part of their own strategies of self-help. Some of this was authorized by the Philippine government, which gave business firms and local elites permission to form their own CHDF-type units to protect their property.[168] Taken together, these non-state sources of physical insecurity had the same effect on the growth of the insurgency as those emanating from state-affiliated actors: they increased incentives for the poor to seek out the Communists for protection. After traveling through the Philippines with the rebels, William Chapman observed that,

> in village after village, the NPA's initial appeal was its role as dispenser of punishment against the ordinary man's enemies. The NPA killed cattle rustlers, "hold-uppers," coconut thieves, molesters of women, arrogant soldiers, even wife-beaters. . . .
>
> [The NPA] flourished and became popular only because it replaced something worse, utter lawlessness. The typical poor community of urban squatters or subsistence farmers was often beyond the reach of civilized law enforcement. The government's writ simply did not run. . . . and the protection of life and property usually fell on ordinary citizens. The NPA filled this gap.[169]

In sum, security dilemma dynamics, fueled by population and environmental pressures and their economic and social effects, were essential to the spectacular growth of the CPP-NPA, and provide the key to understanding the escalating civil war. In the early 1970s the Marcos government was still strong, and dissatisfaction was largely channeled into calls for political reform. But a creeping anarchy beset the country in the late 1970s and early 1980s.[170] Population growth, land inequality, and environmental degradation were all severe, economic deprivation worsened, and much of the archipelago fell into a condition of lawlessness. Fear, mobilization, countermobilization, and the use of violence set in motion the spiral dynamics characteristic of an acute security dilemma. In the first stage of this spiral, peasants increasingly turned to the Communists as a means of economic survival, as well as protection against the physical threats they faced at the hands of paramilitary groups, regular military units, criminals, and private armed forces. Whether they joined the CPP-NPA as fighters or provided other forms of support, the motivations of poor Filipinos were largely the same. In a 1983 interview Brigadier General Dionisio Tan-Gatue, the Constabulary Commander in southeastern Mindanao, noted: "I often question captured NPA guerrillas and ask them why they joined. They tell me that either the army killed their brothers or the government took their land."[171] Similarly one prominent Negros businessman commented, "most of those that join [the CPP-NPA] are not communists at all. They are just the victims of the military and the landlords."[172] In exchange for peasant support, the Communists promised increased access to land and greater economic security. They also killed abusive militiamen, policemen, and soldiers in ambushes or, with special liquidation squads called "Sparrow Units," punished or deterred landgrabbers, and provided a semblance of law and order. In other words, as one NPA rebel put it at the time, the Communists simply did "what the government ought to be doing."[173]

This primarily defensive behavior which poor Filipinos engaged in created insecurity on the part of other groups, namely, elements of the state and landed elites whose interests were threatened by surging CPP-NPA support. As the logic of the security dilemma would lead us to expect, local officials, military detachments, and private armies responded to growing political and material support for the Communists by taking additional measures to ensure their own economic and physical survival. In practice, this meant a ratcheting up of oppression, counterinsurgency activities, and land evictions, which only served to feed the cycle of insecurity motivating peasant support for the CPP-NPA in the first place.[174] A Filipino lawyer in Butuan City in Mindanao nicely summarized this action-reaction spiral in 1984. Commenting on the spreading influence of the Communists in the surrounding countryside, the lawyer remarked:

> The first entry of the NPA in our area took place when certain lands already cultivated by farmers were taken over by a lumber company. The NPA started ambushing the security guards of the company. . . . [When other corporations came in and drove away the settlers] the NPA was always available . . . So in this area a lot of farmers joined the NPA . . . The response of the government was always the same: send the military. And the more military you put in an area, the more abuses there will be, and the more abuses there are, the more the NPA is able to recruit.[175]

Conclusions

The Philippines case provides clear support for the modified version of the state failure hypothesis discussed in chapter 2. DES created intense pressures on Filipino society and contributed substantially to the collapse of state authority. As a consequence, in the late 1970s and early 1980s, increasing numbers of poor Filipinos turned to the Communists as their last best hope for economic and physical survival.

This explanation is more persuasive than accounts that marginalize or ignore the role of demographic and environmental variables. Purely geopolitical or political explanations fail. Although the rebels in the Philippines subscribed to a communist ideology and opposed the U.S. military presence in the country, an explanation centered on Cold War politics cannot explain the conflict. During its period of growth, the CPP-NPA never received significant support from China or the Soviet Union. Nor does reaction to Marcos's authoritarian rule fully explain the communist rebellion. The exclusive nature of Filipino institutions under Marcos was an important source of CPP-NPA support (see chapter 5), but the timing of this support is simply not consistent with a singular emphasis on the character of the regime. Marcos declared martial law in 1972, but the spectacular rise in communist strength did not begin until the end of the decade.

Existing accounts that emphasize demographic or environmental factors point to a number of important dimensions of civil strife in the Philippines, but they also fall short. Norman Myers, for example, in advancing the Neo-Malthusian deprivation hypothesis, uses the communist insurgency in the Philippines to illustrate his position. According to Myers, population growth, deforestation, soil erosion, and coastal degradation combined to create "growing throngs of disaffected peasantry" whose deprivation left them little alternative but to flock to the CPP-NPA. Indeed, Myers argues that deprivation was so central to the insurgency that the Philippine government's efforts to stem the tide of communist success would ultimately make "little headway with rural communities, disenchanted as they are with the degradation of the environmental basis of their livelihood."[176]

The findings in this chapter substantiate the claim that DES-induced poverty and inequality created incentives for poor Filipinos to throw their support behind the Communists. However, overemphasizing deprivation as the source of strife is highly problematic. The deprivation hypothesis fails to explain the variation in CPP-NPA support over time. Deprivation certainly increased under Marcos and accelerated in the early 1980s as a result of DES. But it is impossible to fully explain trends in communist support without tracking variables associated with the state. Support for the CPP-NPA skyrocketed because the state weakened. The erosion of state authority created numerous additional threats to the economic and physical security of poor Filipinos that were layered on top of existing poverty and inequality. In particular, the absence of state services, the growing threats from military and paramilitary forces, and the lack of peaceful alternatives owing to the exclusive nature of Marcos-era institutions encouraged the poor to turn to the Communists for help and protection.[177]

Thomas Homer-Dixon also cites the Philippines as an example to support his version of the state failure hypothesis. Like Myers, Homer-Dixon contends that "unequal access to rich agricultural lowlands combined with population growth to cause migration to easily degraded upland areas; erosion and deforestation contributed to economic hardship that spurred insurgency and rebellion."[178] Unlike Myers, however, Homer-Dixon points out that both deprivation and the opportunities created by state weakness were important: "The country's upland insurgency . . . was motivated by the relative deprivation of landless agricultural laborers and poor farmers displaced into the remote hills . . . and it exploited the structural opportunities provided by the central government's weakness in the country's hinterland."[179]

Despite sharing broad similarities with the findings presented here, Homer-Dixon's brief discussion of the Philippines is still somewhat incomplete. First, although he recognizes the role played by the debt crisis and the resulting incapacity of the Marcos regime in the spread of communist support and influence, he fails to analyze or demonstrate any link between demographic and environmental pressures and this incapacity. Strangely he actually undersells the causal power of his state failure explanation by ignoring the myriad pressures DES placed on the Philippine state, pressures which were central to the state crisis that emerged in the early 1980s. Second, Homer-Dixon sees state failure as a purely permissive cause of violence in the Philippines. "Permissive" causes allow events to unfold, whereas "efficient" causes exert a much more direct and forceful influence on outcomes. For Homer-Dixon, state failure is important in the Philippines case only in so far as it created "structural opportunities" for communist rebels to flourish. But this misses the critical importance played by state failure in generating the security dilemma dynamics driving the civil war. The anarchy that emerged in the Philippines did not simply permit CPP-NPA growth; rather, it actually inspired it by creating powerful incentives for impoverished and increasingly vulnerable Filipinos to turn to the CPP-NPA as their best self-help option.

but if they had always been scarce...

Neoclassical hypotheses also have trouble accounting for the communist insurgency in the Philippines. According to the honey pot hypothesis, conflict emerges when rebel groups form and fight over abundant supplies of valuable natural resources. In the Philippines, however, conflicts that centered on resources such as land and forests did not emerge until *after* these resources became scarce. In addition, the honey pot hypothesis assumes that conflicts are primarily driven by greed (i.e., that the goal is to plunder and profit from the sale of natural resources), but in the Philippines the grievances caused by DES were much more powerful motivations for communist rebels than greed.

Nor can the resource curse adequately account for civil strife in the Philippines. The economic variant of the resource curse suggests that abundant local supplies of valuable natural resources create economic distortions, channeling investment away from labor-intensive manufacturing. This hampers the kind of economic diversification essential for long-term growth and makes countries vulnerable to rapid deterioration in terms of trade as a result of declining prices for primary commodities. In the Philippines the economy has long been dependent on natural resources, and falling prices for primary commodities in the early 1980s played an important role in triggering the onset of economic crisis.

Nevertheless economic distortions related to the resource curse do not account for the collapse of the Philippine economy and the failure of the state. First, although investments were shifted toward export agriculture and capital-intensive industrialization to the detriment of small-scale agriculture and labor-intensive manufacturing during the Marcos years, this was largely a consequence of the regime's development policies. In particular, the government's commitment to import substitution industrialization was responsible for the failure to diversify the economy, and these policies were *not* driven chiefly by calculations of natural resource abundance. Second, as noted in chapter 1, the economic dislocations produced by abundant natural resources are most likely to occur in the context of abundant supplies of nonrenewable mineral resources; however, in the Philippines, renewable resources such as arable land, forests, and fisheries, not minerals, were central. Third, to the degree that renewable resources were implicated in economic decline, it was their growing scarcity and *not* their local abundance that created so many problems. Agricultural land, forests, and fisheries were relatively abundant until the 1960s and all were important components of the country's economy, but they became increasingly depleted and degraded over time as a result of unsustainable exploitation and population growth. And as the natural resource

I think dev. strat. caused stresses on DES

base eroded, the negative effects on the economy were substantial. It was therefore the synergistic interaction between a shortsighted development strategy and the intense demands placed on the system by DES, not resource abundance, that made the economy so vulnerable to collapse in the early 1980s.

An explanation emphasizing the political dimensions of the resource curse fairs no better. At first blush, the pathologies characteristic of "rentier states" appear to apply to the Philippines, although in a somewhat different manner than normally discussed. As in most countries the vast majority of forestland in the Philippines is owned and controlled by the state. Consequently, control over the extraordinary rents stemming from logging could conceivably have unhinged the Philippine state from its reliance on extracting revenue from, and bargaining away concessions to, society. If the Philippines had followed the expected pattern, the state would have calibrated licensing costs, taxes, and other charges on private timber companies to ensure that much of the revenue from logging flowed to the government. This would have generated an enormous amount of revenue during the post–World War II period when forests were abundant and export restrictions were lifted. As noted above, however, in actuality the state captured very little of the rent from logging. Instead, access to inexpensive timber licenses was granted to politically connected individuals and firms who themselves captured 70 to 95 percent of the profits. Prior to Marcos, power over the granting of timber licenses was dispersed; the president and the legislature, as well as the majority and minority political parties, all had a say. Under Marcos, however, authority over the granting of timber licenses was concentrated in the executive, and access to inexpensive timber licenses was used as a means of rewarding the president's closest allies and family members.[180] Therefore, abundant forest resources did contribute to patterns of corruption and unaccountability, which, in turn, contributed to grievances against the regime.

Still, this line of argument has its limitations. Forests were *a* contributor to unaccountable and exclusive government under Marcos but hardly the most important one. On balance, the ability to use funds from foreign loans for patronage was much more important to Marcos's ability to purchase loyalty and maintain authoritarian rule, especially as forests became increasingly scarce during the martial law period. Furthermore, as indicated above, the exclusive nature of the regime alone cannot explain the timing of the growth of support for the communist rebels; mounting grievances and insecurities generated by DES and state disintegration were central here.

Finally, the alternative explanation offered by political ecologists, the distributional hypothesis, only offers limited insight into the events described in this chapter. Political ecologists believe that population growth is relatively unimportant as a contributor to environmental degradation, resource scarcity, or violent conflict. Instead, patterns of resource distribution are central. In the Philippines the distributional hypothesis would suggest that upland migration and mounting economic marginalization resulted primarily from the skewed distribution of land in lowland growing regions. To the extent that environmental degradation contributed to increasing impoverishment and support for the CPP-NPA, political ecologists also contend that this had little to do with population growth. In challenging the neo-Malthusian account, for example, Betsy Hartmann argues that rapid population growth had no significant effects on deforestation rates in the Philippines during the postwar period. Instead, she claims that corrupt timber licensing practices under Marcos and the voracious international demand for wood products combined to produce unsustainable deforestation by landed elites and timber companies. Upland farmers were thus largely victims of environmental degradation rather than its source.[181]

The refusal on the part of political ecologists to consider the ways in which population growth conspires with natural resource inequality to produce hardship and environmental degradation makes their accounts inherently incomplete. First, although the land frontier undoubtedly closed prematurely because of the concentration of land in lowland areas, this concentration would have been much less consequential in the absence of rapid population growth. The point is *not* that population growth was the *only* factor that mattered, although it was clearly very important. Rather, the point is that ignoring population growth obscures as much as it reveals. Second, it is equally problematic to ignore the role population growth played in environmental degradation and mounting economic marginalization. Hartmann's account of the origins of deforestation in the Philippines is largely correct, but it is not accurate to conclude that upland residents played no part in this process. As millions of peasants moved to fragile, sloped land, many were forced to rely on slash-and-burn agriculture to survive. While this was not the major source of the clearing of primary forests (since logging was driven by international demand, and obtaining access to agricultural plots in upland areas required prior clearing and road access provided by timber companies), slash-and-burn agriculture *did* result in the removal of residual secondary forests, a process that itself contributed to substantial soil erosion. This degradation, in turn, made desperate farmers more desperate, since they were continuously forced to move on to more vulnerable land when soil fertility declined. The result was not only additional environmental degradation but also increasing support for communist rebels who promised peasants and indigenous communities in densely populated areas a better life.

In short, demographic and environmental factors were powerful causes of civil strife in the Philippines, but the causal processes involved differed in important ways from the ones highlighted by alternative hypotheses. Instead, the evidence strongly supports the state failure hypothesis presented in chapter 2.

4

Land and Lies: Ethnic Clashes in Kenya

Land is Kenya's obsession, as order is
Germany's and self-sufficiency is Israel's.
  —Christopher Leo, *Land and Class in Kenya*

Kenya has a long history of land conflicts. The
recent ethnic clashes have been an
ethnicization of the land problem.
  —Situma Mwichabe, *Environmental
    Problems in Kenya*

It appears that disputes over land triggered a
chain of events that quickly escalated in
scope and took on the dimensions of an ethnic
war. The tripling of Kenya's population
since independence resulted in tremendous
hunger for land.
  —Akbarali Thobhani, "Political
    Developments during the 1990s"

SINCE INDEPENDENCE, Kenya has been an island of political tranquil-
ity in the turbulent seas of sub-Saharan Africa. In the 1990s this image
of stability was shattered. From 1991 to 1995 a wave of rural ethnic
violence swept over large portions of Kenya's Rift Valley, Nyanza,
and Western Provinces, killing at least fifteen hundred people and
displacing more than three hundred thousand. In 1997 another round
of ethnic bloodshed occurred in several towns in Coast Province. The
violence claimed approximately one hundred lives and drove one
hundred thousand people from their homes. Taken together, the "ethnic clashes," as they are commonly called in Kenya, represented the
worst violence in the country's post-independence history. Given
Kenya's history of relative prosperity and peace, what explains this
violence?

When addressing this puzzle, it is tempting to point to the process
of democratization as the chief culprit; after all, ethnic clashes occurred
in the period after Kenya began its transition to democracy, and the
violence was concentrated around times of national elections. Never-

theless, ethnic conflict in Kenya should not be viewed as the inevitable outgrowth of greater pluralism in an ethnically diverse country. Such a purely political explanation for the violence misses the powerful causal role played by demographic and environmental forces. Rapid urbanization resulting from Kenya's rural population explosion and scarcity of arable land contributed to a number of economic and social problems that, in turn, prompted a coalition of city dwellers to pressure President Daniel arap Moi to democratize. The threat to Moi's power engendered by these demands encouraged the president and his allies to search for ways to polarize ethnic sentiments in Kenyan society in order to perpetuate their rule. A set of demographically, environmentally, and historically rooted grievances over land in the Rift Valley and at the Coast provided golden opportunities for state elites to exploit rising intergroup competition to cling to power. Thus, I contend that DES provided both the incentives and the opportunities for the instigation of large-scale, organized ethnic violence.

This chapter is divided into four sections. The first provides a brief discussion of Kenya's political history. The second and third sections discuss the violence in and around the Rift Valley and at the Coast, respectively. The final section summarizes the results and compares my argument to a number of alternative explanations.

Historical Background

Kenya was declared a British protectorate in 1895 and officially became a British colony in 1920. Beginning in the early 1950s the Mau Mau rebellion forced Britain to reevaluate its colonial rule. At a constitutional conference held in London in early 1960 a transitional constitution permitting political parties and giving Africans a majority on the legislative council was created. The Kenya African National Union (KANU) was quickly formed under the leadership of Tom M'boya, Jaramogi Oginga Odinga, and James Gichuru. Jomo Kenyatta accepted the KANU presidency after his release from detention in 1961. KANU took a radical nationalist stance and attracted supporters from the Kamba, Kikuyu (and the closely related Embu and Meru), Kisii, Luo, and Taita ethnic communities. Fearing Kikuyu-Luo political domination, a number of prominent leaders from Kenya's smaller ethnic groups, including the future president Daniel arap Moi, formed the Kenya African Democratic Union (KADU). KADU, a more conservative party with closer ties to the colonial establishment, rejected KANU's call for a strong centralized state and argued instead for a *majimbo* (meaning "regionalism" in Swahili) system of government.

In May 1963 KANU won an overall majority of seats in the newly created National Assembly. Soon thereafter a series of defections led to the collapse of KADU. A formal declaration of independence from Britain followed in December, and, one year later, the country became a republic under the presidential leadership of Kenyatta. The collapse of KADU left Kenya a de facto one-party state. This status was temporarily challenged when Odinga resigned as vice president in 1966 to form the left-leaning Kenya People's Union (KPU), but the KPU was subsequently banned in 1969.

Kenyatta died in August 1978 and the presidency passed to Moi, a member of the Tugen subgroup of the Kalenjin ethnic community who had been vice president since 1967. Under Moi, Kenya moved even further in the direction of authoritarian rule. In 1982 section 2(a) was added to the constitution making Kenya a de jure one-party state with KANU as the sole legal party. Moi also shifted the ethnic bias of the state away from the Kikuyu community and toward Kalenjins and their allies among smaller ethnic groups. The trend toward consolidating authority in the office of the presidency, the Kalenjin community, and KANU continued unabated for nearly ten years. In December 1991, however, section 2(a) was repealed under growing domestic and international pressure to democratize. This opened the way for multiparty elections in late 1992.[1]

Violence in and around the Rift Valley, 1991–1995

Almost immediately after Kenya began the transition to a more pluralistic society, widespread ethnic violence erupted in Rift Valley Province and in adjoining districts in Nyanza and Western Provinces (see map). Under British colonial rule the violence-affected area was the heart of what came to be known as the "White Highlands," an area containing much of Kenya's most fertile agricultural land. The clashes pitted members of Moi's own ethnic group, the Kalenjin, as well as members of the Maasai, Samburu, and Turkana communities aligned with the Moi regime, against the Kikuyu, Kisii, Luhya, and Luo communities, all associated with the opposition.[2]

The ethnic clashes began on October 29, 1991, at Meteitei Farm, a cooperative located in the Nandi District of Rift Valley Province near the borders of Nyanza and Western Provinces. The Meteitei farm was similar to thousands of other cooperatives formed as a result of the redistribution of white settler land. Meteitei was jointly owned by 310 Kalenjin and 280 non-Kalenjin farmers (Kikuyu, Kisii, Luhya, and Luo). Violence erupted on the farm after Kalenjin members of the collective, with the encouragement of local administrators and politicians, claimed sole ownership of the land and expelled non-Kalenjins. Those who refused to leave were killed or had their houses and property destroyed.[3]

Within days the fighting spread from Nandi to neighboring Kericho District. Soon ongoing ethnic fighting was affecting large areas running along the borders of Rift Valley, Nyanza, and Western Provinces. The main targets were the Kikuyu, Kisii, Luhya, and Luo communities living in "Kalenjin areas." In 1992 the violence spread south to Kisumu District (Nyanza Province) and Nakuru District (Rift Valley Province), and north to Kakamega and Bungoma Districts (Western Province), the Burnt Forest area near Eldoret in Uasin Gishu District (Rift Valley Province), and the border area of West Pokot and Trans Nzoia Districts (Rift Valley Province).[4]

The carnage did not end once elections were held in December 1992. Large organized attacks by Kalenjins and Maasai continued in many areas.[5] In 1993 the violence was concentrated in the Trans Nzoia and Bungoma Districts, as well as the Molo and Burnt Forest areas of Nakuru District and Uasin Gishu District, and spread to the previously unaffected Narok District in the south of the Rift Valley, where Kikuyu farms were attacked by members of the Maasai community.[6] In 1994– 95 clashes became more sporadic, but strife continued in Molo and Burnt Forest, internally displaced persons were targeted in Kericho and Nakuru Districts, and smaller-scale attacks occurred elsewhere.[7]

Throughout this period violence fed on itself through a vicious spiral of fear, preemption, and retaliation. Kalenjin attacks inspired reprisals by Kikuyus and others, contributing to further Kalenjin attacks, and so on.[8] For example, when five hundred Kalenjin warriors attacked Kikuyus, Luhyas, and Kisiis in Olegurone, Nakuru District, in the summer of 1992, the Kalenjin community justified their actions by claiming that they were simply "preempting an anticipated attack by the Kikuyu community."[9] Hundreds died in the ensuing bloodshed and thousands of families were forced to flee.

The violence created a situation in which members of ethnic groups formally capable of peaceful coexistence increasingly came to view one another with suspicion and fear. As one Luo leader put it in May 1993: "The air is now pregnant with hate, revenge and destruction by people who have peacefully co-existed as brothers and sisters since the last 20 years."[10] A report on the violence in Uasin Gishu in the Nairobi newspaper *Daily Nation* came to a similar conclusion when it noted that "the people are so scared even to trust their neighbors."[11]

The insecurity felt by victimized groups was heightened by the strong pro-Kalenjin, pro-Maasai bias evident in the statements of lead-

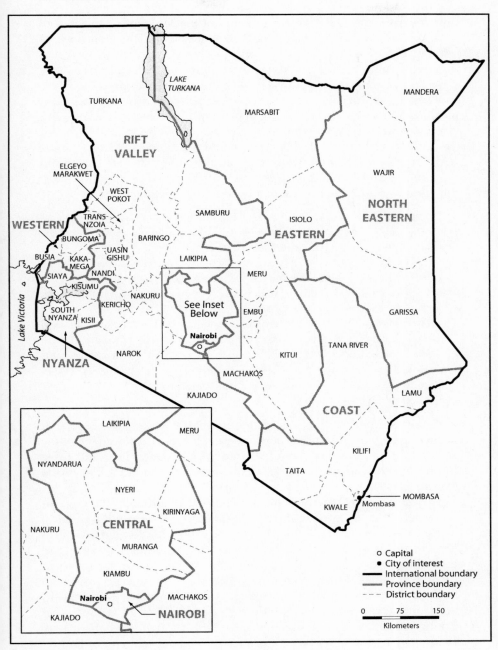

Adminstrative Map of Kenya.

ing government officials and the failure of the Moi regime to act decisively to stop the violence. As one diplomat noted: "The government's
efforts to provide security have only been cosmetic. . . . Even if it is
relatively calm, people are afraid to go home and do not feel safe."[12]
This lack of confidence in the state as neutral arbiter and protector encouraged victimized groups to resort to self-help options, including
arming themselves and engaging in preemptive violence. In early 1992,
for example, Miruka Owuon, the Member of Parliament (MP) for
Nyando, declared that, "if the government could not protect its people
as it had promised, then the people had the right to take up arms and
go to war against their attackers."[13] A 1993 National Election Monitoring Unit (NEMU) Report reached a similar conclusion:

> Throughout the affected areas, a palpable sense that the state does not care
> for the victims of the violence is evident, and the only option left is for the
> affected people to protect and resettle themselves. . . .
>
> It is ironic that the government has reacted with so much speed to these
> efforts to provide self-help security [by disarming victimized groups]. The
> attitude of self-help would certainly not have been as prevalent had the state
> curbed the clashes before they spread. . . .
>
> The rise of the self-help and resistance option is both understandable and
> worrying. Understandable because human beings will normally defend
> themselves. Indeed, it is difficult to keep on entreating a government that is
> unmoved by such suffering. Worrying because violence always begets vio-
> lence, the consequences of which will put Kenya on the path to civil strife
> and self destruction.[14]

Within the first six months of fighting alone it was estimated that
approximately one hundred thousand people were displaced by ethnic
strife. All told, at least fifteen hundred people were killed and three
hundred thousand displaced by ethnic clashes in the first half of the
1990s.[15]

The clashes were clearly politically motivated, although the government denied it. To the extent that President Moi recognized a political
cause to the clashes, he tended to blame unnamed "foreign conspira-
tors"[16] and the opposition, "perversely casting the Kikuyu as perpetrators rather than victims."[17] But, as Nairobi's *Weekly Review* noted in
early 1992, "that simply does not explain why the Kalenjin appear to
be the ones on a war-path against neighboring communities."[18] Indeed,
every major report on the clashes, including reports by the National
Council of Churches of Kenya (NCCK), NEMU, the Inter-Parties Task
Force,[19] a Parliamentary Select Committee made up entirely of KANU
members, and the report of the special judicial commission appointed
in 1998 to inquire into the clashes (known as the "Akiwumi Commis-

sion")[20] all concluded that the role played by the opposition was minor. Instead, the finger was pointed squarely at Moi's regime. The reports all agreed that high-ranking politicians and KANU officials, including a number of close advisers to the president, purposefully set out to incite and orchestrate ethnic violence in a desperate and cynical campaign to hold onto power in the face of pressures to democratize.[21] As Ndinga Mwana A'Nzeki, the Roman Catholic bishop of Nakuru, put it in 1993: "These are not tribal clashes. . . . They are politically motivated clashes fully supported by the Kenyan government. These are meant to cause terrible hardship."[22]

Several indicators demonstrated the involvement of national and local government elites in inciting and facilitating the violence. Numerous statements by national and local officials were clearly designed to spark conflict. Government elites, including many high-ranking Kalenjins, incited violence through a series of rallies calling for the establishment of a majimbo system of government based primarily on ethnicity. Advocates of *majimboism* called for the expulsion of the Kikuyu and other farming communities from land occupied during the precolonial period by the Kalenjin, the Maasai, and other pastoral groups.[23] Little action was taken to check or punish officials who used incendiary rhetoric to incite pastoral communities to violence.[24] On the contrary, the assistant minister Sharif Nassir, a close associate to Moi, revealed the extent of Moi's support when he remarked in February 1993 that the clashes would continue as long as the opposition continued to insult President Moi. "If you do not want the clashes," he is reported to have stated, "tell [Paul] Muite and [Mwai] Kibaki [prominent opposition leaders] to respect Moi."[25]

In addition, the attacks were surprisingly similar, suggesting coordination by elites.[26] In most instances hundreds of so-called Kalenjin warriors attacked the farms of non-Kalenjins, looted and burned houses, and killed and terrorized their inhabitants. The attackers typically dressed in an informal uniform of shorts and red or black T-shirts (some also marked their faces with clay), and they were consistently armed with traditional weapons, including bows, arrows, spears, shields, pangas (machetes), and, later, homemade firearms.[27] Available evidence also suggests that a number of prominent national and local KANU officials went so far as to directly support attackers by providing training, transportation, and sometimes payment.[28]

Finally, state complicity is strongly suggested by the failure of Moi's government to prevent the spread of violence.[29] The Kenyan police and other state security apparatuses have traditionally acted quickly to contain real or perceived insecurity and violence in the country. This was not the case in 1991–95, even though the state clearly had the capability to successfully intervene. As one Luhya farmer lamented: "The Kalenjin . . . are the people who did this to us. But it's their leaders who began this violence. If it were just a question of tribes fighting each other, then the government would have intervened."[30] An editorial in the Nairobi daily *The Standard* agreed: "The government has the machinery to contain the situation. . . . [I]n the past the government is known for having acted swiftly in riotous situations. . . . There is no reason it cannot do it now."[31] At the local level police and judicial authorities were reluctant to arrest attackers, and those they did arrest were frequently turned loose without any punishment. At the national level, although Moi did not hesitate to crack heads during both peaceful and violent protests in Nairobi, few attempts were made to quell the bloodshed in rural areas until late 1993.[32] In September 1993, after the outbreak of fresh clashes in the Molo area of Nakuru District, the government finally responded to the violence by making three areas—Molo, Burnt Forest, and Londiani (in Kericho District)—"security operation zones." These areas were sealed off by security forces, and outside individuals, including journalists and relief organizations, were prevented from entering. These actions were taken primarily to deflect domestic and international criticism while simultaneously increasing government control over the flow of information surrounding the clashes; they were not a sign of genuine government concern over the violence. Indeed, violence persisted in these areas.[33]

Sources of Strife

Mounting demographic and environmental pressures resulted in acute land scarcity and urban social problems in Kenya during the 1980s. By way of these ecological and social effects, DES reverberated into Kenyan politics, providing both the incentives and the opportunities for state-sponsored ethnic violence.

POPULATION GROWTH, ENVIRONMENTAL DEGRADATION,
AND LAND SCARCITY

Compared to most sub-Saharan African nations, Kenya has relatively reliable demographic data predating independence in 1963.[34] These data show that Kenya's population skyrocketed in the post–World War II period. In 1948 Kenya was home to approximately 5.4 million people. By 1969 the population had doubled to almost 11 million.[35] Over the next twenty years the population doubled again. In 1979 Kenya's total population was approximately 15.3 million, and, by 1989, the population had ballooned to 21.4 million. This represented a 40 percent increase in only ten years and an average annual growth rate of 3.4 percent (see Table 4.1), one of the highest rates of population growth in the world. This rate of growth emerged from an extremely high total fertility rate and declining mortality (see Table 4.2). The TFR was highest in Central, Rift Valley, Nyanza, and Western Provinces, averaging more than 7.0.[36] Decades of high fertility and declining infant mortality also produced a significant youth bulge in Kenya. In 1979 7.4 million Kenyans (48.3 percent of the population) were under the age of fifteen and 10.4 million (68.4 percent) were under the age of twenty-five. In 1989 the absolute number of Kenyans under fifteen had grown to 10.3 million (47.8 percent of the population) and 14.5 million (67.8 percent) were under twenty-five.[37]

These demographic pressures combined with significant environmental degradation and a highly uneven distribution of good agricultural land to produce an acute scarcity of arable land in Kenya. Temperature, rainfall, and soil differences create a diverse ecological landscape in Kenya that ranges from inhospitable deserts in the north to broad semiarid plateaus in the south to fertile, rolling highlands in the center. Rainfall varies considerably across the country, with more than 1,000 millimeters (mm) falling annually in the highlands and around the lakes, while arid and semiarid lands (ASALs) experience as little as 200 mm per year. More than 80 percent of Kenya's land (473,000 square kilometers [km^2]), and 94 percent of the land open for new settlement, is considered arid or semiarid.[38] Despite the fact that urban areas have grown twice as fast as the rural population since 1965, 81 percent of Kenyans still resided in rural areas and nearly 80 percent still depended on agriculture for their livelihood in the early 1990s. Given Kenya's predominantly rural and agricultural orientation, the marginal nature of most of the country's land directly impacts the lives of the majority of the populace. Indeed, although livestock can be raised on both arable and marginal lands, most crops are produced on the 18 percent of land that makes up the country's medium- and high-potential areas. Not surprisingly Kenya's population has been highly concentrated in these areas. In 1989, for example, the country's overall population density was low (37 per km^2), but, in the medium- and high-potential areas of western and central Kenya, densities regularly reached 200 to 300 per km^2 and sometimes higher (see Table 4.1). All told, throughout the period under investigation here, roughly two-thirds of Kenya's population was dependent on less than one-third of the country's land.[39]

Since independence rapid population growth has resulted in the division and subdivision of the already limited supply of good agricul-

TABLE 4.1
Population Growth, Population Density, and Land Potential in Kenya

	1979		1989		Intercensal Population Growth Rate	Land Potential**
	Population	Density	Population	Density		
Kenya	15,327,061	27	21,443,636	37	3.4	low
Central Province	2,345,833	178	3,116,703	235	2.9	medium/high
Kiambu	686,290	280	914,412	353	2.9	high
Kirinyaga	291,431	202	391,516	264	3.0	medium
Muranga	648,333	261	858,063	340	2.8	high
Nyandarua	233,302	66	345,420	102	4.0	medium
Nyeri	486,477	148	607,292	186	2.2	medium/high
Coast Province	1,342,794	16	1,829,191	22	3.1	low
Kilifi	430,986	34	591,903	46	3.2	low
Kwale	288,363	34	383,053	46	2.9	low
Lamu	42,299	6	56,783	8	3.0	medium
Mombasa	341,148	1,622	461,752	1,637	3.1	na
Taita Taveta	147,597	8	207,273	12	3.5	low
Tana River	92,401	2	128,426	3	3.3	low
Eastern Province	2,719,851	17	3,768,677	24	3.3	low
Embu	263,173	96	370,138	132	3.5	low
Isiolo	43,478	1	70,078	3	4.9	???
Kitui	464,283	15	652,603	22	3.5	low
Machakos	1,022,522	72	1,402,002	100	3.2	low
Marasabit	96,216	1	129,262	2	3.0	???
Meru	830,179	83	1,144,594	116	3.3	low
Northeastern Province	373,787	2	371,391	3	−0.1	???
Garissa	128,867	2	124,835	3	−0.3	???
Mandera	105,601	3	123,787	5	1.6	???
Wajir	139,319	2	122,769	2	−1.3	???

Source: Republic of Kenya, Ministry of Economic Planning and Development, *Kenya Population Census, 1979*, Vols. 1, 2 (Nairobi, Kenya: Central Bureau of Statistics, 1981); Republic of Kenya, Office of the Vice President, Ministry of Planning and National Development, *Kenya Population Census, 1989*, Vols. 1, 2 (Nairobi, Kenya: Central Bureau of Statistics, 1994). Data on land potential are taken from Uma J. Lele and Steven W. Stone, "Population Pressure, the Environment, and Agricultural Intensification in Sub-Saharan Africa: Variations on the Boserup Hypotheses," Report Prepared for the Managing Development in Africa (MADIA) Symposium, World Bank, 1989, p. 55, Table 2.

* Districts affected by ethnic violence, 1991–95.

** Land is classified as "high," "medium," or "low" potential if the largest percentage of land falls within that category.

TABLE 4.1
Population Growth, Population Density, and Land Potential in Kenya (*cont'd*)

| | 1979 | | 1989 | | Intercensal Population | Land |
	Population	Density	Population	Density	Growth Rate	Potential**
Kenya	15,327,061	27	21,443,636	37	3.4	low
Nyanza Province	2,643,956	211	3,507,162	280	2.9	high
Kisii	869,512	395	1,137,054	517	2.7	high
Kisumu*	482,327	230	664,086	320	3.2	medium
Siaya	474,516	188	639,439	253	3.0	medium
South Nyanza	817,601	143	1,066,583	187	2.7	medium/high
Rift Valley Province	3,240,402	19	4,981,613	27	4.4	low
Baringo	203,792	20	347,990	32	5.5	low
E. Marakwet	148,868	65	216,487	71	3.8	high
Kajiado	149,005	7	258,659	12	5.7	low
Kericho*	633,348	161	900,934	182	3.6	high
Laikipra	134,524	13	218,957	24	5.0	low
Nakuru*	522,709	90	849,096	118	5.0	medium
Nandi*	299,319	109	433,613	156	3.8	high
Narok*	210,306	13	398,272	22	6.6	low
Sambura	76,908	4	108,884	5	3.5	???
Trans Nzoia*	259,503	124	393,682	160	4.3	medium
Turkana	142,702	2	184,060	3	2.6	???
Uasin Gishu*	300,766	89	445,530	138	4.0	medium
West Pokot*	158,652	19	225,449	25	3.6	low
Western Province	1,832,663	223	2,544,329	307	3.3	high
Bungoma*	503,935	163	679,146	221	3.0	high
Busia	297,841	???	213,093	243	-3.3	high
Kakemega*	1,030,887	294	1,463,525	411	3.6	high
Nairobi	827,775	1,210	1,324,570	1911	4.8	na

tural land into smaller and smaller units for subsistence and small-holder farming. Smallholders have long dominated the agricultural sector in Kenya. As of the late 1980s smallholders accounted for nearly 75 percent of agricultural output, 55 percent of the marketed yield, more than 60 percent of the land devoted to arable agriculture, around 85 percent of total agricultural employment, and almost 70 percent of Kenya's total employment. Although smallholders are technically defined as farmers owning 20 ha or less of land, the holding of the average smallholder was only 2 ha in the late 1980s. Additionally, more

TABLE 4.2
Changes in Fertility and Mortality in Kenya

	Total Fertility Rate	Probability of Dying by Age 5 (per 1,000)	Life Expectancy at Birth
ca 1940	5.5	270	37
1958–62	7.0	220	43
1965–69	7.6	190	49
1975–79	7.9	150	54
1985–89	6.7	110	59

Source: William Brass and Carole L. Jolly, eds., *Population Dynamics of Kenya* (Washington D.C.: National Academy Press, 1993), p. 20; Robert A. Wortham, "Prospects for Fertility Reduction and Projections for Future Population Growth in Kenya," *Population Research and Policy Review* 14, no. 1 (March 1995); 115.

than 75 percent of smallholders owned less than 2 ha during this period and more than half owned less than 1 ha.[40]

A regional picture is provided in Table 4.3, which details the estimated availability of good agricultural land (defined as hectares of high-potential land equivalents) per person, per district, for the years 1969, 1979, and 1989. The data show that twelve districts had more than 1 ha of good agricultural land per person in 1969. By 1979 the number had fallen to seven, and by 1989 the total had plummeted to three.

By itself, however, such a rough measure of demand-induced scarcity only provides a partial picture of the land crisis in Kenya, because it neglects land degradation (supply-induced sources of scarcity) and the unequal distribution of land (structural scarcity). Although a comprehensive quantification of land degradation in Kenya does not exist, there is no doubt that soil erosion, desertification, and deforestation became significant problems during the period being investigated here.[41] As Situma Mwichabe observes, "the increased number of people [in Kenya] searching for economic security has lead to intensification of cultivation, expansion of cultivatable land, overgrazing on the range, and harvesting of trees for fuelwood leading to deforestation and an acute water crisis as well as loss of biological diversity and soil erosion."[42] In 1984 Kenya's Population Policy Guidelines noted that trends in population growth and land suggested "increasing pressure on land, accompanied by farm fragmentation, land degradation through soil erosion and unplanned settlement in marginal lands, resulting in slower growth of agricultural output."[43]

TABLE 4.3

Estimated Availability of Good Agricultural Land (Hectares of High Potential Land Equivalents) Per Person, Per Selected Districts, 1969–1989

Province District	Population (× 1000)			Hectares (× 1000)	Hectares of Good Agricultural Land per Person		
	1969	1979	1989		1969	1979	1989
Central Province							
Kiambu	476	686	914	170	0.36	0.25	0.19
Kirinyaga	217	291	392	100	0.46	0.34	0.26
Muranga	445	648	858	217	0.49	0.33	0.25
Nyandarua	177	233	345	265	1.50	1.14	0.77
Nyeri	361	486	607	160	0.44	0.33	0.26
Coast Province							
Kilifi	308	431	592	162	0.53	0.38	0.27
Kwale	206	288	383	163	0.79	0.57	0.43
Lamu	22	42	57	74	3.36	1.76	1.30
Taita Taveta	111	148	207	50	0.45	0.34	0.24
Tana River	51	92	128	119	2.33	1.29	0.93
Eastern Province							
Embu	179	263	370	103	0.58	0.39	0.28
Kitui	343	464	653	305	0.89	0.66	0.47
Machakos	707	1,023	1,402	284	0.40	0.28	0.20
Meru	597	830	1,145	263	0.44	0.32	0.23
Nyanza Province							
Kisii	675	870	1,137	220	0.33	0.25	0.19
Kisumu and Siaya*	784	957	1,304	438	0.56	0.46	0.34
S. Nyanza	663	818	1,067	567	0.86	0.69	0.53
Rift Valley Province							
Baringo	162	204	348	190	1.17	0.93	0.55
E. Marakwet	159	149	216	105	0.66	0.70	0.49
Kericho*	479	633	901	380	0.79	0.60	0.42
Laikipra	66	135	219	138	2.09	1.02	0.63
Nakuru*	291	523	849	301	1.03	0.58	0.35
Nandi*	209	299	434	234	1.12	0.78	0.54
Narok*	125	210	398	915	7.32	4.36	2.30
Samburu	70	77	109	156	2.09	2.03	1.43
Trans Nzoia*	124	260	394	208	1.68	0.80	0.53
West Pokot	82	159	225	107	1.30	0.67	0.48
Uasin Gishu	191	301	446	327	1.71	1.09	0.73
Western Province							
Bungoma*	345	504	679	253	0.73	0.50	0.37
Busia	200	298	213	163	0.82	0.55	0.77
Kakemega*	783	1,031	1,464	325	0.42	0.32	0.22

Source: Data on 1969 population levels and hectares of high potential land equivalents are from Ian Livingston, *Rural Development, Employment and Incomes in Kenya* (Brooksfield, Vt.: Gower, 1986), p. 11. Livingston's data exclude some arid and semiarid regions. Figures for 1979 and 1989 are adapted from Livingston using population data from Republic of Kenya, *Kenya Population Census, 1979*; and Republic of Kenya, *Kenya Population Census, 1989*.

* Districts affected by ethnic violence, 1991–95.

Numerous studies have found significant rates of soil loss in medi-um- and high-potential areas, as well as in Kenya's ASALs, as a result of rapid population growth and intensified land use. The main forms of soil degradation have been erosion by wind and water, soil nutrient depletion (loss of fertility), salinity, acidity, structural deterioration (compaction and surface sealing), reduction of organic matter, and the effects of toxic chemicals and pollutants.[44] Some parts of Central Province, for example, recorded annual soil losses of 20 tons per ha, a rate two orders of magnitude greater than the rate of soil formation. Soil losses in Kajiado, Nakuru, and West Pokot (all in Rift Valley Province), Kitui (in Nyanza Province), Embu (in Eastern Province), and Taita Taveta (in Coast Province) were even higher, exceeding 32 tons per ha per year. Gully erosion was common in medium- and high-potential areas of Bungoma (in Western Province) and parts of Central, Eastern, and Nyanza Provinces. This soil loss reduced rooting depth, depleted available plant nutrients, and undermined the soil's capacity to retain water, placing significant strains on agricultural production.[45] If left unchecked, soil erosion ultimately leads to desertification, which is largely irreversible. As of the late 1980s about 83 percent of Kenya's total land area was affected by some degree of desertification, and 19 percent was severely affected.[46] One estimate suggests that soil erosion and desertification were costing Kenya between .5 and 1.5 percent of its GNP by the 1990s.[47]

In some areas of Kenya population pressures and a favorable economic climate actually spurred incentives to employ conservation efforts.[48] Unfortunately, these areas appear to have been the exception rather than the rule. Although numerous communities in Kenya are environmentally aware, poverty has undermined the capacity for many to practice conservation.[49] Thus, despite some conservation efforts, the overall land degradation problem remained substantial during the period investigated here.[50]

Finally, to fully appreciate the degree to which average rural residents in Kenya experienced land scarcity it is also essential to recognize the extremely uneven distribution of land in the countryside in the decades prior to the onset of violence. Because of the political sensitivity of land ownership in Kenya, recent data are difficult to find. Nevertheless, data from the late 1970s suggest a highly skewed concentration of land. Although the total number of large farms—owned by a combination of individuals, partnerships, cooperatives, and domestic and foreign companies—was only 0.14 percent of the number of small farms in 1979, these relatively few large farms represented 71.1 percent as much land as those held by smallholders. Moreover, the average size of large farms was 1,000 ha compared to 2 ha for farms owned by smallholders.[51] Anecdotal evidence suggests that land ownership has since become even more concentrated and that much of this land is not used for agricultural production.[52] By the late 1980s large farms of more than 200 ha accounted for 33 percent of registered landholdings.[53] Demand- and supply-induced scarcity further aggravated unequal land distribution by both expanding the number of individuals requiring a slice of a shrinking pie of available land and by making land more valuable. The high value of land made it the subject for considerable speculation, and, as a consequence, large chunks, estimated at around 35 percent of all arable land, were not in production as of the late 1980s.[54]

In sum, prior to the ethnic clashes of 1991–95 land scarcity was a large and growing problem in Kenya. A large portion of the country's good arable land was and still is controlled by a small number of large-scale farmers and foreign companies, while soil erosion, creeping desertification, and deforestation reduced the supply of land, and rapid population growth led to the division and subdivision of what remained into increasingly smaller units for subsistence and smallholder farming.[55]

PRESSURES ON SOCIETY

As the rural population ballooned and the supply of arable land shrank, the number of economically marginalized individuals in rural areas rose substantially. A 1991 report by the Kenyan government prepared for the 1992 Earth Summit concluded that,

> Population increase in the last 20 or so years has placed tremendous pressure on available land resources. In high and medium potential areas, the carrying capacity of the land has been stretched to its limits. A large portion of the population has been squeezed out of these areas . . . Others have been rendered completely landless.[56]

As of the mid-1970s 11.4 percent of rural households were landless. Although more recent statistics are difficult to secure, there is every reason to believe that population growth and shrinking land availability led to a worsening of the situation in the 1980s. Indeed, by the mid-1980s, it was estimated that half a million Kenyan families were landless.[57]

While landlessness was not the only cause of poverty in Kenya, it was a powerful contributor during the time under investigation here. Another report by the Kenyan government observed that,

> Landlessness was identified by many communities as a major underlying cause of poverty. Rural communities are dependent on land for production. However, many people have been rendered landless or squatters. The causes of landlessness vary from community to community. In some communities it is the result of high population growth, while in others it is due to poor

land tenure systems . . . Related to landlessness is the fragmentation of land into smaller uneconomical units in parts of the country. This is predominant in high and medium potential areas where there is high population growth.[58]

A 1987 Norwegian country study and aid review reached a similar conclusion. "In its degree and prevalence, absolute poverty is overwhelmingly a rural problem in Kenya, where, because of land and population pressures and increasing landlessness, rural poverty appears to be rising in many areas."[59]

If one follows the World Bank's definition of the "poverty line" (U.S.$370 per capita), approximately 70 percent of Kenya's rural population and 30 percent of its urban population were impoverished in the late 1980s. Moreover, surveys suggest that around half the rural population had a per capita income below the 1988 figure of K£166 (Ksh3,320; U.S.$130).[60] Data on per capita food production provide another sign of rising rural marginalization in the decades prior to the ethnic clashes. Per capita food production, which grew by 0.1 percent a year from 1961 to 1970, declined by −1.6 percent from 1971 to 1979 and by −2.0 percent from 1980 to 1984.[61] As a consequence, by the end of the 1980s, 30 percent of the population suffered from nutritional deficiencies.[62]

Finally, income inequality was a growing problem during this period. In 1982 the bottom 20 percent of the Kenyan population received 4.9 percent of the national income, whereas the top 20 percent received 56.9 percent. By 1992 the distribution was 3.5 percent and 60.2 percent, respectively. In urban areas the situation was worse. In 1992 the lowest 20 percent received 2.9 percent and the top 20 percent received 58.8 percent.[63]

Population growth, land pressures, and escalating economic marginalization forced many of Kenya's rural poor and land deprived to leave medium- and high-potential agricultural areas in search of land and employment. This resulted in increased migration to arid and semiarid regions and urban areas.[64] Rapid rural-to-urban migration was the more important trend in terms of explaining the ethnic conflict that erupted in the 1990s. In 1989 only 18.1 percent of Kenya's population lived in urban areas. Still, the rate of urban population growth has long surpassed the national growth rate. Between 1979 and 1989 urban areas grew at an average annual rate of 5.2 percent. Over the same period Nairobi, where about one-third of all urbanites reside, grew at an annual rate of 4.9 percent.[65] All told, Nairobi's population nearly quadrupled between independence and the late 1980s, bulging from nearly 343,000 inhabitants in 1963 to more than 1.3 million in 1989; between 1979 and 1989 alone the population of the capital city grew by 62 percent. That urban growth was considerably higher than the national rate suggests significant rural-to-urban migration.[66]

Dramatic urban population growth contributed to significant social problems during the 1980s. The exodus from rural areas to urban centers raised the ratio of economically dependent urban dwellers from 14 percent of the national total to 23 percent, imposing severe socioeconomic stress on individuals. This problem was compounded by Kenya's rapid population growth, which outpaced the country's ability to create jobs by a wide margin. Of the 6.6 million economically active Kenyans in 1979, only 1.9 million were wage earners and the rest were nonwage rural workers. Between 1979 and 1989 2 million additional individuals joined the labor force.[67] Toward the end of the decade, 300,000 people were added to Kenya's labor force *each year*. Unfortunately, job creation failed to keep up with this pace of employment during the 1980s. In 1984–85, for example, wage employment in the modern sector increased by 4.9 percent, representing a total increase of 54,700 new jobs. Over the same one-year period the informal sector created 18,100 new jobs. The combined total of 72,800 fell far short of the quarter of a million new jobs required by additions to the labor force that year.[68]

Infrastructure and services were also pushed beyond their limits by urban population growth. As the Kenyan government acknowledged in 1991: "The enormous increase in urban areas in the last decade, caused by high rural-urban migration and natural urban population growth, has put an added strain on basic services and facilities resulting in an immeasurable number of environmental and socio-economic problems."[69] Serious constraints were placed on the provision of housing, health care, education, sanitation, and transportation services.[70] In the late 1960s the Kenyan government estimated that meeting annual housing demands required seventy-six hundred new urban housing units a year. By 1983 the actual demand had increased to sixty thousand a year.[71] Health costs also increased dramatically. In 1981 the recurrent budget for health care was K£40 million. As a result of population growth, costs were estimated to rise to K£67 million by 1995.[72] Other services were also strained. In the early 1990s over 50 percent of the inhabitants in Kenya's large cities (e.g., Nairobi, Mombasa, Kisumu, and Nakuru) lacked adequate and safe sanitation, and urban growth significantly outpaced the expansion of transportation systems, such as adequate roads and mass transit.[73]

The link between demographic pressure and strained services was especially evident in the case of education. The Kenyan government has invested substantially in educating its people since independence. Between 1965 and 1986 the primary school enrollment ratio increased from 54 percent to 94 percent, and the secondary school enrollment ratio increased from 4 percent to 20 percent.[74] Given this commitment and the explosive increase in the size of Kenya's youth population, it should not be surprising that education expenses rose substantially. The number of university students, for example, grew from fewer than nine thousand in 1981 to almost thirty thousand in the early 1990s. Primary school enrollment increased by 35 percent during the 1980s, and secondary school and university enrollments increased by 38 percent and 200 percent, respectively.[75] By the end of the 1980s education was consuming 40 percent of the recurrent national budget. In 1991 the Kenyan government admitted that "providing education through public funding is a burden that is having serious impact on the Government's ability to allocate financial resources to other services and other productive investments."[76]

Employment problems and inadequate social services led to an enormous expansion in urban slums.[77] Nowhere was this situation more acute than in Nairobi, where between 1979 and 1992 the population of the city's slums doubled. In the early 1990s ten of Nairobi's sublocations were predominantly slums. This area made up less than 5 percent of Nairobi's inhabitable land but was home to 30 percent of the city's people.[78] Other estimates suggest that as much as 70 percent of Nairobi's population lived in slums or slum-like conditions during this period.[79]

Finally, population growth also contributed to Kenya's general economic malaise during the 1980s. Over the past several decades Kenya's economy has performed reasonably well, especially when compared to the dismal performance of other sub-Saharan African countries. Between 1965 and 1979 the real GDP growth rate was 5.8 percent, the average GDP growth per capita was 2.8 percent, and agricultural production and industrial production per capita grew by 1.3 and 6.7 percent a year, respectively. Between 1980 and 1990, however, the average GDP growth slumped to 4.2 percent a year, and per capita GDP, agricultural production, and industrial production dipped to –0.3, –0.7, and –4.4 percent, respectively. Furthermore, by 1990 real wages for both public- and private-sector employees, who made up the bulk of the modern sector, may have fallen to only 70 percent of their 1970 level.[80] The proximate causes of Kenya's economic woes included the oil shock of the late 1970s, declining coffee prices in the early 1980s (which hurt agricultural exports), and the drought of 1983–84.[81] However, the country's rapid rate of population growth made the economy considerably more vulnerable to these shocks. As a 1990 World Bank report noted:

The impacts of demography on the economy are . . . long-run in nature . . . In the Kenyan case, the primary cause of short-term variability in [economic] output performance have been largely exogenous . . . However, the vulnerability of the economy to accommodate such exogenous shocks is indeed conditioned by the rapid pace of demographic change.[82]

In short, the report concluded, rapid population growth created a situation in which there was "little margin to cushion the downside shocks that appear to be endemic to Kenya's economic structure."[83] Moreover, once growth resumed in the second half of the 1980s, population growth prevented these gains from being translated into improvements for the average Kenyan. As the Kenyan government lamented in 1991: "High population growth itself makes it impossible to achieve faster rates of economic growth to allow for increases in per capita incomes."[84]

PRESSURES ON THE STATE AND INCENTIVES FOR STATE EXPLOITATION

Kenya's social problems and economic stagnation during the 1980s, stemming from and exacerbated by enormous demographic and environmental pressures, directly threatened Moi's regime, generating powerful incentives for state-sponsored violence during the 1990s. Under Kenyatta, the Kenyan state was able to secure the loyalty of a wide array of social actors through a complex system of patronage. The availability of white settler land for redistribution provided the Kenyatta regime with ample opportunities to reward supporters by providing access to the country's most coveted natural resource. Strong economic growth, fueled by booming cash crop and tourism sectors, also provided Kenyatta's government the financial capacity to purchase support through the provision of government and civil service jobs, low-interest loans, and government contracts. By the time Moi came to power, however, the rapid expansion of Kenya's rural population tightly constricted the ability of the regime to offer land to a broad cross-section of Kenya's ethnic communities. Instead, wealthy Kalenjins and their allies became increasingly favored to the exclusion of other groups, driving up anti-regime sentiments among Kikuyus, Luos, and others.[85]

At the same time, rapid population growth in Kenya's urban areas and the economic contraction the country experienced in the 1980s devastated the regime's support, contributing to growing pressures on the state to reform the economic and political systems. Economic recession led to declining real incomes for most Kenyans. As incomes declined among the urban, educated, mostly Kikuyu and Luo middle class, any residual support for Moi and KANU dissipated.[86] Population dynamics played an important role here. Most directly urban population growth contributed to numerous problems for city dwellers. The ability of the economy to absorb a rapidly growing labor force declined as the private sector slumped and the number of jobs in the public sector, Kenya's single largest source of employment, failed to keep pace with the number of individuals graduating from secondary schools and universities. As a result, un- and underemployment increased substantially, Nairobi and other urban areas witnessed a dramatic expansion of shantytowns and slums, and crime rates escalated.[87]

Politically the level of expectations created by Kenya's educational system made shrinking economic opportunities even more troublesome. In the 1980s three hundred thousand individuals graduated from Kenya's schools each year, but only 7 percent were able to secure jobs in the wage sector.[88] In 1986 urban unemployment stood at 16.2 percent. Unemployment was highest among those aged fifteen to nineteen and twenty to twenty-four, with rates of 47.9 and 38.6 percent, respectively.[89] In 1989 these two age groups made up 22 percent of Kenya's urban population and 25 percent of Nairobi's population. They also represented recent graduates from Kenya's relatively extensive educational system (about half of Nairobi's youth aged fifteen to twenty-four, representing 12 percent of the city's population, had at least some secondary or university education), and therefore their expectations for employment were quite high.[90] This combination of high expectations and low opportunities was a clear recipe for frustration and rising antistate grievances.[91] Moreover, in the context of rapid urban population growth, the government's pro-minority bias significantly increased the sense of relative deprivation perceived by Kikuyus, Luos, and other non-Kalenjin ethnic groups. In particular, Kikuyu urbanites, businessmen, and recent graduates looking for work in the civil service became increasingly concerned with Moi's ethnic bias against them and became more willing to take their grievances to the streets.[92]

Moi's fear of growing opposition to his rule from urban quarters led him to seek to further consolidate his rule and strengthen KANU's claims as the only legal political party.[93] Moi's turn toward greater repression and arbitrary rule, in turn, only served to enhance dissatisfaction with his regime.[94] In sum, the combination of population growth, declining urban conditions, preferential access for Kalenjins and other minority allies to higher education, administrative offices, and public funds, and growing state repression generated considerable antistate grievances.[95]

By 1990 support for the regime was in steep decline. The urban middle class and various civil society organizations, in particular, became increasingly committed to pushing for political liberalization. Leading the charge were powerful church groups (such as the Protestant clergy in the NCCK and the Kenya National Catholic Bishops), legal associations (most notably the Law Society of Kenya), and a number of prominent liberal politicians.[96] The specific trigger for the first wave of mass protests calling for political liberalization came from a political controversy: the suspicious murder in February 1990 of Robert Ouko, the Luo minister of foreign affairs.[97] The Ouko murder brought to the surface escalating urban grievances and created a focal point for opposition. As Africa Watch noted: "Popular dissatisfaction had found new bravado during the Ouko demonstrations. For many, life had become increasingly difficult because of unemployment, rising prices, lack of land, police harassment and a corrupt and aggressive administration."[98] Protests accelerated during the summer of 1990 when the arrest of several high-profile liberal politicians, most notably the former Kikuyu ministers Kenneth Matiba and Charles Rubia, sparked a series of demonstrations and riots in Nairobi.[99] Protests occurred in other locales as well, including Nakuru in Rift Valley Province and in Kikuyu-dominated Central Province, where paramilitary forces were called in to put down protests in Nyeri, Nivasha, Muranga, Limuru, and Kiambu. These areas, among those hardest hit by DES, experienced rapid population growth, acute land shortages, and high levels of unemployment.[100]

Urban protests directly threatened Moi and KANU by raising the long-feared specter of a Kikuyu-Luo political alliance in opposition to the regime.[101] Moi took active and aggressive measures to forcibly contain urban protest.[102] Nevertheless, the president finally succumbed to pressure for political reform in late 1991. Here, escalating levels of internal dissent were crucial to opening the door for reform, but the withdrawal of foreign aid from international and bilateral lenders pushed the regime through it.[103] In November 1991 Western public donors withheld more than $350 million in balance of payments assistance and conditioned its reinstatement on Moi's acceptance of economic and political reforms.[104] Very soon thereafter section 2(a) of the constitution was repealed, opening the way for multiparty elections.

The call for greater pluralism produced a substantial challenge for Moi and KANU. The president, his fellow Kalenjin, and their allies among Kenya's smaller ethnic communities perceived the calls for multipartyism as an attempt to remove their fragile coalition of minority groups from power.[105] In this context, Moi and KANU faced enormous incentives to exploit existing societal schisms in order to discredit and punish pro-democracy forces and thereby prolong Moi's rule.

LAND COMPETITION AND OPPORTUNITIES FOR STATE EXPLOITATION

If the pressure to democratize created the incentive to exploit DES-induced societal animosities to remain in power, rising intergroup competition over land also provided a golden opportunity to do so. The violence that swept Kenya from 1991 to 1995 was located primarily in Rift Valley Province and the adjoining districts of Nyanza and Western Provinces. These regions contain much of Kenya's best farmland. As noted above, since independence land pressure has been intense and growing in these areas, which regularly had some of the highest fertility rates in the country. By the mid-1980s the British Overseas Development Administration estimated that average population densities in these areas, as well as in Central Province, had already reached the level where the ability of land resources to accommodate more people was severely limited. "Everywhere there is competition for limited land and water resources, the potential for further gains in production being limited in many areas to yield increases derived from more intensive use of farm inputs and improved management. As the population increases . . . highland farms are increasingly fragmented and people are forced into semiarid margins."[106]

The overcrowding of the violence-affected areas is obvious from the data provided in Tables 4.1 and 4.3 (see districts noted with an asterisk). While the population density of Kenya as a whole averaged 27 people per km^2 in 1979 and 37 in 1989, population densities in the districts hit by ethnic strife averaged 129 in 1979 and increased to 175 by 1989, with some of the affected districts having densities as high as 300 to 400 people per km^2. The availability of good agricultural land in these areas also diminished significantly, from an average of 1.66 ha per person in 1969 to 1.02 in 1979 and 0.63 in 1989 (see Table 4.3). Furthermore, in six out of the ten districts affected, the average amount of good agricultural land had dipped to less than half a hectare per person by 1989. The end result of rapid population growth, environmental degradation, and unequal land distribution was thus an increasingly fierce competition between individuals and social groups for arable land. Around the time of the violence Norman Miller and Rodger Yeager observed:

> The majority of Kenyans will soon have lost the ability to fall back on the land, but this is still what most people, if all else fails, long for. Issues of land and inequality are the driving forces behind the daily perturbations of modern Kenyan politics and government.

... In a setting of epidemic landlessness, desperate attempts to bring arid and semiarid tracts into cultivation, and forced migration to already overcrowded towns and cities, those left behind have become increasingly polarized.[107]

Layered on top of escalating demographically and environmentally induced competition over arable land were a set of existing intergroup land grievances rooted in Kenya's colonial experience. These historical grievances added an ethnic component to competition over land and are therefore critical to understanding the exact nature of the violence Kenya experienced in the first half of the 1990s.

Prior to British colonization, the Rift Valley was sparsely populated by pastoral nomadic groups. During the colonial period, however, these pastoral communities were alienated from their land as the Rift Valley was transformed into the heart of the "White Highlands."[108] In the late nineteenth century Britain built a rail line between Mombasa on the East African coast and Uganda as part of its attempt to control the Nile Headwaters. Nairobi, one of the railway's stops, became an administrative headquarters and eventually the national capital. Nairobi lay at the foot of the fertile highland areas, and the completed railway link with the lakes, coupled with a desire to generate revenue, encouraged the British to press forward and offer land to potential European and South African settlers. The highlands area was attractive to European settlers in British East Africa because of its temperate climate, fertile soils, and relatively disease-free environment.[109] Between 1899 and 1915 a succession of land regulations expropriated much of the best land in the central highlands and reserved it exclusively for white settlers. Africans were prohibited from buying land in this region and were banished to native reserves. As populations grew, pastoralist inhabitants, such as the Maasai, Sambura, Turkana, and various subgroups of the Kalenjin, were prevented from using their traditional grazing grounds, and cultivators, such as the Kikuyu, were restricted to areas too small to sustain the subdivisions of land dictated by their lineage-based system of land rights.[110] Alienation accelerated after the First World War as British soldiers were encouraged to settle in Kenya and allowed to acquire land at concessionary rates. The ex-soldier Settlement Scheme and the 1921 Crown Ordinance had the effect of expanding settlement away from the railway line. Thus, between 1902 and 1922, significant and rapid alienation took place, and by 1926 the alienation of land was virtually complete in the White Highlands.[111]

Substantial changes in the ethnic composition of the Rift Valley occurred as a result of the introduction of a number of coercive policies designed to create a reliable and cheap agricultural labor force for set-

tlers. The British introduced a hut tax as a means of generating revenue for colonial administration and coercing Africans to leave their traditional subsistence lifestyles to work as laborers on European farms. After an initial period Africans were required to pay the hut taxes in cash. This forced Africans to work for wages at least part of the year. Members from ethnic communities with farming experience migrated from areas now known as Central, Nyanza, and Western Provinces to farms in the Rift Valley to be squatters or laborers on settler farms. These migrants were predominantly from the Kikuyu, Kisii, Luhya, and Luo communities who had been alienated from their ancestral lands in other parts of the White Highlands and "required to live in marginal reserves, often in large numbers, which led to significant overpopulation on their lands."[112] Outside groups thus moved into the Rift Valley partly because they faced a population explosion on their reserves. The largest single contingent of labor came from landless Kikuyu from the overcrowded reserves in Central Province.[113]

By the 1950s population pressures combined synergistically with unequal land distribution and the lack of political progress to trigger violent insurrection in the White Highlands. In 1952 the Mau Mau, a secret society made up largely of Kikuyus, initiated a campaign of terror against settlers in the highlands and their allies among the Kikuyu elite. Many Luo, Luhya, Kalenjin, and other groups in the Rift Valley and at the Coast chose to sit out the rebellion, reluctant to follow the Kikuyu lead and uncertain about the outcome of the struggle.[114] All told, between 1952 and 1959 the Mau Mau uprising led to more than eleven thousand casualties, mostly among Kikuyus.[115] The nationalist rebellion compelled the British to modify their land policy. In 1954 the Swynnerton Plan, first implemented in Central Province, gave African farmers in the highlands land titles for the first time, facilitated the acquisition of credit, and removed the restriction on the cultivation of export crops by Africans. The British also began to give Africans representation in national politics. In March 1960 KANU was formed and quickly adopted a strong position on land settlement in the highlands. In an attempt to neutralize KANU's support among the landless, unused land and large tracts of land from departing European settlers were acquired and then redistributed to the landless through a program that became known as the Million Acre Scheme. Britain, the Commonwealth Development Corporation, and the World Bank provided assistance in buying and developing this land.[116]

Upon independence in 1963 land policy was further modified but not as radically as many had hoped. The interests of white settlers were still protected by allowing them to maintain ownership over expropriated land. Arrangements were made to transfer land ownership from

Europeans to Africans on a "willing buyer, willing seller" basis, and agricultural banks were established to assist in the financing of such transfers. Under this policy Kenyans were able to purchase land, either individually or through collective schemes such as cooperative societies and companies.[117] Since population pressures were intense in Kikuyu-dominated Central Province, which borders the Rift Valley, Kikuyus were eager to take advantage of this new opportunity. The Kenyatta regime also encouraged and assisted Kikuyus to buy land. Consequently, during the 1960s and 1970s, Rift Valley Province became a magnet for rural-to-rural migration from Central Province, as well as from overcrowded portions of Nyanza and Western Provinces. Large numbers of Kikuyus and other outside groups bought land and set up farms. The biggest losers were traditional pastoral groups who were pushed aside to make room for Kikuyu farmers.[118]

In sum, after independence, many of the squatters and workers originally from other parts of Kenya remained in the Rift Valley, where they settled or bought farms from Europeans, either individually or collectively. Others also migrated to the area and bought land under various settlement schemes. These settlement farms were the locus of much of the violence that erupted in 1991.[119]

All told, by the early 1990s the mix of demographically and environmentally induced land competition and historically related grievances provided a situation ripe for exploitation by Moi and KANU.[120] The Parliamentary Sub-Committee investigating the clashes noted that Kalenjin elites sought to exploit and "awaken" latent grievances over "lesser causes imbedded in . . . common place distrusts, disputes, animosities, and parochial considerations to which it [elite incitement] served as an impetus for fulfillment or realization." These disputes included "disputed sub-divisions in land buying co-operative societies, companies and partnerships," "disputed transfers of land sold through individual agreements," and "perennial ancestral claims to some portions of land dismembered from one ethnic community and apparently given to the other." The report concluded that the clashes "(1) were politically motivated and fueled by some officers in the Provincial administration; and (2) were instigated in the misconception that some ethnic communities could chase away other ethnic communities in order to acquire their land."[121]

Other reports reached similar conclusions. Human Rights Watch, for example, observed that,

> the clashes were deliberately instigated and manipulated by KANU politicians anxious to retain their hold on power in the face of mounting internal and external pressure for change in government. . . .

The government has capitalized on unaddressed issues of land ownership and tenure, dating back to the colonial period, between those pastoral groups who were originally ousted from the Rift Valley Province area by the British colonial government and subsequent squatter labor which settled on the land following independence. The clashes drew on these competing claims in order to inflame violence among certain ethnic groups. Land has been a crucial source of dispute between different ethnic groups. Yet no systematic effort has been made to address the shortage of arable land that faces a growing population. Instead, the Moi government has manipulated these pressing problems to polarize ethnic sentiments to its political and economic advantage.[122]

Once it became clear to Moi and his clique that they would not be able to resist calls for greater pluralism, KANU officials and MPs, mostly from the Kalenjin and Maasai communities, began to call for the forced removal of other ethnic communities from "their land" in the Rift Valley.[123] Majimboism became the rallying cry for protecting minority rights. The calls for a majimbo system in the early 1990s differed from those made by KADU in the 1960s in that state elites explicitly called for the expulsion of all non-Kalenjin, non-Maasai, non-Sambura, and non-Turkana groups from the Rift Valley.[124] The call for majimboism and the ethnic cleansing such calls incited were "part of a general strategy to press once more for a form of regional government in which KANU's minority communities would be able to seize enough land and resources to secure permanent control over the state."[125]

A broad cross-section of Kenyan observers agree that majimbo talk played a pivotal role in inciting groups to violence.[126] Five important mass majimbo rallies were held over a period of six weeks in late 1991. The first two rallies were held in Kapsabet (Nandi District) and Kapkatet (Kericho District) in the Kalenjin heartland of Rift Valley Province. The next three were held in Narok, Machakos, and Mombasa. Each rally was conducted under the watchful eye of national and local political elites aligned with Moi and determined to fight off the advocates of multipartyism. The 1991 majimbo rallies were convened and addressed by senior government ministers and KANU officials including the then vice president George Saitoti; the MP and minister Nicholas Biwott; the ministers William ole Ntimama, John Cheruiyot, Timothy Mibei, Kipkalia Kones, Eric Bomett, Willy Kamuren, Paul Chepkok, Francis Mutwol, William Kikwai, John Terrer, Lawi Kiplagat, Chistopher Lomada, and Peter Nangole; the Rift Valley MPs Ayub Chepkwony, Robert Kipkorir, and Samson Ole Tuya; and numerous local KANU officials.[127]

Most observers agree that the chief architect of the majimbo scheme was Biwott. Biwott started out as Moi's personal secretary before winning an unopposed MP seat from Elgeyo-Marakwet (a Kalenjin-dominated area bordering Moi's own Baringo District) in 1979. Over the course of Moi's tenure Biwott served in a number of positions in the cabinet, including a long stint as the minister for energy. Biwott was temporarily demoted, and then sacked and arrested in late 1991 stemming from suspicions over corruption and his involvement in the infamous Ouko murder. He was quickly released, however, and immediately resumed an active role in KANU as a strategist. Later, Biwott was brought back into the government. Regardless of the nature of his official positions, Biwott enjoyed enormous influence throughout the Moi era. He was the president's closest political confidant and, as early as the mid-1980s, was widely seen as the second most powerful man in the country. Indeed, considerable evidence suggests that Biwott was the behind-the-scenes organizer for much of the regime's dirty work, including the effort to incite widespread violence in and around the Rift Valley in the first half of the 1990s and again at the Coast in 1997 through the use of majimbo rhetoric (see also the discussion of the Coast violence below).[128]

The majimbo rallies represented a coordinated effort by the Moi regime and KANU to maintain their monopoly on power. At a September 1991 rally in Narok, Ntimama proclaimed that "all the Ministers and KANU leaders you see here have resolved to fight together and follow President Moi together."[129] Moreover, Joseph Misoi, the KANU MP for Eldoret South and one of the convenors of the rallies, revealed KANU's agenda when he declared that, "unless those clamouring for political pluralism stop, we must devise a protective mechanism by launching this movement."[130]

The violence that first erupted on Meteitei farm occurred less than two months from the first majimbo rally held in nearby Kapsabet.[131] Critical to the successful mobilization of ethnic groups at these rallies was the invocation by elites of minority land rights. As Stephen Ndegwa notes, the majimbo rallies "introduced a new lexicon of difference and intimidation, *especially with reference to the rights of access to and settlement on land* and rights of political participation in selected regions."[132] State elites consistently referred to the contamination of the ancestral lands of the Kalenjin and Maasai communities by *madoadoa* ("spots") and *kwekwe* ("blemishes"). These terms directly referred to ethnic groups, especially Kikuyu, that had migrated to Rift Valley Province during the colonial and postcolonial periods. By referring to Kikuyus, Luos, and others as *chui* ("leopards"), Kalenjin and Maasai elites consistently sought to convince their mass audience that minority groups were victims of land-grabbers who had to be cleansed from the Rift Valley and sent back to their "motherland" (meaning Central Province).[133]

The need for violence to defend land rights was also clearly stated by Kalenjin politicians. At the Kapsabet rally officials present resolved "to fight anti-establishment figures using all means at their disposal so as to protect the government and the ruling party." In a similar vein, Biwott reportedly stated that supporters should be "ready to fight to the last person to protect the Government of President Moi. . . . Kalenjins were not cowards and . . . they were ready to counter attempts to relegate them from leadership."[134] At a November 1993 rally at Makutano Stadium in Kapenguria, the home affairs minister Francis Lotodo gave a speech telling Kikuyus that they had forty-eight hours to depart West Pokot District, and warned that the Pokot (a Kalenjin subgroup) would "take the law into their own hands" if they refused to leave. Following his visit two town councilors repeated the threat, warning Kikuyus that they had two weeks to dispose of their property and move out before "Kalenjins would take over their land." Also in November Biwott declared, at a majimbo rally in Kericho District, that other ethnic groups were welcome in the Rift Valley only as long they respected the rights of the original inhabitants (Kalenjins, Maasais, Samburu, and Turkanas).[135]

Similar provocative statements were made in other venues as well. In a February 1993 speech the KANU veteran Sharif Nassir bluntly warned, "If you insult Moi, you are looking for clashes."[136] And in June 1993 Wiberforce Kisiero, the MP from Mt. Elgon, referred to Kikuyus in a speech delivered in Parliament as "black colonialists," claiming that they had taken over land from "indigenous" owners.[137] Furthermore, government incitement to violence went beyond statements by KANU ministers. As noted earlier, national and local elites assisted attackers by providing training, transport, and sometimes payment.[138]

The violence between the Sabaot (a Kalenjin subgroup) and the Bukusu (a Luhya subgroup) in Trans Nzoia District of the Rift Valley in late 1991 provides an excellent example of the dynamics involved in the exploitation of land grievances by state elites. The Parliamentary Sub-Committee Report on the clashes concluded that the violence in Trans Nzoia stemmed largely from "the hunger for land by the Sabaot, . . . [the] perceived domination of the Sabaot who feel that they are the 'rightful' residents of the area, by the Bukusa, . . . utterances by political and administrative leaders which . . . created more tension, . . . [and] the 'majimbo' rallies of 1991."[139] Population growth in Trans Nzoia averaged 4.3 percent a year during the 1980s. In addition, the population density of the area increased from 124 per km^2 to 160 per km² between 1979 and 1989, while the availability of good agricultural land plummeted from 1.68 ha per person in 1969 to 0.80 ha in 1979 and to 0.53 ha in 1989 (see Tables 4.1 and 4.3). Moreover, while the exact number is probably unreliable, as many as forty thousand Sabaot may have been landless in the region at the time. Layered on top of this demographically induced competition was a long-standing dispute between the Sabaot and Bukusu over land rights in the area.[140] Elites in the district were able to capitalize on the Sabaot's concern for land, as well as their fears that if the opposition came to power through multiparty elections then they would be forced into Uganda. Sabaots were encouraged to chase away their rivals in order to establish their own district and acquire additional rights to land. In December 1991 the district commissioner Changole made public remarks at the Chemoge Market in which he urged Sabaot to remove "madoadoa" and "chui" from their midst.[141] When violence between the two groups broke out in December 1991, the local chief Rotich accused the Luhya of "bringing trouble on themselves because of supporting the opposition."[142]

Clashes pitting the Maasai and Kalenjin against the Kikuyu and Kisii in Narok District provide another interesting example. Although Narok was one of the most sparsely populated areas affected by the violence, it had experienced significant population growth, and land in the area tends to be of low agricultural potential (see Table 4.1). Furthermore, Narok was the locus of considerable intergroup land competition stemming from the migration of Kikuyu and Kisii, caused by demographic pressure in *neighboring* regions, onto land traditionally occupied by the Kalenjin and Maasai. The Kisii, for example, settled in the area in large numbers after independence as a result of the "population explosion and . . . [their] heritage of agricultural enterprise."[143] Beginning in early 1992 KANU elites who were aligned with the Moi regime sought to exploit the pool of land grievances in the area to incite their followers to violence. In February 1992 Ntimama, who was a Narok MP in addition to being the minister for local government, argued at a public meeting that non-Maasai living on Maasai land should respect Maasai rights, and assured his kinsmen that land title deeds held by such non-Maasai were "mere pieces of paper that could be disregarded at any time."[144]

In October 1993 Maasai attacked Kikuyus in the Enoosupukia hills in Narok, leaving dozens dead and displacing more than thirty thousand. Prior to the clashes, Ntimama had tapped into the escalating demographic competition between Maasai and Kikuyu by arguing that contraception was a ploy by more populous tribes to dominate smaller ones, telling the Maasai to no longer be duped into family planning.[145] Ntimama also argued that Kikuyus living in the Enoosupukia hills were destroying local forests, despoiling the environment, and threatening the supply of water needed by Maasai living downstream from them. As Jacqueline Klopp argues, "Ntimama's appeal to local pastoralists, many of whom saw him as a champion of their rights against 'foreigners,' was that he provided an easy 'solution' to very real problems of insecurity of pastoralist land rights and environmental degradation."[146] When a group of opposition MPs criticized Ntimama for instigating the violence, he defended his actions by saying that the attacks had been justified because "during colonial times the Maasai were suppressed and isolated. Some people [the Kikuyu] took the same advantage to suppress us and invade our land."[147] Ntimama also declared that the Kikuyu "had suppressed the Maasai, taken their land and degraded their environment. . . . We had to say enough is enough. I had to lead the Maasai in protecting their rights."[148]

The Narok violence also illustrated the degree of Moi's complicity with the violence. When dozens of opposition MPs threatened to paralyze the government unless Ntimama was dismissed from the government, Moi ignored the demands. And at a late October 1993 rally Biwott defended Ntimama, claiming that the Maasai had "been oppressed for too long by the Kikuyus in Enoosupukia."[149]

As these examples illustrate, population and land pressures in and around the Rift Valley played a critical role in the 1991–95 clashes. An acute scarcity of land, the most valuable natural resource for rural Kenyans, contributed to significant intergroup grievances, grievances that KANU elites could draw on to instigate violence. Moreover, throughout clash-affected areas, the prospect of gaining access to land was used by KANU elites as a powerful selective incentive to encourage individuals to drive away their neighbors.[150] This was captured in an account provided by Naftali Nyaoma, a victim of the Rift Valley violence who testified before the Akiwumi Commission appointed to investigate the clashes. Nyamoa was asked why he and his neighbors had been attacked. He replied: "So that they may occupy the farms we had. . . . [W]hen I met some of these people [attackers] who had taken beer, they used to tell me that some houses . . . were meant to be used by some of them after we had gone." According to Nyaoma, the attackers admitted that "some of our youths had burnt the houses of Kisiis and Kikuyus, because they were promised to get pieces of land."[151] In general, as a Kenya Human Rights Commission (KHRC) report documents,

The Government rewarded handsomely those members of the Kalenjin and Maasai communities who participated in the clashes. By closing its eyes to and often sanctioning fraudulent land transfers, illegal occupation, pressured land sales and exchanges, the government enabled the Kalenjin and the Maasai to acquire land formerly owned by the displaced population in the Rift Valley Province, the most fertile farmlands in the country.[152]

The instigation of rural violence from 1991 to 1995 ultimately served a number of parochial political and economic interests held by state elites and their allies. Both before and after the 1992 election the violence served as a form of punishment for Kikuyu, Kisii, Luhya, and Luo supporters of the political opposition.[153] No less important, however, was the way Moi sought to use the violence to cast doubt among the general populace about the desirability of a return to multiparty politics.[154] As early as January 1990, when Kenyans began seriously agitating for a return to multipartyism, Moi and members of his clique attacked their foes with warnings that pluralism would lead to "tribal conflicts" and unrest in the country. By instigating ethnic violence, Moi's regime made this warning a self-fulfilling prophecy in an attempt to discredit the process.[155] Once the violence began Moi was quick to point out that "since multi-partyism came, you can see tribal clashes have started. I warned of such violence earlier."[156]

Violence was also used after the election to consolidate KANU gains in the Rift Valley, take revenge against those who voted against KANU, and justify repression against regime opponents.[157] More broadly the violence served to reward and empower the Kalenjin and Maasai communities by allowing their members to illegally occupy valuable land in the Rift Valley or purchase it from clash victims at wildly reduced prices. Most of the hundreds of thousands of people internally displaced by the violence were unable to resettle because of sporadic outbreaks of violence and fear of attack.[158] As one Luhya victim noted: "People have not gone back [to their land] because they are afraid and their homes destroyed. . . . They go back to cultivate during the day, but the Kalenjins graze their cattle on our land and steal things and if we tell them to move, they threaten to attack us."[159] Much of their vacated land was illegally occupied by Kalenjins and their allies, and other land was sold for sums significantly below market value because non-Kalenjins feared returning to their farms.[160] In the fertile Uasin Gishu District, for example, the sale price for land declined 75 to 80 percent from pre-clash levels. The displaced were typically offered Ksh20,000 (U.S.$250) instead of the pre-clash level of Ksh80,000–100,000 (U.S.$1,000–$1,200) per acre.[161]

Providing access to seized land helped ensure that communities allied to Moi and KANU would remain loyal in the multiparty era. The violence instigated between Maasais and Kikuyus in Narok by Ntimama in 1993, for example, served to tie the Maasai more closely to the fate of Ntimama and the party. "The cleared land opened up new resources to buy support through patronage and raised the stakes in the fight for change. By effectively taking land claimed by others, Ntimama's supporters now had a stronger stake in maintaining KANU and Ntimama in power."[162] Overall, by chasing ethnic rivals out of Rift Valley Province, the government hoped to consolidate its political power by transforming the entire region into a Kalenjin and Maasai land-owning area.

As a consequence of state-sponsored violence, patterns of land ownership in the Rift Valley were significantly altered, to the benefit of Moi and KANU. Since the largest number of parliamentary seats were allocated to Rift Valley Province, the violence promised substantial gains for KANU in the 1992 election, as well as subsequent elections, by solidifying Kalenjin domination of the province, and by guaranteeing support for the government among the Kalenjin and allied comunities.[163] The regime's strategy clearly reaped electoral rewards. Many would-be opposition supporters were intimidated, and KANU won the majority of parliamentary seats in Rift Valley Province. Perhaps most telling, all ten candidates who ran unopposed in 1992, including Moi himself, were from the Rift Valley.[164]

Violent Reprise: The Coast, 1997

From late August to November 1997 a new wave of ethnic violence occurred in Kenya, this time in Coast Province near the port city of Mombasa.[165] The bloodshed was smaller in scale than the Rift Valley violence, but it was politically very significant. The Coast clashes were concentrated in the Likoni Division of Mombasa and the nearby areas of Matuga, Msawmweni, and Ukunda in Kwale District.[166]

Most of the attackers were of the Digo subgroup of the Mijikenda community[167] At the time of the clashes, around 80 percent of the residents of the Likoni-Kwale area were of the Digo and Duruma subgroups of the Mijikenda, with the Digo comprising a large majority. Most of the victims of the attacks were Kamba, Kikuyus, Luhya, Luo, and other communities that the Digo and their backers labeled *Wabara* ("up-country people") or *Wakirienge* ("those who speak alien dialects").[168] These groups were migrant settlers from other parts of Kenya. Notwithstanding their "up-country" label, most were long-term settlers, although some still owned land in their regions of origin.[169]

The violence started on August 13 when a large gang of around two hundred armed Digo raiders attacked the Likoni Police Station, murdering several police officers—whom the raiders viewed as dominated by up-country residents and abusive of their community—and stealing guns and ammunition to be used to terrorize surrounding residents.[170] Within a number of days the violence spread to other locations on the south coast and, briefly, the north coast of Mombasa.[171] Between August and November there were numerous instances of killings, lootings, rape, and displacement directed against up-country groups in these areas. All told, around one hundred people were killed and perhaps as many as one hundred thousand were displaced. Some estimates suggest that between 75 and 100 percent of up-country residents may have been displaced in violence-affected areas.[172]

As with the violence in the first part of the decade, hard-liners within Moi's regime and KANU engineered the clashes. Moi, of course, denied that the regime had anything to do with violence at the Coast, declaring that the clashes were largely fueled by tribal sentiments and opposition agitation.[173] Shortly after the violence began, Moi insisted that "KANU is a party which advocates peace and unity and at no time can it perpetrate violence."[174] Nevertheless, most observers at the time and since have argued that state elites played a prominent role in instigating and facilitating the violence.

Interviews with Digo attackers indicate that local-level KANU politicians were directly involved in recruiting and organizing the attacks, and other evidence suggests that higher-level government officials and politicians were active behind the scenes.[175] Recruits reported visits to their camps by local politicians who invoked the name "Mzee" (President Moi) to suggest high-level political support.[176] Indeed, as early as 1993, one former KANU politician from Coast Province claimed to have been summoned to the Office of the President and instructed by a high-level official to mobilize a group to drive away up-country voters prior to the 1997 elections. According to the KANU politician involved, the high-level official reportedly stated, "We've got the blessing of Mzee."[177]

Among the KANU elites commonly listed as architects of the Coast clashes were Biwott, Mohammed Sajjad (a KANU-nominated MP and campaign coordinator for Coast Province for the 1997 elections), Boy Juma Boy (the KANU MP for Matuga), Suleiman Kamole (the KANU candidate for Parliament who won the Matuga nomination from Boy prior to the December 1997 election), Kassim Mwamzandi (KANU MP for Msambweni), Karisa Maitha, Omar Masumbuko, Mwalimu Masoud Mwahima (all influential local KANU members), Suleiman Rashid Shakombo (a KANU candidate for Likoni District who defected from the party in November and eventually won the seat), and Swaleh Salim bin Alfan (the Digo spiritual leader widely viewd as a local proxy for KANU).[178]

In a December 1997 interview with the Kenyan Weekly *The Star* Maitha admitted that "The recent 'tribal' clashes at the Coast are part of a larger KANU scheme to rig the December elections."[179] The veteran Mombasa KANU politician Sharif Nassir is reported to have said, in reference to the raid on the Likoni police station, "This matter was political and it will not end until the elections were over."[180] Moreover, shortly after the clashes began Biwott and Sajjad were named in Parliament as the underwriters of the violence, although, of course, both denied the accusation.[181]

Some evidence suggests that plans for the clashes may have been initiated as early as February or March 1997, and as early as May veiled threats were issued to up-country people by some of their Mijikenda neighbors.[182] Over the course of the violence, evidence suggests that KANU politicians supported the raiders by pressuring for the release of the Digo spiritual leader Alfan, visiting the raiders' hidden bases, and providing funding. Other evidence of government complicity included the failure to act to stop the raiders at an early stage despite advance warning, the slow response of government security forces (in part because of pressure from KANU politicians), intrusions into police investigations, pressure to release arrested politicians, and the insufficient protection provided to victims of the attacks.[183]

Sources of Strife

In many respects the violence at the Coast paralleled earlier episodes in the Rift Valley, Nyanza, and Western Provinces. Kenya's continuing social problems, aggravated by DES, kept the pressure on the regime to further reform the country's political and economic system. As before, Moi and KANU reacted to these threats by instigating intergroup violence meant to derail reform efforts, punish opponents, and consolidate KANU power. And the regime once again seized on patterns of economic marginalization and land-related grievances to incite violence and recruit attackers.

PRESSURES ON THE STATE AND INCENTIVES FOR STATE EXPLOITATION

During the 1990s Kenya's population continued to expand, albeit at a somewhat slower rate than in the previous two decades. By 1999 the total population had grown from 21.4 million in 1989 to 28.7 million. This represented an average annual increase of approximately 3 percent during the 1990s and a 34 percent total increase over the course of the decade.[184] During the same period the Kenyan economy only grew by 2.4 percent per year between 1990 and 2000, compared to 5.8 percent and 4.2 percent in the 1965–79 and 1980–90 periods, respectively. The decline in economic growth was widely attributed to a combination of inconsistent macroeconomic policies, the slow pace of structural changes in the economy, and high levels of corruption.[185]

Because economic growth was sluggish and the population was still growing rapidly, there was an overall decline in per capita income during the 1990s. Per person, Kenyans were poorer during the 1990s than they were at independence in 1963.[186] The 1997 Welfare Monitoring Survey estimated that the 1997 national incidence of absolute poverty (i.e., the level at which minimum calorie requirements cannot be met even if all spending is concentrated on food) was 52 percent, and the number of Kenyans living in absolute poverty increased from 11.5 million in 1994 to 12.6 million in 1997.[187] Economic hardships were compounded by the continuing shortage of critical social services. As the economy stagnated and structural adjustment programs required greater fiscal discipline, the government increased fees for education and health services, putting them out of reach for a growing number of Kenyans.[188] The gap between rich and poor also increased during the 1990s. By 1997 the United Nations Development Programme ranked Kenya among the five most economically unequal countries in the world.[189]

Not surprisingly, given these economic problems and the continued corruption and repression engaged in by Moi's government, dissatisfaction with the regime among those groups that had pushed for reforms in the first part of the decade continued. The return of multipartyism had also facilitated the growth of civil society organizations, increasing the number and influence of groups making demands on the state for reform.[190]

In 1994 the KHRC, the Law Society of Kenya, and the Kenya section of the International Commission of Jurists produced a "Proposal for a Model Constitution." The document was intended to inspire a national dialogue on the need for fundamental constitutional change. The groups behind the document also initiated a large-scale public education campaign related to the proposed reforms through the Citizens Coalition for Constitutional Change (CCCC). The CCCC eventually succeeded in convincing the opposition political parties that they would be unable to defeat Moi and KANU in the 1997 elections unless the constitution was first altered.[191] Indeed, as the 1997 presidential and parliamentary elections approached it became increasingly clear that "the manipulation of laws, constitutional gaps, repressive administrative practices against opposition parties, and limitations to independent democratic activity" would make it impossible for the opposition to defeat Moi and KANU.[192]

Consequently, the push for reform escalated. The CCCC organized the first attempt at a people's constitutional convention in Kenya known as the National Convention Assembly (NCA). The NCA's operation and political activities were led by the National Convention Executive Committee (NCEC), a group established by leaders from three opposition parties—most notably Raila Odinga, Kenneth Matiba, and Paul Muite—and several civil society organizations.[193] The NCEC organized mass-action activities and rallies across Kenya to generate broader grass-roots support for reform, and the move attracted significant support across Kenyan society.[194] Eventually, to level the playing field, the NCEC agreed to a minimum agenda for reforms to be implemented prior to the 1997 elections; more ambitious reforms designed to transform Kenya into a real democracy would be pursued after the elections. If these minimal reforms were not enacted, the NCEC threatened to organize a widespread boycott of the elections.[195]

The constitutional reform movement represented a huge threat to Moi and KANU. Nevertheless, when pressure first emerged in 1994 to reform the constitution, KANU's initial response was not an outright rejection of the prospect. Instead, some hard-liners, led by Biwott and Ntimama, hoped to take advantage of the constitutional reform process to create a majimbo system. As David Throup and Charles Hornsby explain:

> The key goal seemed to be to ensure that the Kalenjin and Maasai could rule the Rift and expel the Kikuyu, since land ownership remained at the core of the argument. Indeed, there were rumours that Nicholas Biwott wished to be made Premier of the Rift Valley region, and even that he intended to take over when Moi finally died or retired. No one had a clear concept of what this would entail, however, or whether such a system of government would be remotely practical.[196]

After the release of the Law Society of Kenya draft constitution at the end of 1994, Moi even went so far as to publicly endorse the call for a new regional structure.[197]

As civil society groups succeeded in generating momentum for constitutional changes, however, the threats to KANU's rule became increasingly clear. A KHRC report observed that,

> The organizational success of the NCA and its executive wing, the National Convention Executive Council (NCEC), the mass support that it enjoyed, and the national unity that it was able to forge, all left a Moi-KANU regime that felt threatened and increasingly under siege. . . .

... [R]ather than accept the popular will of the people, the Moi-KANU regime turned around like a cornered rat, and proceeded to unleash another wave of violence against Kenyans.[198]

Vice President George Saitoti accused the NCA of having an "evil mission of changing the government of Kenya by revolution."[199] The government backed up this view by violently breaking up "illegal" rallies sponsored by the NCEC. The conflict reached its high point on July 7, 1997 (Saba Saba Day; seven seven, in Swahili), when security forces responded to pro-reform rallies in Nairobi and elsewhere around the country with tear gas and beatings. Overall, more than twenty people were killed and the main Anglican cathedral in Nairobi was desecrated. The events shocked many Kenyans as well as the international donor community, and were broadcast around the world on CNN.[200]

The violence in Coast Province started in August and occurred as the constitutional reform movement was gaining ground among coastal inhabitants, challenging KANU's traditional hold over the area. The answer to this threat was to encourage "indigenous" constituencies traditionally aligned with KANU to drive out "alien" pro-opposition groups, just as the regime had done in and around the Rift Valley. At the Coast this goal was captured in the phrase "up-country people go away," written by Digo raiders on some of the farmhouses of their victims.[201]

One motivation for state-instigated intergroup violence at the Coast was thus to intimidate the opposition and create an electoral landscape more amenable to Moi and KANU. This motivation was widely recognized at the time of the clashes. As the *Update* noted on September 30, 1997, "KANU had to plan and execute the clashes so that the majority of the up-country people supporting the opposition could be evicted."[202] The Akiwumi Commission investigating the violence reached similar conclusions:

> The introduction of multi-party politics in 1991 gave the coastal people a chance to express themselves politically and the result of this was a serious set back [*sic*] for the ruling KANU party. Politics had by then become polarized along tribal lines and of all the four coastal parliamentary seats in the Mombasa District, KANU only managed in the first multi-party general elections held in 1992 to win one seat which was in Mombasa Island. . . .
>
> This meant that come the next presidential and general elections which were to be held at the end of 1997, KANU would have to take appropriate steps to ensure that this time around it did much better in the general elections and secured the twenty-five percent Coast Province vote in favour of President Moi.
>
> In the Likoni-Kwale area, the only strategy that . . . would yield durable results for KANU would be to ensure that the upcountry people, namely the

Luo, Kikuyu and Luhya, who were seen as supporters of the opposition parties, did not vote for these parties. And how best to achieve this than to exploit existing and latent animosity which the coastal people might have against the upcountry inhabitants, which had hitherto not led to any violence, so that the former can intimidate or drive away the latter from voting for the opposition parties.[203]

To a large degree this aspect of KANU's strategy succeeded. The evidence suggests that a large number of registered up-country residents of Likoni-Kwale were disenfranchised to the advantage of KANU. In the 1997 election KANU gained one net seat in Mombasa and retained all the seats in Kwale District, and Moi led in all constituencies at the Coast including traditional opposition strongholds.[204]

Beyond the immediate electoral benefits, however, the regime also hoped that violence would derail the demands by civil society organizations for constitutional reform. A KHRC report released in late 1997 observed that "the Likoni-Kwale tragedy was ... an initial phase of a larger state-sponsored plan to undermine the constitutional reform movement and provide a reconfigured political space that would allow KANU to recapture the political initiative it had lost to the National Convention Assembly (NCA) and its executive arm, the National Convention Executive Committee (NCEC) after [the NCA's First Plenary Session] Limura I [Convention held on August 6, 1997]."[205] Many observers speculate that Moi's regime may have wanted to use the violence at the Coast to justify a nationwide state of emergency, allowing the elections to be postponed and legitimating a further crack down on opposition groups.[206]

The option to declare a state of emergency and cancel elections may have been abandoned primarily because the constitutional reform movement was mainstreamed by the Inter-Parties Parliamentary Group (IPPG), which allowed the regime greater control over the process.[207] The violence at the Coast refocused international attention on political instability in Kenya. The valuable tourist sector in the area declined, and donors moved to cut off aid to the government. In response, Moi agreed to consider passing a number of reforms prior to the election but only on the condition that the process was dominated by members of Parliament rather than civic organizations.[208] The goal was to weaken the NCEC and take over the initiative for reforms. This was acceptable to KANU elites as long as it did not result in a reform package that undermined the party's monopoly over power.[209] The long-term effects of these reforms is discussed in the next chapter.

ECONOMIC MARGINALIZATION, LAND COMPETITION,
AND OPPORTUNITIES FOR STATE EXPLOITATION

In order to instigate violence at the Coast, KANU elites exploited a set
of Mijikenda (especially Digo) grievances centered around patterns
of land ownership, population pressures, and employment problems.
To some degree the land-starved Mijikenda were aggrieved because
settlement schemes in the area had attracted substantial in-migration
by up-country groups from other overpopulated areas of the country.[210] More important, however, was the "land-grabbing mania" that
emerged in Kenya in the 1990s. Over the course of the decade numerous politically connected individuals and land-buying companies
were granted "free" public land by the government, including forestland and land reserved for playgrounds, markets, hospitals, dem-
onstration farms, research institutions, and other public goods. Irregular privatizations and evictions also occurred on rural settlements and
group ranches, with land ending up in the hands of affluent regime
supporters and politicians. These individuals could then turn around
and sell the land to developers for large sums of money.[211]

Prior to the 1997 clashes land-grabbing had become a very contentious issue in the Likoni-Kwale area. At the time much of the land was
designated as government, unregistered, or trust land; less than 10 percent was categorized as freehold and registered. This opened up substantial opportunities for the regime to use land for patronage. The
irregular acquisition of valuable land associated with the tourism industry at the Coast was particularly rampant.[212]

Land-grabbing during the 1990s was encouraged by a number of factors. Structural adjustment programs implemented under pressure from
the IMF and the World Bank required a certain amount of fiscal discipline, the abandonment or auctioning off of inefficient parastatal firms,
and limitations on the government's ability to print money. All these
measures reduced the patronage resources available to Moi's regime.
Compounding matters, these new constraints occurred at the very time
when multipartyism was increasing the costs of preventing defections
from KANU to opposition parties. It was thus essential for Moi and
KANU to find new avenues for purchasing and maintaining political
allies. Since public land, including a considerable amount at the Coast,
was both highly accessible and less prone to international scrutiny, it
became an appealing patronage asset for the regime.[213] Moreover, acute
land scarcity throughout Kenya furthered the usefulness of public land
as a means of purchasing and rewarding political support because, "as
land diminished, the remainder . . . increased in value."[214]

Beyond the issue of land, the inability of the local economy at the Coast to accommodate population increases also contributed to Mijikenda grievances. In Mombasa District, of which Likoni is a division, the annual population growth rate was 3.1 percent from 1979 to 1989 and 3.7 percent from 1989 to 1999; over the same period the annual rate for Kwale District were 2.9 percent and 2.6 percent, respectively.[215] Population growth in excess of economic opportunities contributed to escalating impoverishment. Between 1994 and 1997 the prevalence of absolute poverty in Coast Province increased from 55 percent to 62 percent, with the number of rural poor in the Coast totaling 883,667 and the number of poor in Mombasa totaling 217,402 in 1997.[216] During this period impoverished women in Coast Province—along with those in Eastern Province—also had the highest total fertility rates in Kenya, resulting in the highest mean household sizes among the poor.[217]

Unemployment in the areas affected by the violence was also substantial. According to government data for Kiwale District, only 9.4 percent of the local labor force was engaged in the public sector, 5.9 percent in the formal sector, and 12.7 percent in the informal sector. This represents a total of only 28 percent of the labor force that could be considered to have had stable employment during the time of the clashes; the rest of the labor force was engaged in casual labor or unpaid family labor or was unemployed.[218] All told, at the time of the clashes, the Likoni-Kwale area had a total population of about half a million people, of which only about 50 percent were employed. The Mijikenda constituted most of the unemployed in areas affected by the clashes because of higher rates of illiteracy and substantial ethnic biases in hiring practices. This latter factor was significant given that upcountry communities controlled about 80 percent of the local commercial and business sector.[219]

Finally, economic grievances in the Likoni-Kwale area were also magnified by the widespread perception among the Mijikenda that little of the wealth generated from the lucrative tourist industry in the area was used to improve the socioeconomic condition of the local population and by wide disparities in access to health care, sanitation, clean water, and educational opportunities.[220]

Economic marginalization among the Mijikenda provided enormous opportunities for troublemaking by KANU elites. Many in the Mijikenda community were landless, while up-country people were perceived to own large tracts of land; many of the Mijikenda were poor and unemployed, while up-country people and foreigners were perceived to dominate the jobs available in the tourism industry and government. Most of the perpetrators of the Coast attacks were young Digo men who were angry over their landlessness, poverty, unemployment, and inadequate educational opportunities, and blamed up-country residents for their plight.[221] These grievances were clearly spelled out in an open letter by Stambuli Abdillahi Nassir, the secretary general of the Coast People's Party-Mwambao, to President Moi, dated October 25, 1996:

> It has been thirty-three (33) years since Kenya attained its independence, but we people of the Coast are still in the dark. Until today, we have no right to govern ourselves. It is now thirty-three years and the Digo still do not possess titles of ownership to their farms. It is now thirty-three years and the Bajuni still do not have titles of ownership of the farms and plots of land. Some are still squatters to this very day. Do you consider it right that we should be made to feel like foreigners to this day? . . . We can no longer remain silent in the face of continuing deprivation of the rights of the coastal people by foreigners. The people of the Coast must be free to have sovereignty over themselves. The truth must be told, bitter as it may be. Freedom for the Coast, Let the foreigners go!![222]

In this context, KANU elites reinforced the belief that up-country people were to blame. Karuti Kanyinga of the Institute of Development Studies at Nairobi University notes that the instigators of the clashes told people, "You are poor not because we [the government] stole your land, but because the Kikuyu dominate economic activities."[223] KANU elites offered an easy solution to all the suffering experienced by the Mijikenda: drive away up-country communities.

In the first half of 1997 local leaders approached numerous Digo men in their twenties and thirties to encourage them to terrorize their up-country neighbors. Other recruitment occurred by word of mouth. Local leaders promised participants that they would accrue certain rewards for joining in attacks, including help in obtaining the farmland, houses, and jobs left behind by the victims. Indeed, interviews with raiders indicated that their primary motivation was obtaining access to "their" lands, property, and jobs.[224] These motivations were not kept secret. During the attacks leaflets in Swahili were distributed in some areas declaring, "The time has come for us original inhabitants of the coast to claim what is rightfully ours. We must remove these invaders from our land."[225]

As with the violence in and around the Rift Valley in the first part of the 1990s, majimbo rhetoric was used to instigate violence at the Coast. Participants were told that the purpose of the attacks was to bring about a majimbo system that would ensure greater Mijikenda control over local affairs. As one raider put it, the area councilor who recruited him told him that "people wanted to start majimbo . . . [O]nce we chased away the up-country people we would have the area, we would take control." Another attacker explained further: "It was already known from the Rift Valley how to chase people out—by clashes—so it was copied. The idea was to organize the youth to evict up-country people. . . . If you say 'majimbo,' you mean driving non-indigenous people out."[226]

In short, as with earlier episodes of ethnic bloodshed, the pool of grievances among the Mijikenda was drawn upon by KANU elites to instigate intergroup conflict in an effort to maintain and consolidate political power. The efforts at the Coast in 1997 were especially cynical since regime-sponsored land-grabbing, and the actions of local politicians and a small number of wealthy up-country individuals, was much more responsible for the plight of the Mijikenda than the largely poor up-country migrants who were chased away during the attacks.[227]

Conclusions

Land scarcity resulting from DES was a fundamental cause of the ethnic clashes that plagued Kenya throughout the 1990s. Because of the predominately rural character of the Kenyan economy and the small amount of good arable land, land was, and remains, the most valuable natural resource for most Kenyans. In the post-independence period, land scarcity became acute as Kenya's population soared and land was substantially degraded. These pressures were magnified by significant land inequalities left over from colonial times and postcolonial settlement schemes, and made worse by the Moi regime's policies of using access to land resources for political patronage. As good farmland became increasingly difficult to secure, many impoverished rural residents left for urban centers. This dramatically escalated Kenya's social problems and contributed to demands on the government for reform which Moi and KANU perceived as highly threatening. At the same time, economic marginalization rooted in land scarcity generated a number of grievances that KANU elites could use to pit ethnic groups against one another in a bid to stay in power, as well as opportunities for the state to use promises of access to land as selective incentives to encourage attacks. The centrality of land to the clashes was noted by a commentary in the *Daily Nation* on May 8, 2000:

> There is no denying that land is one of the most vexed questions in this country. Virtually every Kenyan takes his or her cultural identity from a piece of land somewhere. . . .
>
> The modern economy has not lessened our fixation on land. This is still largely an agricultural country. Most Kenyans eke out a livelihood from the

soil. Never mind that, in the more densely-populated districts, there is barely any land to speak of beyond the circumference of your hut. The land has been sub-divided so extensively that it is no longer possible to make any meaningful living from it. . . .

If you are a squatter somewhere in the Rift Valley or at the Coast, the idea of getting your hands on a reasonable chunk of prime agricultural land would probably sound great. There is something obscene about individuals owning huge tracts of arable land . . . while others are reduced to beggars in their own country. . . .

It is precisely these "ancestral land" sentiments that ignited and sustained tribal clashes in the Rift Valley, parts of Nyanza and Western Kenya and the Coast throughout the 1990s.[228]

Ironically, although some of the attackers involved in the various clashes directly profited from their activities, the general problem of landlessness among the Kalenjin, Maasai, and Mijikenda communities in areas affected by the clashes was not really altered. The promise of majimbo rhetoric, especially the claim that there would be more local control over land resources, proved to be a lie. Much of the land previously occupied by victims in violence-affected areas was ultimately grabbed up by affluent regime supporters rather than redistributed to the local landless.[229]

The clashes throughout the 1990s worked to the political advantage of Moi and KANU. The violence allowed the regime to intimidate, chase away, and punish communities aligned with opposition parties, creating KANU zones in large swaths of the country. By producing a general climate of insecurity, KANU elites were also able to ensure the loyalty of "their" communities; after all, continued support for KANU elites was essential if the attackers wished to maintain their gains in land and influence and if their broader communities were to be protected against violent reprisals by victimized groups. Lastly, the polarization of violence-affected areas discouraged the kinds of cross-ethnic alliances in those areas that might have threatened the regime.[230]

Alternative explanations that ignore demographic and environmental factors are far less persuasive. One possible explanation might point to long-standing hatreds between ethnic groups in rural areas as the primary cause. This explanation, however, fails to account for the fact that contending groups in and around the Rift Valley and at the Coast managed to live side by side for decades without killing one another. As noted by one Kikuyu farmer who had lived alongside Kalenjins for almost three decades prior to the onset of violence: "We could not understand it when our Kalenjin neighbors with whom we have been on good terms for years descended on us like animals."[231] The violence was not a spontaneous eruption of ethnic hatred. It was the result of cold-blooded calculations made by state elites who manipulated rising interethnic competition over scarce land resources to serve their own narrow interests.

A second, more plausible explanation would point to democratization as the main cause of ethnic strife. According to this argument, pressures to democratize threatened President Moi and KANU, polarized ethnic sentiments throughout Kenya, and encouraged national and local elites to incite their supporters to violence.[232] As the discussion of the democratization process in this chapter demonstrates, this explanation certainly captures essential parts of the story, but it is incomplete. It ignores the importance of DES in generating the pressures to democratize in the first place. It also fails to account for the critical importance of interethnic land competition, which created the grievances and selective incentives that state elites seized upon to instigate the violence. Without these demographically and environmentally induced grievances and selective incentives, the democratization process may not have been initiated and would not have been nearly as prone to violence.

Although DES was clearly a central cause of ethnic clashes in Kenya, the neo-Malthusian deprivation hypothesis discussed in chapter 1 cannot adequately explain the violence. Growing DES-induced absolute and relative deprivation were certainly essential to the rising grievances that both threatened the Kenyan state and provided opportunities for Moi and other elites to pit ethnic groups against one another. Yet the deprivation hypothesis by itself is inadequate, because it has no political component and envisions conflicts purely in terms of bottom-up dynamics; it has nothing to say about the top-down state exploitation processes at work in Kenya.

The hypotheses advanced by neoclassical economists hold up no better. The honey pot hypothesis presumes that conflict occurs between groups competing over valuable and abundant natural resources. In Kenya, however, land was scarce and its value was inflated by this scarcity.

Resource curse arguments also fail. Economic variants suggest that abundant natural resources undermine diversification and make countries vulnerable to price volatility for primary commodities. Kenya's dependence on natural resources certainly made it vulnerable to declining prices for coffee, as well as other exogenous shocks such as drought during the 1980s, that contributed to the country's economic troubles. However, as noted above, the inability of the economy to accommodate these shocks was also substantially affected by rapid popula-

as well

tion growth. Moreover, the specific socioeconomic problems that triggered the crisis for the Moi regime, and inspired the effort to engineer ethnic violence, were related to land scarcity in rural areas and rapid urbanization; they were not consequences of abundance.

Political variants of the resource curse also fail to account for the violence. As I argued in chapter 1, the pathologies of rentier states apply mainly in the context of abundant supplies of highly valuable mineral resources whose rents accrue directly to the state. In Kenya, however, land—the resource at the center of ethnic bloodshed—was defuse, largely privately owned, and did not provide revenue streams sufficiently captured by the state to explain the overall pattern of authoritarianism and misrule. Additionally, the regime actually became narrower, more corrupt, and more prone to generating widespread grievances as a consequence of land scarcity rather than abundance. Under Kenyatta, there was a large amount of white settler land to redistribute to both landless Kikuyus and elites from nearly all of Kenya's ethnic communities. This helped the Kenyatta regime to co-opt many potential challengers and build a solid foundation of trans-ethnic support. In contrast, by the time Moi took power, demographic expansion and environmental degradation had significantly reduced the amount of available land, and land shortages became even more acute during the 1980s and 1990s. As a consequence, the government tilted its land policies toward a much narrower coalition of regime supporters (this is discussed further in chapter 5).

Finally, the distribution hypothesis advanced by political ecologists does not provide a satisfactory explanation either. Political ecologists would emphasize the ways that colonial and postcolonial land policies concentrated land so as to generate artificial scarcity and a related set of grievances. The analysis provided in this chapter confirms that contemporary land inequality, as well as historically rooted perceptions of injustice, were crucial contributors to ethnic violence. Nevertheless, an account that *only* focuses on the distribution of resources and ignores the effects of population growth and environmental degradation misses fundamental dynamics of the land problem and cannot explain the timing of the land crisis. Land became such a contentious issue in Kenya during the 1990s because it was unequally distributed and increasingly fragmented among more and more people *and* increasingly degraded. Population growth and environmental degradation increased the demand for, and reduced the supply of, high-quality land, increasing its value and encouraging both competition among rural residents and additional land-grabbing by elites. Thus, as the Kenya Section of the International Commission of Jurists observed in an account that is largely sympathetic to the position held by political ecologists, "Ethnic strife [in Kenya] must be seen as a symptom of competition for property rights, such as land and capital, *under conditions of [a] diminishing resource base.*"[233]

In sum, an analysis of ethnic clashes in Kenya during the 1990s clearly supports the state exploitation hypothesis presented in chapter 2. It also demonstrates the explanatory power of my theoretical argument in comparison with its rivals.

5

From Chaos to Calm: Explaining Variations in Violence in the Philippines and Kenya

DEMOGRAPHIC and environmental stress can be a powerful cause of civil strife in developing countries, but DES does not produce civil strife in a vacuum. Patterns of social organization and the characteristics of political institutions mediate the causal relationship. This chapter examines the importance of social and political intervening variables by revisiting the communist insurgency in the Philippines and ethnic clashes in Kenya. In both countries DES led to violence, but the amount of violence varied over time and space. In the Philippines the communist insurgency, which had become a potent political force by the 1980s, began its descent into irrelevance once Ferdinand Marcos was removed from power. In Kenya ethnic violence was widespread in and around the Rift Valley and at the Coast in the 1990s but failed to engulf the entire country. Moreover, the state-sponsored ethnic clashes that surrounded the 1992 and 1997 elections in Kenya failed to recur in the lead-up to the 2002 elections. There was thus considerable temporal and spatial variation in the level of violence in the two countries. I argue that this variation is explained by the intervening variables discussed in chapter 2: groupness and institutional inclusivity.

Intervening Variables in the Philippines

The social and political context in which DES occurred in the Philippines mediated the effects of population and environmental pressures. Increasing levels of groupness over time helped communist recruitment efforts, while exclusive institutions left individuals who were desirous of positive political action no alternative but to address their plight through violence. The situation remained unaltered until these political institutions began to change under Corazon Aquino.

High Levels of Groupness

In the post–World War II period vertical ties between landlords and tenants broke down in rural areas in the Philippines. The result was a

significant increase in class consciousness. Because ethno-cultural affiliations did not crosscut these class cleavages, groupness was high.
Communist rebels were able to capitalize on this high degree of
groupness to mobilize marginalized Filipinos in support of their cause.

GROUP IDENTIFICATION IN THE PHILIPPINES

Although the Philippines has a diverse ethno-cultural and religious
landscape, the division of Filipino society along ethno-cultural and religious lines was relatively limited during the Marcos years. In the four
hundred years since the Spanish first set foot in the archipelago, Filipinos have evolved into a relatively homogeneous population, at least
in terms of the key identity markers around which individuals organize. Over the course of four centuries Filipinos have emerged as an
ethno-cultural blend of Malay, Chinese, Spanish, Negrito, and American. In terms of religion, Christianity (particularly Catholicism) has
been dominant nationally since Spain colonized the country in the sixteenth century; in 1990 so-called Christian Malays made up 91.5 percent of the population. Among Christian Filipinos, regional language
differences represent the main form of cultural differentiation. Some
eleven languages and eighty-seven dialects are spoken in the Philippines. Four major languages—Tagalog, Cebuano, Ilongo, and Illo-
cano—are the native tongues of more than two-thirds of the populace,
while the eight most widely spoken languages, all belonging to the
Malay-Polynesian language family, account for nearly 90 percent.

In the contemporary period, however, these distinctions have not
been particularly crucial to how the vast majority of individuals identify and organize. A long history of cross-group interaction, internal migration, urbanization, and intermarriage, in addition to the spread of
public education and national communications and transportation networks have all helped to break down ethno-cultural boundaries. The
widespread use of English (in big business, government, and education), Tagalog (in mass media), and the more recent government emphasis on Pilipino (a somewhat modified version of Tagalog introduced
in 1974 to gradually phase out the primacy of English) were important
to this process as well. Relevant distinctions between ethno-cultural
groups were also diminshed as a result of growing national opposition
to Spanish rule in the nineteenth century and the war against American
troops at the beginning of the twentieth century. All told, these dynamics worked in tandem to produce a strong sense of Filipino national identity. The Philippines, as David Wurfel notes, "though not a
nation before colonial rule, has since independence enjoyed a na-

tional cohesion greater than that found in most postcolonial states";[1] therefore more narrow ethno-cultural affiliations have become increasingly insignificant.[2]

There are, of course, exceptions to this broad generalization. Two important sets of minorities subscribing to religious beliefs that reinforce linguistic boundaries have continued to define their identities in more parochial terms. The first is the Muslim minority, or Moros. Islam was introduced into the southern parts of the archipelago in the fifteenth century, and Muslim sultanates remained impervious to Christian conversion during the Spanish colonial period. In the late twentieth century approximately 5 percent of the Philippine population adhered to the Islamic faith, making Muslims the country's largest minority. The Muslim community is regionally concentrated in southern and western Mindanao, southern Palawan, and the Sulu archipelago. Despite being ethnically undifferentiated from the majority of Filipinos, the Muslim community has a long history of viewing itself as distinct and independent. Indeed, Muslim groups initiated an insurgency of their own against Marcos in the 1970s. Between 1948 and 1960 immigrants, mostly Christians, resettled in southwestern Mindanao and Sulu at twice the rate as those that immigrated to any other region except Manila. By the late 1960s tensions between Christians and Muslims increased in Mindanao as northern Christian immigrants threatened to make Muslims the minority on what they felt was their own land. After the imposition of martial law, the Moro National Liberation Front launched a violent drive for independence. Talks between the government and the Moro insurgents began in 1976, and Muslims were granted limited autonomy in Mindanao under Aquino.[3]

The roughly one hundred indigenous upland communities make up a second important group of minorities. These communities, each with its own linguistic and animistic tradition, are scattered throughout the mountains of Luzon and Mindanao. In 1990 these groups made up 3 percent of the Filipino population. Like the Muslim community, the Spanish never succeeded in converting upland tribal groups. Moreover, their long-standing physical isolation from broader Filipino society has encouraged these communities to maintain distinct ethno-cultural identities.[4]

Nevertheless, with the important exception of these two minority groups, ethno-cultural and religious cleavages were not the most important ways in which Filipino society was divided during the period under investigation here. More important to the central identity and organization of most Filipinos was, and remains, extensive webs of kinship and personal alliance systems. This includes family and extended family ties, ritual kinship (personal alliances sealed by baptism, confirmation, and marriage), and networks of patron-client relations and obligations that bind Filipinos via vertical lines to other members of their local community. The latter set of ties is particularly important to understanding how the Philippines became increasingly cleaved along class lines.

Patron-client ties between tenant farmers and their landlords have historically been an essential element of rural community in the Philippines. These ties involved a social web of reciprocal obligations whereby the landlord provided farmers a means of earning a living, other material help (often in the form of loans), intervention in local disputes, and protection, while the client provided labor and personal favors, ranging from household tasks to political support. Beyond this material component lay reinforcing cultural ones: in Filipino culture the extension of favors tends to bind the giver and the recipient together in a network of mutual obligation and interdependency (known as *utang na loób*, the debt of gratitude); and patron-client relationships often evolve into forms of ritual kinship that serve to strengthen the bond further.[5]

Prior to the Second World War landlords and tenants normally lived in close proximity, encouraging the development of strong patron-client relationships often infused with mutual affection. These strong vertical ties across socioeconomic classes discouraged peasants from developing strong horizontal group loyalties outside their kinship network. Consequently, despite the bifurcation of Philippine society into wealthy and poor, class consciousness was not high. In the postwar period, however, landlords began to leave the countryside en masse for new homes and businesses in towns and urban centers, leaving their farms to be managed by overseers. In addition, as elite interests diversified beyond agriculture to include commerce, manufacturing, and finance, many became less dependent on land-based resources altogether, coming instead to rely on opportunities provided by external resources (often loans) and "office-based" resources (i.e., positions granted by the state). The migration of elites to urban centers, especially Manila, accelerated under Marcos as he concentrated economic decisions and development in the capital and went about destroying rural political machines that encouraged landowners to build bases of support in the countryside. By the mid-1980s, when the disparity between rich and poor was greater than ever, most large landowners no longer lived in rural communities, even if they often maintained a second residence in these areas. The exodus of elites severed the vertical chord between patron and client since, in Filipino society, "closeness in relationship [beyond the nuclear family] depends very much on physical proximity."[6]

Failed land reform efforts during the Marcos era reinforced the growing landlord-tenant divide, as expectations were first raised and then dashed. The conflict over land reform highlighted class differences and conflicts of interest, reducing still further the vertical bonds linking peasants to landlords.[7] At the same time population growth and the lack of alternative employment increased the supply of prospective tenants and increased the number of landless laborers and subsistence upland farmers. This eased pressure on landlords and overseers to fulfill their side of the patron-client bargain and encouraged them to shift to hired labor instead of a tenancy arrangement. This created a growing pool of individuals lacking any stable bonds of dependency with landowners.[8] Together these trends contributed to growing class consciousness among the poor. Wurfel nicely summarizes these changes in social structure:

> The transformation of many rural landlords into urban capitalists and the intrusion into village life of moneylenders and political leaders seeking electoral support undermined traditional, all-purpose, patron-client relationships, which had been a key element in the social structure. Among some urban workers, plantation laborers, and tenants on large haciendas a much more impersonal relationship with employer or overseer developed. The seeds of class consciousness were being planted by many who moved into the new social space to serve as peasant or labor leaders. . . .
>
> . . . Even land reform . . . exacerbated landlord-tenant conflict and thus contributed to the break-up in patron-client ties and ultimately the reemergence of clandestine opposition in several land reform areas. . . .
>
> . . . [B]y the early 1970s . . . [p]atron-client relationships were losing their binding force. . . . More and more men of means were finding obligations of patronage too onerous. And group membership provided the disaffected with a psychological security from which they could launch their salvos against those identified as political or economic exploiters.[9]

Lastly, to the extent that ethno-cultural, religious, and class-based group affiliations overlapped, they did not crosscut one another in ways that reduced groupness during the Marcos years. In fact, ethno-cultural, religious, and class-based affiliations intersected in such a way as to reinforce groupness. Since disadvantaged ethno-cultural and religious groups *also* found themselves on the lower rungs of the socio-economic ladder, multiple forms of identification did not operate to demobilize groups. On the contrary, the Communists actually capitalized on reinforcing forms of exploitation and oppression to help galvanize support among indigenous upland communities.

EFFECTS ON THE COMMUNIST INSURGENCY

Growing social cleavages made communist mobilization efforts much easier, evidenced by the fact that landless agricultural wage laborers, marginalized tenants, upland farmers, and upland tribal communities made up the main social base of support for the CPP-NPA.[10] By providing material and physical protection, the CPP-NPA took on many of the roles, and reaped many of the loyalties, previously accorded to landlord patrons. In Negros, for example, interviews with government and Catholic Church leaders in the early 1980s emphasized that the Communists were successful in moving into this vacuum, becoming a new kind of patron for vulnerable sugar workers.[11]

Communist organizers coupled the provision of material needs and security with efforts at peasant education, thereby entrenching class awareness. The CPP placed an enormous emphasis on political education. The purpose was to gradually change attitudes by encouraging peasants to view the problems of poverty and exploitation in a different way, connecting them with the experiences of both impoverished farmers in neighboring barrios and struggling laborers in urban slums.[12] Communist leadership also forced NPA regulars to assist peasants during harvest time in order to ensure, as one regional commander put it, that "fighters remember their class origins as peasants."[13] These communist education efforts solidified class consciousness. In the words of one U.S. Embassy official in 1981, the Communists were able to build "political awareness among farmers whose traditionally restricted outlook has led them to expect little from their national government."[14]

However, rising class identification should not be confused with strict adherence to Maoist ideology. As one Manila opposition member adroitly commented in 1985:

> Ninety percent of the guerrillas are not committed to the Communist ideology. They are just people reacting to circumstances—poverty and military abuses. At present, with Marcos's power, they are not given a decent alternative to joining the N.P.A. But the Filipino is not a Bolshevik. He doesn't want that much. He wants to be left alone, to earn a decent living and have enough to send his kids to school.[15]

To the extent that CPP-NPA organizers spoke of Maoist ideology at the grassroots, they made every attempt to translate abstract concepts like feudalism and imperialism into examples peasants could understand: low wages, high rents, the absence of available land, government, and military abuses, and so on. Their offered solutions were equally flexibly and pragmatic in nature: higher wages, lower rents, land reform, and physical protection. By adapting their message to local needs, including the needs of specific indigenous upland communities, the Communists achieved far greater success than they would have with a more dogmatic ideological approach.[16]

Overall, high levels of groupness had several interrelated effects. First, it created a discrete pool of individuals that communist organizers could easily target for mobilization efforts. Second, the growing sense of class consciousness, solidified further by communist propaganda and educational programs, helped poor Filipinos conceptualize their interests in collective class-based terms rather than in individual terms. Lastly, the set of reciprocal obligations established between poor farmers and the CPP-NPA replaced the sense of community that previously existed between landlords and the poor, thereby creating a host of benefits to continued cooperation and discouraging individuals from defecting in the absence of a better alternative for securing their everyday needs.

Exclusive Institutions Under Marcos

The exclusive nature of the Philippines' political institutions under Marcos also played an important facilitating role in the civil war. By eliminating peaceful institutional mechanisms for addressing rising grievances, exclusive political institutions encouraged marginalized Filipinos to turn to extra-institutional means, including support for violent rebellion.

THE EVOLUTION OF EXCLUSIVE INSTITUTIONS IN THE PHILIPPINES

Prior to Marcos's declaration of martial law, the Philippines could be described as a quasi-democracy. Upon independence, the Philippines adopted institutions modeled on the U.S. system, with a president, a Senate, and a House of Representatives. Two political parties, the Nacionalista Party that formed in 1907 and the Liberal Party that formed from a Nacionalista splinter group in 1947, dominated politics. The president and members of the Senate and House were elected, and the president could serve a maximum of two four-year terms (although, until the reelection of Marcos in 1969, no one party had succeeded in maintaining control of Malacanang Palace for more than one term). However, despite the veneer of democracy, the Philippines was controlled by a collection of extended families (or "political clans") whose wealth and influence stemmed largely from their control over land. The two major parties had few discernible ideological differences and were both dominated by these elites. Patron-client relationships determined politics and elections: national leaders had connections to local leaders responsible for mobilizing peasant support during elections. Electoral success was ultimately based more on material incentives than policy platforms; electoral rhetoric catered to mass demands, but these demands were usually neglected once politicians were elected.[17]

Marcos's 1972 declaration of martial law radically altered the country's political institutions, erasing any vestiges of democracy and replacing them with one-man authoritarian rule. The writ of habeas corpus was suspended, Congress and free elections were done away with, civil rights and civil liberties were sharply curtailed, and the power of the military and technocrats was enhanced. Martial law also broke the dominance of traditional elites over the state and consolidated authority within the office of the presidency. Under martial law the authority of the traditional landed elite families was absorbed by the state, since Marcos could, at any time, declare that their property was no longer theirs. Indeed, shortly after imposing martial law, Marcos seized the assets of a number of powerful families perceived to be political enemies, most notably the Aquino and Lopez clans. Foreign investors and some domestic firms were also forced to pay 10–25 percent of their equity to Marcos or his associates as an extortion fee to guarantee necessary government permits. While the landed elite continued to dominate nonstate sectors of Filipino society, they became wholly dependent on the good graces of the Marcos regime for their continued prosperity. If one wanted cheap credit, an import license, tax incentives, or monopoly privileges, one had to go through the state to get them and one had to remain loyal to the Marcos regime to keep them. The highly personalistic dictatorship also funneled the bulk of the political and economic benefits to the president, his family, and his allies. Marcos created monopolies to control the export of coconuts and sugar, and placed these monopolies under the control of friends and family members. He then used them to generate revenue to fill the coffers of the regime. Many members of the Marcos-Romualdez family, for example, were given positions within the state or state-controlled corporations, which increased in number from sixty-five in 1970 to more that three hundred in 1985. Billions of dollars in foreign aid and loans were directed to the private bank accounts of the president, his wife Imelda, and their allies. Government financial institutions were also raided and the country's gold reserves mysteriously evaporated.[18]

In 1978 Marcos reinstated some elections as part of a policy of "normalization," and in early 1981 he lifted martial law. Press freedoms were increased and some opposition demonstrations were tolerated. However, the formal ending of martial law "made no difference in the power of the regime over the people. It did not even affect the distribution of power within ruling circles."[19] In fact, at the same time that Marcos lifted martial law, he signed an order providing that all previous decrees and instructions by which he ruled under martial law would remain in force. Thus, although habeas corpus was formally restored (except in Mindanao), the president could still detain anyone in the name of "public safety" or "security of the state"; individuals deemed to be political offenders could be robbed of their citizenship or property, or sentenced to death or life in prison; Marcos maintained concurrent legislative authority with the reconstituted National Assembly; the president continued to control the media and the Commission on Elections, which determined voter lists and balloting; and elections were rigged to ensure continued control over the reigns of government. In short, liberalization meant an easing of repression, not a transition to democracy.[20]

EFFECTS ON THE COMMUNIST INSURGENCY

The exclusive nature of political institutions under Marcos contributed to the communist insurgency in several ways. First, the system facilitated counterproductive development and borrowing practices, as well as the plundering of the environment, thereby increasing the incentives to rebel. As we saw above and in chapter 3, Marcos's grip on the state allowed him to place the control of natural resources in the hands of a relative few closely aligned with his regime. Exclusive institutions also permitted the flawed capital-intensive, import-substituting development strategy to persist to the detriment of more broad-based industrial or agricultural development. The strategy subsidized the activities of entrepreneurs from wealthy landed families who had invested heavily in the manufacture of consumer goods largely aimed at those same families. Exclusive institutions also encouraged Marcos's borrowing spree. Since the regime was able to capture the short-term benefits from new loans and "invest" the money in any way Marcos saw fit, while passing the long-term costs on to politically important segments of society, there was little incentive for the state to be fiscally responsible. The inability of the majority of Filipinos to thwart or alter the course of development had disastrous implications: profits from export agriculture, logging, and manufacturing filled the bank accounts of state elites and the wealthy, while the environment was severely degraded, millions were displaced and impoverished, and little of the revenue was redistributed throughout society.[21]

Second, exclusive institutions left the dispossessed little option but to support the communist rebels if they hoped to have any chance of improving their economic and physical security. If martial law had not been imposed and the country's institutions had remained at least quasi-democratic, some of the government's opponents would undoubtedly have been co-opted by the political system. Yet in the absence of more inclusive institutions, poor Filipinos had few nonviolent self-help options. The following example of political impotence was typical. In 1975 Marcopper, a giant copper-mining concession in Marinduque Province given to Marcos's cronies, Jose Campos and Rolando Gapud, began dumping highly toxic mine trailings into Calacan Bay. The trailings threatened marine life and the livelihood of thousands of fishermen. Nevertheless, protests made by the fishermen to the National Pollution Control Commission were ignored because of the close connections between Marcopper and the Marcos government.[22]

In contrast to this exclusion, the CPP-NPA promised to create a social system that worked for the poor. As Wurfel notes, "just as Marcos ['s] policies were creating more hardship at the mass level, the only possible organizational channels to mobilize discontent were underground or disguised . . . Communist Party leadership provided an alternative model of development to millions of Filipinos who saw no livelihood, nor personal security, nor hope in the economic and political institutions spawned by Marcos."[23] Consequently, by the late 1970s, a growing number of poor Filipinos turned away from peaceful alternatives and toward the extra-institutional alternative offered by the CPP-NPA. While traveling with the NPA, one journalist observed this dynamic in action: "Frustrated by their defeats through legal methods, many peasants [in Mindanao] supported the rebels who came to their barrios promising 'land for the landless.' "[24] Similarly the former Philippine Senator Jose Diokno, chairman of the Civil Liberties Union of the Philippines, noted in 1981 that "more and more people are becoming convinced that short of an act of God, there is no way to get Marcos out and restore freedom in the country. This hopelessness has made the Communist Party of the Philippines the best organized party politically outside the government."[25] And in 1983 the former Philippine president Diosdado Macapagal concluded: "Ironically, the martial government was imposed to save the country from 1,500 Communist rebels. But after a decade they're much stronger. Now they're all over the country. It's precisely this regime that has brought danger to the country."[26]

The leadership of the CPP-NPA was sensitive to the important permissive role exclusive institutions played in the party's success. In a 1972 policy statement the party claimed that the imposition of martial law had made the situation "far more favorable to the revolutionary movement than ever before."[27] And communist literature in the early 1980s suggested that the biggest fear of the CPP-NPA was *not* losing to Marcos but rather that a liberal government would replace Marcos and lessen the appeal of violent revolution.[28] This fear was realized, of course, in 1986.

Institutional Change in the Post–Marcos Era

The importance of institutional exclusivity to the success of the CPP-NPA is perhaps best demonstrated by the effect the return to more inclusive institutions had on the insurgency. Indeed, as the country's institutions became more democratic, widespread support for the communist rebels evaporated.

INSTITUTIONS AFTER MARCOS

In 1986 Marcos was driven from office by Corazon Aquino's famous "people power" revolution. The chain of events leading up to his demise began in 1981. In that year Marcos lifted martial law and then proceeded to hold a rigged election to keep himself in office. In 1983 Benigno Aquino, who had been allowed to go into exile in 1980, attempted to return to the Philippines to challenge Marcos directly. Upon his arrival in Manila security forces working for General Fabian Ver, Marcos's trusted chief of staff, assassinated him. Attempts by Marcos to blame the murder on the Communists failed. Hundreds of thousands of Filipinos took to the streets in protest, and the United States and the Catholic Church began to demand an end to his reign. Marcos ignored his plummeting support and failing health, and attempted to cling to office by calling a snap election in February 1986. In the lead-up to the election, the opposition managed to form a united front around Corazon Aquino, Benigno's widow, as their candidate. Once again, Marcos used fraud to claim victory, but the fraud was so blatant that Aquino announced that she was the true winner of the election. Defense Minister Juan Ponce Enrile and Lt. Gen. Fidel Ramos then defected to the Aquino camp, and their supporters seized control of military headquarters. Marcos ordered military units to stop the mutiny, but their efforts were blockaded by hundreds of thousands of unarmed civilians. Marcos attempted to have himself inaugurated, but he no longer enjoyed the support of the armed forces and police. Under American pressure he finally admitted defeat and fled the country.[29]

Shortly after taking power from Marcos, Aquino oversaw the construction of a new constitution establishing democratic procedures and civil liberties. The constitution was overwhelmingly approved in February 1987, and by 1988 all major politicians in the country were popularly elected.[30] Still, Aquino's rise to power simply marked the beginning of the transition to more inclusive institutions. Throughout the early part of her term in office, Aquino faced threats from Marcos loyalists and other elites who stood to lose wealth and power if significant socioeconomic reforms were implemented. Aquino also confronted the constant threat of military revolt, especially from Enrile and the Reform the Armed Forces Movement, who saw themselves as the true victors in the anti-Marcos struggle and only reluctantly supported the new president. Indeed, Enrile secretly backed loyalist ambitions in an attempt to build his own power base, and pro-Marcos politicians and military officers staged numerous coup attempts intended to block each step in the new electoral constitutional system. Even after a RAM-supported coup attempt by Marcos loyalists in November 1986 resulted in Enrile's removal as defense minister, his influence continued to hold sway over some factions in the armed forces, and the threat of military revolt remained. All told, by the end of 1989 at least six major coup attempts had been launched against Aquino.[31]

Fending off these threats required Aquino to provide concessions to both the elite and military communities. During her campaign against Marcos, Aquino concentrated on attacking personal corruption and calling for a return to democracy; large-scale socioeconomic changes were not emphasized. However, after a group of farmers demanding land redistribution were gunned down by marines near Malacanang Palace in January 1987, and a national poll suggested that two-thirds of the public wanted the president to use her decree powers to institute land reform prior to the convening of the new Congress, Aquino put forth a draft proposal for significant land reform. Despite calls by the World Bank and the Catholic Bishops' Conference to strengthen the proposal, conservative politicians and landowners vehemently attacked the land reform plan. It was eventually watered down and then sent to Congress, which further eroded its provisions before passing it in 1988.[32] Aquino also chose not to challenge the country's inefficient industries, bowing to huge opposition from the beneficiaries of Marcos-era crony capitalism. These interests strongly opposed breaking up monopolies and state-run firms, and lobbied against lifting protectionist barriers shielding inefficient import-substituting industries from international competition. Consequently, reforms aimed at increasing privatization and trade liberalization were slowed and often circumvented until an emerging balance of payments crisis in 1990 forced the government to give in to pressure from the IMF and renew its commitment to structural adjustment.[33]

Aquino was also forced to make concessions to the military. The military budget was increased in October 1986 in order to guarantee the loyalty of Ramos, whom the president appointed chief of staff of the armed forces. Under military pressure Aquino backed off her pledge to reach a negotiated peace with the CPP-NPA. During her presidential campaign Aquino promised to release political prisoners and she followed through with this promise, releasing a number of top CPP officials, most notably the CPP-founder José Sison. In addition, in late 1986 Aquino initiated cease-fire negotiations with the CPP-NPA—which was represented at the talks by the National Democratic Front—over the strong opposition of the military. The Communists were highly suspicious of the new government, however, and the government was unwilling to compromise on a number of key communist demands, including the removal of American military bases. After a short cease-fire, talks broke down. Aquino then caved in to military demands to abandon peace gestures and allowed the armed forces to go on the offensive against the Communists. She also authorized the formation of military-backed anticommunist vigilante groups to replace the Civilian Home Defense Forces, which were technically disbanded by the new constitution. Aquino also purged several cabinet members considered "leftist" by the armed forces and stalled efforts to investigate human rights abuses by the military.

These efforts were probably essential to the new president's survival. Ramos became defense minister after Enrile's dismissal and remained Aquino's key ally during the tumultuous period of 1987–90. This guaranteed that the military would not stand united against Aquino's government. After the last coup attempt in December 1989, democracy appeared to turn the corner in the Philippines. A series of arrests cut into the ranks of rebellious leadership within the armed forces, and the violent nature of the 1989 coup left the military with little stomach to initiate another round of internal conflict.[34]

Aquino's concessions to elites and the military had an ironic effect on the process of democratic consolidation. On the one hand, the concessions made the government less inclusive than many had initially hoped. The broad base that made up the people power revolution was not institutionalized. Instead, the political party structure that emerged mirrored the pre–martial law, elite-controlled system. It was estimated that more than 80 percent of the congressmen elected in 1987 belonged to the powerful families long at the center of Filipino politics.[35] On the other hand, these concessions were probably a necessary evil, since united opposition from the economic oligarchy and the military would have been too much for the vulnerable president to survive. Avoiding drastic socioeconomic reform was essential to placate landed and business elites, and concessions to the military were required to keep the bulk of the armed forces in the president's camp. As Mark Thompson explains, "The compromises Aquino made adversely affected the quality of democracy being restored in the Philippines, but it gave her the breathing space needed to seek democratic consolidation slowly through electoral means."[36]

Consequently, by the time Aquino left office, the legitimacy of democracy in the eyes of the social elite and military had been solidified, opponents increasingly relied on electoral strategies for change rather than violence, the military assumed a neutral stance in politics, and election fraud was largely eliminated (at least at the national level). The election of Ramos to the presidency in May 1992 and the congressional elections that same year were widely seen as a sign that democracy had become consolidated in the Philippines. Although Ramos won with less than 24 percent of the vote, five of his six major opponents conceded defeat, and he was successful in developing a working relationship with both houses of Congress. Moreover, the remaining military troublemakers agreed to surrender to Ramos in exchange for amnesty.[37]

Even as democracy was taking hold, however, the material conditions of most poor Filipinos did not substantially improve, especially under Aquino.[38] Demographic and environmental pressures remained significant. Population growth slowed, but the average annual rate was still 2.3 percent between 1980 and 1990 (see Table 3.2). Land pressures also remained. Aquino took some steps to limit deforestation, including a ban on log exports in 1986 (with the exception of exports from tree plantations), efforts to curtail illegal logging, and an increased commitment to reforestation. But reforestation efforts suffered from limited financial resources, and the Department of Environment and Natural Resources admitted that it lacked the funding necessary to enforce the logging ban. As a result, forest destruction was still estimated to be 100,000 ha per year in 1991.[39] Furthermore, since no significant efforts at land redistribution or radical changes in development were adopted, structural land scarcity remained a serious problem.

The economy also failed to thrive through much of Aquino's tenure. The new president was saddled with an inefficient and highly protected industrial base with a strong anti-export bias, a bloated public sector, local governments in financial disarray, and $30 billion in debt left over from the Marcos years. The need to service the huge debt led to a diversion of resources away from much needed infrastructural development and social services. In 1989, for example, 43.9 percent of the national budget was devoted to debt service compared to 38.7 percent for economic and social services.[40] Economic growth was also unsteady. Between 1986 and 1988 the GNP grew by an annual clip of almost 5 percent. But GNP growth slipped to 2 percent in 1990, before falling to 1 percent in 1991 and 1.6 percent in 1992, in part a result of short-term dislocations from the restrictive macroeconomic adjustment program adopted at the behest of the IMF.[41]

When Ramos won the presidency in 1992, the new administration recognized the need to liberalize the economy. With broad support among the military, little owed to traditional elites, and skillful alliance building, Ramos undertook economic reforms. These reforms were designed to reduce the influence of the major oligarchic families, dismantle monopolies and cartels, substantially reduce protectionist barriers to trade and encourage export-based manufacturing, liberalize control over foreign exchange and foreign investment, reform the tax system and prosecute tax evaders to raise government revenue, encourage family planning (despite strong opposition from the Catholic Church), and further poverty reduction through infrastructural development and economic growth. The government also took steps, albeit small, to put in place safety nets for vulnerable groups, including measures to increase access to health, nutrition, education, and shelter services to hedge against the inevitable hardships associated with additional structural adjustment.

Ramos's government reaped the benefits of these reforms—as well as the eventual payoffs from the previous decade of haphazard stabilization and structural adjustment efforts—in the form of accelerating economic growth. Annual growth in the GNP was 2.1 percent in 1993, 5.3 percent in 1994, 5.5 percent in 1995, and 6.9 percent in 1996. Unlike previous waves of growth, this one emerged from investment and expansion in the productive capacity of the economy rather than from external debt and aid. And since economic growth outpaced the annual rate of population increase, even after the onset of the Asian financial crisis in 1997, the poor made modest strides under Ramos. Efforts to promote major infrastructural projects and slow population growth and environmental degradation, however, were often dwarfed by the magnitude of the challenges being addressed. Consequently, the problems of the poor did not vanish. Extreme inequality persisted and more than half of all Filipinos remained below the poverty line.[42]

INSTITUTIONAL INCLUSIVITY AND DESTRUCTION OF THE CPP

Despite their emergence as a potent political force, the Communists were largely bystanders during the events that swept Marcos from power. The proximate source of this marginalization was the Communist Party's decision to boycott the snap presidential election of 1986. The deeper cause, however, was the inability of the Communists and their various front organizations to garner widespread support from the urban middle class and the church. These groups increasingly despised Marcos but were also fearful of communism and weary of escalating violence in the countryside. As a result, the CPP-NPA, which many inside and outside the party believed to be on the brink of political and military success, found themselves left out in the cold. Over the next decade the Communists saw their support and influence largely blown away by the winds of democratic change.[43] Indeed, two years before Marcos fled the country, a government prosecutor noted in an interview, "If we had a president we could follow, the Communists would not stand a chance."[44] This prediction proved to be right on the mark.

Despite only slight material improvements for the poor, the move toward greater institutional inclusivity still sapped the strength out of the communist movement. As early as 1988 the U.S. assistant secretary of defense Richard Armitage reversed his pessimistic assessment made only a few years earlier and argued that the CPP-NPA were losing strength because of political changes, "the most noteworthy of which is the enfranchisement of the Filipino people and the election of president Aquino and the inauguration of constitutional government."[45] And in 1991 Aquino herself declared: "The restoration of democracy has destroyed the moral pretensions of the [communist] insurgency, and left only its hardened elements clinging to its dying branches."[46]

The effect that democratic institutions had on the insurgency is best illustrated by the steep declines in both NPA fighting forces and in the CPP's mass base. According to government estimates, the number of NPA fighters declined from more than twenty-five thousand in 1988 to fewer than twelve thousand by the end of 1992. The number again fell to around eighty-four hundred by the end of 1993 and then to around seven thousand in 1995.[47] Documents from the Executive Committee of the Party's Central Committee also noted a significant erosion of the Communists' mass base:

> From 1987 to 1990, Party membership decreased by 15 percent, the total number of barrios under its coverage by 16 percent, the total number of members of the people's army by 28 percent, and the total membership in the rural mass organizations by 60 percent. The army's rifles increased in number, but the number added each year went down—to the same proportion as in 1976–78. A big number of cadres at the provincial, front and district levels were lost due to arrest, death, or demoralization.[48]

By the time Aquino left office the Communists were even losing ground in such former strongholds as northern Luzon, Samar, Negros, and throughout Mindanao.[49] According to estimates by the AFP, the number of NPA fronts declined from seventy-one to fifty-

seven between 1988 and 1991, an estimate the insurgents did not dispute.[50] The erosion of communist support only accelerated under
Ramos. In 1993 alone the government estimated that the number of
areas under CPP-NPA control decreased by 52 percent, declining still
further in the following years. By 1995 the government estimated that
the CPA-NPA controlled or influenced only about 2.6 percent of all
barangays.[51]

Other indicators also revealed the party's demise. One was the party's decision in 1988 to seek financial assistance and arms from abroad,
something they had resisted doing since the early days of the insurgency. The end of the Cold War, however, made such assistance difficult to secure. The insurgents were also hurt by improved government
tactics, including better military coordination and intelligence gather-
ing, the redeployment of elite forces to the countryside that had previously been assigned to guard Manila, and the arrests of several top
party leaders.[52]

Most substantially the CPP began to implode at the top. The loss of
support after Aquino's election was devastating to the party's leadership. Paranoid about government infiltration, CPP ideologues instigated a series of bloody purges, including purges of party ranks in
Mindanao in 1985–87 and again in Southern Tagalog in 1988–89, killing
more than one thousand cadres, activists, and guerrillas. In the early
1990s splits also emerged between hard-line CPP leaders in exile in the
Netherlands, led by Sison, who demanded a commitment to a "pro-
tracted people's war," and more pragmatic factions on the ground in
the Philippines, including some who sought to abandon rebellion altogether in favor of legal and electoral struggle. By 1993 the rift within
the CPP had "reached a point of no return" as a result of its "mix of
strategic, ideological and personal hostility." Discontent among party
cadres was "very high" and guerrilla units were "very demoralized."[53]

Why did the move toward democracy have such a dramatic effect
even though material conditions did not improve significantly? Undoubtedly one important factor, at least initially, was Aquino's personal popularity. In late 1986, 87 percent of Filipinos expressed their
approval of Aquino, and in 1987 the new constitution, which was
largely seen as a referendum on Aquino's administration, was approved by 75 percent of the 22 million people who voted. Moreover,
the constitution was overwhelmingly affirmed *even in CPP-NPA strongholds*, demonstrating the deep appeal of the new government.[54]

Second, and more fundamental, the confusion created by the new
government and the allure of competing in fair elections created serious divisions within the CPP-NPA. As a CPP statement discussing the
immediate aftermath of Marcos's defeat revealed, there was an "inde-

cisiveness brought about by internal debates regarding the new regime and the democratic possibilities it offered."[55] Aquino's rise to power came as a total shock to the CPP. In January 1985 the NDF's twelve-point program, a document meant to map the Communists' road to power, stated that "armed struggle is the primary form of struggle that we must wage. This is starkly clear, especially in the face of the fascist dictatorship." Yet in 1986 the CPP was forced to concede that "the Marcos fascist regime has been overthrown . . . his fall hastened by direct popular struggle of the Filipino people."[56] This declaration was ironic given the Communists' absence from direct involvement in the events that brought Marcos down owing to the party's calamitous decision to boycott the 1986 presidential election. The CPP's own newspaper, *Ang Bayan*, candidly admitted as much in May 1986:

> For more than 17 of the 20 years that the Marcos puppet regime was in power, the Communist Party of the Philippines . . . played a leading role in our people's anti-fascist, anti-imperialist and anti-feudal struggle. In all those 17 years, the Party and the revolutionary forces that it leads contributed tremendously to exposing, isolating and weakening the regime, leading to its eventual downfall. Yet, where the people saw in the February 7 snap election a chance to deliver a crippling blow on the Marcos regime, a memorandum by the Executive Committee of the Party Central Committee (EC-CC) saw it merely as a "noisy and empty political battle" among factions of the ruling classes. And when the aroused and militant moved spontaneously but resolutely to oust the hated regime last February 22–25, the Party and its forces were not there to lead them. In large measure the Party and its forces were on the sidelines, unable to lead or influence the hundreds of thousands of people who moved with amazing speed and decisiveness to overthrow the regime.[57]

The Communists thus found themselves excluded from the new government, and their hopes of forging greater alliances with moderate political forces were ended. The fall of Marcos cost the CPP and its front organizations any hope of support from middle-class groups and the church. These groups abandoned their flirtation with the Communists once Aquino provided the possibility for peaceful social change.[58] In the words of one communist front organizer shortly after Marcos's demise,

> We have found that some [moderate supporters] whom we thought we had convinced to rationally understand the structural problems were in fact only anti-Marcos and anti-military. We had tried to teach them that the problems were not caused by evil men but by an unjust system. . . . [T]he victory of Cory is a real dilemma for us.[59]

The crisis that emerged within the CPP-NPA in 1986–87 was significant. Both the CPP chairman Rodolfo Salas and the head of the NPA Juanito Rivera were replaced. And although the official party view remained that the class composition of the Aquino government was no different from Marcos's, a contentious debate emerged within the CPP and its affiliated organizations as to the best way to further their revolutionary goals. Many within the party came to see the traditional primacy of armed struggle over political struggle as too narrow a strategy.[60] As noted above, in December 1986 the CPP-NPA yielded to public pressure and calls from within the movement and agreed to participate in cease-fire negotiations. When cease-fire talks collapsed in late January 1987, the core of the party redoubled its efforts to inflame insurgency in the countryside, seeking to take advantage of Aquino's apparently tenuous grip on power. Yet others close to the party chose to pursue nonviolent means of struggle. The phrase "democratic space" became popular among those who wished to explore alternative avenues for advancing the communist agenda.[61] In preparation for the May 1987 congressional election, activists close to the CPP formed the Alliance for New Politics, the first leftist party to participate in elections in forty years. The largest component of the Alliance for New Politics was the Partido ng Bayan, whose candidates for office included some of the most prominent Communists released from prison, including Bernabe Buscayno (Commander Dante). Nevertheless, pro-Aquino candidates swept the polls and leftist politicians received limited support from the core of the CPP.[62]

This defeat convinced many fence sitters within the Communist Party to abandon the electoral approach and return to the hills to fight.[63] The revised version of the CPP's party program, "Onward to Victory: Program for a People's Democratic Revolution, 1987," stated:

> In waging revolution, the Party wields armed struggle and the united front as its powerful weapons. . . . It wages all forms of struggle but armed struggle is the principal form . . . The Party adheres to the principle of encircling the cities from the countryside. It should never give up or prejudice the depth in strength of the people's army.[64]

Between 1987 and 1990 orthodoxy reasserted itself within the CPP-NPA. And as Aquino became more conservative to placate elite and military interests, and as military and vigilante abuses resumed, support for the Communists among rural residents briefly increased.[65] This bump in support proved short-lived. By the time Ramos became president, the party was permanently torn into openly warring camps, some advocating violence and others calling for political strategies.[66] Ramos sought to exploit these divisions by adopting a series of accommodationist and inclusive policies, including the legalization of the CPP, amnesty for "rebel returnees," and extensive negotiations with the NDF. By 1993 internal feuds, defections, and a series of government military actions relegated the communist rebels to a marginal force in all but a few outlying provinces.[67]

A final source of declining support for the CPP-NPA was the legitimacy of democratic institutions in the eyes of the populace. Even after economic growth slumped and Aquino's approval ratings declined, faith in democracy remained steady. Opinion polls conducted in the early 1990s showed that public support for persons and institutions that behaved democratically—namely, Aquino, Ramos, and Congress—was high. In contrast, individuals considered to be disloyal opponents of democracy, such as Aquino's vice president Salvador H. Laurel, Imelda Marcos, Gregorio Honasan (the RAM instigator of coup attempts in 1987 and 1989), and CPP head Sison, consistently received negative ratings.[68] Thus, even if, in practice, the government was not sufficiently responsive to the will of the masses, there was a general perception that a free press, free speech, and free and fair elections opened up the formulation and implementation of state policies to considerably more public input than was the case under Marcos.[69]

As institutions gradually became more inclusive, the poor increasingly saw nonviolent political action as a preferable alternative to joining the CPP-NPA. The appeal of nonviolent struggle was apparent as early as 1986 when so many ignored the CPP's call to boycott the presidential elections that led to Marcos's downfall. In May 1986 the Central Committee's Political Bureau was forced to acknowledge that a "large . . . part of our own mass base did not heed the boycott call and voted for the opposition."[70] Aquino's success in holding off early challenges to democracy only furthered the decline in popular support for the Communists. As the CPP party secretary for the southeast region of Mindanao observed in 1987, "Many people are asking us, 'Why are you fighting Cory?' It's hard to explain."[71] Another NPA organizer based in a northeast Quezon fishing village admitted in 1988 that "the people are no longer convinced that armed struggle is the way to end their poverty."[72]

Observers outside the CPP also noted the trends. An editorial in the *Manila Chronicle* in 1989 stated: "The departure of the dictator seems to have changed the entire picture and cut short the people's deadly flirtation with violent revolution." And in the same year a Western defense analyst declared: "Now the frail Madonna of Aquino is far more palatable to Filipinos than Marxism."[73] The siphoning effect of inclusive institutions on potential communist supporters became even more pronounced as the economy rebounded and democracy consolidated under Ramos.[74]

As the CPP-NPA became more and more desperate they resorted to actions that alienated their base. Splits within the party reduced centralized control, and radicalized elements increasingly resorted to indiscriminate main force and Sparrow Unit attacks that harmed innocent civilians. This frightened the party's supporters among the poor and crystallized the notion among moderate political forces that the Communists were dangerous. As one Western diplomat put it in 1992, "Economic conditions have not improved much under Corey. But there is a definite disenchantment with the violent excesses of the insurgents." In contrast, "the military has become more professional."[75] Resentment within the party's mass base also increased as financial problems forced the Communists to impose taxes on residents in the areas under their control.[76] The Robin Hood image of the Communists as protectors and providers evaporated, as did their remaining popular support.

Intervening Variables in Kenya

Intervening variables also played crucial roles in explaining the onset and extent of ethnic conflict in Kenya in the 1990s. The high degree of groupness in the countryside helps to explain the successful mobilization of rural conflict groups by state elites. Groupness was not high throughout Kenya, however. In urban areas, in particular, ethnic and class ties created a set of crosscutting allegiances and interests. This helps to explain why Kenya did not descend into all-out civil war between 1991 and 1995, despite many commentators at the time predicting just such a descent. The nature of Kenya's political institutions also shaped the prospects for violence. For most of the 1990s Kenya's exclusive political institutions permitted Moi and his clique to exploit DES-induced grievances in order to pit ethnic groups against one another. But, by 2002, a number of constitutional changes had increased the inclusivity of the country's institutions, putting constraints on the ability of state elites to engineer another round of ethnic bloodshed.

High Groupness in Clash-Affected Areas

The nature of social identification in Kenya is critical to understanding the onset and extent of ethnic violence during the 1990s. In rural areas strong commitments to particular ethnic identities created opportunities for KANU elites to mobilize supporters and encourage them to terrorize their neighbors.

ETHNIC IDENTIFICATION IN KENYA

In rural parts of Kenya an individual's ethnic and clan membership remain key indicators of social identity.[77] During the period of the clashes, 40 indigenous ethnic groups, representing about 120 dialectically distinct subgroups belonging to the Bantu, Nilotic, Nilo-Hamitic, and Cushitic language groups, accounted for 98 percent of Kenya's population, with Asians, Arabs, and Europeans comprising the remaining 2 percent.[78] The relative numbers of Kenya's myriad ethnic groups range from several million to a few hundred. In 1989 the four largest groups were the Kikuyu, Luhya,[79] Luo, and the Kalenjin.[80] The sixteen largest ethnic groups, as indicated by the 1989 census, are listed in Table 5.1.

As Norman Miller and Rodger Yeager note, ethnic labels in Kenya tend to "denote formerly independent societies once characterized by common patterns of kinship, language, and custom, distinctive types of economic and political systems, and some sense of collective identity. Today, ethnicity is largely based on one's geographic origins, extended family ties, and cross-kinship affiliations."[81] More often than not contemporary ethnic categories represent social constructions rather than authentic names for, or primordial linkages between, African communities. Prior to colonization many individuals moved in and out of multiple identities; firm and fixed tribal affiliations were not the norm. Contemporary ethnic constructions emerged and "hardened" over the course of the twentieth century as a result of British colonial policies that redefined groups, linked these identities to particular territories, and apportioned benefits and political power based on ethnic categories. The system of "Native Reservations" established by the British, for example, played an important role in solidifying and policing previously fluid boundaries between specific named groups. As discussed in chapter 4, ethnic divisions and antagonisms were further magnified by British agricultural policies, which encouraged the migration of traditional farming communities (such as the Kikuyu) into the fertile hills of the Central Highlands and Rift Valley, much of which had been formerly occupied by nomadic pastoralists (Kalenjin and Maasai). British policies of indirect rule also elevated certain "natives" into positions of authority, destabilizing the more egalitarian and decentralized systems in place in most communities prior to colonization. This created a set of pro-British elites whose authority and actions reinforced ethnic classifications. In the post-independence period, ethnic identification was further reified by Kenyan elites from across the political spectrum who seized on ethnic symbols and rhetoric to garner political support. Finally, the ethnic patronage networks established by Kenyatta and Moi

TABLE 5.1
Ethnic Composition of Kenya's Population in 1989 (percent)

Ethnic Group	Kenya	Nairobi	Central Province	Coast Province	Eastern Province	North-eastern Province	Nyanza Province	Rift Valley Province	Western Province
Kikuyu	20.78	32.37	93.82	3.20	1.57	0.69	0.25	19.32	0.89
Luhya	14.38	16.46	1.23	3.03	0.18	0.32	2.59	9.73	86.16
Luo	12.38	18.49	0.88	4.54	0.22	0.43	57.89	3.89	2.57
Kalenjin	11.46	1.66	0.24	0.24	0.06	0.17	0.19	46.36	3.24
Kamba	11.42	13.50	1.79	6.94	53.91	0.71	0.10	0.92	0.12
Kisii	6.15	2.64	0.28	0.37	2.48	0.12	32.42	2.48	0.21
Meru	5.07	1.60	0.36	0.36	27.37	0.05	0.02	0.31	0.02
Miji-kenda	4.70	0.47	0.03	54.35	0.04	0.09	0.02	0.06	0.02
Maasai	1.76	0.37	0.08	0.20	0.04	0.02	0.01	7.33	0.13
Turkana	1.32	0.11	0.12	0.04	0.45	0.02	0.02	5.23	0.09
Embu	1.20	0.91	0.24	0.15	6.07	0.05	0.02	0.07	0.05
Taita	0.95	0.81	0.04	10.20	0.03	0.03	0.02	0.04	0.02
Teso	0.83	0.27	0.05	0.07	0.02	0.03	0.07	0.48	5.70
Kuria	0.52	0.18	0.02	0.06	0.01	0.02	2.81	0.15	0.07
Basuba	0.50	0.09	0.01	0.04	0.00	0.00	2.97	0.03	0.01
Sambura	0.50	0.12	0.05	0.03	0.35	0.02	0.00	1.82	0.01

Source: Republic of Kenya, Office of the Vice President, Ministry of Planning and National Development, *Kenya Population Census, 1989.*

helped to maintain and entrench notions of ethnic identification and link this identification to tangible rewards.[82]

EFFECTS ON ELITE MOBILIZATION EFFORTS

High levels of groupness greatly facilitated state-sponsored violence during the 1990s. As we saw in chapter 4, extreme DES in Rift Valley, Nyanza, and Western Provinces created latent yet volatile conflicts of interest over land between Kalenjins, Maasai, and other pastoralists, on the one hand, and Kikuyu, Kisii, Luhya, and Luo, on the other, that erupted into violence in the 1991–95 period. State elites were able to capitalize on the salience of ethnic identification and intergroup land competition, play the ethnic card, and incite individuals to violence in protection of their group's rights. State elites "asserted and invigorated the integrity of Kalenjin ethnicity, claiming that there was no such identity as Nandi, Tugen, or Kipsigis (all subgroups)—only Kalenjin. Moi also forged a wider collaboration with other minority groups through leaders willing to invoke minority ethnic identity or reformulate new identities to balance 'Kikuyu-Luo' multi-party advocates."[83] State elites systematically linked defense of ethnic rights with access to land. As a 1992 report by the Inter-Parties Task Force noted, there was "extensive indoctrination of the Kalenjin society by politicians who, in doing so, have exploited ethnic differences and greed for land within the community. Fear has been instilled in the [Kalenjin] community of possible persecution or retribution in the event of KANU losing power, and in particular President Moi."[84]

Groupness was also high in Coast Province. Here religious cleavages reinforced ethnic ones; the predominantly Muslim Digo and Duruma were pitted against the predominately Christian up-country groups.[85] A KHRC report on the 1997 clashes found that, although both attackers and victims were ethnically heterogeneous, "the developing polity has been regionally and religiously dual—predominantly Muslim *wapwani* (coastal people) versus predominantly Christian *wabara* (upcountry people), and this duality has remained unmediated by other potentially neutralizing forces."[86] Thus, the areas of the Coast hit by violence shared certain similarities with those in and around the Rift Valley: a high level of ethnic identification and the absence of significant cross-cutting affiliations and interests among the conflict groups. As in 1991–95 KANU elites seized on these ethnic cleavages, consistently invoking the "indigenous" rights of the Mijikenda peoples to control "their" land. As in the Rift Valley, majimbo rhetoric was deployed by KANU leaders seeking to reinforce ethnic divides and to fuel intergroup conflict by suggesting that the Mijikenda should drive off their neighbors and rule themselves. As the KHRC report noted, there was "unusually high ethno-nationalist consciousness in the area" which contributed to growing support for a majimbo system that would allow "the Digo and the coastal people in general to have more control over their socioeconomic destiny."[87]

 Overall, the nature of group identification and the degree of intergroup competition in violence-affected areas helps to explain why individual Kalenjins, Maasais, and Mijikenda were able to overcome the free-riding dilemmas normally associated with violent collective action. Residents in clash-affected areas tended to define their interests collectively in terms of the broader interests of their ethnic community.

They also received a host of benefits from group membership, not the least of which was privileged political and economic resources from the Moi regime. This made it easier for KANU elites to rally preexisting groups to engage in violence on the basis that minority rights and their own communities' privileged access to wealth and power would be in jeopardy if they failed to drive Kikuyus and other "foreigners" off "their" land. The promise of additional land and protection against political domination by larger ethnic groups, particularly the Kikuyu, also provided concrete benefits to be accrued if indigenous groups succeeded in chasing their rivals out of the Rift Valley and sections of Coast Province.[88]

Low Groupness in Urban Areas

When large-scale ethnic clashes first began in late 1991, a wide range of commentators predicted that Kenya would fall into the abyss of societywide ethnic war. The NCCK, for example, warned in 1992 that "the current situation . . . is heading towards a state of lawlessness and civil strife . . . Since violence begets violence it is likely that this civil strife will eventually get hold of the whole nation."[89] In a similar vein Nairobi's *Weekly Review* argued that,

> people in the affected areas live in fear and uncertainty, which has spread even to parts of the country that have not been affected by the fighting. If the violence continues much longer, it will be difficult to avert a national catastrophe similar to that which has affected many of Kenya's neighbors in Africa.[90]

Such dire warnings continued in 1993. The NEMU Report claimed that the violence "could well engulf the entire country before too long. . . . Unless the violence and insecurity is contained soon, Kenya as a nation runs the serious risk of instability and disintegration."[91] And *The Economist* declared: "Kenya, once a prosperous paradise amid the chaos of the Horn of Africa, is fast becoming a shambles."[92]

The greatest risk of a downward spiral to all-out civil war came in the 1991–95 period when violence in the countryside reached levels not seen since the Mau Mau rebellion against the British in the 1950s. How did Kenya manage to avoid this tragedy? To answer this question, a deeper inquiry into the nature of groupness in Kenya is required.

CROSSCUTTING TIES IN URBAN AREAS

While ethnicity tended to be the key form of collective identification in clash-affected areas, class identifications increasingly cut across ethnic ones in Kenya's major urban centers.[93] Groupness was therefore much lower in urban areas. This is not meant to suggest that ethnic affiliations were irrelevant to urbanites; they clearly still mattered. And as ethnic strife raged in the countryside, ethnic tensions also increased in Nairobi and other urban locations.[94] Urban areas nevertheless remained relatively quiet and key urban groups refused to join in an ethnic war against the Moi government.

During the period investigated here, Kenya's upper class included owners of large parcels of land and urban professionals, businessmen, physicians, high-ranking politicians and civil servants, and senior Kenyan associates in resident multinational corporations. One notch below was an emerging and increasingly cohesive urban middle class, including small businessmen, lesser government employees, nurses, teachers, artisans, mechanics, plant supervisors, and skilled factory workers. Kenya's upper and middle classes cut horizontally across ethnic lines. Kikuyus, the largest victims in the ethnic clashes, have long dominated Kenya's economy, making up the largest proportion of prominent Africans in business and agriculture. Along with Luos, Kikuyus also made up the largest segment of Kenya's growing middle class.[95]

EFFECTS ON THE LEVEL OF VIOLENCE

Despite the fact that their kinsmen were being brutalized in the countryside, Kikuyu and Luo members of the upper and middle classes were, and remain, wary of action that would polarize the entire country along ethnic lines. Their class-based interests were best served by pushing for political reform that would increase their access to the state on policy matters, not by escalating ethnic violence.[96] Political reform held out the promise that Kikuyu and Luo members of the middle class would have greater access to state funds, civil service positions, and the like, whereas violence would only bring destruction. Kikuyu and Luo members of the business community also shared this desire for political reform. Although they had become increasingly critical of government corruption and Moi's pro-Kalenjin bias, their heavy dependence on government capital, contracts, and services gave them a huge stake in seeing a *peaceful* transition away from authoritarian rule rather than ethnic war.[97] Consequently, as David Throup and Charles Hornsby note, during the widespread rural violence of the early 1990s "Kikuyu did little but complain. Their leaders remained too well-educated, wealthy, and with too much to lose to support 'direct action' or open conflict."[98] These sentiments were echoed at the time of the Rift Valley clashes by Gibson Kamau Kuria, a Kikuyu lawyer and human rights leader:

The Kikuyus and the Luos are most involved in the market economy, and they were at the forefront of the struggle for independence, as well as in the move toward democracy. They understand that the problem is one of bad government and corrupt economics, not bad tribes. Once you conceptualize the problem as dealing with bad governance, then you know the solution lies in good government, human rights, and sound economic management, not tribal warfare.[99]

A growing number of civil society groups also became intertwined with class affiliations during this period. Prior to the clashes the fairly advanced state of capitalism in Kenya produced a civil society that was strong relative to many of the country's sub-Saharan African neighbors.[100] Prominent civil society groups included churches, legal associations, university students, and private voluntary organizations advocating environmental and development causes, women's interests, and civil liberties. These groups were, and remain, the leading domestic proponents of political reform. Although the country's larger ethnic clusters were strongly represented in these groups, the issues they raised were class-based rather than communal. Civil society groups demanded sweeping political change, not a reorientation of ethnic favoritism.[101]

These overlapping and crosscutting group affiliations and interests in urban areas helped Kenya avoid all-out civil war. Most directly they served to dampen the possibility of ethnic violence in urban areas, without which full-scale escalation was unlikely. Less directly low urban groupness may have served as some brake on wider rural violence. Kenya's urbanites typically maintain substantial ties and influence over kinsmen in the countryside. Their strong preference for peaceful change over ethnic warfare may have therefore helped limit the expansion of rural conflict.[102]

Exclusive Institutions Under Moi

Patterns of social organization were not the only intervening factors that shaped and shoved violent events in Kenya. Variations in the inclusivity of the country's political institutions over time also had profound effects, accounting for the structural opportunities and constraints confronting KANU elites looking to instigate intergroup conflict.

FROM KENYATTA TO MOI

Throughout most of the postcolonial period, Kenya's governing institutions could be described as exclusive and authoritarian. Jomo Kenyatta, Kenya's first president, built a quasi-authoritarian state, with a strong executive, a relatively weak Parliament dominated by a single political party (KANU), and an intricate system of ethnically based patronage used to secure societal support for the regime. Under Daniel arap Moi, Kenyatta's successor, the country's institutions became even more exclusive, concentrating greater power in the executive and KANU. This exclusivity left KANU elites relatively unconstrained during the 1990s, when state-sponsored ethnic violence was used to keep the Moi regime in power.

The first Kenyan election in which Africans could vote was held in 1957, six years before the country gained its formal independence from Great Britain. Prior to this time all African members of the colonial Legislative Council had to be appointed by the governor. Between 1957 and 1960 a growing political schism emerged between many of Kenya's larger ethnic communities, who were confrontational toward the colonial establishment, and those communities that feared a transition to a government dominated by these groups. In early 1960 the British legalized the formation of political parties, signaling their intent to allow majoritarian rule and full independence. Two new political parties immediately appeared on the scene: KANU and KADU. KANU drew the bulk of its support from several ethnic communities—the Kamba, Kikuyu, Kisii, Luo, and Taita communities, as well as the Embu and Meru, two groups closely related to the Kikuyu—living in Central Province, Nyanza Province, and Nairobi. KADU, in contrast, represented a coalition of smaller, less economically advanced ethnic groups—including Kalenjins, Maasai, Mijikenda, Sambura, Turkana, and some sections of the Luhya community—concentrated in the Rift Valley, Coast Province, and the semiarid far north. In 1961 Kenyatta, whom colonial authorities suspected of engineering the Mau Mau revolt, was released from detention. As the country's most famous Kikuyu, Kenyatta quickly took over the leadership of KANU and led the party to victory in the May 1963 elections for the National Assembly. In December of that year, with Kenyatta at the helm, Kenya gained its full independence.[103]

At independence Kenya was governed by a constitution providing for a strong Parliament (the National Assembly) and a significant degree of regional authority. However, Kenyatta and KANU quickly succeeded in defeating KADU's attempt to fully institutionalize a majimbo system that would have ensured substantial regional autonomy. Kenyatta succeeded in concentrating political power in Nairobi by first curtailing and then abolishing regional administrations. A system of eight provinces—Central, Coast, Eastern, Nairobi, North-Eastern, Nyanza, Rift Valley, and Western—with forty-one districts was created, with provincial administrations and district commissioners made directly accountable to Kenyatta's office. In 1964 Kenyatta converted his position from prime minister to president.[104]

The political dominance of KANU also grew in the immediate aftermath of independence. As a consequence of mass defections from KADU to KANU, KADU was dissolved in December 1964, producing a de facto one-party state. This status was temporarily challenged when the prominent Luo politician Jaramogi Oginga Odinga resigned as vice president in 1966 to form the left-leaning KPU, but three years later the party was banned.[105]

Kenyatta also helped to establish another mainstay of Kenyan politics: ethnic patronage.[106] For most of his tenure Kenyatta's patronage system depended on two factors: the ability to allocate land to supporters and the relative strength of the Kenyan economy, with the latter factor driven by high commodity prices for Kenya's chief export crops (coffee, tea, and pyrethrum) and a booming tourist industry. Kenyatta used rural land grants and the redistribution of white settler land in the Rift Valley (through the Million Acre Scheme, for example), as well as other forms of patronage, such as access to civil service and parastatal jobs, low interest loans, government contracts, and urban land grants, to purchase loyalty among landless Kikuyus and to enlist support from Kikuyu elites. The president also made efforts to distribute patronage resources to leaders from nearly every other ethnic community, but Kikuyus accrued significantly more benefits than less populous ethnic groups. Kikuyus came to dominate business, commerce, the civil service, many high-prestige professions, and politics. As noted in chapter 4, many Kikuyus also migrated from their traditional homelands in Central Province and secured access to valuable land in Rift Valley and Coast Provinces during the Kenyatta era as a result of land grants and purchases facilitated by the government.[107]

In 1967 Moi, who had been a prominent figure with KADU before joining KANU, was made vice president. At the time Kenyatta and KANU were facing pressure from the KPU, and giving Moi the vice presidency was seen as a way of building broader support for KANU among the country's smaller ethnic communities.[108] This decision would prove decisive in determining the political trajectory of Kenya after Kenyatta's death in 1978.

Initially upon taking office Moi espoused a policy of *Nyayo* (or "footsteps") meant to signify his desire to stay the course established by Kenyatta. However, as Moi consolidated his power and became increasingly intolerant of opposition, the policy was transformed to mean "follow in *my* footsteps."[109] Those challenging KANU's one-party rule were accused of "treason," labeled "subversive," and targeted for detention, criminal prosecution, publication bans, and violent harassment. Freedoms of speech, press, and association were far from guaranteed, and Moi's regime tolerated criticism only when it served a particular short-term interest, such as deflecting international pressure.[110]

In the wake of a failed coup attempt in 1982, Moi made Kenya's institutions even more exclusive and intolerant of criticism. The coup attempt occurred in August 1982 and was initiated by members of the Kenyan Air Force.[111] Moi reacted to the coup threat by further insulating the executive from societal pressures and clamping down on dissent. Moi assumed that Kikuyu and Luo grievances lay behind the coup attempt.[112] As a result, the president became even more unwilling to trust the small number of Kikuyu advisers still in his government, and the high profile Luo politicians Jaramogi Oginga Odinga and his son, Raila, were detained.[113]

In addition to consolidating his personal authority, Moi also took steps to elevate the role that KANU played in controlling the political landscape. Under Kenyatta KANU had remained organizationally weak, because Kenyatta preferred to rule more directly through the complex patronage system he had constructed. This changed under Moi.[114] In 1982 a constitutional amendment was adopted, section 2(a), transforming Kenya from a de facto one-party state to a de jure one-party state in which only KANU members were allowed to serve in the National Assembly. Beginning in 1983 Moi also sought to transform KANU into a "mass political movement" wielding much greater political power.[115] He initiated a coercive campaign to substantially increase KANU membership, and by 1988 the number of KANU members had grown from several hundred thousand to eight million. The mass recruitment drive was achieved largely by depriving non-KANU members of certain basic rights, including access to rural produce markets, trading licenses, education, administrative services, and land. Recruitment was carried out by force in some cases and was assisted by provincial administrations and administration police.[116]

Simultaneously Moi made moves to increase and institutionalize party discipline. In the mid-1980s the KANU Disciplinary Committee was empowered to deal with a broad range of "misconduct," defined as "undermining" the presidency of KANU, the head of state, the party constitution, the country's constitution, the KANU government, or party activities. The committee was also given the authority to withdraw "the protection, rights, and privileges" of persons deemed by the committee to be an "offender" even if they were not members of KANU. The committee was disbanded in 1987, because Moi feared it would become too powerful. However, its demise was functionally irrelevant since KANU party branches continued to meet and expel or suspend any leader or private citizen they deemed "disloyal."[117]

Moi also succeeded in shifting the ethnic bias of the state away from Kikuyus. As Kenya's population ballooned and its economy slumped, there were fewer patronage resources to go around and benefits were increasingly targeted toward Kalenjins and other minorities aligned with the regime. Moreover, while Kikuyu dominance in the *economic* sphere still persisted, Moi took great strides to undercut the remaining political power of the Kikuyu community.[118] He initiated this campaign in 1980 by outlawing the Gikuyu, Embu, and Meru Association and other similar ethnic welfare associations.[119] After the 1982 coup attempt Moi moved to replace many senior Kikuyu officers with Kalenjins.[120] In 1984–85 the "Njonjo affair," in which a former Kikuyu minister of constitutional affairs was brought down, allowed Moi to purge the government of a leading Kikuyu politician and many of his supporters within KANU. And in 1989–90 the dismissal and then detention of Kenneth Matiba and Charles Rubia, two Kikuyu ministers and leading critics of the regime, served similar purposes.[121] Consequently, by the late 1980s, most power rested in the hands of the president and his party apparatus, and the state became dominated by elites from the Kalenjin and other minority tribes, with most senior positions in government, the military, security agencies, and state-owned enterprises held by Kalenjins and their allies.[122]

Not surprisingly the consolidation of presidential authority and KANU power, as well as the narrowing base of societal influence on the regime, led to a shrinking of the institutional relevance of the National Assembly.[123] In 1986 the National Assembly adopted a series of constitutional amendments transferring control of the civil service to the Office of the President and giving Moi the power to dismiss at will the attorney general, auditor general, and judges. The secret ballot in primary elections was also eliminated in favor of a queue voting system, in which individuals were forced to form specific lines to show their support for the candidate they preferred. This new system substantially increased the ability of the executive and KANU to coerce and rig election results and thereby keep MPs in line with the regime.[124]

Any residual independence of the National Assembly was effectively destroyed; for the first time in the country's history the influence of MPs was subordinated to the authority of the party, and only close associates of the president were put in leadership positions within the party.[125] The National Assembly became "an impotent talking shop"[126] and "a rubber stamp for advice received from an inner circle of trusted security officials and ethnic kinsmen."[127] All these changes had the effect of lessening even further the state's accountability to the majority of the Kenyan people. As one former MP lamented:

> Parliament is now treated as a livelihood and it's done for the money—if you're loyal, you can get the money. The *wananchi* [people] feel no one takes their complaints to parliament anymore—but they have so many complaints. Unemployment, education, high costs of living, harassment by the police, land—you hear it all the time. And you know the card-carrying members of KANU are a minority, so what is there for the majority non-card carrying [citizens]?[128]

THE RETURN OF MULTIPARTYISM

As we saw in chapter 4, domestic pressure combined with international pressure to force an eventual return to multipartyism. In early December 1991 KANU convened a leadership meeting chaired by Moi and agreed to remove section 2(a) from the constitution, thereby legalizing the existence of other parties. A week later the National Assembly codified this decision by passing the Constitution of Kenya (Amendment) Act No. 12 of 1991. In addition to removing section 2(a), this act repealed the sections of the constitution that gave effect to 2(a), such as those requiring that KANU nominate all candidates for Parliament.[129] Other modifications to the constitution were also adopted. In 1992 the constitution was changed to require that, to be elected, a Kenyan presidential candidate had to not only win a plurality of the nationwide vote but also to exceed 25 percent of the votes in at least five of the country's eight provinces. Moi designed this provision to sabotage the presidential prospects of popular Kikuyu and Luo opposition figures, who drew most of their support from their ethnic homelands.[130] Finally, the constitution was further amended to limit the president's tenure to two five-year terms. This term limit was to start with the 1992 elections; thus, although Moi had already served two terms, he would be eligible for two more.[131]

Despite these constitutional revisions, many aspects of Kenya's political system were incompatible with open and competitive politics and executive power remained largely unconstrained.[132] Central in this regard were several laws, most of them dating back to the Mau Mau rebellion, originally intended to restrict anticolonial political activity by Africans. As Stephen Ndegwa argues, upon the return to multipartyism, these laws "ensured an intimidated civic space and undermined the rights of individuals and groups to participate in the public arena and to effectively challenge incumbent officials. Left intact during the 1991 transition, these laws severely curtailed any democratizing effect that the return of multipartyism was expected to have."[133]

Numerous laws inhibited the formation of political parties and frustrated campaign meetings and other activities by opposition politicians. The Societies Act, for example, required that all organizations, including political parties, be formally registered, allowing the government to deny or delay the registration of groups it deemed threatening. The ability of opposition parties to raise funds, hold events, and mobilize supporters was also curtailed. The Public Collections Act was used to limit opposition fund-raising activities through biased licensing procedures. Under the Public Order Act, District Commissioners, who were appointees of the president, controlled the licenses required for all public meetings, including opposition political rallies and other campaign events, allowing the government to sharply limit opposition activities. The Chiefs' Authority Act also gave chiefs (the local representatives of the Provincial Administration) the ability to restrict opposition party meetings, even those held in private residences. Finally, the Preservation of Public Security Act, which allowed for the detention of persons deemed a risk to public security for indefinite periods, and other restrictions on movement were used to detain and restrain pro-reform politicians.[134]

Other laws set limits on freedom of speech. A section of the Kenyan penal code, for example, allowed the government to ban, censor, and impose stiff penalties on publications engaging in "seditious activities." The law was used to harass newspaper editors and writers, especially in the alternative press, and it had the effect of discouraging publishers, printers, and advertisers from supporting publications that were overly critical of Moi or KANU. Two other laws, the Outlying Districts Act and the Special District (Administration) Act, allowed the government to limit travel into, and movement within, areas declared to be security zones. These emergency laws also permitted warrantless searches, as well as emergency decrees and actions curtailing the rights of residents. This severely limited the ability of opposition parties to gain access to remote areas of the country, such as Northeastern Province, or areas, such as parts of Rift Valley Province, affected by ethnic clashes.[135]

There were also substantial institutionalized biases in elections and in the organization of the National Assembly. Although the constitution ostensibly created an independent Electoral Commission of Kenya (ECK) to organize multiparty elections, the president appointed all eleven commission members, giving Moi considerable power to shape election outcomes.[136] Indeed, the chair of the commission at the time of the 1992 elections, Justice Zacheus Chesoni, was on record as an opponent of multipartyism.[137] Electoral rules providing for a plurality system with single-member constituencies for the election of MPs also worked in KANU's favor. This system hurt opposition parties whose support was not sufficiently concentrated to capture a constituency seat, even though their supporters might have represented a majority over a wider area. Additionally, although the Kenyan constitution required that constituencies be drawn in roughly equal populations and the ECK was empowered to make efforts to create more equitable representation, in practice the system allowed for the manipulation of the size and boundaries of single-member constituencies by the ECK to maximize the chances of a KANU victory. The system overrepresented the members of Kenya's smallest and most spatially dispersed ethnic groups historically aligned with Moi's regime by giving them more constituencies than larger and more concentrated groups.[138] In late 1996 Moi reappointed seven of eleven ECK members, including Justice Chesoni, signaling Moi's willingness to ignore criticism by the opposition and continue to manipulate the process. The ECK established a new set of boundaries for 210 parliamentary constituencies, resulting in twenty-two additional seats. Although the seats were distributed across all of Kenya's provinces in a rough approximation of their relative populations, no new seats were given to Nairobi, the area with the greatest population growth. This omission was significant, since Nairobi was an opposition stronghold.[139]

Finally, KANU benefited from media bias that was both considerable and institutionalized. Radio broadcasts were heavily slanted in favor of KANU. This was of great importance considering that radio reaches nearly 90 percent of Kenya's population, half of which is illiterate. KANU also enjoyed biased coverage by the Kenya Broadcasting Company (KBC), the only source of local news for most Kenyans outside the capital. These media advantages gave KANU candidates a decisive advantage in framing election issues and tarring opposition candidates.[140]

The nature of Kenya's political institutions was central to the ability of Moi and KANU to remain in power from 1992 to 2002 despite the emergence of opposition parties. Residue from the authoritarian, one-party past created a landscape predisposed toward opposition factionalism. Because the power of the executive remained great, as did the executive's ability to dispense ethnic patronage, the stakes involved in elections were perceived by many opposition figures to be very high for whichever ethnic community secured the presidency. This encouraged a zero-sum competition among the powerful political leaders within each of the communities excluded from Moi's government, frustrating efforts to present a united front and contributing to the proliferation of political parties.[141]

Prior to the move to multipartyism, Jaramogi Oginga Odinga formed the Forum for the Restoration of Democracy (FORD), a nonpartisan group made up of churches, politicians, and lawyers interested in the legalization of opposition parties and fundamental constitutional reform. When section 2(a) of the constitution was removed, FORD reinvented itself as a political party. However, this transformation exposed personal rivalries and ethnic tensions that previously had been kept under wraps.[142] Fearing that a newly elected government would continue the Kenyatta/Moi precedent of favoring ethnic supporters, powerful politicians from different ethnic communities jockeyed for control within FORD in order to maximize the chances that their constituents would reap the benefits of electoral success. This generated ferocious infighting over who was to be FORD's presidential candidate in the 1992 election and divided the opposition into competing factions. Kenneth Matiba, a Kikuyu, attempted to wrestle the leadership of FORD away from the ageing Odinga, breaking FORD into two parties: FORD-Kenya led by Odinga and FORD-Asli led by Matiba. After the 1992 election the opposition fragmented even more, splitting up into at least six major factions.[143]

Opposition disunity, Moi's ability to nominate the ECK, gerrymandering, campaign support from provincial and district administrations aligned with KANU, a near KANU monopoly on radio and television coverage, better KANU funding, and various election "irregularities" all worked in tandem to keep Moi and KANU in power.[144] In the 1992 presidential election Odinga, Matiba, and Mwai Kibaki, the Kikuyu leader of the Democratic Party of Kenya (DP), split the opposition vote. As a result, Moi managed to win the presidency with only 36 percent of the vote; the three major opposition candidates combined earned 62 percent of the vote. Gerrymandering and the creation of legislative districts with vastly unequal numbers of voters also helped KANU to capture one hundred seats in Parliament (53 percent of the total) in 1992, despite winning less than 30 percent of the vote. The results were similar in 1997. There were fifteen presidential candidates on the ballot, although only Moi (KANU), Kibaki (DP), Raila Odinga (National Development Party [NDP]), Kijana Wamalwa (FORD-Kenya), and Charity Ngilu (Social Democratic Party) were serious contenders. Moi was reelected with 40.5 percent of the total national vote. The next two top vote getters were Kibaki and Odinga with 31 percent and 8.2 percent, respectively. As in 1992 Moi was the only candidate to obtain at least 25 percent of the vote in five provinces, with Kibaki being the only other candidate to garner at least 25 percent in more than one province. In the National Assembly KANU won 107 of the 210 National Assembly seats (51 percent of the total). After Moi appointed six additional MPs, KANU's edge had 113 seats to the combined total of 109 for the opposition.[145]

Despite losing a majority of the overall votes cast in the 1992 and 1997 presidential and parliamentary elections, Moi and KANU acted as if they had a powerful mandate to go about business as usual. As Joel Barkan observes:

> Moi and the KANU leadership refused to recognize the opposition as the legitimate, albeit fragmented, voice of a substantial majority of Kenyans. Instead of bargaining with its adversaries to establish a modus operandi for Kenyan politics in the multiparty era, the regime behaved as if nothing had changed while pursuing a three-pronged strategy of co-optation, intimidation, and divide and rule.[146]

STRUCTURAL OPPORTUNITIES FOR STATE EXPLOITATION

In chapter 2 I argued that exclusive institutions leave state elites with structural opportunities to instigate and organize intergroup violence to further their parochial interests. Kenya provides convincing empirical support for this argument. Throughout the 1990s Kenya's exclusive political institutions allowed KANU politicians to incite violence with impunity. The structure of Kenya's political institutions was such that access to the state on policy matters was ad hoc and highly contingent on personal relationships with key civil servants and politicians. To the extent that these relationships were determined by ethnic affiliations, excluded groups had few protections against the whims of ruling elites. Moreover, groups traditionally receiving the short end of the stick under Moi's rule did not see their influence increase in the multiparty era.[147] In the immediate aftermath of the 1992 and 1997 elections, Kikuyus and Luo were almost completely excluded from the cabinet and had very little direct influence over the president.[148] Many former Kikuyu and Luo members of KANU defected to the opposition, but KANU's opponents within the National Assembly "were unable to convert the existing structure into a significant additional legislative function or a substantive watchdog on the executive."[149]

The groups targeted in the 1991–95 and 1997 attacks were therefore institutionally impotent to constrain KANU elites bent on exploiting land grievances to advance their political agenda. When Kikuyu and Luo MPs *within* KANU complained about the majimbo campaign pushed by Kalenjin and Maasai leaders in the early 1990s, for example, they were largely ignored. Nor were members of targeted groups who had joined the opposition any more capable of preventing the president and other KANU elites from stirring up trouble.[150] When Kikuyu- and Luo-based opposition groups blamed the government for instigating ethnic strife in the Rift Valley, the Moi regime responded by stating that "the government will not spare anybody bent on spreading rumours aimed at causing fear and despondency among the peace loving *wananchi*. Every Kenyan should, therefore, ignore rumours."[151]

Toward Institutional Inclusivity and the End of the Moi Era

Important constraints on the executive were enacted just before the 1997 elections. These reforms were passed *after* the violence at the Coast and were too late to have much effect on the 1997 elections. But by the 2002 general elections, these constraints, in conjunction with some of the positive changes enacted in 1991–92, were pivotal in constraining KANU elites from instigating another round of ethnic clashes.

PRESSURES TO REFORM AND THE IPPG PACKAGE

In 1993 the IMF and the World Bank resumed assistance to Kenya, and most bilateral donors followed suit despite their misgivings about the stalled democratization process.[152] In 1997, however, pressure on the Moi government from international donors began to build again as a consequence of several factors. There was growing concern among donors over the regime's unwillingness to crack down on rampant corruption, which had been catapulted to front-page news by a series of high-profile scandals, including the infamous Goldenberg affair allegedly involving embezzlement by several high-ranking political and business figures.[153]

Donor concerns were also heightened by upward trends in political violence. In particular, the widely publicized attacks by Kenyan security forces against pro-reform protestors on July 7, 1997 (*Saba Saba* Day) encouraged the IMF to suspend its $220 million Enhanced Structural Adjustment program. The World Bank and bilateral donors followed the IMF's lead, bringing the total amount of suspended aid to more than $400 million. This inspired a substantial flight of short-term capital investment that devalued the Kenyan shilling by around 20 percent. The local business community and bilateral donors such as the United States stepped up the pressure on Moi to engage the constitutional reform movement led by the National Convention Assembly and its leadership group, the National Convention Executive Committee.[154] The determining factor, however, may have been the fallout from the August–November clashes at the Coast. Demands for reform were intensified by the public outcry over the clashes, as well as the economic turmoil inflicted on the tourism industry around Mombasa. "The attacks provoked a broad-based response by the opposition parties and civil society—including the Catholic Church and the (Anglican) Church of the Province of Kenya—as well as the donor community. All demanded reform, fearing that Kenya, like some of its neighbors, might descend into civil war."[155]

Moi finally agreed to initiate a dialogue on new constitutional changes. However, the president successfully framed the dialogue so as to make the best of a bad situation. Moi agreed to work toward a reform package on the condition that negotiations involve only MPs, *not* a national convention involving both MPs and representatives from the civil society groups affiliated with NCA/NCEC. This had the effect of driving a wedge between "official" opposition party leaders and "unofficial" ones in civil society. Although the latter group initiated the constitutional reform movement and were very critical of Moi's attempt to co-opt the process, many established opposition politicians jumped at the opportunity to improve their political stature. Most opposition parties asked the NCA/NCEC to step back and allow negotiations between MPs under the newly created Inter-Parties Parliamentary Group.[156]

Because of KANU's parliamentary majority and the exclusive role given to established KANU and opposition politicians (most with less ambitious reform agendas), the Moi regime was able to gain a degree of control over the IPPG process, derailing, or at least delaying, the more radical demands emanating from civil society groups. Still, the IPPG process managed to produce a series of legal, administrative, and constitutional changes that were passed by the Kenyan Parliament in November 1997. The IPPG reforms were composed of the Constitution of Kenya Amendment Bill, omnibus legislation repealing and amending a number of repressive laws, and legislation establishing the Constitution of Kenya Review Commission, charged with proposing further reforms after the election.

The IPPG reforms increased the inclusivity of the country's institutions by creating a number of new constraints on executive power.[157] Under the reform package the requirement that the president only appoint government ministers from MPs of the ruling party was repealed, and the president's unilateral authority to appoint twelve MPs was replaced with a system based on the proportional representation of the various parties in the National Assembly. The size of the ECK was also expanded from eleven to twenty-one members, with the additional ten members recommended by opposition parties, and the ECK's independence was enhanced. The ECK was empowered to be the sole determinant of almost all election-related decisions, with the exception of the president's continued ability to force elections by dissolving Parliament, and the commission was given the authority to monitor coverage of parties on state-owned media and to hire its own prosecutors to pursue election offenses.[158]

Several important legislative changes were also made. The Societies Act was amended to eliminate the registrar's discretion in determining which parties qualified for registration and a new requirement of reasonable cause to deny or rescind party registration was established. Registration decisions were also shortened to a maximum of 120 days and parties were allowed to appeal to the High Court for a decision within 90 days. The Preservation of Public Security Act was amended to prohibit detentions resulting from one's political beliefs and activities, and the Public Order Act and the Chiefs' Act were altered to ease licensing requirements and limit the ability of officials to interfere with the activities of political parties. Clauses of the penal code were also changed so that critical speech was no longer considered seditious. And the Outlying Districts Act and the Special District (Administration) Act were repealed, as was the Vagrancy Act, enhancing the right of movement in urban areas.

Lastly, the IPPG reform package included some important nonlegislative administrative agreements. To avoid state interference and partiality, Provincial Administration and other senior civil servants were to be restrained from participating in elections. Steps were taken to lessen media bias via an agreement that all political parties would be given equal coverage in state-owned media, especially radio and television, and the registration of pending private radio and television applications was ensured.[159]

Although they were widely viewed as a "minimal" set of reforms, the IPPG package created the possibility for a much more level political playing field and put fresh limits on the ability of the executive to manipulate the electoral process. This was not immediately evident. Because the reforms passed less than two months before the 1997 election, there was not enough time for the change to dramatically improve the opposition's prospects.[160] Moreover, as noted above, the opposition remained fragmented and this continued to work to Moi's and KANU's advantage.

STRUCTURAL CONSTRAINTS AND THE PEACEFUL END TO THE MOI ERA

The real effects of the 1997 reforms would not be clear until the 2002 election. Together with a number of positive changes enacted in 1991–92, the IPPG reforms placed a number of important restrictions on the regime that both assisted the opposition and limited the ability of KANU politicians to instigate additional interethnic violence.

According to the constitution, Moi had to step aside when his second term ended in 2002. Given the narrowing prospects for manipulating elections in the wake of the IPPG changes, it was vital that Moi pick a successor with appeal beyond the narrow group of minority communities that had long propped up his regime. In practice this meant making KANU more inclusive by courting Kikuyus and Luos. As the 2002 elections loomed, Moi initially turned his attention to the Luo community. This led to a series of engagements with Odinga's NDP culminating with the NDP's merger with KANU in March 2002. Nevertheless, Moi apparently felt that electoral success still depended on winning at least some of the Kikuyu vote. There had long been considerable speculation about who Moi would pick to run for office under the KANU banner, and Odinga clearly believed that the NDP-KANU merger gave him the inside track to being named Moi's successor.[161] Moi kept the decision to himself until July 2002 when he chose Uhuru Kenyatta, the son of Kenya's first president. Moi clearly sought to use the choice of Kenyatta to court long-alienated Kikuyu voters.[162] However, many Kikuyu perceived Kenyatta as too beholden to Moi and too likely to protect top Kalenjin politicians, including many of those responsible for ethnic clashes during the 1990s.[163] Ironically, the choice of Kenyatta not only failed to build KANU's support base, but it actually reduced that base by producing outrage among other ambitious KANU leaders. Kenyatta was widely viewed as an ineffective campaigner, illustrated by the fact that he had never won an election.[164] Fearing personal marginalization and a possible KANU defeat, several leading KANU politicians, including members of the NDP, bolted and formed the ad hoc Rainbow Alliance and later the Liberal Democratic Party (LDP), both led by Odinga.[165]

The other major opposition group, the National Alliance of Kenya (NAK), was formed five months before the 2002 elections. The NAK was a coalition of various parties, including Kibaki's DP, FORD-Kenya, the National Party of Kenya, and a number of other ethno-regional parties. On October 22 NAK and the LDP signed a memorandum of understanding creating the National Alliance Rainbow Coalition (NARC), putting forth Kibaki as the presidential candidate of the newly unified opposition.[166]

Thus, in the 2002 election, Kenya had two large trans-ethnic parties (KANU and NARC), in contrast to the two previous elections when KANU confronted several competing ethnically and regionally based opposition parties. NARC represented a fragile coalition comprised as it was by as many as fifteen parties.[167] Still, several factors helped to hold NARC together. First, "Kibaki proved to be the man of the hour—a credible reformer, experienced, not an ethnic chauvinist, and a self-declared one-term president. He was also a good coalition leader who did not try to overwhelm other coalition figures."[168] Second, sustained pressure was exerted on the opposition to stay unified by numerous segments of Kenyan society long frustrated with the fragmented nature of the opposition and eager to move into a post-Moi/post-KANU era.[169] Here an institutional feature, the 25 percent rule, may have played an important role. Initially the rule benefited Moi; as the only truly national candidate, Moi twice defeated a split opposition by being the only candidate to cross the 25 percent threshold in a sufficient number of provinces. As long as the opposition remained divided into factions competing for narrow ethnic constituencies, they would have a difficult time gaining enough cross-ethnic votes to secure a victory against KANU. Thus, over the long run, the 25 percent rule made a divided opposition untenable and probably encouraged unification. Unfortunately for Kenyan democracy, this lesson took two elections to learn.

The combination of Moi's immanent departure and a unified opposition obviously represented huge threats to KANU's monopoly on power. In the early 1990s, and again in 1997, KANU elites had responded to similar threats by capitalizing on land grievances to instigate intergroup violence designed to keep them in office. And as the 2002 election approached, many observers feared a replay of past events.[170] Indeed, as early as 1998, the KHRC warned that "Kenya is now confronted with increasing, rather than diminishing, chances of political violence as more and more KANU hawks close to the president feel increasingly threatened by the impending end of Moi's rule by the year 2002."[171] As the opposition unified in the months before the election, the threats to KANU, and the incentives to resort to state-sponsored violence, grew even more acute.

Even though many believed that Moi and KANU would work aggressively and violently to ensure that NARC did not achieve victory, there was no repeat of the state-instigated ethnic cleansings that occurred around the two previous elections.[172] In 2002 there were reports of sporadic violence, but the incidents were localized rather than orchestrated large-scale efforts.[173] As Anders Wijkman, the head of the European Union Observer Mission,[174] noted at the time: "These elections mark an important step forward in the process of development of democracy in Kenya. The political parties were able to campaign actively in a far more peaceful and conducive atmosphere than in previous elections."[175] After the elections passed peacefully, Kenyan society appeared to release a collective sigh of relief. As John Githongo, a Kenyan anticorruption activist, put it: "If we got this wrong, there would have been civil strife. This country would have gone down the drain."[176]

Why did Kenya "get it right" in 2002 and avoid another round of state-sponsored bloodshed? The answer appears to be the growing inclusivity of the country's political institutions resulting from a combination of changes put in place in 1991–92 and 1997.[177] First, the same term limits that forced Moi to step down and directly threatened KANU's power *also* deterred KANU elites from instigating violence. After all, in a post-Moi world, there was no guarantee that KANU-instigators of election-related violence would escape justice.[178] The departing president reinforced this conclusion by signaling that he would not intervene in the political process after the election to protect troublemakers. Upon his return from a trip to the United States a few weeks before the election, Moi gave a widely publicized speech in which he failed to put in a strong pitch for a KANU victory, reiterated his commitment to leaving office, and declared that "Kenyans must be free to vote in a calm and peaceful atmosphere. And Kenyans equally must accept the results that the polls deliver. This is democracy."[179]

Second, the IPPG reforms helped to make the ECK substantially more independent. This independence was given a further boost by the absence of an incumbent presidential candidate to whom the ECK was beholden.[180] In the lead-up to the 2002 election, the newly empowered ECK played a critical role in constraining state elite behavior. The ECK, together with a number of civil society groups (including the Central Depository Unit, the NCCK, the Catholic Justice and Peace Commission, Peace Net, the Kenya Domestic Observation Programme, the Coalition for Peaceful Elections, the KHRC, and the CCCC), repeatedly called on the public to shun leaders who promoted violence and warned that such leaders would be punished.[181] Samuel Kivuitu, then chairman of the ECK, acknowledged in March 2002, that "The biggest challenge to Kenya's electoral process is violence. . . . A mechanism must be put in place to curb these occurrences."[182] In late October Kivuitu again observed that "there's a lot of tension, which could lead to violence. . . . These elections are crucial. So we urge calmness and peace."[183] The ECK set up peace committees in all constituencies to enforce the Electoral Code of Conduct, to assist in conflict resolution and management, and to promote nonviolent campaigns. The ECK also managed and implemented a nationwide media campaign aimed at deterring election violence. The campaign utilized radio, television, and print media, huge roadside billboards, and posters distributed to different institutions around the country.[184] Letters and other warnings were sent to some of Moi's top aides and to Kenyatta insisting that they refrain from inciting violence.[185] The ECK also threatened legal action against the state-owned KBC following complaints that its campaign coverage was unfairly biased in Kenyatta's favor, and, as a result, KBC began to provide fairer coverage.[186] All told, the Institute for Education in Democracy, a local election observer group, concluded:

The [ECK] campaign had a remarkable impact; it directly deterred electoral violence and also provided voter education. . . .

In the 2002 General Election, the ECK showed a remarkable difference in the exercise of its powers. It seems to have "grown some teeth" and was able to summon and fine several politicians who were reported to have breached the Electoral Code of Conduct. Logistically, the ECK was definitely more organized and well prepared to conduct elections than in any previous election.[187]

The ECK campaign was buttressed by the commitment of the press and civil society groups to vigorously respond to any hint of KANU-organized violence. For example, there was widespread outrage when KANU brought the Mungiki, a proscribed Kikuyu militant group, into the fold a few months before the election. In October, when Mungiki members, including some with machetes, marched in Nairobi in support of Kenyatta and KANU, the "subsequent outcry from the press and civil society leadership forced Kenyatta to distance himself from the group. The option of mayhem and disorder disappeared in its wake."[188]

Finally, Moi seems to have come around to the conclusion that few additional electoral gains could be made from another round of electoral violence targeting Kikuyus. After all, Moi handpicked Kenyatta to replace him precisely because of the recognition that electoral victory for KANU required siphoning off some Kikuyu votes from the opposition. Moreover, Moi undoubtedly calculated that a co-opted Kikuyu candidate would be less likely to retaliate against the Kalenjin for the election violence perpetrated during the 1990s.[189] The need to include Kikuyus within the increasingly democratic process thus placed progressively tighter constraints on the ability of the executive to profit from interethnic violence.[190]

In the election Kibaki decisively beat Kenyatta, winning just over 62 percent of the vote. The NARC took 125 of the 224 seats in Parliament, and KANU received only 64 (smaller parties took up the remaining 21 elected seats). Ten of Moi's thirteen ministers lost their seats. With additional appointed members, NARC totaled 132 MPs.[191]

The degree to which politics in Kenya had changed by 2002 was symbolized by the way power was peacefully transferred to Kibaki. As election returns were coming in and it became apparent that Kenyatta had lost, an interviewer asked Moi for his reaction. Moi responded: "That's the way democracy goes. . . . [A]s far as I am concerned, Kenyans have demonstrated well, surrounded by countries that are not stable and therefore I feel happy to leave them peaceful."[192] The actual handover of presidential power took place in Nairobi's

Uhura Park almost immediately after the final vote tallies were clear. The event was attended by thousands of jubilant spectators. During Moi's speech clumps of mud were thrown at him and chants of "mwizi, mwizi" (Swahili for "thief, thief") could be heard from the crowd.[193] Adding insult to injury, when Kibaki took the stage he was blunt in his criticism of the regime he was replacing. The new president stated that he was "inheriting a country which has been badly ravaged by years of misrule and ineptitude. There has been a wide disconnect between the people and the government." In the face of these personal attacks, the now ex-president Moi, who had fought so fiercely and violently to hold onto power during the 1990s, sat expressionless in the background.[194]

The 2002 election offered hopeful signs that Kenya might be starting a transition away from a political system dominated by ethnicity. Although leaders from the country's various ethnic communities still indicated which candidates "their" groups should back, many people "crossed new ethnic borders with their vote, while others, completely dissatisfied with the old regime, voted for reform above all considerations."[195] Yash Pal Ghai, the head of the Kenya Constitutional Review Commission, related the sense of optimism that many Kenyans had in the immediate aftermath of the elections, declaring that the country was "moving to trans-tribal alliances now, because most political leaders realize the only way to hold on to power is to ensure resources are fairly distributed."[196] Whether this will last in the years ahead without Moi and KANU to unite disparate opposition groups and suppress inflated egos remains to be seen.

Conclusions

Two key intervening variables, groupness and institutional inclusivity, mediate the relationship between DES, on the one hand, and civil strife, on the other. High levels of groupness help to overcome collective action problems, facilitating the formation of conflict groups by aggrieved individuals and political entrepreneurs, whereas low levels of groupness frustrate such efforts. Evidence from the Philippines and Kenya bear this out. In the Philippines the erosion of landlord-tenant ties in the post–World War II period cut vertical chords between social groups and contributed to growing class consciousness. As groupness increased, communist organizers found it much easier to foment a truly national rebellion than did similar political entrepreneurs in previous periods. In Kenya spatial variations in the degree of groupness were crucial in determining *both* the violence seen in and around the Rift Valley and at the Coast *and* the failure of this violence to engulf the entire country. In clash-affected areas KANU elites were able to play off strong ethnic bonds so as to mobilize preexisting communities to drive off their neighbors. Widespread violence in the countryside failed to escalate, however, because the cities, especially Nairobi, stayed relatively quiet. Here class-based affiliations and interests cut across ethnic ones, discouraging urban individuals with ties to victims in the countryside from engaging in violent struggle against the Moi regime.

The degree of institutional inclusivity also matters. Exclusive institutions give aggrieved individuals few outlets to advance their cause peacefully and leave state elites free to instigate violence to serve their parochial interests. This makes both state failure and state exploitation conflicts more likely. Inclusive institutions, in contrast, decrease these risks. As institutions become more inclusive, support for rebel groups is siphoned off by the perception of nonviolent institutional alternatives. State elites are also less likely to stir up trouble, because they face greater constraints on their activities. Once again, evidence from the Philippines and Kenya support these propositions. Both countries experienced long periods of institutional exclusivity followed by a period of democratization. When institutions were exclusive, the insurgents in the Philippines were able to convince struggling peasants, urban slum dwellers, and marginalized indigenous communities that the CPP-NPA represented their last best hope for economic and physical survival. Once Marcos was deposed, however, and the country became more democratic, the mere perception of additional institutional routes for addressing grievances gutted most of the support for the Communists. In Kenya the country's exclusive political institutions gave victimized groups few mechanisms to influence KANU elites, leaving Moi and his alies free to instigate attacks. However, a number of constitutional changes made in 1991–92, and especially in 1997, eventually placed new constraints on the executive, preventing a violent replay of ethnic clashes in the crucial 2002 election that swept KANU from power.

The evidence presented in the previous three chapters, taken together, clearly demonstrates that severe population and environmental pressures are important causes of civil strife but do not lead to violence in a social and political vacuum. This insight is a useful corrective to the kinds of demographic and environmental determinism that creep into some existing accounts of the population—environment—civil strife connection. Both neo-Malthusian deprivation claims and neoclassical honey pot arguments, for example, assume that demographic and environmental forces provide incentives for social actors to engage in violence, yet neither specifies the social and political contexts that make violence more likely or prevent it altogether. Similarly, although both existing neo-Malthusian state failure accounts and neoclassical resource curse arguments acknowledge the importance of state institutions, they view institutions primarily through the lens of the state's capacity to maintain order and do not sufficiently explore the relationship between DES and institutional inclusivity. They also fail to adequately theorize the importance of patterns of social organization to violent conflict.

Finally, while some neo-Malthusians, as well their critics among political ecologists, recognize the role intervening variables play in influencing demographically and environmentally induced conflict, they have typically offered laundry lists of contextual factors without identifying which variables matter most. It is not enough simply to acknowledge that social and political factors mediate the causal relationship; the variables need to be clearly specified, and evidence needs to be brought to bear to demonstrate their effects. The discussion in this chapter shows that such an analysis is both possible and empirically fruitful.

6

Conclusions and Implications

FOR MORE THAN a decade the study of international security has opened up to include an analysis of nontraditional threats to political stability, including the possible connection between population growth, environmental degradation, resource scarcity, and civil strife. I have argued that existing causal accounts provide an incomplete understanding of these linkages. To improve our understanding of the population–environment–civil strife connection, I have advanced an alternative state-centric theory that builds on the best insights of existing hypotheses and adds a number of others gleaned from broader scholarly work on the causes of internal wars. I have argued that demographic and environmental stress can lead to strife by creating various pressures on societies and states in the developing world, setting in motion two potential pathways to conflict: state failure and state exploitation. I have also contended that two key intervening variables, groupness and institutional inclusivity, mediate the relationship between DES and civil strife, helping to determine which countries are most likely to become embroiled in large-scale internal violence.

In this chapter I summarize the theoretical and empirical findings of this volume and demonstrate that the causal dynamics and processes at work in the Philippines and Kenya are not unique to those countries. To this end I briefly examine a number of other cases of violent conflict and nonconflict in the context of severe DES. These examples are not meant to represent a definitive scientific "test" of my theoretical argument but rather to suggest its plausible generalizability across a wider universe of cases. I then revisit the theoretical disputes discussed in chapter 1, drawing lessons from my findings for existing theory. Finally, in the last section of the chapter, I discuss the implications of my argument for the future of international security, suggesting that emerging demographic, economic, and environmental trends will pose significant challenges in the years ahead.

Theoretical Expectations and Empirical Support

The theory outlined in chapter 2 makes both conjunctural and process predictions. Its conjunctural predictions describe the theory's expectations regarding "under what conditions" we would expect population growth, environmental degradation, and natural resource inequality to produce large-scale violence within developing countries. These predictions, which are summarized in Table 2.1, map the posited relationship between DES (the independent variable), groupness and institutional inclusivity (the intervening variables), and civil strife (the dependent variable). When DES is high, groupness is high, and institutions are exclusive, then civil strife is likely. But if groupness is low, institutions are inclusive, or both, large-scale internal violence is unlikely even if DES is severe.

Beyond these conjunctural predictions, the core of the analysis presented in this book relates to the theory's process predictions. These are the theory's expectations regarding "how" the causal processes are expected to operate. At the broadest level my theoretical argument claims that DES will lead to civil strife via state failure and state exploitation dynamics. The theory also makes a number of process predictions concerning the operation of the intervening variables: (1) high groupness will facilitate conflict group mobilization; (2) low groupness will frustrate or minimize conflict group mobilization; (3) exclusive institutions limit nonviolent self-help options and facilitate state exploitation; and (4) inclusive institutions increase the menu of nonviolent self-help options and place constraints on state exploitation.

Two Hypothesized Pathways to Civil Strife

DES does not directly produce civil strife; the causal relationship is more complex. Severe DES can generate intense pressures on both societies and states in developing countries. When these pressures are refracted through certain forms of social organization and certain types of political institutions, the prospects for violent internal conflict escalate dramatically.

DES can produce several kinds of strains on society. These include rising scarcities of renewable natural resources, increased economic marginalization, and demographic shifts (such as youth bulges and rapid urbanization). These pressures can ratchet up the level of absolute and relative deprivation experienced by disadvantaged individuals and groups, and increase the pool of grievances directed against the state or other societal actors. At the same time, DES can also undermine the administrative and coercive capacity, legitimacy, and cohesion of the state. DES can increase the demands placed on the state to invest in costly assistance, services, and development projects, and can also erode economic productivity and the state's ability to meet these demands.

As government revenues become more limited, the administrative and coercive capacities of the state are likely to decline, as will the state's legitimacy in the eyes of disadvantaged segments of society. Intrastate cohesion may also be placed in doubt as elites compete for shrinking resources and bicker over the best way to respond to societal grievances.

These pressures on society and the state generate two hypothesized pathways to civil strife.

STATE FAILURE CONFLICTS

State failure conflicts are "bottom-up" conflicts that result when DES and state weakness interact to produce an internal security dilemma. As the state's administrative and coercive capacity, legitimacy, and cohesion decline, it can generate an enormous amount of insecurity among social groups that normally depend on a strong neutral state to provide economic and physical security. State weakness encourages groups from across the social spectrum (including remnants of the declining state itself) to engage in self-help strategies designed to ensure their economic and physical survival. However, as each group acts to preserve its own security, it can inspire fear in other groups. The inability of one group to trust the motivations and commitments of other groups in an ever more anarchic context creates a volatile social climate in which small actions and incidents can spark spiraling hostilities, resulting in violent antistate and intergroup conflict.

The security dilemma that emerges as the state weakness is likely to be particularly acute under conditions of severe DES for at least two reasons. First, resource scarcity, economic marginalization, demographic shifts, and the associated grievances and intergroup competition emanating from DES produce a host of additional threats to the economic and physical security of individuals and groups that get layered on top of those created by a weakened state. Second, DES makes it easier for political entrepreneurs to mobilize individuals into contending conflict groups, because organizers can use access to scarce economic and natural resources as powerful selective incentives. This assists in overcoming the free-riding problems inherent in violent collective action. If only participants enjoy access to natural resources essential to survival, individuals will be much less likely to conclude that it is rational to sit on the sidelines and let others do the fighting.

The analysis of the communist insurgency in the Philippines presented in chapter 3 strongly supports the state failure hypothesis. In the Philippines rapid population growth, environmental degradation, and extreme inequalities in land distribution substantially increased poverty and deprivation from the late 1960s on. DES also placed significant strains on the Philippine state. Population and environmental pressures generated escalating demands on Ferdinand Marcos's regime to invest in costly rural and urban infrastructural projects. Population growth, environmental degradation, and resource inequality also ate into domestic savings and undermined economic productivity. In conjunction with a deeply flawed capital-intensive import substitution development strategy, DES was an important contributor to the debt crisis that threw the Philippine economy into a tailspin in the early 1980s and crippled the state's ability to control and service the countryside.

DES and an emerging anarchy in the Philippines created a highly insecure social landscape. Groups across the entire social spectrum, including poor peasants and fishermen, urban slum dwellers, indigenous tribal communities, landlords, and organizations and individuals within the state itself, experienced growing economic and physical insecurity. As these groups positioned themselves to ensure their survival, the self-help strategies they employed set in motion the spiral dynamics of the security dilemma. Dire economic insecurity brought on by DES and the absence of social services drove poor Filipinos and indigenous communities in ever increasing numbers into the waiting arms of a small but highly motivated band of communist rebels. The CPP-NPA promised land reform and a fundamental reordering of Filipino society, and appeared to offer the poor the last best option for survival. As CPP-NPA support surged, the weakened Marcos regime and its allies among the landed elite turned to their own self-help strategies. Government reliance on poorly trained, poorly equipped, and poorly controlled military and paramilitary units increased, and some landlords formed private armies. These actions, in turn, created additional physical threats to poor Filipinos, in the form of growing human rights abuses, layered on top of worsening economic insecurities. The CPP-NPA promised, and often delivered, protection from these threats in exchange for peasant participation and material support for the insurgency. In this way an acute security dilemma emerged in the Philippines during the early 1980s, transforming a communist nuisance into a nationwide rebellion.

In addition to supporting the basic claims of the state failure hypothesis, evidence from the Philippines also suggests that the state need not completely disappear for the security dilemma to take hold. In fact, the logic of the security dilemma posits that a strong and *neutral* state is what keeps the peace. In situations where the state is weakened and simultaneously tilts heavily in favor of one segment of society over another, as occurred in the Philippines, the state is transformed into just another social group jockeying for its economic and physical security, not a neutral arbiter of disputes between groups. If victims of a weak and biased state feel that their future survival has been placed in jeopardy by the actions of the state and its allies, the threshold of state weakness required to create a security dilemma will be lowered, and disadvantaged groups may be tempted to engage in a risky gamble for survival.

This dynamic of deep insecurity helps us to understand why relatively weak social groups in other parts of the world have occasionally embarked on "now or never" attacks on the state even when the balance of forces on the ground suggests that their prospects for success are grim. The 1994 rebellion in the Mexican state of Chiapas nicely illustrates this causal logic. On January 1, 1994, about two thousand members of the Zapatista National Liberation Army (Ejército Zapatista de Liberación Nacional, or EZLN) launched a string of attacks, occupying several towns in Chiapas. The Mexican army deployed thousands of troops to the region and eventually succeeded in driving the rebels into the mountains but not before a series of fierce battles produced hundreds of casualties.

The roots of the rebellion can be traced to both a history of marginalization and severe population and environmental pressures in the contemporary period. Chiapas has one of the largest concentrations of indigenous peoples in Mexico, and the vast majority of Zapatista rebels and supporters were young peasants from among the ethnically Mayan indigenous peoples living in the eastern lowlands and the central highlands. Since Spain colonized the area in the sixteenth century, indigenous communities in Chiapas have gradually been pushed out of the lowland areas of the Soconusco coast and the fertile slopes of the Sierra Madre and the Grijalva river valley and forced to farm on the steep, rocky, and erosion-prone slopes of the central highlands. This process continued in the twentieth century, as large landowners in Chiapas conspired with the Mexican government to manipulate land tenure arrangements, agricultural prices, and access to credit all to the disadvantage of small commercial and subsistence farmers. As a result, the best land throughout Chiapas came under the control of wealthy and politically connected plantation owners and cattle ranchers.[1]

Even if land had been distributed more equitably, however, it would have been difficult to accommodate the rapid population growth and environmental degradation experienced in the region. Between 1940 and 1990 the population of the area grew from nearly 680,000 to more than 3.2 million (almost a fivefold increase). Population growth in Chiapas averaged 4.4 percent from 1980 to 1990 (more than double the national average), and some areas saw demographic expansion over this period of 5.6 percent per year. As population growth exceeded the capacity of the central highlands to support agriculture, many of the poor-

est residents migrated to the last remaining frontiers in the eastern lowlands, especially the Lacandón rain forest. Between 1970 and 1990 the
population of indigenous peoples tripled from 288,000 to 716,000, and
as many as 300,000 were concentrated in the Lacandón and other parts
of the eastern lowlands by the time of the rebellion. As the number of
impoverished farmers in the jungle multiplied, so did deforestation and
soil erosion, and a familiar feedback loop emerged between economic
marginalization, migration, and environmental degradation. In the
years before the 1994 revolt indigenous peasants living in the central
highlands and the Lacandón rain forest ranked among the poorest and
most desperate individuals in Mexico, and the frontier settlement areas
in the Lacandón jungle became a hotbed of EZLN recruitment.[2]

Coterminous with these pressures, the Mexican state weakened as a
consequence of the country's debt crisis in the early 1980s, the rapid
liberalization of the Mexican economy, and austerity measures under-
taken by President Carlos Salinas de Gotari in the late 1980s to comply
with the demands of international lenders. Fiscal constraints increased
the political space for protest by undermining the ability of the corpo-
ratist government to dispense patronage and co-opt opposition, especially among labor and peasants.[3] That said, the Mexican state did not
collapse. Instead, as the state weakened, it tilted toward landed elites
in Chiapas and abandoned any residual support for peasant agricul-
turalists, leaving them to fend for themselves.

The state took several steps that directly threatened the survival of
indigenous peasants in Chiapas. The Mexican Coffee Institute was disbanded, exposing coffee producers to volatile market prices, and subsidies for agricultural inputs that many peasants relied on to make
poor soils productive were cut. There were also concerns that lower
tariffs for agricultural imports under the North American Free Trade
Agreement would sharply reduce coffee and corn prices, undermining
incomes further.[4] By far the most important indication that the Mexican
state had abandoned indigenous peasants in Chiapas, however, was
the decision made by Salinas in 1992 to push through changes to Article 27 of the Mexican Constitution and the Agrarian Code that removed the prohibition on the sale of communal landholdings. This
was a boon for powerful landed elites seeking to clear out subsistence
farmers to make room for expanded exports, and was widely perceived among peasants in Chiapas as destroying future prospects for
land redistribution.[5] Since the 1930s the Mexican state and its dominant
political party, the Institutional Revolutionary Party (Partido Revolucionario Institucional, or PRI), had succeeded in co-opting indigenous
communities and peasants in Chiapas with continual promises of
agrarian reform. As George Collier notes:

It is difficult to overstate the power of land reform in winning peasants to the side of the state. Even when land grants were agonizingly slow in coming—and they often were—the federal government was able to hold out the _promise_ of land reform as a way of retaining peasant loyalty. By positioning itself, at least symbolically, as the champion of the peasants and the poor, the government was able to inspire tremendous popular support for its programs. . . .

By co-opting one group after another with land redistribution, the government ensured that the peasants' primary loyalty would be to the state and not to their class. The factionalism that developed as each community struggled for its own land helped to contain the potential for organized dissidence because it meant that each village or _municipio_ (township) concentrated more on maintaining strong ties with the national government than with other native communities that might well compete for the same land.[6]

By altering Article 27 of the Constitution and the Agrarian Code, Salinas shattered any remaining perception among indigenous peasants in Chiapas that the Mexican state would ensure their survival. Indeed, as Collier concludes, "In Chiapas, where many land claims have yet to be resolved after languishing in the state bureaucracy for years, repeal of land reform robbed many peasants not just of the possibility of gaining a piece of land, but, quite simply, of hope."[7]

The beneficiary of this desperation was the EZLN, which appeared to offer some possibility, however slight, of providing for the basic survival of indigenous peasants. Although their prospects for success were small, indigenous peasants in Chiapas perceived the status quo as so intolerable and their security situation as so dire that some were willing to undertake a desperate gamble by taking up arms against the government.[8] Indeed, the Mexican newspaper _Tiempo_ observed shortly after the uprising that,

> As far as the peasants are concerned, the EZLN arose as a self-defense group to defend against the ranchers' hired gunmen, who try to take their land and maltreat them, limiting the social and political advancement of Indians. So they took up arms so as not to be defenseless. Then, later, the comrades saw it wasn't enough to do self-defense of a single _ejido_ or community but rather to establish alliances with others and to begin to make up military and paramilitary contingents on a larger scale, still for the purpose of self-defense. . . . The reforms [of Article 27 of the Constitution and the Agrarian Code] negated any legal possibility of obtaining land, and it was land that was the basis of peasants' self-defense.[9]

The self-help logic driving the rebellion was understood by the EZLN. The Zapatista leadership argued passionately and consistently that the government had abandoned indigenous peasants in Chiapas and that their only chance for survival was to use violence to force the government to redistribute land and enact political reforms. This was clearly articulated by the Zapatistas in their 1993 *Declaration of the Lacandón Jungle*:

> We have nothing to lose, absolutely nothing, no decent roof over our heads, no land, no work, poor health, no food, no education, no right to freely and democratically choose our leaders, no independence from foreign interests, and no justice for ourselves or our children. But we say enough is enough! We are the descendants of those that built this nation, we are the millions of dispossessed, we call upon all of our brethren to join our crusade, the only option to avoid dying of starvation![10]

The notion of a security dilemma caused by *both* state weakness *and* DES also suggests a number of other possibilities not sufficiently recognized by the current literature on demographic and environmental conflict. It suggests that population and environmental pressures can lead to conflict in countries that have had weak states for quite some time but have managed to avoid conflict prior to the onset of severe DES. And it opens the possibility that population growth and environmental pressures can play an important causal role in state failure conflicts even in situations where the state was weakened by *non*-demographic and *non*-environmental forces.

In Somalia, for example, the state collapsed for reasons that were not directly related to demographic and environmental change. The economic troubles following the Somali defeat in the 1977–78 Ogaadeen war against Ethiopia, the ensuing refugee crisis, the proliferation of small arms (which eliminated the state's monopoly on violence), and the end of the Cold War (which stripped the country of external support) combined to cripple the capacity of Siyaad Barre's government to maintain order. As the state's authority waned and Somalia's economic conditions deteriorated during the 1980s, individuals retreated to their clan-based groups for economic and physical security and began arming themselves to protect their interests. In 1990 the Somali National Movement (SNM), an Isaaq clan-based group that had been battling the regime for two years, joined forces with the Ogaadeeni-based Somali Patriotic Movement (SPM) and the Hawiye-based United Somali Congress (USC), and, in January 1991, they succeeded in violently toppling the government.[11]

With the collapse of the regime Somalia completed its descent into utter lawlessness and the security dilemma intensified. As Ioan Lewis obseves, "The general tendency was for every major Somali clan to form its own militia movement. Thus clans were becoming effectively

self-governing entities throughout the Somali region as they carved
out spheres of influence in a process which, with the abundance of
modern weapons, frequently entailed savage battles at a high toll of
civilian casualties."[12] The alliance that defeated Siyaad Barre quickly
disintegrated into both inter-clan and intra-clan bloodshed over which
group would dominate the new government. In particular, a sub-clan
split emerged within the USC and two powerful groups—the Habar
Gidir faction led by General Mohammed Farah Aideed and the Ab-
gaal-based faction led by Ali Mahdi—waged war throughout the capital Mogadishu and much of the southern part of the country for control
of the state. The conflict destroyed what remained of the country's government and infrastructure, directly killed tens of thousands, and resulted in hundreds of thousands of additional deaths from starvation
and disease.[13]

To stop the story here, however, would be to miss the important
role DES played in the conflict. Although DES was not chiefly responsible for state failure in Somalia, it did contribute to violent clan competition and exacerbate the security dilemma in the context of a state
weakened by other factors. In the years leading up to civil war,
roughly 60 percent of Somalia's people were nomadic pastoralists or
seminomadic herders, and around 25 percent were cultivators. During the 1980s rapid population growth (the country's population expanded from 3.3 million in 1975 to 7.7 million by 1991), overgrazing,
soil erosion, desertification, excessive fuelwood cutting, extensive
land-grabbing by Siyaad Barre's regime and its allies in southern Somalia, and rising demand for meat and vegetables stemming from
rapid urbanization in Mogadishu (where the population grew from
50,000 in 1960 to more than 1 million by the mid-1980s) all conspired
to increase the value of land and aggravate inter-clan competition
over water, grazing rights, and farmland.[14] When crop failures and
famines devastated southern Somalia in the late 1980s, the movement
of people and livestock across traditional clan-territorial boundaries
helped to spark deadly inter-clan conflict over access to wells and
crops.[15] As David Laitin notes,

> It seems clear that the ecological conditions in the bush exacerbated clan
> conflict in the late 1980s. These conflicts became heavily militarized due to
> the seeding to clans among Siyaad's allies weapons that the President re-
> ceived due to his international diplomatic forays. The militarized conflicts
> in the bush gave added power to warlords within the clans, and diminished
> the power of those who had peace interests. With the collapse of the regime,
> these forces engendered a dynamic that no indigenous actors had the power
> or legitimacy to stop.[16]

Once the regime was overthrown, insecurity and violence deepened as warlords and militias engaged in both offensive and preemptive violence to seize land resources from their rivals. Lee Cassenelli contends that, "Warlords . . . were not simply clan leaders intent on destroying their rivals but competitors using weapons, alliances, and propaganda to gain access to productive land, port facilities, and urban real estate, which in turn could be used to sustain networks of patronage and support." Thus, "below the surface of militia mobilization was a struggle to secure resources in an increasingly resource-poor country."[17] As a result, rural violence was endemic in southern Somalia throughout the 1990s wherever productive or potentially productive land remained in dispute.[18]

The importance of DES becomes even clearer when the experiences of northern and southern Somalia are compared. The relative calm that was maintained in northern Somalia, where drought and its dislocations were far less severe and land was less valuable, and the chaos in the fertile south, where clans increasingly engaged in deadly competition for access to natural resources, suggests that any explanation focusing on the collapse of the state as the sole cause of conflict is suspect.[19] Both state weakness and DES were important.

STATE EXPLOITATION CONFLICTS

A second hypothesized pathway to DES-induced civil strife is state exploitation. State exploitation involves primarily "top-down" causal processes and can occur at levels of state weakness far short of total collapse.

Rising grievances and intergroup competition stemming from DES, if left unchecked or unchanneled, can pose significant threats to elites in control of the state. In conditions of state weakness, elites may fear that their grasp on the reigns of power will slip away unless drastic measures are taken to secure their base of support and co-opt or crush opponents. Unfortunately, state elites sometimes conclude that the instigation of intergroup violence is an appropriate strategy to advance these goals. In addition to increasing incentives for state exploitations, severe DES also presents state elites with opportunities to cause trouble. If they are so inclined, grievances and animosities stemming from population and environmental pressures can be capitalized on by state elites to pit groups against one another to serve the regime's narrow parochial interests. Furthermore, as in state failure conflicts, political entrepreneurs (in this case agents of the state) can often regulate access to coveted and scarce natural resources to encourage some groups to attack others.

The analysis of ethnic clashes in Kenya provided in chapter 4 provides clear support for the state exploitation hypothesis. During the 1980s population growth averaging 3.4 percent a year combined with soil erosion, desertification, and unequal land access to create an extreme scarcity of arable land, economic marginalization in the countryside, and substantial rural-to-urban migration. As the population of Nairobi and other urban centers soared, and related social and economic problems worsened, pressure mounted on President Daniel arap Moi's regime to forsake one-party rule and allow multiparty elections. This posed a significant challenge to Moi, the ruling KANU party, and their coalition of minority ethnic groups. Between 1991 and 1995 the president, many of his close associates, and numerous lower-level KANU politicians set out to discredit the democratization process and to consolidate their control over the fertile Rift Valley by orchestrating ethnic violence. To implement this strategy, state elites capitalized on and manipulated a set of demographically, environmentally, and historically rooted land grievances between the Kalenjin, Maasai, and other pastoral groups, on the one hand, and the Kikuyu, Kissii, Luhya, and Luo farming communities that had moved onto traditionally pastoral land during the colonial and postcolonial periods, on the other. In 1997 similar dynamics ignited ethnic bloodshed in Coast Province. Once again, threatened KANU elites sought to derail calls for political reform by manipulating land and economic grievances, this time pitting the "indigenous" Mijikenda community against "up-country" communities aligned with the opposition. The resulting violence displaced thousands and helped KANU consolidate its political dominance at the Coast.

The causal processes at work in Kenya can be seen elsewhere. In the 1994 genocide in Rwanda, for example, state exploitation dynamics were central. By the early 1990s Juvénal Habyarimana's Hutu-dominated regime was besieged on all fronts. Collapsing prices for coffee and tea (Rwanda's leading exports), serious drought and famine, mounting foreign debt, dislocations from structural adjustment policies, and growing domestic and international pressure to democratize all created intense strains on the Rwandan state.[20] Starting in October 1990 the regime also found itself embroiled in a civil war with the Rwandan Patriotic Front (RPF), a Tutsi rebel group based in Uganda. Habyarimana's government and its Forces Armées Rwandaise (FAR) were only saved from defeat by the timely deployment of French and Zairian troops. Still, the RPF eventually made significant headway in the north of the country, and in 1993 the rebels launched a major offensive, advancing to within twenty-three kilometers of the capital Kigali. Again the French sent in reinforcements to assist the FAR, and the Tutsi rebels came under international pressure to reach a settlement. The result was the 1993 Arusha Accords, which called for a cessation of hostilities and provided for extensive power sharing between Hutus and Tutsis, including the RPF.[21]

While Habyarimana signed on to the agreement, many in his inner circle feared an imminent loss of power. The government had long been controlled by northern Hutu clans and the Mouvement Republicain National pour le Developpement (MRND), the country's only legal political party. Most real power, however, rested with a clique of Hutu extremists from Habyarimana's clan family known by the nickname *akazu* ("little house"), and the akazu were unwilling to give up their privileged position without a fight. In response to the Arusha Accords, the akazu began organizing militias and stepped up efforts to foment anti-Tutsi and anti-RPF sentiment among the Hutu majority. Upon Habyarimana's death in a suspicious plane explosion on April 6, 1994, the akazu launched the genocide. Much of the violence was carried out by the FAR and government-backed militias (especially the MRND youth wing known as the *interhamwe*, or "those who work together"), but a large number of ordinary Hutus also joined in the carnage. Some did so willingly, and others were coerced. All told, some eight hundred thousand Tutsis and moderate Hutus were killed.[22]

Opportunities for state exploitation created by DES were critical to the ability of Hutu genocidaires to execute their vicious campaign. From 1985 to 1990 the annual population growth rate in Rwanda was 3.3 percent. With a population density of around 290 people per km², and an adjusted density of 422 per km² (if lakes, national parks, and forest reserves are excluded), Rwanda ranked as Africa's most overcrowded country. Given the predominantly rural nature of Rwanda's economy, population growth generated competition over increasingly scarce land, competition that was further compounded by falling soil fertility stemming from overcultivation and erosion. By the late 1980s most available land was under cultivation and agricultural production was no longer outpacing demographic expansion.[23] DES was therefore already increasing interpersonal and intergroup tensions before the economic and military shocks of the late 1980s and early 1990s made conditions even more desperate for both the populace and the regime.[24]

DES in Rwanda contributed to social conditions, fears, and grievances that were easy for Hutu extremists to manipulate. In particular, from the late 1980s on, a growing number of young men perceived diminishing prospects for land, jobs, schooling, and marriage (which, by custom and statute, required ownership of land and a dwelling). This created a large pool of aggrieved individuals from which Hutu extremists could draw. Based on intensive fieldwork in northwestern Rwanda in the years prior to the genocide, Catherine André and Jean-Philippe Platteau conclude that "the prevailing state of extreme land hunger [in Rwanda] created a troubled environment which made the most desperate people (particularly young people with only bleak prospects) ready to seize any opportunity to change their present predicament or reverse the present order of things."[25] Young men flocked to the FAR, which increased eightfold in the early 1990s, and, most notably, to Hutu militias in search of basic training and a sense of belonging. These were the "shock troops of the extremist factions within the army, the parties, and the government. It was these militias—formed mostly of disaffected youth—which were to carry out the genocide."[26]

Beyond assisting in the recruitment of armed forces and militias prior to the genocide, DES created direct incentives for individuals to engage in violence against their neighbors once the slaughter began. In the years before the genocide Hutu propaganda exploited mounting population pressures, poverty, and land scarcity to portray Tutsis as *inyenzi* ("cockroaches") hell-bent on seizing Hutu jobs and farms. These fears escalated after the RPF invasion and the Arusha Accords, which raised the possibility of a Tutsi-dominated government that might reverse Hutu privileges. State elites played on these concerns to incite individual Hutus to participate in the genocide while simultaneously capitalizing on acute land scarcity to overcome incentives to free-ride. Indeed, land shortages may have been a major reason why some ordinary people chose to take part in the bloodshed, since peasants could reap private gains by possessing the land and livestock of those they killed. As Gérard Prunier explains:

> Grim as it may seem, the genocidal violence of the spring of 1994 can be partly attributed to . . . population density. The decision to kill was of course made by politicians, for political reasons. But at least part of the reason why it was carried out so thoroughly by the ordinary rank-and-file peasants in their *ingo* [small administrative units comprised of ten households] was a feeling that there were too many people on too little land, and that with a reduction in their numbers, there would be more for the survivors.[27]

Understanding and explaining the genocide in Rwanda therefore requires recognition of the ways in which Hutu extremists were able to exploit DES-related grievances and the opportunities for private gain arising from land scarcity to mobilize their brethren to engage in violence against those supposedly responsible for their misfortune.[28]

In contrast to this conclusion, Valerie Percival and Thomas Homer-Dixon argue that DES was *not* a major source of the civil strife in

Rwanda. They base this finding on two arguments: (1) there is no evidence that a large number of Rwandans participated in the genocide; and (2) Hutus in southern Rwanda, where, according to the authors, land pressures were most acute, initially abstained from the killing and only joined in when they were coerced by northern militias and local authorities.[29] Contrary to these claims, however, there *is* evidence of mass participation, even if it was often coerced, and, for at least some of the participants, DES provided powerful incentives to join in the violence. Moreover, the reason the south initially stayed calm was the unique restraining influence of Tutsi opposition leaders in positions of political power there. Once these leaders were purged, the killing began.[30] It should also be noted that population and land pressures were substantial in the fertile northern and northwestern regions of the country where violence was intense. Indeed, the northwest of the country was the *most* densely populated region, with population densities as high as one thousand people per km^2 in some areas prior to the genocide. Although there may have been less interethnic competition for land in the north and northwest, many Hutu militia members were recruited from these areas, and evidence also suggests that scarcity drove *intra*-ethnic violence between land-hungry Hutus and large Hutu landowners.[31]

Finally, Percival and Homer-Dixon fail to find a causal connection between DES and strife in Rwanda in part because they chose to focus on bottom-up dynamics (i.e., rising social grievances as a cause of spontaneous violence) rather than top-down state exploitation of social grievances. To the extent that Percival and Homer-Dixon consider what I call state exploitation, it is only with regard to the role that DES played in increasing the salience of ethnic identity, which they conclude was negligible. What this misses is the important role that population growth and land scarcity played in providing elites with opportunities to stir up ethnic bloodshed by exploiting fears of domination and private incentives to seize victims' land and livestock. In short, although the primacy of population and environmental pressures as a cause of genocide in Rwanda should not be overstated, to ignore DES is to ignore an essential contributing factor to the violence.

Groupness

Many countries experiencing significant DES remain peaceful. The key to the success of any theory of demographically and environmentally induced civil strife is to identify the conditions under which violence is most likely. The effects of DES are always mediated by intervening social and political variables that increase or decrease the likelihood of antistate or intergroup conflict. In chapter 2 I argued that two such intervening variables, groupness and institutional inclusivity, are particularly important. The evidence provided in the empirical chapters, as well as evidence from a number of additional cases discussed below, lend support to this claim.

Groupness represents the degree to which a given society is sharply cleaved along ethno-cultural, religious, or class lines. Countries with high degrees of groupness tend to be heterogeneous societies in which individuals give their primary allegiance to relatively distinct, non-overlapping, non-crosscutting identity groups in order to provide for their basic needs. Societies with low groupness, on the other hand, are either homogeneous or, more often, heterogeneous with numerous overlapping and crosscutting group affiliations and interests.

GROUPNESS AND STATE FAILURE CONFLICTS

High groupness increases the likelihood of DES-induced state failure conflicts. Strong group identification contributes to conflict group formation by encouraging individuals to conceptualize costs and benefits in collective terms and by embedding individuals within a web of interconnected social relations that facilitate conditional cooperation. High groupness also eases the ability of political entrepreneurs to target discrete groups for organizational purposes. These three effects greatly improve the chances that individuals will overcome collective action problems associated with organized antistate or intergroup violence. And because high groupness facilitates conflict group mobilization, the starting point for the action-reaction dynamics driving the security dilemma, it makes state failure conflicts more likely.

Evidence from the Philippines bears this out. In the Philippines class consciousness increased sharply in the post–World War II period as a consequence of socioeconomic changes that eroded traditional patron-client bonds between landlords and peasants. And, although the Philippines is home to many diverse peoples, ethno-cultural and religious affiliations and interests failed to crosscut class lines in a way that reduced conflict potential. Class cleavages were thus sufficient to produce a high degree of groupness.

High groupness proved very helpful to communist organizers by creating a discrete set of individuals who could easily be targeted by the CPP-NPA for mobilizational purposes. The Communists were also skillful in using flexible propaganda and educational programs to tap into, and expand, class consciousness. This encouraged many among the poor to conceive of their interests in collective terms. Similar techniques were used to win the allegiance of upland indigenous communities. And as the CPP-NPA stepped in to fill roles traditionally held by landlord patrons, a set of reciprocal obligations emerged, discouraging individuals from defecting from the communist cause in the absence of a better alternative.

High levels of groupness also mediated the relationship between DES and the other instances of state failure conflict discussed above. In Chiapas, for example, centuries of racism and discrimination emanating from the dominant *landino* society (people of mixed Spanish and Indian descent), government neglect, and economic marginalization worked together to forge a distinct sense of collective identity among indigenous peoples in the area. By and large these groups also ranked lowest on the socioeconomic ladder, adding a class-component that reinforced, rather than crosscut, ethno-cultural identity. The EZLN leadership actively tapped into this sense of collective identity and interest to build support for their movement.[32] For example, many of the demands made in the Zapatistas "34-Point Agenda for Negotiation in 1994" were framed in precisely the same manner as those made twenty years earlier by the 1974 Indigenous Congress. The EZLN consistently argued that "land [in Chiapas] is for the Indians and peasants who work it, not for the large landlords. We demand that the copious lands in the hands of ranchers, foreign and national landlords, and other non-peasants be turned over to our communities, which totally lack land."[33]

In Somalia clan divisions were central to the organization of armed conflict. Although Somalia is relatively homogeneous in terms of culture, language, and religion, important cleavages along clan-based lines provided the foundation for the formation of conflict groups in the country's civil war. Clans rooted in lineage and kinship have historically been the primary source of economic and physical security in Somalia, and the bedrock for political power. These cleavages hardened in the decades before the collapse of the Somali state. In the precolonial period a set of traditional dispute resolution mechanisms involving assemblies of elders allowed for shifting and crosscutting alliances among clans, sub-clans, and sub-sub-clans. British colonialism in the North and Italian colonialism in the South, however, led to the centralization of governance structures, undermining the legitimacy of local brokers between the clans. The Somali defeat in the Ogaadeen war also reified clan loyalties as different groups sought to blame the demoralizing defeat on others. The result was a Somali society increasingly characterized by sharper divides and militarized rivalries among powerful clans, divides that exploded into open warfare as a consequence of DES and state failure.[34]

In contrast to these examples, mobilizing support for rebel groups should be more difficult when groupness is low, the security dilemma should be less acute, and state failure conflicts should be less likely. Crosscutting group affiliations and interests complicate the formation of conflict groups. Since organized violence on behalf of a particular group has costly effects on both the individual and society as a whole, choosing to fight on behalf of one group will frequently be at odds with the interests of other groups that the individual is affiliated with. Consequently, multiple overlapping allegiances reduce the incentives for individuals to engage in violence. The ability of an individual to turn to multiple groups to secure basic needs also reduces the probability that social sanctions emanating from a particular group will overcome collective action problems, making the formation of conflict groups less likely. Finally, low groupness increases the costs for political entrepreneurs and thus makes mobilization more difficult.

The experience of Costa Rica during the turbulent 1980s provides an excellent illustration of low groupness helping to defuse a potentially destabilizing situation. At the very time that DES drove support for communist rebels to an all-time high in the Philippines, Costa Rica was experiencing similar demographic and environmental pressures. Between 1950 and 1990 the population of tiny Costa Rica increased from only 862,000 to more than 3 million. The annual rate of population growth during this period averaged between 2.8 and 3.8 percent a year, one of the fastest rates of increase in the world.[35] The country also experienced significant land degradation. Most of the country remained under forest cover until the 1950s, and even as late as 1970 more than half of Costa Rica's total land area was forestland. However, annual rates of forest loss accelerated throughout the 1970s. By the early 1980s Costa Rica was losing 4 percent of its forests every year, the highest rate of deforestation in the Western Hemisphere. Between 1970 and 1980 alone forest cover was reduced from 51 percent of total land area to 36 percent. Moreover, these statistics undoubtedly understate the extent of deforestation, since they do not include the large amount of illegal forest clearing during this period.[36] This deforestation, in combination with other forms of poor land use, produced an enormous amount of soil erosion. A World Resources Institute study estimated that Costa Rica lost 2.2 billion metric tons of soil between 1970 and 1989.[37] Other studies suggest that eroded or degraded land amounted to 17 percent of total land area by the end of the 1980s, and that two-thirds of land under pasture and nearly all the land under permanent crops were at "high to very high" risk of erosion.[38]

This degradation stemmed from the interaction between population growth, extremely unequal land access, the clearing of forests by cattle

ranchers and poor squatters for use as pastureland, the expansion of
land devoted to plantations growing bananas and other export crops,
an increase in timber extraction, the invasion of marginal lands by impoverished and landless farmers, and urban sprawl.[39] As in the Philippines, land degradation in Costa Rica undermined crop production,
eroded river banks, silted rivers and watersheds, made cycles of flood
and drought more extreme, disrupted fishing grounds, and interfered
with the normal operation of hydroelectric facilities.[40] Not surprisingly
the pressures on disadvantaged segments of Costa Rican society were
significant. Nearly half the country's population was forced to live in
areas with broken terrain and steep slopes, poor tropical soils, or heavy
rainfall that made cultivation difficult, and 42 percent of all farms in
the mid-1980s were considered to be *minifundios*, farms too small to
support a family.[41] Further, although only 20 percent of the country's
population fell below the poverty line in the 1980s, income inequality
was very high. In 1986 the poorest one-fifth of Costa Ricans received
only 3.3 percent of national income compared to the 38.8 percent of
national income received by the richest 10 percent of the population.[42]

Like the Philippines, Costa Rica also experienced an economic crisis
in the early 1980s stemming from rising oil prices, falling commodity
prices, rising interest rates, and an inability to make payments on its
escalating foreign debt. The crisis was shorter than the one in the Philippines, but in some respects it was more severe. In 1981 inflation
reached triple digits and the Costa Rican currency was devalued 400
percent. Also, in 1981 and 1982 real wages fell by 30 percent in the
private sector and 40 percent in the large public sector, and unemployment doubled. Overall Costa Rica experienced a 9 percent decline in
GDP between 1981 and 1987.[43]

Despite these pressures, Costa Rica managed to avoid large-scale violence. Two factors, low groupness and the country's status as Latin
America's oldest democracy (discussed below), go a long way toward
explaining Costa Rica's ability to ride out the types of crises that sent
the Philippines, not to mention Costa Rica's neighbors El Salvador,
Guatemala, and Nicaragua, spinning into civil war.

In sharp contrast to other Central American countries, Costa Rica's
ethno-cultural composition has, historically, been fairly homogeneous.
Costa Rica was sparsely populated when Spain colonized the Meso-
american isthmus in the early sixteenth century. Very little of the original Indian population inhabiting Costa Rica survived, and the country's relatively small indigenous and Afro-Caribbean populations were
largely assimilated into the predominantly mestizo, culturally His-
panic population. Consequently, despite the presence of a small Afro-
Caribbean population (around 3 percent of the total) concentrated in

the Atlantic Coast Province of Limón, "the racial homogeneity of most Costa Ricans living in the central valley [where the majority of the population resides] has prevented the emergence of virulent and ethnically based politics."[44]

In terms of class cleavages, Costa Rica has a small upper class, fairly sizable middle and working classes, and a large lower class of landless and land-poor peasants, domestic servants, unskilled urban laborers, and urban informal workers. Costa Rica also has a dense array of civil society organizations (e.g., labor unions, community-based development organizations, organizations of housing squatters, farmers associations, professional associations, church groups, business organizations, etc.) that cut across class lines and one another. As John Booth notes, Costa Ricans "tend to belong to groups of many sorts and [act] through them to mobilize and press demands upon the government."[45] Ethno-cultural homogeneity and the crosscutting nature of other forms of social organization thus discouraged the formation of narrow conflict groups in Costa Rica. As a result, despite severe rural and urban population growth, environmental stress, and economic crisis during the 1980s, conflicts between landlords and landless peasants were muted, and there were no large urban uprisings.[46]

GROUPNESS AND STATE EXPLOITATION CONFLICTS

Because high groupness eases the formation of conflict groups, it also assists state elites interested in instigating intergroup violence. In clash-affected areas of Kenya, for example, state elites were able to exploit strong ethnic and clan identification to instigate violence. During the 1990s high degrees of groupness encouraged individual Kalenjins, Maasais, and Mijikenda to define their interests in terms of the broader interests of their ethnic groups. Residents in clash-affected areas also received a host of benefits from group membership, including privileged treatment by the Kenyan state, which created high costs to defection. Together with the promise of access to valued land, strong group identification greatly assisted Moi and his allies in rallying "indigenous" groups to kill and chase off their neighbors in and around the Rift Valley and at the Coast.

Similar dynamics were also at work in Rwanda. Before the arrival of Western colonial powers at the end of the nineteenth century, ethnic boundaries between Hutus and Tutsis in Rwanda were not central to society or politics. Hutus and Tutsis spoke the same language, practiced the same religion, lived among one another, intermarried, and were governed by the same system of small chiefdoms. The labels "Hutu" and "Tutsi" basically represented a class distinction: Hutus

Franch

vs.

were typically farmers, and Tutsis were pastoralists. Since cattle represented the most valuable asset in Rwandan society, the word Tutsi became affiliated with elite status. Under colonial rule (first by Germany and then, after World War I, by Belgium) these relatively minor distinctions were magnified, and a strong sense of ethnic identity was cultivated around a set of supposedly distinctive physical characteristics: Hutus were short, stocky, round-faced, dark-skinned, flat-nosed, thick-lipped, and square jawed; Tutsis were tall, thin, long-faced, lighter in complexion, narrow-nosed, thin-lipped, and narrow-chinned. The Belgians especially viewed Tutsis as Rwanda's natural aristocracy and elevated them to a position of political privilege. Ethnicity became central to the allocation of material resources, educational placement, and job opportunities, and Hutus faced extensive discrimination in these areas. The Belgians also sought to reify and police ethnic boundaries by establishing a "scientific" basis for ethnic difference, and by issuing identification cards indicating whether an individual was Hutu or Tutsi. As a result, racist myths and notions of collective identity hardened. Groupness increased further as the Hutu majority seized political power through a revolution in the late 1950s, the country gained its independence, and the new Hutu dictatorship began to systematically marginalize Tutsis.[47]

Prior to and during the genocide Hutu extremists capitalized on these ethnic divisions. Government propaganda conflated Tutsis in the general population with the threat posed by the RPF, and both were portrayed as mortal enemies to the collective interests of all Hutus. As noted above, Tutsis were depicted as cockroaches determined to infest Hutu lands, and the genocidaires urged all Hutus to stick together to ward off the threat to their collective survival. Crucial to the success of this project was the ability of Hutu extremists to manipulate ethnic stereotypes and spread hate and fear through pamphlets, songs, speeches, official documents, and, most notably, the radio.[48]

In contrast to rural parts of Kenya and the situation in Rwanda, an analysis of the failure of urban Kenyans to engage in organized violence during the 1990s supports the contention that low groupness can limit state exploitation conflicts even in conditions of significant DES. In urban parts of Kenya, Kikuyus and Luos make up a large percentage of the upper class and growing middle class. Individuals from these communities were also prominent members of civil society organizations at the heart of the democratic reform movement. Thus, unlike the situation in clash-affected areas, ethnic- and class-based affiliations and interests overlapped and crosscut one another. The available evidence suggests that these crosscutting affiliations and interests discouraged urbanites from joining the fight. Urban Kikuyus and Luos acted on behalf of their class interests, and remained committed to pushing for peaceful change rather than seeking violent revenge against the Moi regime. Since the existence of ongoing bloodshed directed at a particular group, by its very nature, increases the sense of insecurity among the members of the victimized group, the fact that urban compatriots of those being persecuted in the Kenyan countryside stayed calm provides especially powerful support for the proposition that low groupness limits violence.

Institutional Inclusivity

A second important intervening variable is institutional inclusivity. Inclusive political institutions allow a broad array of social groups to influence and constrain decision makers within the state. States with exclusive political institutions, on the other hand, provide no such guarantees of influence and tend to be controlled by a narrow cadre of elites at the top.

INSTITUTIONAL INCLUSIVITY AND STATE FAILURE CONFLICTS

Countries with weak states and exclusive political institutions are incredibly vulnerable to state failure conflicts. In such circumstances, the weakened state will be decidedly tilted toward a narrow slice of society. Excluded individuals and groups will thus have little faith that the government can or will provide for their security. Unless disadvantaged groups are willing to suffer in silence or engage in prolonged peaceful struggle with little hope of success, their only other option for securing their economic and physical survival is to prepare to fight.

In the Philippines, exclusive institutions under Marcos presented marginalized Filipinos with exactly this choice. The system left the impoverished no hope of influencing the counterproductive development strategies responsible for their economic plight. Moreover, as the state weakened and economic and physical threats mounted, poor farmers, fishermen, slum dwellers, and indigenous upland communities had no institutional option to ensure their survival. They turned, therefore, to the extrainstitutional option represented by the CPP-NPA.

The volatile mix of severe DES, state failure, and exclusive institutions has manifested itself in violence in other countries as well. Given the exclusive nature of political institutions in Mexico, for example, it was not difficult for the Zapatistas to convince indigenous communities in Chiapas that they had little hope of peacefully addressing their plight. For most of the twentieth century Mexico was a one-party authoritarian state dominated by the PRI. Although the country had a bicameral national legislature, most central authority was concentrated in the office of the president. Under Salinas a number of political reforms were enacted in the years before the Chiapas rebellion, but the PRI's monopoly on power and the government's general lack of accountability remained intact.[49] Political exclusion also existed at the local level. Although indigenous peasants made up the vast majority of residents in eastern Chiapas, for example, local government was thoroughly dominated by large landowners and ranchers, leaving indigenous peasants with few prospects of influencing local decision making, obtaining public services, or securing justice.[50] Furthermore, in the years before the rebellion, local authorities lost their ability to peacefully co-opt opposition in Chiapas and relied heavily on repression. Hundreds of Mayan activists and demonstrators were imprisoned on flimsy charges, and human rights abuses by Mexican troops deployed in Chiapas increased.[51] It was therefore easy for the Zapatista's to declare that "constitutional laws have not been complied with by those who govern the country, while, on the contrary, we peasants and Indians are made to pay for the tiniest error, under the full weight of the laws drawn up by those who are the first to violate them."[52] In the absence of institutional channels to address their grievances, an increasing number of peasants in Chiapas threw their support to the Zapatistas, siding with Sub-Comandante Marcos when he argued that "we did everything legal that we could so far as elections and organizations were concerned, and to no avail."[53] For many, the only alternative left was to use violence to call international and domestic attention to their plight and force the Mexican government to reform its policies.

Exclusive political institutions also encouraged armed resistance to the state in Somalia. Prior to his overthrow, Siyaad Barre sat atop a regime that was highly centralized, authoritarian, and corrupt. In the years following the Ogaadeen war, the regime increasingly tilted toward its clan allies—especially the Marrehaan, Ogaadeen, and Dulbahante, known as MOD—and became harsher in its treatment of opposition clans.[54] This bias produced a significant threat to excluded groups. During the 1980s, for example, the regime funneled U.S. military assistance to its allies in the countryside to help them secure vital water holes and grazing lands from rivals, jeopardizing the core economic and survival interests of disempowered groups.[55] With few peaceful institutional avenues to address their grievances, a growing number of excluded groups sought to change their status through force.

In contrast, when political institutions are inclusive, as they are in most consolidated democracies, state failure conflicts are less likely because individuals and groups have a greater menu of nonviolent self-help options. Since organized violence is incredibly risky and costly for participants, the possibility of advancing one's interests through normal political means is very seductive. Because of this, we would expect inclusive institutions to siphon off support for groups looking to engage in violent collective action. Since the trigger for the spiral dynamics of the security dilemma is the mobilization of potential conflict groups, anything that acts to complicate mobilization by these groups will make the security dilemma less acute. Moreover, inclusive institutions also provide a forum for compromise and repeated cooperation between social groups with a basic common interest in peaceful coexistence. This helps to build a foundation of trust and respect, and reduces the perception among disadvantaged groups that stronger groups will exploit their weakness.

These theoretical expectations are borne out by the events in the Philippines after the fall of Marcos. As the country's institutions became more democratic under Aquino and Ramos, previously disenfranchised individuals and groups felt much more confident in the possibility of securing their interests through nonviolent means, even if, in practice, this did not always produce the desired result. State legitimacy increased, splits emerged within the Communist Party between factions supportive of an electoral strategy and factions committed to armed struggle, and support for communist insurgents in the countryside plummeted. In only a few years inclusive institutions sent the Communists hurling back from the brink of success. By the early 1990s the once potent CPP-NPA was reduced to a relatively trivial force in Filipino society and politics.

Inclusive institutions had a similar pacifying influence in Costa Rica. The country's 1949 constitution established three independent branches of government, a series of checks and balances, and a separate and independent electoral institution called the Supreme Electoral Tribunal tasked with ensuring fair elections. Costa Rica's constitution also prohibits the existence of a standing army (although it allows for police forces) and guarantees freedoms of speech, the press, association, due process, and other basic civil rights and civil liberties. Together these institutions provide a "national political climate with few institutional barriers to citizen political participation."[56] The nature of Costa Rica's political system, along with low levels of groupness, helped the country avoid civil strife during the 1980s despite severe DES and a potentially destabilizing economic crisis. During the deep recession of the early 1980s, for example, grievances directed against the state by impoverished and landless peasants increased significantly, as did grievances by poor squatters and slum residents in Costa Rica's overcrowded urban areas. Yet the expression of grievances by the rural and urban poor most often took the form of peaceful organization, protests, petitions, and lawsuits. Even in those rare instances where grievances boiled over into violence, the violence tended to be sporadic and unorganized, relatively low-level, and was quickly deescalated through policy concessions made by the government. Indeed, throughout the 1980s the Costa Rican state consistently demonstrated its willingness to accommodate mass participation and even confrontational protests with very little repression, in sharp contrast to the policies pursued by the Marcos regime in the Philippines and Moi's government in Kenya. Furthermore, unlike the situation in the Philippines, there was almost no violent revolutionary activity by the Costa Rican Left during the 1980s, even after private and governmental fears of the spread of communism throughout Central America produced an increase in the membership of right-leaning paramilitary organizations.[57] Thus, as Booth concludes: "The shared ideals of consensus, peaceful problem-solving, and equality of opportunity . . . encourage[d] Costa Ricans, rulers and ruled alike, to treat each other with a restraint and respect often absent in several neighboring countries."[58] In short, it appears that the long-standing strength of Costa Rican democracy fostered both an institutional and normative commitment to peaceful conflict resolution that dramatically reduced the prospects for large-scale violence.

INSTITUTIONAL INCLUSIVITY AND STATE EXPLOITATION

Institutional inclusivity is also an important determinant of a country's vulnerability to DES-induced state exploitation conflicts. Exclusive institutions increase the likelihood that DES will lead to state exploitation, whereas inclusive institutions make such exploitation much more difficult. In countries with exclusive political institutions, state elites and their allies have both the power and the incentive to manipulate social grievances emanating from DES to serve their interests. Exclusionary political landscapes allow state elites to accrue all the potential benefits of risky strategies of exploitation while also allowing them to pass the costs of such policies on to disempowered segments of society.

In Kenya during the 1990s, for example, the country's political institutions vested the majority of political power in the executive and the ruling KANU party, both of which Moi controlled. Moi also ensured that Kalenjins and other members of minority tribes dominated most senior positions in government, the military, security organizations, and state-owned enterprises. The exclusion of Kikuyus, Kisiis, Luhyas, and Luos from positions of influence within the government left them powerless to prevent the instigation of violence by KANU elites.

In Rwanda, too, state exploitation dynamics were greatly assisted by exclusive institutions. Under Habyarimana, political power was highly concentrated. MRND party members and supporters were given privileged positions throughout the bureaucracy, state enterprises, the FAR, and the church, and the akazu oligarchy controlled state banks, many leading enterprises, the tourism and coffee industries (the two biggest earners of foreign currency), and, most crucially, the armed forces and the Presidential Guard.[59] In the early 1990s, under pressure from domestic opposition and international lenders, the regime enacted a set of half-hearted political reforms, but it was not until the 1993 Arusha Accords that the prospects emerged for real power sharing with the RPF and with Tutsis more broadly. The genocide was initiated by the akazu to forestall this loss of power.[60] The exclusive nature of Rwanda's political institutions was thus an important intervening variable in the process leading to genocide. As in Kenya, but on a much greater scale, state elites reacted to threats to their rule by taking advantage of an institutional context that left them unconstrained to manipulate DES-related grievances and selective incentives to orchestrate mass murder.

Such exploitation is much less likely in countries with inclusive institutions for the obvious reason that inclusive institutions, by definition, provide potential victims ways of influencing their fate and constraining predatory elites. Indeed, as additional constraints were placed on the executive in Kenya, especially in the wake of the 1997 IPPG reforms, KANU elites were deterred from instigating another round of ethnic clashes in the months before the crucial 2002 elections that swept KANU from power.

Support for the constraining power of inclusive institutions can also be found in Mali, where inclusive institutions have helped to prevent both state failure *and* state exploitation dynamics from emerging, despite significant DES. At independence in 1960 Mali's population totaled 4.6 million, mainly consisting of subsistence farmers and pastoral nomads. Thirty years later, in 1990, the population had doubled to 9.2 million, and by 2003 Mali's population had reached 11.6 million. For most of this period the average annual rate of population growth was around 2 percent. During the 1990s, however, the population grew at an annual clip of 2.8 percent, and in 2003 the total fertility rate was 6.6 children per woman.[61] Land and water stress is severe in Mali as well. Although Mali has twice the land area of modern France, most of this land is either desert or unusable wasteland; the majority of arable land is concentrated along the Niger River, and only 2 percent of the total land in the country is cultivated. Given the nature of Mali's climate, which spans the transition zone between the arid Sahelian savannah and the Sahara desert, the country is also incredibly vulnerable to severe periodic drought. The combination of population pressures, poor land use practices, and a fragile ecology has made soil erosion, desertification, and freshwater scarcity serious problems. Not surprisingly, daily life is precarious for the three-fourths of Mali's population that is involved in agriculture (largely at subsistence levels).[62]

Ethno-culturally Mali is quite diverse. The population has been classified into five or six ethno-linguistic groups, representing numerous distinct communities and several dozen different languages. The country is also regionally divided. The South is dominated by crop farmers, villagers, and town residents, and is home to 80 percent of the country's population. In contrast, the North is home to nomadic pastoralist groups, most notably the Tuaregs.[63]

Regional cleavages have been a powerful political force since independence, and Mali has experienced both state failure and state exploitation dynamics centered in the North. In the wake of independence, poor economic performance and bad governance dashed the rising expectations of the Malian populace. Tuaregs, in particular, felt they were the victims of significant discrimination in the distribution of benefits from the new government lead by Modibo Keita, in part because they were seriously underrepresented in the new civil administration and military establishment. In 1962 the Tuaregs rebelled, but the government succeeded in violently crushing the insurgents and erecting a repressive military administration in the North. This did nothing to resolve the ultimate causes of the rebellion. The government's strong-arm tactics completely failed to address Tuareg grievances and only served to alienate many Tuaregs who had not originally supported the rebels. Moreover, in the context of highly exclusive political institutions, the Tuaregs had no means of influencing, or even communicating, their concerns to the government.

In 1968 Keita was overthrown and replaced by a group of young army officers led by Lieutenant (later General) Moussa Traore. The new military government sought to turn away from Keita's socialist leanings and rejuvenate Mali's stagnant economy, but foreign investment and economic recovery were not forthcoming. Compounding matters, the region was besieged by a series of severe droughts between 1968 and 1974, and then again between 1980 and 1985. These droughts devastated Mali's economy and undermined the livelihood of nomadic peoples throughout the Sahel, killing a high proportion of livestock and forcing many Tuaregs to relocate to squalid refugee camps and urban areas in the South. Meanwhile, Mali's national debt escalated, corruption mounted, and population growth consistently outstripped the economy's capacity to produce jobs.[64]

As the state weakened and development efforts continued to privilege the more populated, economically viable southern regions of the country over the North, the Tuaregs rebelled for a second time in June of 1990. This rebellion exhibited both state failure and state exploitation characteristics. On the one hand, the bottom-up aspects of the rebellion were partially driven by the Tuaregs' security fears. Toward the end of the 1980s the view solidified among many Tuaregs that the central government was weak, unresponsive, and hostile. Fears of cultural genocide also arose from the biased manner in which the government handled famine relief during periods of drought. On the other hand, the conflict also exhibited top-down dynamics characteristic of state exploitation conflicts. As the Tuareg threat to the government increased, state elites encouraged non-Tuareg portions of the population in the North to attack Tuaregs in the hopes of crushing opposition to the regime. This state-sponsored violence only added to cycles of fear, insecurity, mobilization, and countermobilization. Many of the farming communities in the North formed self-defense militias, some of which were armed by Malian security forces, and fighting escalated.[65]

Violence did not subside until Mali's political institutions became more inclusive. In 1991, while the civil war raged on in the North, domestic opposition to the Malian government increased sharply, culminating in a coup led by Lt. Col. Amadou Toumany Toure that toppled the Traore regime. Soon after coming to power Toure initiated a transition to democracy, resulting in the election of a former opposition leader, Alpha Oumar Konaré, to the presidency in 1992. Since 1992 Mali has been widely viewed as one of the most stable and promising democracies in Africa. Mali's new institutions allow for frequent and fair elections of national and local officials, ensure an annual public forum in which all Malians are allowed to directly question the government on any subject (the proceedings of which are broadcast live to almost universal listenership), and provide protections for basic civil rights and civil liberties. The country's political institutions were also redesigned to provide the previously disempowered Tuaregs considerably more influence: Tuaregs were integrated into the Malian army, police, and civil service; the North was guaranteed a fixed proportion of Mali's national infrastructure investment funding; authority over many administrative decisions were decentralized, devolving considerable power to local and regional communities, including the Tuaregs; and promises were made, and measures taken, to ensure that Tuareg culture would be maintained and respected, including the initiation of an education campaign within the military to increase awareness of Tuareg culture.[66]

Mali's more inclusive institutions had a great deal of mutual insecurity to overcome. By the end of 1992 violence and pervasive fears of reprisals plagued the Tuareg communities in the North. The Malian army and many of the Tuareg's northern neighbors were also highly distrustful and fearful of Tuareg attacks. Nevertheless, by 1996, the civil war in the North had ended and most Tuareg communities had overcome their fear of the Malian army. Mali has remained relatively calm ever since.[67] This stability is striking given that demographic and environmental pressures continue to mount and Mali remains one of the poorest countries in the world.[68]

Inclusive institutions also placed constraints on state exploitation in Mali. As Kalifa Keita notes, since all major ethnic groups are capable of influencing government decision making, "no national government can afford to alienate ethnic blocs. As a result, Mali's senior leaders have endeavored to avoid the appearance of ethnic favoritism while tolerating a considerable amount of 'ethnic patronage.' "[69] State elites in Mali have also allowed the media to criticize the government and support opposition politicians. Most substantially, in 2002, Konaré made no attempt to circumvent the constitutional limit of two five-year terms, and the presidency was transferred peacefully to the winner of the national election, Amadou Toumany Toure, the man who had liberated the country from dictatorship in 1991. All told, democracy in Mali appears to have limited corruption, facilitated consensual politics, and reduced the prospects of the state stirring up trouble.[70]

Implications for Existing Theory

These theoretical and empirical findings have substantial implications for existing accounts of the population—environment—civil strife connection. In this section I revisit the theoretical perspectives discussed in chapter 1, and discuss their analytical and empirical limitations.

Neo-Malthusian Hypotheses

Neo-Malthusians contend that rapid population growth, environmental degradation, and resource inequality conspire to produce civil strife. The findings presented in this study suggest that existing neo-Malthusian arguments get much right but are incomplete.

The neo-Malthusian deprivation hypothesis posits that demographically and environmentally induced poverty and inequality contribute to the grievances underlying rebellion. Evidence from cases of demographically and environmentally induced conflict in the Philippines, Kenya, and elsewhere strongly support the notion that DES can worsen poverty and inequality. Empirically this deprivation has fueled antistate and intergroup grievances and competition, but these grievances alone do not lead to civil strife. Civil strife is only likely when grievances are accompanied by the weakening of the state and when individuals are able to overcome the inherent collective action problems plaguing the mobilization of conflict groups.

The version of the neo-Malthusian state failure hypothesis advanced by Jack Goldstone and Homer-Dixon partially corrects for this problem by pointing out that civil strife only occurs when DES simultaneously generates grievances and incapacitates the state, thereby opening the political space for the expression of grievances. The findings of this study support this basic claim but push it further by suggesting that state failure does more than just permit violence to occur. The analysis of the communist insurgency in the Philippines, as well as the shorter discussions of Chiapas and Somali, indicate that state failure opens structural opportunities for civil strife *and* provides powerful incentives for violence in and of itself by producing a security dilemma.

Finally, existing neo-Malthusian claims are incomplete because they largely envision violence as a bottom-up process; that is, given sufficient structural opportunities, DES-induced grievances and resource competition are seen to motivate social groups to direct violence upward toward the state or sideways toward other groups. However, civil strife can also result from top-down state exploitation dynamics, as evidenced by the ethnic violence in both Kenya and Rwanda.

Neoclassical Hypotheses

Neoclassical economists advance conflict hypotheses that appear to turn neo-Malthusian hypotheses (including my own) on their heads; an abundance of natural resources, rather than scarcity, is argued to produce civil strife. A closer look at these contentions reveals two things. First, neo-Malthusian and neoclassical arguments are not as diametrically opposed as they initially appear; and, second, neoclassical hypotheses in isolation cannot account for demographically and environmentally induced conflicts.

The neoclassical honey pot hypothesis suggests that locally abundant supplies of valuable natural resources create greed-based incentives for rebel groups to form and fight to seize control of these resources. Once captured, valuable natural resources also produce revenue streams that keep rebels in business. Evidence from several contemporary conflicts indicates that the honey pot hypothesis identifies some important dynamics. The civil wars in Sierra Leone and the Democratic Republic of Congo (DRC, the former Zaire), for example, clearly demonstrate the honey pot effect in action. In Sierra Leone, the Revolutionary United Front (RUF), a rebel group formed by disgruntled Sierra Leone officials and supported by Liberia's Charles Taylor, invaded the country from Liberia in 1991. The RUF was chiefly interested in capturing the Sierra Leone's mineral wealth. Indeed, the group's first act was to seize control of the Kono diamond fields and then, throughout the conflict, it sustained its operations with diamond revenues.[71] In the DRC the attempt by local actors and neighboring armies to profit from the country's valuable supply of diamonds, gold, copper, coltan, and timber resources was not the initial source of turmoil, but plunder eventually became a powerful contributor to the escalation and endurance of one of the bloodiest wars in recent memory.[72]

These examples notwithstanding, as a general explanation for the relationship between natural resources and civil strife the honey pot hypothesis is plagued by a number of limitations. First, although the argument is framed in terms of conflicts driven by resource abundance, this is a bit misleading. After all, the local resources in question in Sierra Leone and the Congo are only valuable because they are *globally* scarce. Moreover, as *local* natural resources are consumed and degraded at unsustainable rates, thus becoming increasingly scarce over time, their value and conflict potential are likely to increase not decrease. The renewal of civil war in the Sudan in 1983 provides a clear example here. By the end of the 1970s environmental stress in northern Sudan, stemming largely from mechanized farming, increased the value of water, land, and oil resources available in the South. Northern elites, acting in support of allied northern mechanized farm owners, pushed south to capture these valuable resources. This posed an enormous threat to the economic and physical survival of southerners, encouraging them to restart the war against the North. And as the war raged on, oil exports became central to northerners' ability to finance their campaign, encouraging them to seize and exploit oil deposits deeper and deeper into the South.[73]

Second, honey pot dynamics are much more likely to apply to nonrenewable mineral resources (such as oil, precious metals, and gemstones) than renewable resources. Nonrenewable resources typically have much higher value per unit of volume and tend to be geographically concentrated. This makes them much more "lootable" and "seizable" than less valuable, more diffuse renewable resources (with the partial exception of timber). As the conflicts in Chiapas, Kenya, the Philippines, Rwanda, and Somalia clearly suggest, renewable resources, including arable land and forests, are much more likely than nonrenewables to be implicated in grievance-based struggles in which shortages increase the prospects for violence through their widespread socioeconomic effects on marginalized populations.

Third, the honey pot hypothesis fails to consider the possible interactions between the abundance of one resource and emerging scarcities of other resources. The extraction and production activities centered around locally abundant (and usually nonrenewable) resources can lead to environmental degradation and scarcities of *other* (usually renewable) resources, and the synergy may lead to violent conflict. In Bougainville, Papua New Guinea (PNG), for example, huge mining operations centered around a local abundance of copper resulted in both disputes over unequal distributions of copper revenue and grievances stemming from environmental degradation and scarcity. Copper was discovered on Bougainville in the 1960s, and in the 1970s extensive cooperation began between the PNG government and the London-based mining company Rio Tinto Zinc (RTZ). The Panguna copper mine run by RTZ was soon one of the largest mines in the world. The mine became incredibly important to the revenue of the national government, producing 16 percent of PNG's internally generated income and 44 percent of its exports since 1972. Nevertheless, Bougainvilleans grew increasingly resentful that most of the mining revenues went to RTZ (80 percent) and the national government (20 percent) and that many of the mining jobs went to workers from other parts of PNG. Compounding matters, poisonous tailings and chemical pollutants stemming from mining operations destroyed local fisheries, contaminated drinking water, and undermined crop production, threatening the livelihoods of local landowners. When the national government and RTZ ignored Bougainvillean concerns, local landowners started a sabotage campaign against the mine, and the conflict soon escalated to a guerrilla war against troops of the national government.[74]

Similar dynamics have occurred in Nigeria. Revenue streams from the oil-rich Niger Delta have historically filled the coffers of a small minority in Nigeria and propped up a series of repressive regimes. Throughout the 1990s inequities, environmental degradation, pollution, and health problems stemming from the oil industry generated substantial grievances among local communities in the Niger Delta, including the Ogoni people. In the mid-1990s the military dictatorship in Nigeria responded to Ogoni protests with repression and the instigation of interethnic violence.[75]

Finally, the honey pot hypothesis ignores the ways in which state weakness and rising DES-related grievances make even those conflicts centered on locally abundant resources more likely. Returning to the case of Sierra Leone is illustrative here. In the early 1990s economic mismanagement crippled the functional capacity of the state and drastically reduced state-centered education and employment opportunities. In the context of 2 percent annual population growth, a fertility rate of 6.5, and a large youth cohort traditionally dependent on shrinking economic opportunities, the recruitment efforts of the RUF were significantly aided. And as the state weakened, its ability to maintain order and provide security also dissipated.[76] Thus, although the possibility of profiting from the seizure of diamonds undoubtedly encouraged individuals to join the RUF, and the capture of diamond fields allowed the organization to finance its operations, this account is incomplete. Without the rise of DES-related grievances and the collapse of the central government, RUF recruitment would have been far more difficult and the rebels would have faced fewer opportunities to prosecute the war.

The neoclassical resource curse hypothesis acknowledges the importance of state weakness and accounts for failed states by pointing to a country's resource endowments. The economic variant of the resource curse, sometimes called Dutch Disease, claims that locally abundant supplies of natural resources encourages investment to concentrate in these sectors, undermining economic diversification and making countries vulnerable to rapid declines in prices for primary commodities. This economic weakness, in turn, makes states prone to collapse during times of crisis. The political variant of the resource curse argues that abundant supplies of natural resources make civil strife more likely by producing corrupt and authoritarian rentier states. If states control the revenue streams from valuable natural resources, they need never bargain away rights in exchange for extracting revenue from society through taxes. Instead, the state can rule through a mix of coercion and patronage. Such narrow regimes generate extensive grievances and are therefore prone to rebellion.

There appears to be some strong cross-national evidence for the developmental problems associated with the resource curse. Statistical analyses suggest that countries that are highly dependent on primary commodity exports have, on average, lower rates of economic growth and more unequal distributions of income.[77] Underdevelopment and poor governance, in turn, can generate grievances and open political space for organized violence. For example, many oil-exporting countries, including Algeria, Angola, Ecuador, Indonesia, Iraq, and Nigeria, have historically been prone to authoritarianism, corruption, periodic social protests, and violence.[78] Recently some have also expressed fears that Dutch Disease and rentier state pathologies could pose significant threats to the future stability of post-Saddam Iraq. If an equitable system is not established to manage and distribute the country's oil wealth among the various regions and religious and ethnic communities, it could have a corrupting influence on future political institutions, put any new government's legitimacy at risk, and spur bloody competition between Shiites, Sunnis, Kurds, and Turkmen.[79]

However, these findings need to be qualified somewhat. First, as with the honey-pot hypothesis, Dutch Disease and rentier state dynamics are much more likely to occur in the context of nonrenewable mineral resources, especially oil. Mining is a very capital-intensive enterprise, and mining countries are often economically dependent on a single resource. The economic distortions and sensitivity to price volatility are therefore likely to be especially acute. Furthermore, mineral resources generate extraordinary rents (relative to most renewable resources), and governments in the developing world generally exercise sole ownership rights over subsoil assets. This means that rents from nonrenewable resources typically accrue directly to the state, and the pathologies of rentier state politics are likely to be much greater. Forests are the major exception to the distinction here between nonrenewable and renewable resources, because they, too, are typically owned by the state. Thus, in the Philippines, control over forest resources was one component (although not the most important one) propping up the corrupt Marcos regime. But the ability of regimes to unhinge themselves from society by monopolizing other renewable resources and their revenues is inherently limited. In post-independence Kenya, for example, providing access to both white settler land and public land has at times been an important aspect of ethnic patronage, but, because most land is privately owned, the government has not possessed widespread direct control over the resource.

Second, a good case can also be made that the developmental pathologies of the resource curse and those emerging from DES can both occur and interact with each other within the same country over time. When resources are abundant, a country may become highly dependent on these resources, and elements of the resource curse may take hold. However, precisely because of this dependence, mounting demographic and environmental pressures over time can undermine economic growth. Indeed, many of the world's poorest countries appear to be stuck in a situation in which a high dependence on natural resources (produced by local abundance at some point in the past) has interacted with rapid population growth, environmental degradation, and emerging scarcity in the contemporary period to pose significant challenges for economic growth. These challenges may be self-correct-ing over the long term as countries are forced to diversify their econo-mies, but in the short and medium term the economic and political consequences can be significant.

The collapse of regimes that depend on natural resource revenue is also particularly likely as natural resources become scarce. State control over locally abundant natural resources often promotes corruption and authoritarian rule, as the rentier state argument suggests, but the ability to capture or distribute access to extraordinary rents *also* provides states with considerable opportunities to finance patronage networks and co-ercive institutions, such as the police and army. Regimes in resource-rich countries are thus often able to maintain political order in spite of widespread popular grievances through a mix of bribery, co-optation, and coercion. This narrow foundation for political order, however, is vulnerable to rapid collapse as the resource propping up the regime is depleted or degraded at an unsustainable rate. In the Philippines, for example, extensive deforestation robbed the Marcos government of an important patronage asset. Land scarcity had a similar effect in Kenya under Moi. While Kenyatta was able to use access to white settler land to co-opt landless Kikuyus and important political leaders from many different ethnic communities, demographic expansion and environ-mental degradation during Moi's tenure robbed the regime of similar opportunities to use land to craft a broad political base.

Political Ecology

Political ecologists vehemently reject neo-Malthusian accounts of civil strife, arguing that natural limitations and the demands generated by population growth are not very important contributors to violence. In-stead, for political ecologists, it is crucial to examine the ways that par-ticular historical legacies and the contemporary political economy value and structure the distribution of essential resources in particular ways, producing violent contests over resource control. The evidence from the Philippines and Kenya, as well as the shorter discussions of conflicts in Chiapas, Rwanda, and Somalia, provide some support here. In these cases it is clearly impossible to understand environmen-tal degradation and emerging scarcities of natural resources, or ac-count for their social and political effects, without considering the resi-due of colonial rule, postcolonial patterns of resource distribution, and the broader international and domestic political economy.

That said, the dogmatic rejection of all neo-Malthusian arguments is myopic. In case after case it is the *interactions* between population growth, economic practices that degrade the environment, and natural resource inequality that matters. Focusing on any element to the complete exclusion of the others is nonsensical. Rapid population growth, for example, would be far less consequential if arable land was equally distributed or if conservation measures were in place. By the same token, however, unequal land distribution would be far less consequential if demand for land was not accelerating as a consequence of rapid population growth or if the supply of land was not being degraded by soil erosion.

Finally, the political ecology perspective is undermined by its failure to clearly specify a causal theory of civil strife. Some political ecologists have offered accounts that parallel the arguments made by the honey pot and resource curse hypotheses.[80] More often, however, political ecologists present a laundry list of factors to consider, including the logic of capitalism, discourses about nature, and other characteristics of a country's political and cultural traditions, without tying them together in a systematic causal account. Part of this stems from the tendency among many political ecologists to eschew the project of causal explanation altogether. As a result, their arguments remain underspecified and are rarely tested against their rivals. Until more theoretical work is done, it will be very difficult to evaluate the unique contribution of political ecology to explaining violent conflict.

Future Trends and Their Implications

The world will experience tremendous demographic and environmental change during the twenty-first century. The UN medium projection estimates that, by 2050, the world population will increase by 2.6 billion, that is, from its current level of 6.3 billion to 8.9 billion, with almost the entire increase occurring in developing countries.[81] By 2050 the population of high-income countries is expected to be in the midst of a twenty-year population *decline*, whereas developing countries as a whole are expected to have an annual population growth rate in 2050 of 0.4 percent, and the population of the *least* developed countries will likely still be rising by 1.2 percent a year. As a result, the population of developing countries is projected to increase from 4.9 billion in 2003 to 7.7 billion in 2050, and, over the same period, the population of the least developed countries in the world is projected to more than double from 668 million to 1.7 billion.[82]

It is important to note that these estimates assume continued increases in access to family planning and public health services.[83] Absent greater access, there is the potential for considerably higher population growth. If fertility rates were to remain at their current level, for example, the estimated world population in 2050 would balloon to 12.8 billion (of which 11.6 billion would reside in developing countries). And even if women were to have, on average, only about .5 children more than the current medium projection assumes, world population could increase to 10.6 billion by 2050.[84]

Another wildcard affecting future population growth rates is the HIV/AIDS pandemic. Over the current decade the number of excess deaths from AIDS in the worst-affected countries is estimated at 46 million; this number is projected to rise to 278 million by 2050.[85] However, the horrific death of millions of people is hardly a "solution" to the burdens posed by rapid population growth on the economies of many of the world's least developed countries. Not only will high fertility rates offset deaths that result from AIDS in most places,[86] but the tremendous loss of human potential will pose its own set of unique challenges to struggling societies and economies. The death of so many young adults in their most productive years, coupled with astronomical health costs, may outstrip the ability of many governments to fight the disease and trade off with financial resources that could otherwise be devoted to fostering development.[87]

Beyond these demographic changes, economic growth and consumption are also projected to increase in the decades ahead, spurred on by continued economic globalization. The World Bank projects growth in global income of 3 percent per year over the next fifty years, suggesting a fourfold increase in the world economy (to a total of $140 trillion) by mid-century. Higher income has historically been associated with higher levels of consumption, even though, owing to changes in technology, the relationship has rarely been linear. Consequently, as the world economy expands, strains on the environment are likely to accelerate, especially if too little attention is paid to altering consumption and production patterns.[88]

Consumption by wealthier individuals and nations will likely drive global patterns of natural resource depletion and pollution in the years ahead, but population growth and poverty will continue to have an important impact at the local level. Even as globalization raises the living standards of some countries and peoples, pockets of extreme poverty and yawning inequalities are likely to persist, placing their own strains on the environment. Despite rapid urbanization across the developing world, current projections suggest that the absolute number of individuals living in rural areas will inch slightly upward from 3.2 to 3.3 billion by 2030.[89] Assuming that current patterns persist, hundreds of millions of people will continue to rely on overcrowded and ecologically fragile lands where there is a real danger of becoming trapped in a vicious cycle of poverty and environmental decline.

Another factor likely to add to environmental pressures in the decades ahead is impending climate change. The accumulation of greenhouse gases, particularly carbon dioxide (CO_2) produced by the combustion of fossil fuels, is widely expected to result in dramatic climatic shifts over the next one hundred years. The most recent findings by the UN Intergovernmental Panel on Climate Change (IPCC) estimates that global average surface temperatures will warm 1.4 to 5.8° C by 2100, a rate of warming greater than any experienced in the past ten thousand years. Global warming is projected to raise average sea level by as much as 0.88 meters over the same period. As temperatures and seas rise, the number and severity of extreme weather events such as droughts, floods, and cyclones will increase in many regions, and land and freshwater resources will face growing stress. The effects are likely to be most profound in countries where large segments of the economy remain dependent on climate-sensitive primary product sectors. The rate and magnitude of change may ultimately outpace the adaptation capacities of many natural and social systems, especially in cash-strapped developing nations.[90]

Although it is impossible to predict the future of any complex system, let alone a future based on the interaction of several complex systems (demographic, economic, political, and environmental), some possible scenarios have been offered. Combining UN population growth estimates, IPCC estimates on future CO_2 emissions, and UN Food and Agriculture Organization estimates regarding trends in the consumption of agricultural products (crops, meat, and dairy), forest products (including fuelwood), and fish and seafood, a study by the World Wildlife Fund has projected humanity's ecological footprint (the total area required to produce the renewable resources consumed and to assimilate the wastes generated by humans) forward from 2000 to 2050. The study concludes that "9 billion people in 2050 would require between 1.8 and 2.2 Earth-sized planets in order to sustain current levels of consumption of crops, meat, fish, and wood, and to hold CO_2 levels constant in the atmosphere."[91] Whether this scenario comes about obviously depends on future consumption habits and available technology. Rapid advances in technology that provide for significant improvements in resource efficiency, for example, could allow for long-term sustainability and continued advances in human welfare; however, without significant technological changes, projected consumption would likely become unsustainable.[92]

What are the probable implications of these changes for political stability in the developing world? If the analysis in this book is correct, mounting demographic and environmental pressures will raise the risks of turmoil, especially in the world's least developed countries where fertility rates are expected to remain high, environmental degradation and inequality are likely to worsen, and stagnant economies set the stage for failed states and predatory violence instigated by state elites.

DES will not produce these effects in a social or political vacuum. An especially important political trend to watch relates to the spread and consolidation of democracy. Data from Freedom House suggest that the number of "free" countries (where the rule of law prevails, basic human rights are protected, and there is free political competition, including elections) has increased from 44 in 1973, to 53 in 1983, 72 in 1993, and 88 in 2003. Although there is the widespread notion that democracy cannot flourish in low-income states, thirty-eight of the eighty-eight "free" countries in 2003 had per capita incomes of $3,500 or less.[93] The spread of democracy opens up both promises and perils for developing countries experiencing severe population and environmental pressures in the coming years. Cross-national data suggest that consolidated democracies are relatively immune from civil strife. However, this same data indicate that _democratization itself substantially increases risks of violent political instability._[94] Qualitative studies of this phenomenon argue that democratization puts the political rules of the game up for grabs, potentially threatening existing power holders and their allies, and often produces substantial increases in popular participation prior to the creation of institutions capable of accommodating new demands. As a consequence, some democratizing states experience periods of violence and backsliding to authoritarianism.[95]

The recent history of democratization in the Philippines and Kenya reinforces many of these findings. In both countries the consolidation of more inclusive institutions over time helped to limit the prospects for rebellion and to constrain elites from troublemaking, but the period of democratization itself was a dangerous time. In the Philippines democratization immediately reduced support for the CPP-NPA, but Aquino herself narrowly escaped several coup attempts. Aquino was ultimately forced to slow the pace of democratization in order to avoid alienating the military and powerful landed elites. The destabilizing effects of democratization were even more apparent in Kenya, where constitutional reform threatened Moi and KANU, encouraging them to engineer tribal warfare. Both countries demonstrate that the road to peaceful, consolidated democratic institutions is a bumpy one.

The experience of the Philippines, Kenya, and the other cases surveyed in this chapter also point to another dimension that will likely affect future prospects for DES-related civil strife: patterns of social organization. The potential for violent conflict is likely to vary considerably from country to country depending on the degree of groupness. In societies with deep ethnic, religious, and class-based cleavages, and few crosscutting affiliations and interests, civil strife is more likely. Thus, beyond the spread of democracy, it will be important to watch trends in the growth of civil society in developing countries and, where possible, to encourage the growth of groups and organizations that cut across, and against, the identity-based fault lines around which violent antagonisms often emerge.

Taking Demographic and Environmental Stress Seriously

In a well-known critique of the environmental security literature, Marc Levy argued that,

> Better research and better advice can grow out of an understanding that environmental factors interact with a variety of other factors to spawn violent conflict. . . . There appears to be *no interesting mechanisms that are purely and discretely environmental*. Therefore any research strategy aimed at deepening our understanding of security problems by studying *only* environmental connections can never succeed. . . . Instead, for those who worry about global conflict, the attention ought to be on how the constellation of factors that promote or impede violence operate.[96]

Levy has a point. Demographic and environmental variables are neither universally necessary nor wholly sufficient causes of civil strife in developing countries. DES is always embedded within a complex causal chain; DES only results in civil strife in conjunction and synergistic interaction with other intervening social and political variables that make societies prone to conflict. Nevertheless, Levy's suggestion that we abandon focused research on environmental (and presumably demographic) sources of violence in favor of a more general research program on civil and regional conflict forces an unnecessary choice. Adopting a generic research program is not the only way to make a valuable contribution to the study and practice of international security. The empirical evidence presented in this book suggests that DES is a potentially powerful contributor to civil strife and, as such, deserves careful study. Moreover, a research program focusing on DES is important if we are to fully evaluate the political effects of future population growth, accelerating economic activities, mounting environmental degradation, and widening income disparities in the developing world.[97]

This book has presented a new state-centric theory of demographically and environmentally induced civil strife in the hope of improving our understanding of the causal dynamics involved. Although I have not provided a definitive test of the theory, the evidence from detailed case studies of civil strife in the Philippines and Kenya, as well as a cursory look at a number of other conflicts around the globe, provide strong preliminary support for my argument. The next challenge for scholars is to conduct additional empirical tests. Unlike much of the research conducted up to this point, however, analysts should pay much more attention to the social and political variables that mediate the relationship between DES, the state, and internal conflicts. This is essential if scholars are to identify when and where demographic and environmental forces are most likely to lead to violence, and how this complex process will unfold. Only then will we be capable of addressing one of the most pressing security challenges of our day.

Notes

Chapter 1
Plight, Plunder, and Political Ecology

1. Here, "civil strife" refers to large-scale, sustained, and organized violent conflict within a country.

2. For excellent discussions of trends over this period, see Ted Robert Gurr, *Peoples Versus States: Minorities at Risk in the New Century* (Washington, D.C.: United States Institute of Peace Press, 2000); Kalevi J. Holsti, *The State, War, and the State of War* (New York: Cambridge University Press, 1996); and Mary Kaldor, *New and Old Wars: Organized Violence in a Global Era* (Stanford, Calif.: Stanford University Press, 1999).

3. Milton Leitenberg, "Deaths in Wars and Conflicts between 1945 and 2000," Occassional Paper #29, Cornell University Peace Studies Program, July 2003.

4. See Paul Collier et al., *Breaking the Conflict Trap: Civil War and Development Policy* (Washington, D.C.: The World Bank and Oxford University Press, 2003), chap. 1.

5. See ibid., chap. 2; Chester A. Crocker, "Engaging Failed States," *Foreign Affairs* 82, no. 5 (September/October 2003): 32–44; and Monty G. Marshall and Ted Robert Gurr, *Peace and Conflict 2003* (College Park, Md.: Center for International Development and Conflict Management, University of Maryland, 2003).

6. Since the early 1990s Thomas Homer-Dixon and his colleagues at the University of Toronto have been at the forefront of theoretical and empirical work in this area, conducting three major research projects: the Project on Environmental Change and Acute Conflict; the Project on Environment, Population, and Security; and the Project on Environmental Scarcities, State Capacity, and Civil Violence. For a summary of this work, see Thomas F. Homer-Dixon and Jessica Blitt, eds., *Ecoviolence: Links among Environment, Population, and Security* (Lanham, Md.: Rowan and Littlefield, 1998); and Thomas Homer-Dixon, *Environment, Scarcity, and Violence* (Princeton, N.J.: Princeton University Press, 1999). Homer-Dixon's work has also been influential in shaping the Swiss Environment and Conflict Project (ENCOP), as well as research conducted by two prominent Norwegian groups, the International Peace Research Institute, Oslo (PRIO) and the Fridtjof Nansen Institute (FIN). See Günther Baechler, "Why Environmental Transformation Causes Violence: A Synthesis," *Environmental Change and Security Project Report*, Woodrow Wilson Center, Issue 4 (spring 1998): 24–44; Günther Baechler et al., *Environmental Degradation as a Cause of War: Environmental Conflicts in the Third World and Ways for Their Peaceful Resolution*, Vol. 1 (Berne: Swiss Peace Foundation/Swiss Federal Institute of Technology, 1996); Günther Baechler and Kurt R. Spillmann, eds., *Environmental Degradation as a Cause of War: Regional and Country Studies*, Vols. 2 and 3 (Berne: Swiss Peace Founda-

tion/Swiss Federal Institute of Technology, 1996); and Dan Smith and Willy Østreng, eds., *Research on Environment, Poverty, and Conflict: A Proposal* (Oslo: International Peace Research Institute/The Fridtjof Nansen Institute, 1997).

7. On population size and density as correlates of internal war, see Jack A. Goldstone et al., *State Failure Task Force Report: Phase III Findings* (McLean, Va.: Science Applications International Corporation, 2000), p. 18. Analyzing data from the post–Cold War period, Indra de Soysa also finds that population size and population density, in a context of economic stagnation, are significantly correlated with internal conflicts resulting in at least twenty-five battle fatalities. See Indra de Soysa, "The Resource Curse: Are Civil Wars Driven by Rapacity or Paucity?" in *Greed and Grievance: Economic Agendas in Civil Wars*, ed., Mats Berdal and David M. Malone (Boulder, Colo.: Lynne Rienner, 2000), p. 124; Indra de Soysa, "Paradise Is a Bazaar? Greed, Creed, and Governance in Civil War, 1989–99," *Journal of Peace Research* 39, no. 4 (July 2002): 407–10. For other findings on population size, see Paul Collier and Anke Hoeffler, "Greed and Grievance in Civil War," rev. version, World Bank, October 21, 2001, pp. 8, 17; and James D. Fearon and David D. Laitin, "Ethnicity, Insurgency, and Civil War," *American Political Science Review* 97, no. 1 (February 2003): 85. It should be noted that although Fearon and Laitin find that population size is correlated with internal war, population growth (measured using an average growth rate for the prior three years) has no significant impact. However, since population growth is only likely to have effects over the long term and under certain economic, social, and political conditions, this measure may be missing important effects.

8. Richard P. Cincotta et al., *The Security Demographic: Population and Civil Conflict after the Cold War* (Washington, D.C.: Population Action International, 2003). The demographic transition refers to the historical transformation away from societies characterized by large families and short lives to societies characterized by small families and long lives. Many countries in the world have successfully made it through the demographic transition, but a significant number of low-income countries in the contemporary period remain stuck in the early or middle phases of this transition.

9. A series of studies conducted by Paul Collier and his research associates for the World Bank suggest that the percentage of a country's exports made up of primary commodity exports is a significant risk factor for internal war. Although some, including at times the authors themselves, infer from this finding that resource abundance is a risk factor, the measure used only points to the level of resource dependence, not abundance or scarcity *per se*. See Paul Collier and Anke Hoeffler, "On Economic Causes of Civil War," *Oxford Economic Papers* 50 (1998): 563–73; idem, "Justice-Seeking and Loot-Seeking in Civil War," World Bank, February 17, 1999; idem, "Greed and Grievance in Civil War," World Bank Policy Research Paper 2355, April 12, 2000; idem, "Greed and Grievance in Civil War," rev. version; Paul Collier, "Economic Causes of Civil Conflict and Their Implications for Policy," World Bank, June 15, 2000; idem, "The Market for Civil War," *Foreign Policy* (May/June 2003): 38–45; and Collier et al., *The Conflict Trap*, chap. 3.

10. Wenche Hauge and Tanja Ellingsen have found statistical evidence linking forest loss, soil degradation, and freshwater availability to internal conflict during the 1980–92 period. See Hauge and Ellingsen, "Beyond Environmental Scarcity: Causal Pathways to Conflict," *Journal of Peace Research* 35, no. 3 (May 1998): 299–317. On the statistical relationship between per capita availability of cropland and freshwater and internal conflict, see Cincotta et al., *The Security Demographic*, chap. 5. It should be noted that all these studies argue that the risk of environmentally induced violence varies depending on the interaction between environmental degradation, natural resource endowments, and other economic, social, and political variables. This supports the point made later in this chapter that much more work needs to be done to analyze the intervening variables involved in the population–environment–civil strife connection.

11. Quoted in Simon Dalby, "Threats from the South? Geopolitics, Equity, and Environmental Security," in *Contested Ground: Security and Conflict in the New Environmental Politics*, ed. Daniel H. Deudney and Richard A. Matthew (Albany, N.Y.: State University of New York Press, 1999), p. 162. NATO's Strategic Concept now includes environmental components, and members of the European Union appear to believe that demographic and environmental forces in East-Central Europe, the Middle East, and Africa pose threats to European security. See Kent Hughes Butts, "National Security, the Environment and DOD," *Environmental Change and Security Project Report*, Woodrow Wilson Center, Issue 2 (spring 1996): 22–27.

12. Robert D. Kaplan, "The Coming Anarchy," *Atlantic Monthly*, February 1994, p. 58.

13. Nafis Sadik, "Population Growth and Global Stability," in *Population and Global Security*, ed. Nicholas Polunin (New York: Cambridge University Press, 1998), pp. 1–2, 12.

14. *A National Security Strategy of Engagement and Enlargement* (Washington, D.C.: The White House, 1996), preface.

15. "2015 Outlook: Enough Food, Scarce Water, Porous Borders," *New York Times*, 18 December 2000, p. A6. For the original, see National Intelligence Council, *Global Trends 2015: A Dialogue about the Future with Nongovernmental Experts* (NIC 2000–2, December 2000).

16. *The National Security Strategy of the United States of America* (Washington, D.C.: The White House, September 2000).

17. Colin L. Powell, Remarks at State Department Conference, Meridian International Center, Washington, D.C., 12 July 2002; available at http://www.state.gov/secretary/rm/2002/11822.htm (accessed 10/2/03).

18. Peter Schwartz and Doug Randall, *An Abrupt Climate Change Scenario and Its Implications for United States National Security*, October 2003, pp. 1–3, available at http://www.ems.org/climate/pentagon_climate_change.pdf (accessed 2/24/04). The Pentagon did not intend for the findings to be made public, but the report was leaked to the British press. See Mark Townsend and Paul Harris, "Now the Pentagon Tells Bush: Climate Change Will Destroy Us," *The Observer*, 22 February 2004, p. Lexis-Nexis.

19. Thomas Malthus, *An Essay on the Principles of Population* (New York: Penguin Books, 1985 [1798]). Classic texts in the neo-Malthusian tradition include Paul Ehrlich, *The Population Bomb* (New York: Ballantine Books, 1968); Paul R. Ehrlich and Anne H. Ehrlich, *The Population Explosion* (New York: Touchstone/ Simon and Schuster, 1990); and Donella Meadows et al., *The Limits to Growth: A Report for the Club of Rome's Project on the Predicament of Mankind* (New York: Signet, 1972). In more recent years the Washington, D.C.-based Worldwatch Institute has served as a standard bearer for the neo-Malthusian position. See, for example, Lester R. Brown et al., *Beyond Malthus: Nineteen Dimensions of the Population Challenge* (New York: W.W. Norton, 1999).

20. United Nations Population Division (UNPD), *World Population Prospects: The 2002 Revision* (New York: UNPD, 2003); World Bank, *World Development Report 2003: Sustainable Development in a Dynamic World* (Washington, D.C. and New York: World Bank and Oxford University Press, 2003), p. 7; Worldwatch Institute, *Vital Signs 2003* (New York: W.W. Norton, 2003), p. 67.

21. UNPD, *Population, Environment, and Development: The Concise Report* (New York: UNPD, 2001), p. 5; and UNPD, *World Population Prospects: The 2002 Revision*, p. vi.

22. UNPD, *Population, Environment, and Development*, p. 1; and Worldwatch Institute, *Vital Signs 2003*, pp. 44-45.

23. United Nations Development Programme (UNDP), *Human Development Report 2003* (New York: Oxford University Press, 2003), p. 16.

24. Of these fifty-four countries, twenty were in sub-Saharan Africa, seventeen in Eastern Europe and the former Soviet Union, six in Latin America and the Caribbean, six in East Asia and the Pacific, and five in the Middle East (UNDP, *Human Development Report 2003*, p. 3).

25. Ibid., pp. 2-3, 5, 34, 40-41; World Bank, *World Development Indicators* (Washington, D.C.: World Bank, 2003), pp. 4-5, 9; and World Bank, *World Development Report 2003*, pp. 1-3.

26. Worldwatch Institute, *Vital Signs 2003*, pp. 18, 88.

27. UNDP, *Human Development Report 2003*, pp. 5, 39-40.

28. World Bank, *World Development Indicators*, p. 118; World Resources Institute, *World Resources 2000-2001* (Oxford: Elsevier Science, 2000), pp. 26-27; and Worldwatch Institute, *Vital Signs 2003*, p. 17.

29. This figure includes 518 million in arid regions with no access to irrigation systems, 430 million on land with soils unsuitable for agriculture, 216 million in slope-dominated regions, and more that 130 million in fragile forest ecosystems (World Bank, *World Development Report 2003*, p. 60).

30. World Bank, *World Development Indicators*, p. 118; World Bank, *World Development Report 2003*, pp. 7-8, 60-67; and Worldwatch Institute, *Vital Signs 2003*, p. 17.

31. Bill McKibben, "A Special Moment in History," *Atlantic Monthly*, May 1998, p. 63.

32. Worldwatch Institute, *Vital Signs 2003*, p. 34.

33. World Bank, *World Development Indicators*, p. 118.

34. Payal Sampat, "Scrapping Mining Dependence," in Worldwatch Institute, *State of the World 2003* (New York: W.W. Norton, 2003), p. 113.

35. Mathis Wackernagel et al., "Tracking the Ecological Overshoot of the Human Economy," *Proceedings of the National Academy of Sciences* 99, no.14 (2002): 9266–71; and World Wildlife Fund (WWF), *Living Planet Report 2002* (Gland, Switzerland: WWF, 2002).

36. UNDP, *Human Development Report 2003*, p. 10; and World Bank, *World Development Report 2003*, p. 2.

37. World Bank, *World Development Indicators*, p. 118; and idem, *World Development Report 2003*, p. 3.

38. UNDP, *Human Development Report 2003*, pp. 10, 125; World Bank, *World Development Indicators*, p. 118; and idem, *World Development Report 2003*, p. 2.

39. UNDP, *Human Development Report 2003*, p. 10; World Bank, *World Development Report 2003*, p. 3; and World Resources Institute, *World Resources 2000–2001*, p. 70.

40. These labels are meant to capture the distinct causal logic of each hypothesis and provide umbrella terms that encompass the arguments made by the numerous authors advancing them. It should be noted, however, that my labels might differ somewhat from the labels assigned in other research projects. Homer-Dixon, for example, introduced the term *simple scarcity* and uses it in the way I do, but he combines what I call the *deprivation* and *state failure* hypotheses into a single label called *deprivation conflicts* or *insurgencies*. Moreover, what I label the *transboundary migration hypothesis*, Homer-Dixon refers to as *group identity* conflicts. See Thomas F. Homer-Dixon, "On the Threshold: Environmental Changes as Causes of Acute Conflict," *International Security* 16, no. 2 (fall 1991): 104–11; idem, "Environmental Scarcities and Violent Conflict: Evidence from Cases," *International Security* 19, no. 1 (summer 1994): 18–31; and idem, *Environment, Scarcity, and Violence*, chap. 7. The ENCOP project provides seven ideal types of environmental conflict: (1) ethnopolitical conflicts; (2) core-periphery conflicts; (3) regionalist migration/displacement conflicts; (4) transboundary migration conflicts; (5) demographically caused conflicts; (6) international water/river basins conflicts; and (7) global environmental conflicts (owing to climate change, ozone depletion, and other global environmental problems). Types 1–3 and 5 fall under what I call the deprivation hypothesis, 4 (and some examples of 5) fall under the transboundary migration hypothesis, and 6 and 7 fall under the simple scarcity hypothesis. For a brief description of these ideal types, see Baechler, "Why Environmental Transformation Causes Violence"; and idem, "Environmental Degradation in the South as a Cause of Armed Conflict," in *Environmental Change and Security: A European Perspective*, ed. Alexander Carius and Kurt M. Lietzmann (Berlin: Springer, 1999), pp. 107–29.

41. The simple scarcity hypothesis combines the neo-Malthusian emphasis on scarcity with Realist understandings of international relations. Realism posits that the lack of central authority (or, "anarchy") in the international system compels states to focus first and foremost on maintaining their security and political independence in the face of the constant possibility of war. Realists argue that war can result from clashes of interest or spiraling insecurities and miscalculations by states jockeying for position in this anarchic context. The simple scarcity hypothesis builds on this foundation and contends that war

between states may erupt over scarce natural resources if six conditions hold: (1) the resource involved is necessary for a state's survival; (2) the resource is unevenly distributed across the international system; (3) the resource is vulnerable to scarcity or disruption; (4) few cost-effective alternative supplies or substitutes exist; (5) the resource can be seized, controlled, or destroyed through military means; and (6) the aggressor believes it has the military means to be successful. For general discussions of the prospects for international resource wars, see Nazli Choucri and Robert North, *Nations in Conflict* (San Francisco: Freeman, 1975); Peter H. Gleick, "Environment, Resources, and International Security and Politics," in *Science and International Security: Responding to a Changing World*, ed. Eric Arnett, (Washington, D.C.: American Association for the Advancement of Science, 1990), pp. 501–23; Peter H. Gleick, "Water and Conflict: Fresh Water Resources and International Security," *International Security* 18, no. 1 (summer 1993): 79–112; Homer-Dixon, "On the Threshold," pp. 106–8; Homer-Dixon, *Environment, Scarcity, and Violence*, pp. 137–41; Michael T. Klare, *Resource Wars: The New Landscape of International Conflict* (New York: Metropolitan Books, 2001); Miriam R. Lowi, *Water and Power: The Politics of a Scarce Resource in the Jordan River Basin* (Cambridge: Cambridge University Press, 1993); John Orme, "The Utility of Force in a World of Scarcity," *International Security* 22, no. 3 (winter 1997–98), pp. 138-67; Sandra Postel, "The Politics of Water," *Worldwatch* 6, no. 4 (July/August 1993): 10–18; Joyce Starr, "Water Wars," *Foreign Policy*, no. 82 (spring 1991): 17–30; and Arthur Westing, ed., *Global Resources and International Conflict: Environmental Factors in Strategic Policy and Action* (New York: Oxford University Press, 1986).

42. The transboundary migration hypothesis identifies a different causal link between demographic and environmental pressures and international conflict. Here the claim is that environmental degradation and resource scarcity can force marginalized inhabitants of one country to move in order to survive. As these environmentally displaced persons cross borders, regional and international tensions will increase, and conflicts may erupt as potentially hostile ethnic and religious groups are thrown together under conditions of scarcity, deprivation, and intense competition. See Baechler, "Why Environmental Transformation Causes Violence," pp. 28–30; Nazli Choucri, "Environment, Development and International Assistance: Crucial Linkages," in *Resolving Third World Conflict: Challenges for a New Era*, ed. Sheryl J. Brown and Kimber M. Schraub, pp. 89–118 (Washington D.C.: United States Institute of Peace Press, 1992); Sanjoy Hazarika, "Bangladesh and Assam: Land Pressures, Migration and Ethnic Conflict," Occasional Paper No. 3, Project on Environmental Change and Acute Conflict (Washington, D.C.: University of Toronto, the Academy of Arts and Sciences, 1993); Homer-Dixon, "On the Threshold," pp. 108–9; idem, "Environmental Scarcities and Violent Conflict," pp. 20–23; idem, *Environment, Scarcity, and Violence*, pp. 141–42; Jodi L. Jacobson, "Environmental Refugees: A Yardstick of Habitability," *World Watch Paper* 86 (Washington, D.C.: Worldwatch Institute, 1989); and Shin-wha Lee, "A Deadly Triangle: The Environment, Refugees, and Conflict," paper presented at the Annual Meeting of the American Political Science Association, New York, 1–4 September 1994.

43. There is scant empirical evidence supporting a strong link between population growth, environmental degradation, resource scarcity, and international violence. Resource wars between countries are very rare. Nations have only occasionally clashed over oil and other nonrenewable mineral resources, and international violence driven by conflicts over renewable resources is even less common. A simple cost-benefit analysis explains the infrequency of international resource wars. The destructive capacity of modern weaponry makes international warfare an incredibly costly and risky endeavor, creating a general presumption in favor of resolving conflicts peacefully. The relatively low stakes involved in most interstate resource disputes reinforces this general presumption toward nonviolence. While countries may occasionally view certain natural resources, especially oil and water, as critical to short-term national survival, directly transferable into national power, and thus potentially worth fighting over, this is not the case with most natural resources most of the time. Moreover, even when resources are seen as vital, it is almost always cheaper to obtain them through trade or bilateral and multilateral agreements than to fight for them.

Indeed, in the contemporary period, the countries most dependent on natural resources for their national security are either rich enough to purchase them (e.g., Japan), militarily powerful enough to guarantee access through arrangements backed up by the implied threat of force (e.g., the United States and Russia), or so poor and militarily impotent that external aggression is not a viable option (e.g., most countries in the developing world). Thus, given the high costs of war relative to the stakes involved, and the existence of nonviolent alternatives, we would expect the majority of international resource conflicts to be resolved peacefully, if not always fairly. In most cases nations competing for natural resources will avoid war through trade, mutual accommodation, or less symmetric arrangements dictated by the most powerful actors involved. For general criticisms of the simple scarcity hypothesis, see Daniel H. Deudney, "The Case against Linking Environmental Degradation and National Security," *Millennium* 19, no. 3 (winter 1990): 469–74; idem, "Environmental Security: A Critique," pp. 205–8; Jack A. Goldstone, "Demography, Environment, and Security," in *Environmental Conflict*, ed. Paul F. Diehl and Nils Petter Gleditsch, pp. 84–109 (Boulder, Colo.: Westview, 2001); Goldstone, "How Demographic Change Can Lead to Violent Conflict," *Journal of International Affairs* 56, no. 1 (fall 2002): 5–8; Homer-Dixon, *Environment, Scarcity, and Violence*, pp. 138–39; Ronnie D. Lipschutz, *When Nations Clash: Raw Materials, Ideology, and Foreign Policy* (New York: Ballinger, 1989); Ronnie D. Lipschutz and John Holdren, "Crossing Borders: Resource Flows, the Global Environment, and International Security," *Bulletin of Peace Proposals* 21, no. 2 (June 1990): 121–33; and Steve C. Lonegran, "Water and Conflict: Rhetoric and Reality," in Diehl and Gleditsch, *Environmental Conflict*, pp. 109–24. For examples of resource shortages leading to cooperation, see Baechler, "Why Environmental Transformation Causes Violence," pp. 30–31, 38; Peter H. Gleick, "Freshwater in Southern Africa as a Tool of Domestic and International Politics," paper prepared for the Columbia University Environment and Security Project, 1998; and Ronnie D. Lipschutz, "Damming Troubled Waters: Conflict over the Danube, 1950–2000," paper prepared for the Columbia University Environment and Security Project, 1998.

The contention that transboundary migration produces international strife also has a weak empirical foundation. There are a few cases of conflict arising from demographically and environmentally induced population displacements, most notably the violence that followed the flow of Bangladeshi migrants into the Indian states of Assam and Tripura during the 1980s. There are many other cases, however, where similar population displacements have not incited violence. See Astri Suhrke, "Environmental Change, Migration, and Conflict," in *Managing Global Chaos: Sources of and Responses to International Conflict* ed. Chester A. Crocker and Fen Osler Hampson, pp.113–40 (Washington, D.C.: United States Institute of Peace Press, 1996).

44. "Absolute deprivation" refers to a gap between what people want and what they need, whereas "relative deprivation" refers to a gap between what people have and what they think they deserve.

45. See the discussion of "environmental scarcity" in Homer-Dixon, "Environmental Scarcities and Violent Conflict," pp. 8–16; and idem, *Environment, Scarcity, and Violence*, chap. 4.

46. This hypothesis is rooted in early theoretical work by James C. Davies, "Toward a Theory of Revolution," *American Sociological Review* 27, no. 1 (February 1962): 5–19; and Ted Robert Gurr, *Why Men Rebel* (Princeton, N.J.: Princeton University Press, 1970). For a discussion and application to demographic and environmental conflicts, see Homer-Dixon, "On the Threshold," pp. 104–5, 109–11; and idem, *Environment, Scarcity, and Violence*, pp. 142–47. For criticisms, see Deudney, "Environmental Security: A Critique," pp. 210–13.

47. Norman Myers, *Ultimate Security: The Environmental Basis of Political Stability* (New York: W. W. Norton, 1993), p. 22; and Jessica Tuchman Mathews, "Redefining Security," *Foreign Affairs* 68, no. 2 (Spring 1989) pp. 166, 168. See also Ehrlich and Ehrlich, *The Population Explosion*, pp. 178–79.

48. See Jack A. Goldstone, *Revolution and Rebellion in the Early Modern World* (Berkeley: University of California Press, 1991); idem, "Population Growth and Revolutionary Crises," in *Theorizing Revolutions*, ed. John Foran, pp. 102–20 (London: Routledge, 1997); idem, "Demography, Domestic Conflict, and the International Order," in *International Order and the Future of World Politics*, ed. T. V. Paul and John A. Hall, pp. 352–72 (Cambridge: Cambridge University Press, 1999); Homer-Dixon, "On the Threshold"; idem, "Environmental Scarcities and Violent Conflict"; idem, *Environment, Scarcity, and Violence*; and Myron Weiner, "Political Demography: An Inquiry into the Political Consequences of Population Change," in *Rapid Population Growth: Consequences and Policy Implications*, Vol. 2: Research Papers, pp. 567–617 (Baltimore, Md.: Johns Hopkins University Press, 1971). For similar, but less rigorous, arguments, see Kaplan, "The Coming Anarchy"; idem, *The Ends of the Earth: A Journey at the Dawn of the 21st Century* (New York: Random House, 1996); and Paul Kennedy, *Preparing for the Twenty-First Century* (New York: Random House, 1993).

49. Goldstone, "Demography, Domestic Conflict, and the International Order," pp. 360–64; and Homer-Dixon, *Environment, Scarcity, and Violence*, pp. 98–103.

50. On the negative economic effects of population growth, see Dennis A. Ahlburg, "Population Growth and Poverty," in *Population and Development: Old Debates, New Conclusions*, ed. Robert Cassen, pp. 127–47 (New Brunswick, N.J.: Transaction, 1994); Allen C. Kelley, "Economic Consequences of Population Change in the Third World," *Journal of Economic Literature* 26, no. 4 (December 1988): 1685–1728; Allen C. Kelley and William Paul McGreevey, "Population and Development in Historical Perspective," in Cassen, *Population and Development*, pp. 107–26. For the economic challenges posed by environmental degradation and resource scarcity, see Homer-Dixon, "Environmental Scarcities and Violent Conflict," pp. 25–26; and idem, *Environment, Scarcity, and Violence*, pp. 88–93.

51. Goldstone, "Demography, Domestic Conflict, and the International Order," pp. 360–61, 367; and Homer-Dixon, *Environment, Scarcity, and Violence*, pp. 101–2.

52. See Jeffrey Berejikian, "Revolutionary Collective Action and the Agent-Structure Problem," *American Political Science Review* 86, no. 3 (September 1992): 649–51, 655; Mark I. Lichbach, "What Makes Rational Peasants Revolutionary? Dilemma, Paradox, and Irony in Peasant Collective Action." *World Politics* 46, no. 3 (April 1994): 383–418; and Edward N. Muller and Karl-Dieter Opp, "Rational Choice and Rebellious Collective Action," *American Political Science Review* 80, no. 2 (June 1986): 471–73. This line of reasoning builds on the classic work of Mancur Olson, *The Logic of Collective Action* (Cambridge, Mass.: Harvard University Press, 1965).

53. See the discussion of state strength and institutional inclusivity in chapter 2.

54. Jack A. Goldstone, "Debate," *Environmental Change and Security Project Report*, Woodrow Wilson Center, Issue 2 (spring 1996), p. 70 (emphasis added).

55. Baechler, "Why Environmental Transformation Causes Violence," p. 32. A similar point is made by Weiner in, "Political Demography" (p. 573).

56. Homer-Dixon, *Environment, Scarcity, and Violence*, p. 178.

57. Ibid., pp. 143–44, 178–79; idem, "On the Threshold," p. 111; idem, "Environmental Scarcities and Violent Conflict," pp. 26–27; and Valerie Percival and Thomas F. Homer-Dixon, "Environmental Scarcity and Violent Conflict: The Case of South Africa," Occasional Paper, Project on Environment, Population, and Security (Washington, D.C.: University of Toronto, the Academy of Arts and Sciences, 1995), p. 7. See also, Baechler , "Why Environmental Transformation Causes Violence," pp. 32–35; and Goldstone, "Population Growth and Revolutionary Crises," pp. 111–15. Goldstone's classic study of revolutions in early modern Europe and Asia does specify and integrate a number of important intervening variables into its causal account. In particular, Goldstone identified state fiscal strength, intra-elite mobility, and popular mobilization potential as mediating the relationship between demographic pressures and revolution in England, France, China, and elsewhere (*Revolution and Rebellion in the Early Modern World*, chaps. 1, 6). Nevertheless, Goldstone's study includes only a limited discussion of the intervening factors likely to matter most in contemporary civil and ethnic conflict, and factors such as ethnic, religious, and regional cleavages are only discussed in passing in his more recent work.

See Goldstone, "Demography, Domestic Conflict, and the International Order," pp. 352-53, 363-64.

58. For a similar criticism, see Nils Petter Gleditsch, "Armed Conflict and the Environment: A Critique of the Literature," *Journal of Peace Research* 35, no. 1 (May 1998): 389.

59. This research has received a great deal of attention outside academia as well. See, for example, Fred Pearce, "Blood Diamonds and Oil," *New Scientist*, 29 June 2002, pp. 36–41.

60. Classics in this tradition include Ester Boserup, *The Conditions of Agricultural Growth* (Chicago: Aldine, 1965); J. E. Stiglitz, "Neoclassical Analysis of Resource Economics," in *Scarcity and Growth Reconsidered*, ed. K. Smith, pp. 36–66 (Baltimore, Md.: The Johns Hopkins University Press, 1979); Julian L. Simon, *The Ultimate Resource* (Princeton, N.J.: Princeton University Press, 1981); Julian L. Simon and Herman Kahn, eds., *The Resourceful Earth: A Response to Global 2000* (Oxford: Basil Blackwell, 1984); and Julian L. Simon, *Population and Development in Poor Countries* (Princeton, N.J.: Princeton University Press, 1992). For more recent examples, see Nicholas Eberstadt, "Population, Food, and Income: Global Trends in the Twentieth Century," in *The True State of the Planet*, ed. Ronald Bailey, pp. 7–48 (New York: Free Press, 1995); Bjørn Lomborg, *The Skeptical Environmentalist: Measuring the Real State of the World* (New York: Cambridge University Press, 2001 [1998]); and Mark Sagoff, "Do We Consume Too Much?" *Altantic Monthly*, June 1997, pp. 80–96. Within the debate over the prospects for demographic and environmental conflict, this position has been advanced by several critics of the neo-Malthusian view. See Deudney, "Environmental Security: A Critique," pp. 205–6; Gleditsch, "Armed Conflict and the Environment," pp. 383–84; and Hartmann, "Will the Circle Be Unbroken?" pp. 45–46.

61. Bjørn Lomborg, "Resource Constraints or Abundance?" in Diehl and Gleditsch, *Environmental Conflict*, pp. 125–26, 143, 152. For a similar argument, see Richard A. Matthew, "Environment, Population and Conflict: New Modalities of Threat and Vulnerability in South Asia," *Journal of International Affairs* 56, no. 1 (fall 2002): 243–44.

62. For excellent reviews of the debate, see Allen C. Kelley, "The Population Debate in Historical Perspective: Revisionism Revisited," in Birdsall, Kelley, and Sinding, *Population Matters*, pp. 24–54; and Allen C. Kelley and Robert M. Schmidt, "Economic and Demographic Change: A Synthesis of Models, Findings, and Perspectives," in Birdsall, Kelley, and Sinding, *Population Matters*, pp. 67–105.

63. For a discussion of these and related dynamics, as well as relevant empirical findings, see Michael L. Ross, "Natural Resources and Civil War: An Overview," unpublished manuscript, 15 August 2003, pp. 15–26; and Ross, "What Do We Know about Natural Resources and Civil War?" *Journal of Peace Research* 41, no. 3 (May 2004): 337–56. In another article, Ross identifies thirteen different mechanisms whereby natural resources potentially contribute to the onset, duration, and intensity of civil wars. See Ross, "How Do Natural Resources Influence Civil War? Evidence from Thirteen Cases," *International Organization* 58, no. 1 (winter 2004): 35–67. Curiously, despite his extensive review

NOTES TO PAGE 15

of the neoclassical conflict literature, Ross ignores scarcity-related hypotheses. He discusses one "grievance"-related argument—the possibility that resource extraction produces grievances by contributing to economic dislocations and environmental degradation—but even this hypothesis is framed in terms of resource abundance. Moreover, to test competing hypotheses, Ross offers brief descriptions of thirteen cases from a list of thirty-six civil wars during the 1990s. The thirteen cases "were chosen on a 'most likely' basis: the sample includes all civil wars that occurred between 1990 and 2000 in which scholars, nongovernmental organizations, or UN agencies suggested that natural resource wealth, or natural resource dependence, influenced the war's onset, duration, or casualty rate" (ibid., p. 46). Unfortunately, because of his selection criteria, a number of scarcity-driven conflicts from the larger list of civil wars, including the Philippines, Rwanda, and Somalia, were ignored by the analysis. These cases are briefly discussed in chapter 6.

64. A number of studies suggest that a local abundance of valuable natural resources lengthens the duration of civil wars. See Michael W. Doyle and Nicholas Sambanis, "International Peacebuilding: A Theoretical and Quantitative Analysis," *American Political Science Review* 94, no. 4 (December 2000): 785, 789; and James D. Fearon, "Why Do Some Civil Wars Last So Much Longer Than Others?" *Journal of Peace Research* 41, no. 3 (May 2004): 283–84, 295–98. Other research suggests that abundant supplies of valuable resources increases the geographic scope of violent conflicts. See Halvard Buhaug, "The Geography of Civil War," *Journal of Peace Research* 39, no. 4 (July 2002): 422, 427, 430.

65. Collier, "Economic Causes of Civil Conflict and Their Implications for Policy," p. 21. See also Collier and Hoeffler, "On Economic Causes of Civil War"; idem, "Justice-Seeking and Loot-Seeking in Civil War"; idem, "Greed and Grievance in Civil War," rev. ed.; and Collier et al., *The Conflict Trap*, chap. 3.

66. Indra de Soysa, "Natural Resources and Civil Conflict: Shrinking Pie or Honey Pot?" unpublished manuscript, 2000, p. 26. See also idem, "The Resource Curse"; idem, "Paradise Is a Bazaar?"; and Michael Renner, *The Anatomy of Resource Wars*, Worldwatch Paper 162, October 2002.

67. For thorough reviews of these arguments, see Richard M. Auty, "Resource Abundance and Economic Development: Improving the Performance of Resource-Rich Countries," Research for Action 44, World Institute for Development Economics and Research, 1998; and Michael L. Ross, "The Political Economy of the Resource Curse," *World Politics* 51, no. 2 (1999): 297–322.

68. Jeffrey D. Sachs and Andrew M. Warner, "The Big Push, Natural Resource Booms, and Growth," *Journal of Development Economics* 59 (1999): 48.

69. See Auty, "Resource Abundance and Economic Development," pp. 6–8; Richard M. Auty, "The Political Economy of Resource-Driven Growth," *European Economic Review* 45 (2001): 839–846; Terry Lynn Karl, *The Paradox of Plenty: Oil Booms and Petro-States* (Berkeley, Calif.: University of California Press, 1997), pp. 5, 52–53; Edward E. Leamer et al., "Does Natural Resource Abundance Increase Latin American Income Inequality?" *Journal of Development Economics* 59 (1999): 40; Ross, "The Political Economy of the Resource Curse," pp. 305–7; Jeffrey D. Sachs and Andrew M. Warner, *Natural Resource Abundance and Economic Growth*, Development Discussion Paper No. 517a (Cambridge, Mass.:

Harvard Institute for International Development, 1995); idem, "Sources of Slow Growth in African Economies," *Journal of African Economics* 6, no. 3 (1997): 335–80; idem, "The Big Push, Natural Resource Booms and Growth"; idem, "Natural Resources and Economic Development: The Curse of Natural Resources," *European Economic Review* 45 (2001): 827–38.

70. Auty, "Resource Abundance and Economic Development," p. 2; Leamer et al., "Does Natural Resource Abundance Increase Latin American Income Inequality?" p. 5; and Ross, "The Political Economy of the Resource Curse," pp. 301–4.

71. See Richard M. Auty, *Patterns of Development: Resources, Policy and Economic Growth* (London: Edward Arnold, 1995); Karl, *The Paradox of Plenty*; Ross, "The Political Economy of the Resource Curse"; and Michael L. Ross, *Timber Booms and Institutional Breakdown in Southeast Asia* (New York: Cambridge University Press, 2001).

72. See de Soysa, "The Resource Curse," pp. 120–22; Renner, *The Anatomy of Resource Wars*, pp. 14–18; William Reno, *Warlord Politics and African States* (Boulder, Colo.: Lynne Rienner, 1998); and Ross, "Natural Resources and Civil War: An Overview," pp. 7–15.

73. Nancy Birdsall and Steven W. Sinding, "How and Why Population Matters: New Findings, New Issues," in Birdsall and Sinding, *Population Matters*, p. 19.

74. For an excellent discussion of these issues, see Dennis A. Ahlburg, "Julian Simon and the Population Growth Debate," *Population and Development Review* 24, no. 2 (June 1998): 317–27; Thomas F. Homer-Dixon, *The Ingenuity Gap: Facing the Economic, Environmental, and Other Challenges of an Increasingly Complex and Unpredictable Future* (New York: Knopf, 2000); idem, "The Ingenuity Gap: Can Poor Countries Adapt to Resource Scarcity," *Population and Development Review* 21, no. 3 (September 1995): 587–612; and idem, *Environment, Scarcity, and Violence*, chaps. 3, 6.

75. Birdsall and Sinding, "How and Why Population Matters," pp. 9–10; Kelley and Schmidt, "Economic and Demographic Change." Ahlburg argues that there are a number of reasons for the negative relationship that began to appear in the 1980s, including more adverse effects on savings, diminished returns from existing technologies in agriculture, and the adverse effects of environmental degradation on agricultural productivity. ("Julian Simon and the Population Growth Debate," p. 321).

76. Kelley and Schmidt, "Economic and Demographic Change," p. 71.

77. Kelley, "The Population Debate in Historical Perspective," pp. 41–43.

78. Ibid., pp. 42–43.

79. Philippe Le Billon, "The Political Ecology of War: Natural Resources and Armed Conflicts," *Political Geography* 20 (2001): 569–70.

80. In his survey of the literature on resource abundance and civil war, Ross notes that oil is associated with the onset of civil war and that certain lootable natural resources such as diamonds are associated with the duration of civil wars but that an abundance of legal agricultural commodities is not associated with conflict ("What Do We Know about Natural Resources and Civil War?" pp. 346–47). Moreover, de Soysa finds a significant correlation between mineral

wealth and internal armed conflict but no such correlation for natural resource abundance *in general*. ("Paradise Is a Bazaar?" pp. 407–9, 413; and "Natural Resources and Civil Conflict?" pp. 9–10). See also Renner, *The Anatomy of Resource Wars*, pp. 22–39.

81. In some cases extraction and production activities related to nonrenewable resources contribute to the degradation and depletion of renewable resources. Mining, for example, often contaminates nearby cropland and water supplies. Under these circumstances nonrenewable sectors have widespread effects but this is a result of their impact on surrounding renewable resources.

82. Pearce, "Blood Diamonds and Oil," p. 40.

83. Klare, *Resource Wars*, pp. 20–21, chap. 8.

84. Collier et al. acknowledge this point. See idem, *The Conflict Trap*, pp. 70–71.

85. Karl, *The Paradox of Plenty*, pp. 47–48.

86. Sachs and Warner, "Natural Resources and Economic Development," p. 831.

87. Auty, "Resource Abundance and Economic Development," p. 1; Karl, *The Paradox of Plenty*, pp. 15, 48–49, 52, 56–57; and Ross, "The Political Economy of the Resource Curse," pp. 311, 319–20.

88. UNDP, *Human Development Report 2003* (New York: Oxford University Press, 2003), p. 123; World Bank, *World Development Indicators*, p. 119.

89. UNDP, *Human Development Report 2003*, p. 17; see also p. 123.

90. de Soysa, "Paradise Is a Bazaar?" p. 398. See also idem, "Natural Resources and Civil Conflict," p. 11. In an attempt to alleviate this problem and provide a better measure of abundance versus scarcity, de Soysa uses data on the absolute value of the stock of a country's natural resources gleaned from World Bank figures (World Bank, *Expanding the Measure of Wealth: Indicators of Environmental Sustainability* [Washington, D.C.: World Bank, 1997], chap. 3). Nevertheless, de Soysa's methodology is also problematic. First, the data used covers some important resources, namely, cropland, pasture, timber assets, non-timber forest assets, and subsoil (mineral) assets, but omits other important resources, such as freshwater and fisheries.

Second, the World Bank report de Soysa used only provides data on international market prices for the resources in question, adjusted by an estimate of the rent portion of the traded price, not the physical stock of the resource *per se*. See World Bank, *Expanding the Measure of Wealth*, p. 30. Moreover, this is, at best, a very indirect and inaccurate measure of the *quality* of remaining stocks of renewable resources, and no direct figures are provided measuring soil erosion, desertification, salinization, forest degradation, and so on.

Third, de Soysa's method of summing together disparate renewable and nonrenewable resources into only two categories called "renewable resources" and "mineral assets" is questionable. To derive per capita estimates of available renewable resource stocks, de Soysa sums all cropland, pasture, timber, and non-timber forest assets together. He also uses the World Bank's aggregate category "subsoil assets" as a single measure for per capita availability of non-renewables. This technique is problematic since the component resources within these categories are not perfect substitutes for one another; some resources are likely to be particularly important to certain countries, whereas others will be far less important. Consequently, scarcities of economically and politically important resources might be substantially masked by abundance in less vital resources.

Fourth, the World Bank data used by de Soysa is national data that are not collected or presented in a year-by-year fashion. Indeed, for each country as a whole, only a single data point for each resource is presented for a single year, 1994. Thus, at best, de Soysa's measure is capable of static comparisons of differences in average per capita resource availability *across countries at a single point in time*. However, it is completely incapable of measuring changing resource availability (i.e., the emergence of scarcity) *within a single country over time*. Furthermore, since the World Bank only provides aggregate national data, the data say nothing about how the resources in question are distributed. The data used mask potentially large regional and local resource inequalities. These problems rob de Soysa's measures of most of their utility. Scarcity is not a static, objective, aggregate national phenomenon; it is a changing, (inter)subjective, local phenomenon. Indeed, when discussing land quality measures, the very World Bank report de Soysa relies on acknowledges the difficulty of "developing meaningful indicators of land quality, particularly at a national level where averages generally have little meaning. It appears that work at the level of (relatively homogeneous) agro-ecological zones or the local level is more promising" (World Bank, *Expanding the Measure of Wealth*, p. 69).

Finally, de Soysa's analysis of conflict only covers a very short time period (1989–99). This is problematic because scarcities emerge over longer time periods, and their economic, social, and political ramifications may take some time to manifest themselves. Thus, de Soysa's temporal snapshot may miss significant medium- and long-term trends and interactions between natural resources and civil strife.

91. Collier and Hoeffler find that population size is significantly correlated with internal war, whereas de Soysa finds that both population size and density, in the context of poor economic conditions, are risk factors. See note 7, above.

92. For general overviews of political ecology, see Raymond L. Bryant and Sinead Bailey, *Third World Political Ecology* (London: Routledge, 1997); Tim Forsyth, *Critical Political Ecology: The Politics of Environmental Science* (London: Routedge, 2003); Richard Peet and Michael Watts, *Liberation Ecologies: Environment, Development, and Social Movements* (London: Routledge, 1996); and Michael Watts, *Struggles over Geography: Violence, Freedom, and Development at the Millennium* (Cambridge: Polity, 2000). For the most prominent applications of this approach to the study of the environment and conflict, see Nancy Lee Peluso and Michael Watts, eds., *Violent Environments* (Ithaca, N.Y.: Cornell University Press, 2001); and Mohamed Suliman, ed., *Ecology, Politics, and Violent Conflict* (London: Zed Books, 1999). For a general critique, see Andrew P. Vayda and Bradley B. Walters, "Against Political Ecology," *Human Ecology* 27, no. 1 (March 1999): 167–99.

93. Peluso and Watts, "Violent Environments," p. 5.

94. See Simon Dalby, *Environmental Security* (Minneapolis: University of Minnesota Press, 2002); and James Fairhead, "International Dimensions of Conflict over Natural and Environmental Resources," in Peluso and Watts, *Violent Environments*, pp. 213–36.

95. Nicholas Hildyard, "Blood, Babies, and the Social Roots of Conflict," in Suliman, *Ecology, Politics, and Violent Conflict*, p. 14. Hildyard is quoting A. Ross, "The Lonely Hour of Scarcity," *Capitalism, Nature, Socialism*, 7, no. 3 (September 1996): 6.

96. See Betsy Hartmann, "Will the Circle Be Unbroken? A Critique of the Project on Environment, Population, and Security," in Peluso and Watts, *Violent Environments*, pp. 39–62; and Richard Matthew, "Environment, Population, and Conflict," p. 244.

97. See Fairhead, "International Dimensions of Conflict over Natural and Environmental Resources," p. 217; and Hartmann, "Will the Circle Be Unbroken?" p. 43. For Homer-Dixon's description of demand-induced, supply-induced, and structural scarcity, see his *Environment, Scarcity, and Violence*, p. 48; and for Homer-Dixon's response to the political ecology critique, see idem, "Debating *Violent Environments*," *Environmental Change and Security Project Report*, Woodrow Wilson Center, Issue 9 (2003): 89–93.

98. Hildyard, "Blood, Babies, and the Social Roots of Conflict," p. 14. See also Peluso and Watts, "Violent Environments," pp. 18–19.

99. It should be noted that some political ecologists define "violence" as all threats to well-being, not just physical violence, and others reverse the analytical arrow by examining the ways that violence affects the environment. Therefore, the claims advanced by political ecologists often refer to very different independent and dependent variables from those discussed by neo-Malthusian and neoclassical conflict scholars. S. Ravi Rajan's work on the Bhopol Gas accident in India in 1984 offers an extreme example of defining violence to encompass an enormous array of threats to well-being. Rajan argues that the Bhopol Gas explosion represented an act of "environmental violence" that involved and originated from "tehnological violence" (the direct human health harms arising from prior decisions related to technical design and safety measures), "corporate violence" (the reckless behavior and lackluster response by Union Carbide), "distributive violence" (power asymmetries that worked to the advantage of large corporations and exposed marginalized populations to disproportionately high hazard risks), "bureaucratic violence" (the absence of effective governmental regulation or preparation prior to the disaster and the inadequate post-disaster response), and "discursive violence" (the discursive prioritization of economic development above all else by government officials, the discursive attempts by NGOs to appropriate suffering related to the accident to advance their own agendas, and the discursive silence by social scientists who failed to propose workable solutions to these various problems). See S. Ravi Rajan, "Toward a Metaphysic of Environmental Violence: The Case of the Bhopal Gas Disaster," in Peluso and Watts, *Violent Environments*, pp. 380–98. For examples of political ecologists that reverse the causal arrow, looking at the effect of violence on the environment, see Valerie Kuletz, "Invisible Spaces, Violent Places: Cold War Nuclear and Militarized Landscapes," and Paula

Garb and Galina Komarova, "Victims of 'Friendly Fire' at Russia's Nuclear Weapons Sites," both in Peluso and Watts, *Violent Environments*, pp. 237–60 and 287-302, respectively.

100. Peluso and Watts, "Violent Environments," p. 29. Complicating matters further, many political ecologists appear to eschew the project of causal generalization altogether. As Peluso and Watts note: "There is . . . no overarching 'theory of political ecology' that can be used to explore some set of universal or reductionist truths about the politics of human-environmental relationships" (ibid., p. 25 n. 28).

101. See, for example, Aaron Bobrow-Strain, "Between a Ranch and a Hard Place: Violence, Scarcity, and Meaning in Chiapas, Mexico," and Michael Watts, "Petro-Violence: Community, Extraction, and Political Ecology of a Mythic Commodity," both in Peluso and Watts, *Violent Environments*, pp. 155–85 and 189–212, respectively; and Le Billon, "The Political Ecology of War," p. 574.

102. See Le Billon, "The Political Ecology of War," pp. 568–75; and Paul Richards, "Are 'Forest' Wars in Africa Resource Conflicts? The Case of Sierra Leone," in Peluso and Watts, *Violent Environments*, pp. 65–82.

103. Le Billon, "The Political Ecology of War," pp. 564–68.

104. Peluso and Watts, "Violent Environments," p. 18.

105. Hartmann, "Will the Circle Be Unbroken?" pp. 45–50.

106. Peluso and Watts, "Violent Environments," p. 20.

107. The use of quantitative analysis to study demographically and environmentally induced civil strife also faces other limitations. These are discussed at greater length in the methodological section of chapter 2.

108. Deudney, "Environmental Security: A Critique," pp. 203, 212; Gleditsch, "Armed Conflict and the Environment," pp. 391–92; Levy, "Time for a Third Wave of Environment and Security Scholarship," p. 45; and Levy, "Is the Environment a National Security Issue?" pp. 56–57.

109. Homer-Dixon, Environment, Scarcity, and Violence, p. 182.

Chapter 2
States, Scarcity, and Civil Strife: A Theoretical Framework

1. For a discussion of qualitative research in this area, see Günther Baechler, et al., *Environmental Degradation as a Cause of War: Environmental Conflicts in the Third World and Ways for their Peaceful Resolution*, Vol. 1 (Berne: Swiss Peace Foundation/Swiss Federal Institute of Technology, 1996); Günther Baechler and Kurt R. Spillmann, eds., *Environmental Degradation as a Cause of War: Regional and Country Studies*, Vols. 2 and 3 (Berne: Swiss Peace Foundation/Swiss Federal Institute of Technology, 1996); Robert Chase, Emily Hill, Paul Kennedy, eds., *The Pivotal States: A New Framework for U.S. Policy in the Developing World* (New York: W.W. Norton, 1999); Thomas F. Homer-Dixon, "Environmental Scarcities and Violent Conflict: Evidence from Cases," *International Security* 19, no. 1 (summer 1994): 4–40; Thomas F. Homer-Dixon and Jessica Blitt, eds., *Ecoviolence: Links among Environment, Population, and Security* (Lanham, Md.:

Rowan and Littlefield, 1998); and Thomas F. Homer-Dixon, *Environment, Scarcity, and Violence* (Princeton, N.J.: Princeton University Press, 1999). For quantitative studies, see Richard P. Cincotta et al., *The Security Demographic: Population and Civil Conflict after the Cold War* (Washington, D.C.: Population Action International, 2003); and Wenche Hauge and Tanja Ellingsen, "Beyond Environmental Scarcity: Causal Pathways to Conflict," *Journal of Peace Research* 35, no. 3 (May 1998): 299–317. For critical reviews of this research see Daniel H. Deudney, "Environmental Security: A Critique," in *Contested Grounds: Security and Conflict in the New Environmental Politics*, ed. Daniel H. Deudney and Richard A. Matthew (Albany, N.Y.: State University of New York Press, 1999), pp. 187–222; Nils Petter Gleditsch, "Armed Conflict and the Environment: A Critique of the Literature," *Journal of Peace Research* 35, no. 1 (May 1998): 381–400; Jack A. Goldstone, "Demography, Environment, and Security," in *Environmental Conflict*, ed. Paul F. Diehl and Nils Petter Gleditsch, pp. 84–109; (Boulder, Colo.: Westview, 2001); and Marc A. Levy, "Is the Environment a National Security Issue?" *International Security* 20, no. 2 (fall 1995): 35–62.

2. The three components of DES mirror Thomas Homer-Dixon's definition of "environmental scarcity" as scarcity emerging from some combination of "demand-induced," "supply-induced," and "structural" sources. See Homer-Dixon, *Environment, Scarcity, and Violence*, pp. 8–9, 14–16. Nevertheless, I use the concept of DES rather than environmental scarcity to avoid analytical conflation between causes—population growth, environmental degradation, and unequal resource distribution—and possible consequences, including *but not limited to* natural resource scarcity.

3. See George D. Moffett, *Critical Masses: The Global Population Challenge* (New York: Penguin Books, 1994), chap. 3; and the United Nations Population Division (UNPD) online database, available at http://esa.un.org/unpp/index.asp?panel=2. Homer-Dixon calls this dynamic "ecological marginalization." For a discussion, see Homer-Dixon, "Environmental Scarcities and Violent Conflict," pp. 15–16; and idem, *Environment, Scarcity, and Violence*, pp. 77–79.

4. For further discussion, see Homer-Dixon, *Environment, Scarcity, and Violence*, pp. 17–18, 104–6, 179.

5. This definition combines elements found in Max Weber, *The Theory of Social and Economic Organization*, ed. Talcott Parsons (New York: Free Press, 1964), p. 156; Michael Mann, *States, War, and Capitalism* (Cambridge, Mass.: Blackwell, 1988), p. 4; Joel S. Migdal, *Strong States and Weak Societies: State-Society Relations and State Capabilities in the Third World* (Princeton, N.J.: Princeton University Press, 1988), p. 19; Eric Nordlinger, *On the Autonomy of the Democratic State* (Cambridge, Mass.: Harvard University Press, 1981), p. 11; and Gianfranco Pogi, *The Development of the Modern State: A Sociological Introduction* (Stanford, Calif.: Stanford University Press, 1978), p. 1.

6. This definition does not assume that all state preferences are autonomously generated in the sense of arising independently from societal influence. I recognize that the degree of state autonomy vis-à-vis the preferences of societal actors is an empirical question. Likewise, how "unitary" an actor the state is will vary depending on the degree of state cohesion. As I explain later

in this chapter, the degree of state cohesion is an important component determining state "strength."

7. See Fred Block, *Revising State Theory* (Philadelphia: Temple University Press, 1987), p. 84; and Peter A. Hall, *Governing the Economy: The Politics of State Intervention in Britain and France* (New York: Oxford University Press, 1986), chap. 1.

8. If markets, governments, and other social institutions adjust to population and environmental pressures, societies will not necessarily experience scarcity as a result of DES. For excellent discussions of the importance of ingenuity in adapting to DES, see Thomas F. Homer-Dixon, "The Ingenuity Gap: Can Poor Countries Adapt to Resource Scarcity," *Population and Development Review* 21, no. 3 (September 1995): 587–612; and idem, *The Ingenuity Gap: Facing the Economic, Environmental, and Other Challenges of an Increasingly Complex and Unpredictable Future* (New York: Knopf, 2000).

9. Obviously, like all natural resources, renewable resources are "goods" in the sense of being tangible commodities produced, consumed, and otherwise utilized by individuals. Renewable resources also provide "services." By acting as sinks and buffers for wastes and other by-products of human activities, renewable resources provide a valuable service by limiting the harmful effects of human activities on society. For example, the ability of land and ocean plants to serve as carbon sinks helps to limit the destabilizing effect that industrial emissions of carbon dioxide have on the climate, which, in turn, limits the potentially harmful economic and societal effects of climate change. See Stepan Libiszewski, "What Is an *Environmental Conflict*?" Occasional Paper No. 1, Environment and Conflicts Project (Berne and Zurich, Switzerland: Swiss Peace Foundation and Center for Security Studies and Conflict Research, 1992), pp. 3–6.

10. See Jean Dréze and Amartya Sen, *Hunger and Public Action* (New York: Oxford University Press, 1989), p. 30; and Homer-Dixon, "Environmental Scarcities and Violent Conflict," p. 9.

11. For example, the Bangladeshi famine of 1974 was dramatically worsened when the flood-ravaged rice crop led to increased unemployment, which, in turn, made it more difficult for individuals to purchase the primary food crop *aman* (Dréze and Sen, *Hunger and Public Action*, p. 29).

12. Homer-Dixon, "Environmental Scarcities and Violent Conflict," p. 9.

13. World Bank, *World Development Indicators* (Washington, D.C.: World Bank, 2003), pp. 7–8; idem, *World Development Report 2003: Sustainable Development in a Dynamic World* (Washington, D.C., and New York: World Bank and Oxford University Press, 2003), p. 7; Worldwatch Institute, *Vital Signs 2003* (New York: W.W. Norton, 2003), p. 67; United Nations Population Division (UNPD), *Population, Environment, and Development: The Concise Report* (New York: UNPD, 2001), p. 5; and UNPD, *World Population Prospects: The 2002 Revision* (New York: UNPD, 2003).

14. Worldwatch Institute, *Vital Signs 2003* (New York: W.W. Norton, 2003), p. 44.

15. See the discussion in chapter 1.

16. Joel E. Cohen, *How Many People Can the Earth Support* (New York: W. W. Norton, 1995), p. 367.

17. Jack A. Goldstone, "Demography, Domestic Conflict, and International Order," in *International Order and the Future of World Politics*, ed. T.V. Paul and John A. Hall (Cambridge: Cambridge University Press, 1999), p. 355.

18. United Nations Development Programme (UNDP), *Human Development Report 2003* (New York: Oxford University Press, 2003), pp. 10, 123–25; idem, *World Urbanization Prospects: The 2001 Revision* (New York: UNPD, 2002), p. 13; World Bank, *World Development Indicators*, p. 12.

19. See World Bank, *World Development Indicators*, p. 118; idem, *World Development Report 2003*, pp. 7–8, 60–67; World Resources Institute, *World Resources 1992–1993* (New York: Oxford University Press, 1992), pp. 30–31; idem, *World Resources 1994–1995*, pp. 34–35; idem, *World Resources 1998–1999* (New York: Oxford University Press, 1998), pp. 143, 274–75; and Worldwatch Institute, *Vital Signs 2003*, p. 17.

20. International Labour Organization (ILO), *Global Employment Trends* (Gevena, Switzerland: ILO, 2004), pp. 1–2, 18.

21. See the discussion in Jack A. Goldstone, *Revolution and Rebellion in the Early Modern World* (Berkeley.: University of California Press, 1991), p. 33.

22. Homer-Dixon, *Environment, Scarcity, and Violence*, p. 74. See also Goldstone, "Demography, Domestic Conflict, and International Order," p. 360; and Homer-Dixon, "Environmental Scarcities and Violent Conflict," pp. 11–14. For the general logic of this argument, see Margaret Levi, *Of Revenue and Rule* (Berkeley: University of California Press, 1988), pp. 17–23.

23. Homer-Dixon calls this particular form of rent-seeking behavior "resource capture." Homer-Dixon, "Environmental Scarcities and Violent Conflict," pp. 11–14; idem, *Environment, Scarcity, and Violence*, pp. 73–77.

24. Cincotta et al., *The Security Demographic*, pp. 42–44.

25. Calculated using the UNPD online database, available at http://esa.un.org/unpp/index.asp?panel=2.

26. World Resources Institute, *World Resources 1996–1997* (New York: Oxford University Press, 1996), p. 11.

27. Ibid., pp. 10–12; Cincotta et al., *The Security Demographic*, chap. 4; and Peter Gizewski and Thomas F. Homer-Dixon, "Urban Growth and Violence: Will the Future Resemble the Past?" Project on Environment, Population, and Security (Washington, D.C.: University of Toronto, Academy of Arts and Sciences, 1995).

28. UNPD, *World Urbanization Prospects: The 2001 Revision*, pp. 5–34.

29. See Ted Robert Gurr, *Why Men Rebel* (Princeton, N.J.: Princeton University Press, 1970), esp. chaps. 1, 2. For a discussion, see Mark I. Lichbach, "An Evaluation of 'Does Economic Inequality Breed Political Conflict?' Studies," *World Politics* 41, no. 4 (July 1989): 431–71.

30. See Kimberly Kelly and Thomas Homer-Dixon, "Environmental Scarcity and Violent Conflict: The Case of Gaza," Occasional Paper, Project on Environment, Population, and Security (Washington, D.C.: University of Toronto, Academy of Arts and Sciences, 1996); and Miriam R. Lowi, "Bridging the Divide: Transboundary Resource Disputes and the Case of West Bank Water,"

International Security 18, no. 1 (summer 1993): 113–38. The population rate was calculated using the UNPD online database, available at http://esa.un.org/unpp/index.asp?panel=2.

31. In societies with the ability to educate, train, and employ young adults, however, a youth bulge can be a significant economic asset. See Cincotta et al., *The Security Demographic*, p. 42.

32. Gary Fuller, "The Demographic Backdrop to Ethnic Conflict: A Geographic Overview," in *The Challenge of Ethnic Conflict to National and International Order in the 1990s: Geographic Perspectives*, Conference Report, Central Intelligence Agency (Washington, D.C.: Central Intelligence Agency, RTT 95-10039, 1995), pp. 152–54.

33. Cincotta, *The Security Demographic*, chap. 3.

34. UNDP, *Human Development Report 2003*, pp. 103–4; and World Resources Institute, *World Resources 1996–1997*, chap. 1.

35. World Resources Institute, *World Resources 1996–1997*, p. 4.

36. See Norman Myers, *Ultimate Security: The Environmental Basis of Political Stability* (New York: W.W. Norton, 1993), chap. 8.

37. Eric J. Hooglund, *Land and Revolution in Iran, 1960–1980* (Austin: University of Texas Press, 1982), pp. 118–19, 168–69 n. 44; and Jon Tinker and Lloyd Timberlake, "Environment and Conflict," *World Press Review*, April 1985, pp. 29-30. See also Robert D. Kaplan, *The Ends of the Earth: A Journey at the Dawn of the 21st Century* (New York: Random House, 1996), chap. 11.

38. See, for example, Patrick E. Tyler, "In China's Far West, Tensions with Ethnic Muslims Boil Over in Riots and Bombings." *New York Times*, 28 February 1997, p. A8.

39. This conceptualization of state strength and weakness is similar to the one put forth by Michael C. Desch, "War and Strong States, Peace and Weak States?" *International Organization* 50, no. 2 (spring 1996): 240–41. It differs from those who, like Peter Katzenstein, Stephen Krasner, and J. P. Nettl define "strong" and "weak" states in terms of how autonomous the state is from societal actors. See Peter J. Katzenstein, "Conclusion: Domestic Structures and Strategies of Foreign Economic Policy," in *Between Power and Plenty: Foreign Economic Policies of Advanced Industrialized States*, ed. Peter J. Katzenstein, pp. 295-336 (Madison: University of Wisconsin Press, 1978); Stephen D. Krasner, *Defending the National Interest* (Princeton, N.J.: Princeton University Press, 1978); and J. P. Nettl, "The State as a Conceptual Variable," *World Politics* 20, no. 4 (July 1968): 559–92.

40. Adapted from Barry Buzan, Charles Jones, and Richard Little, *The Logic of Anarchy: From Neorealism to Structural Realism* (New York: Columbia University Press, 1993), pp. 35–36.

41. See I. William Zartman, "Introduction: Posing the Problem of State Collapse," in *Collapsed States: The Disintegration and Restoration of Legitimate Authority*, ed. I. William Zartman, pp. 1–14 (Boulder, Colo.: Lynne Rienner, 1995).

42. See Charles Tilly, *From Mobilization to Revolution* (Reading, Mass.: Addison-Wesley, 1978); and Charles Tilly, *European Revolutions, 1492–1992* (Cambridge, Mass.: Blackwell, 1993), chap. 1.

43. Homer-Dixon, "Environmental Scarcities and Violent Conflict," p. 25; and idem, *Environment, Scarcity, and Violence*, pp. 101–2. See also Goldstone, *Revolution and Rebellion in the Early Modern World*, chap. 1; and Jack A. Goldstone, "Population Growth and Revolutionary Crises," in *Theorizing Revolutions*, ed. John Foran (London: Routledge, 1997), p. 108.

44. Homer-Dixon, "Environmental Scarcities and Violent Conflict," p. 26. The degree to which individuals blame the state may depend on how involved the state traditionally is in providing goods and services to the population. See Charles Tilly, "Food Supply and Public Order in Modern Europe," in *The Formation of National States in Western Europe*, ed. Charles Tilly, pp. 380–455 (Princeton, N.J.: Princeton University Press, 1975); and Kale J. Holsti, *The State, War, and the State of War* (New York: Cambridge University Press, 1996), p. 109.

45. Nathan Keyfitz, "Population Growth Can Prevent the Development That Would Slow Population Growth," in *Preserving the Global Environment*, ed. Jessica Tuchman Matthews (New York: W. W. Norton, 1991), p. 66. See also Gizewski and Homer-Dixon, "Urban Growth and Violence."

46. Homer-Dixon, "Environmental Scarcities and Violent Conflict," p. 25.

47. Ibid.; and idem, *Environment, Scarcity, and Violence*, p. 102.

48. Allen C. Kelley, "Economic Consequences of Population Change in the Third World," *Journal of Economic Literature* 26, no. 4 (December 1988): 1685–1728.

49. Ibid., 1699, 1704–5. However, population growth can also reduce wages by creating a surplus of labor. If the cost reduction of labor outpaces the effects of reduced capital per worker, then a country can remain competitive in its exports. But it does so only at the cost of lower incomes for its own people. I am indebted to Jack Goldstone for pointing this out.

50. Cohen, *How Many People Can the Earth Support*, p. 352; and Allen C. Kelley and William Paul McGreevey. "Population and Development in Historical Perspective," in *Population and Development: Old Debates, New Conclusions*, ed. Robert Cassen, pp. 107–26 (New Brunswick, N.J.: Transaction, 1994).

51. Dennis A. Ahlburg, "Population Growth and Poverty," in Cassen, *Population and Development*, pp. 136–37; Jeffrey G. Williamson, "Demographic Change, Economic Growth, and Inequality," in *Population Matters: Demographic Change, Economic Growth, and Poverty in Developing Countries*, ed. Nancy Birdsall, Allen C. Kelley, and Steven W. Sinding (Oxford: Oxford University Press, 2001), pp. 124–28; and Ronald D. Lee, Andrew Mason, and Time Miller, "Savings, Wealth, and Population," in Birdsall, Kelley, and Sinding, *Population Matters*, pp. 137–142.

52. Allen C. Kelley, "The Population Debate in Historical Perspective: Revisionism Revisited," in Birdsall, Kelley, and Sinding, *Population Matters*, p. 35.

53. Thomas F. Homer-Dixon, "On the Threshold: Environmental Changes as Causes of Acute Conflict," *International Security* 16, no. 2 (fall 1991): 94–97.

54. H. Jeffrey Leonard, "Managing Central America's Renewable Resources: The Path to Sustainable Economic Development," *International Environmental Affairs* 1, no. 1 (winter 1989): 38–56. For other excellent examples, see Peter Gizewski and Thomas F. Homer-Dixon, "Environmental Scarcity and Violent Conflict: The Case of Pakistan," Occasional Paper, Project on Environment,

Population, and Security (Washington, D.C.: University of Toronto, Academy of Arts and Sciences, 1996); and Vaclav Smil, *China's Environmental Crisis: An Inquiry into the Limits of National Development* (New York: M. E. Sharpe, 1993).

55. World Bank, *World Development Indicators*, p. 119.

56. For example, this dynamic appears to have driven increased rates of deforestation in Indonesia. See Charles Victor Barber, "Natural Resource Scarcity, Civil Violence, and the State: Indonesia's Forests in a Period of Economic and Political Crisis," paper prepared for the Columbia University Environment and Security Project, 1998, pp. 16–20. An earlier version of this paper was completed as part of the University of Toronto Project on Environmental Scarcities, State Capacity, and Civil Violence, and is available online at: http://www.library.utoronto.ca/pcs/state.htm.

57. See Elizabeth Economy, "The Implications of Water Scarcity for the Chinese State," paper prepared for the Columbia University Environment and Security Project, 1998. An earlier version of this paper is also available online at: http://www.library.utoronto.ca/pcs/state.htm.

58. Goldstone, "Population Growth and Revolutionary Crises," p. 112.

59. See Valerie Percival and Thomas F. Homer-Dixon, "Environmental Scarcity and Violent Conflict: The Case of South Africa," Occasional Paper. Project on Environment, Population, and Security (Washington, D.C.: University of Toronto, Academy of Arts and Sciences, 1995).

60. Economy, "The Implications of Water Scarcity for the Chinese State," p. 30.

61. For examples, see Robert D. Kaplan, "The Coming Anarchy," *Atlantic Monthly*, February 1994, pp. 44–76; and Kaplan, *The Ends of the Earth*.

62. For the bottom-up argument, see James D. Fearon, "Ethnic War as a Commitment Problem," unpublished manuscript, University of Chicago, 1993; Russell Hardin, *One for All* (Princeton, N.J.: Princeton University Press, 1995); David A. Lake and Donald Rothchild, "Containing Fear: The Origins and Management of Ethnic Conflict," *International Security* 21, no. 2 (fall 1996): 41–75; Barry R. Posen, "The Security Dilemma and Ethnic Conflict," in *Ethnic Conflict and International Security*, ed. Michael E. Brown, pp. 103–24 (Princeton, N.J.: Princeton University Press, 1993); Theda Skocpol, *States and Social Revolutions* (Cambridge: Cambridge University Press, 1979); Tilly, *From Mobilization to Revolution*; and Barry R. Weingast, "The Fundamental Political and Economic Puzzles of Ethnic and Regional Violence," unpublished manuscript, Stanford University, May 1996. For the top-down argument, see Rui deFigueiredo and Barry R. Weingast, "The Rationality of Fear: Political Opportunism and Ethnic Conflict," in *Civil Wars, Insecurity, and Intervention* ed. Barbara F. Walter and Jack Snyder, pp. 261–302 (New York: Columbia University Press, 1999); V. P. Gagnon Jr., "Ethnic Nationalism and International Conflict: The Case of Serbia," *International Security* 19, no. 3 (winter 1994/95): 130–66; and Stuart J. Kaufman, "Spiraling to Ethnic War: Elites, Masses, and Moscow in Moldova's Civil War," *International Security* 21, no. 2 (fall 1996): 108–38. For a general survey of recent theories of internal war, see Michael E. Brown, "The Causes of Internal Conflicts: An Overview," in *Nationalism and Ethnic Conflict*, ed. Michael E. Brown, et al., pp. 3–25; rev. ed. (Cambridge, Mass.: MIT Press, 2001); Steven R. David,

"Internal Wars: Causes and Cures," *World Politics* 49, no. 4 (July 1997): 552–76; and Stuart J. Kaufman, *Modern Hatreds: The Symbolic Politics of Ethnic War* (Ithaca, N.Y.: Cornell University Press, 2001), chaps. 1–2.

63. Goldstone, *Revolution and Rebellion in the Early Modern World*; Goldstone, "Population Growth and Revolutionary Crises"; Homer-Dixon, "Environmental Scarcities and Violent Conflict"; and idem, *Environment, Scarcity, and Violence*.

64. See Harry Eckstein, "On the Etiology of Internal Wars," in *Why Revolution?* ed. Clifford T. Paynton and Robert Blackey (Rochester, Vt.: Schenkman Books, 1971), 141–45; Skocpol, *States and Social Revolutions*; and Tilly, *From Mobilization to Revolution*. For a general discussion of the importance of opportunity structures and collective action, see Sidney Tarrow, *Power in Movement: Social Movements, Collective Action, and Politics* (New York: Cambridge University Press, 1994).

65. See Daniel Byman and Stephen Van Evera, "Hypotheses on the Causes of Contemporary Deadly Conflict." *Security Studies* 7, no. 3 (spring 1998): 37–39.

66. See ibid., pp. 31–37; Holsti, *The State, War, and the State of War*, chap. 5; and Migdal, *Strong States and Weak Societies*, pp. 32–33.

67. See Fearon "Rationalist Explanations for War," *International Organization* 49, no. 3 (summer 1995): 379–414; and James D. Fearon and David D. Laitin, "Explaining Interethnic Cooperation," *American Political Science Review* 90, no. 4 (December 1996): 715–35.

68. See, for example, Charles L. Glaser, "The Security Dilemma Revisited," *World Politics* 50, no. 1 (October 1997): 171–201; Robert Jervis, *Perception and Misperception in International Politics* (Princeton, N.J.: Princeton University Press, 1976), chap. 3; idem, "Cooperation under the Security Dilemma," *World Politics* 30, no. 2 (January 1978): 167–214; and Kenneth N. Waltz, *Theory of International Politics* (New York: McGraw-Hill, 1979).

69. Posen, "The Security Dilemma and Ethnic Conflict"; William Rose, "The Security Dilemma and Ethnic Conflict: Some New Hypotheses," *Security Studies* 9, no. 4 (summer 2000): 1–51; and Jack Snyder and Robert Jervis, "Civil War and the Security Dilemma," in Walter and Snyder, *Civil Wars, Insecurity, and Intervention*, pp. 15–38. Ironically, the Hobbesian logic of anarchy, long at the heart of Realist theories of conflict between states, may provide even greater promise for understanding conflict within states. This is because of the simple fact that individuals and social groups are more vulnerable to annihilation than nation-states are. See Hedley Bull, *The Anarchical Society: A Study of Order in World Politics* (New York: Columbia University Press, 1977), pp. 46–51; and Thomas Hobbes, *Leviathan* (New York: Penguin Books, 1985 [1651]).

70. See Jervis, "Cooperation under the Security Dilemma."

71. Goldstone, "Demography, Domestic Conflict, and the International Order," pp. 360–61, 364; Holsti, *The State, War, and the State of War*, 116–22; and Stephen M. Saideman, "Is Pandora's Box Half Empty or Half Full? The Limited Virulence of Secessionism and the Domestic Sources of Disintegration," in *The International Spread of Ethnic Conflict: Fear, Diffusion, and Escalation*, ed.

David A. Lake and Donald Rothchild (Princeton, N.J.: Princeton University Press, 1998), p. 135.

72. John H. Herz, *Political Realism and Political Idealism: A Study in Theories and Realities* (Chicago: University of Chicago Press, 1951), p. 3.

73. Lake and Rothchild, "Containing Fear," pp. 47–48.

74. Groups may misrepresent their intentions to (1) bluff; (2) hide their aggressive intentions; or (3) maintain advantages on the battlefield. See Fearon "Rationalist Explanations for War," pp. 391–401; and Lake and Rothchild, "Containing Fear," pp. 46–47. On attempts to misrepresent the intentions of others, see Gagnon, "Ethnic Nationalism and International Conflict"; and Kaufman, "Spiraling to Ethnic War," pp. 109, 116–18.

75. Jervis, "Cooperation under the Security Dilemma," p. 168.

76. Hardin, *One for All*, p. 144.

77. See Barry R. Weingast, "Constructing Trust: The Political and Economic Roots of Ethnic and Regional Conflict," unpublished manuscript, Stanford University, 1995; and Weingast, "The Fundamental Political and Economic Puzzles of Ethnic and Regional Violence," unpublished manuscript, Stanford University, May 1996. This argument is also implicit in Jervis, "Cooperation under the Security Dilemma," passim.

78. See Fearon, "Ethnic War as a Commitment Problem"; and James D. Fearon, "Commitment Problems and the Spread of Ethnic Conflict," in Lake and Rothchild, *The International Spread of Ethnic Conflict*, pp. 107–26.

79. See Barbara Walter, "Exiting from War: Cooperating under Even the Most Difficult Conditions," unpublished manuscript, University of California–San Diego, February 1996; and Chaim Kaufman, "Possible and Impossible Solutions to Ethnic Civil Wars," *International Security* 20, no. 4 (spring 1996): 147–48.

80. See Jervis, *Perception and Misperception in International Politics*, pp. 75–76.

81. Gagnon, "Ethnic Nationalism and International Conflict," pp. 135–36.

82. For a general discussion of diversionary tactics as a cause of civil and ethnic war, see Michael E. Brown, "The Causes and Regional Dimensions of Internal Conflict," in *The International Dimensions of Internal Conflict*, ed. Michael E. Brown (Cambridge, Mass.: MIT Press, 1996), pp. 585–86; idem, "The Causes of Internal Conflict," pp. 17–23; Gagnon, "Ethnic Nationalism and International Conflict," pp. 134–140; Jack S. Levy, "The Diversionary Theory of War: A Critique," in *Handbook of War Studies*, ed. Manus I. Midlarsky, pp. 259–88 (Ann Arbor: University of Michigan Press, 1993); and Kaufman, "Spiraling to Ethnic War," p. 117.

83. See Jack Snyder and Karen Ballentine, "Nationalism and the Marketplace of Ideas," *International Security* 21, no. 2 (fall 1996): 5–40; and Jack Snyder, *From Voting to Violence: Democratization and Nationalist Conflict* (New York: W.W. Norton, 2000), chap. 2.

84. See Fearon, "Ethnic War as a Commitment Problem"; Lake and Rothchild, "Containing Fear"; and Weingast, "Fundamental Political and Economic Puzzles."

85. Hardin, *One for All*, p. 155.

86. See deFigueiredo and Weingast, "The Rationality of Fear," p. 263; Gagnon, "Ethnic Nationalism and International Conflict," pp. 138; and Jack Snyder, *Myths of Empire: Domestic Politics and International Ambition* (Ithaca, N.Y.: Cornell University Press, 1991), pp. 41–43.

87. For excellent discussions of individual identity and reference group selection, see Morris Rosenberg, "The Self-Concept: Social Product and Social Force," in *Social Psychology: Sociological Perspectives*, ed. Morris Rosenberg and Ralph H. Turner (New York: Basic Books, 1981), pp. 593–624; and John C. Turner, *Rediscovering the Social Group* (New York: Basil Blackwell, 1987).

88. See Edward N. Muller and Karl-Dieter Opp, "Rational Choice and Rebellious Collective Action," *American Political Science Review* 80, no. 2 (June 1986): 471–87.

89. See Michael Taylor, *Community, Anarchy, and Liberty* (Cambridge: Cambridge University Press, 1982), chap. 1.

90. Michael Taylor, "Rationality and Revolutionary Collective Action," in *Rationality and Revolution*. ed. Michael Taylor (Cambridge: Cambridge University Press), pp. 68–69. See also Michael Hechter, *Principles of Group Solidarity* (Berkeley: University of California Press, 1987), p. 50.

91. See Snyder and Ballentine, "Nationalism and the Marketplace of Ideas."

92. For convincing evidence for crosscutting ties limiting intergroup violence, see Marc Howard Ross, *The Culture of Conflict: Interpretations and Interests in Comparative Perspective* (New Haven, Conn.: Yale University Press, 1993), chaps. 3, 9.

93. Lake and Rothchild, "Containing Fear," pp. 58–61; and Arend Lijphart, *Democracy in Plural Societies* (New Haven, Conn.: Yale University Press, 1977), chap. 2.

94. While most inclusive states are democratic, and most exclusionary states are authoritarian, democracy is neither necessary nor sufficient for inclusivity. Democracies vary in the extent to which they include a broad spectrum of social groups in the decision-making process, and some authoritarian states allow for minority participation and influence in executive decision-making processes. Nevertheless, it is undoubtedly the case that democracies, on average, tend to be more inclusive than authoritarian states. See Donald Horowitz, "Democracy in Divided Societies," in *Nationalism, Ethnic Conflict, and Democracy*, ed. Larry Diamond and Marc F. Plattner (Baltimore, Md.: The Johns Hopkins University Press, 1994), pp. 35–55; Lake and Rothchild, "Containing Fear," p. 59; and Mancur Olson, "Dictatorship, Democracy, and Development," *American Political Science Review* 87, no. 3 (September 1993): 579.

95. Samuel P. Huntington, *Political Order in Changing Societies* (New Haven, Conn.: Yale University Press, 1968), p. 275.

96. Jeffrey J. Ryan, "The Impact of Democratization on Revolutionary Movements," *Comparative Politics* 27, no. 1 (October 1994): 29. Some evidence suggests that the spread of democracy is also partly responsible for the declining incidence of ethnic war. See Ted Robert Gurr, "Ethnic Warfare on the Wane," *Foreign Affairs* 79, no. 3 (May/June 2000): 52–64. However, during the transition to consolidated democracy, the prospects for ethnic conflict may increase.

See Snyder, *From Voting to Violence*; and Fareed Zakaria, *The Future of Freedom: Illiberal Democracy at Home and Abroad* (New York: W.W. Norton 2003).

97. Ernesto Guevara, *Guerilla Warfare* (Lincoln: University of Nebraska Press, 1985 [1961]), p. 48.

98. For the logic, see Robert H. Dix, "Why Revolutions Succeed and Fail," *Polity* 16, no. 3 (spring 1984): 423–46; and Ryan, "The Impact of Democratization on Revolutionary Movements." See also Byman and Van Evera, "Hypotheses," pp. 35–36.

99. For discussions of transaction costs, see Thráinn Eggertsson, *Economic Behavior and Institution* (New York: Cambridge University Press, 1990), chap. 1; and Oliver Williamson, *Markets and Hierarchies* (New York: Free Press, 1975).

100. For the logic, see Kenneth Oye, "Explaining Cooperation under Anarchy," in *Cooperation under Anarchy*, ed. Kenneth A. Oye (Princeton, N.J.: Princeton University Press, 1986), pp. 13–18.

101. See Lake and Rothchild, "Containing Fear," pp. 57–58.

102. It should be emphasized that institutional inclusivity will not prevent all state failure conflicts. When conflicts of interest between contending groups are intense and zero-sum, when stronger groups have clear intentions to exploit the opportunities provided by their superior capabilities, and when the stakes for weaker groups of being exploited include physical or cultural annihilation, inclusive institutions may be of little consequence. But when all major political actors ultimately prefer continued peace to bloodshed, inclusive institutions help to avoid conflicts arising from residual conflicts of interest, the security dilemma, and spiral dynamics.

103. This builds on Anthony Downs, *An Economic Theory of Democracy* (New York: Harper and Row, 1957), pp. 96–108; Olson, "Dictatorship, Democracy, and Development," pp. 567–76; Amartya Sen, "Development: Which Way Now?" *Economic Journal* 93, no. 372 (December 1983): 745–62; idem, *Resources, Values, and Development* (Cambridge, Mass.: Harvard University Press, 1984); idem, "Freedom and Needs"; and idem, "Wars and Famines: On Divisions and Incentives," *Disarmament* 19, no. 3 (1996): 18–37.

104. Fearon, "Ethnic War as a Commitment Problem," pp. 16–20; and Weingast, "The Fundamental Political and Economic Puzzles of Ethnic and Regional Violence," p. 14.

105. This builds on an argument made by Jack Snyder in his "Nationalism and the Crisis of the Post-Soviet State," in Brown, *Ethnic Conflict and International Security*, pp. 82, 86. See also Thomas F. Homer-Dixon and Valerie Percival, "Environmental Scarcity and Violent Conflict: Briefing Book," Occasional Paper, Project on Environment, Population, and Security (Washington, D.C.: University of Toronto, the Academy of Arts and Sciences, 1996), p. 8.

106. Michael Ignatieff, *The Warrior's Honor: Ethnic War and the Modern Conscience* (New York: Metropolitan Books, 1997), p. 45.

107. Quoted in Moffett, *Critical Masses*, p. 48.

108. See the discussion of "privileged" groups in Mancur Olson, *The Logic of Collective Action* (Cambridge, Mass.: Harvard University Press, 1965), pp. 48–50; and Todd Sandler, *Collective Action: Theory and Applications* (Ann Arbor: University of Michigan Press, 1992), pp. 9–10, 24, 35. For an empirical assess-

ment of the use of selective incentives in rebellious collective action, see Samuel Popkin, *The Rational Peasant: The Political Economy of Rural Society in Vietnam* (Berkeley: University of California Press, 1979).

109. Homer-Dixon, "On the Threshold," p. 113.

110. Horowitz, "Democracy in Divided Societies."

111. For a defense of this approach, see Timothy McKeown, "Case Studies and the Statistical Worldview: Review of King, Keohane, and Verba's *Designing Social Inquiry: Scientific Inference in Qualitative Research*," *International Organization* 53, no. 1 (winter 1999): 161–90.

112. Nils Petter Gleditsch, "Armed Conflict and the Environment: A Critique of the Literature," *Journal of Peace Research* 35, no. 1 (May 1998): 396.

113. Stephen M. Walt, "Rethinking Revolution and War: A Reply to Goldstone and Dassel," *Security Studies* 6, no. 2 (winter 1996/97): 177. See also James D. Fearon, "Counterfactuals and Hypothesis Testing in Political Science," *World Politics* 43, no. 2 (January 1991): 169–95, 174–75; Barbara Geddes, "How the Cases You Choose Affect the Answers You Get: Selection Bias in Comparative Politics," *Political Analysis* 2 (1990): 141–43; and Gary King, Robert O. Keohane, and Sidney Verba, *Designing Social Inquiry* (Princeton, N.J.: Princeton University Press, 1994).

114. Jack A. Goldstone, "Revolution, War, and Security," *Security Studies* 6, no. 2 (winter 1996/97): 131. See also Thomas F. Homer-Dixon, "Strategies for Studying Causation in Complex Ecological Political Systems," Occasional Paper, Project on Environment, Population, and Security (Washington, D.C.: University of Toronto, Academy of Arts and Sciences, 1995). Statistical models assuming linear relationships are simply inappropriate for studying nonlinear systems, and models capable of accommodating nonlinear equations must operate under the assumption that the same equation applies across all cases, which is often a difficult assumption to maintain.

115. Alexander L. George, "Case Studies and Theory Development: The Method of Structured, Focused Comparison," in *Diplomacy: New Approaches in History, Theory, and Policy*, ed. Paul Gordon Lauren (New York: Free Press, 1979), p. 60. See also Ronald Mitchell and Thomas Bernauer, "Empirical Research on International Environmental Policy: Designing Qualitative Case Studies," *Journal of Environment and Development* 7, no. 1 (March 1998): pp. 6–7.

116. For a discussion of process tracing, see Alexander L. George and Timothy J. McKeown, "Case Studies and Theories of Organizational Decision Making," *Advances in Information Processing in Organizations* 2 (1985): 21–58.

117. "It is . . . essential to distinguish between the number of cases and the number of observations. The former may be of some interest for some purposes, but only the latter is of importance in judging the amount of information a study brings to bear on a theoretical question" (King, Keohane, and Verba, *Designing Social Inquiry*, p. 52). See also Harry Eckstein, "Case Study and Theory in Political Science," in *Handbook of Political Science*, Vol. 7, *Strategies for Inquiry* ed. Fred I. Greenstein and Nelson W. Polsby, (Reading, Mass.: Addison-Wesley, 1975), pp. 85, 119, 126; Mitchell and Bernauer, "Empirical Research on International Environmental Policy," p. 15; and Stephen Van Evera, *Guide to*

Methodology for Students of Political Science, Working Paper, Defense and Arms Control Studies Program (Cambridge, Mass.: MIT), pp. 45–46.

118. See King, Keohane, and Verba, *Designing Social Inquiry*, pp. 219–23.

119. A second potential drawback to reliance on within-case temporal and spatial variation is the lack of "independence" between the cases. Nevertheless, dependence among observations "does not disqualify these new tests unless the dependence is perfect—that is, unless we can perfectly predict the new data from the existing data. Short of this unlikely case, there does exist at least some new information in the new data, and it will help to analyze these data. These new observations, based on non-independent information, do not add as much information as fully independent observations, but they can still be useful" (King, Keohane, and Verba, *Designing Social Inquiry*, p. 222).

120. For a discussion, see Kaufman, "Possible and Impossible Solutions to Ethnic Civil Wars"; Walter, "Exiting from War"; and Barbara F. Walter, "The Critical Barrier to Civil War Settlement," *International Organization* 51, no. 3 (summer 1997): 335–64.

121. For a discussion of strong and weak tests of a theory, see Eckstein, "Case Study and Theory in Political Science," pp. 113–31; Arthur L. Stinchcombe, *Constructing Social Theories* (Chicago: University of Chicago Press, 1968), pp. 20–22; and Van Evera, *Guide to Methodology*, pp. 40–41.

Chapter 3
Green Crisis, Red Rebels: Communist Insurgency in the Philippines

1. The brief history recounted up to this point is based on James K. Boyce, *The Philippines: The Political Economy of Growth and Impoverishment in the Marcos Era* (London: MacMillan, 1993), pp. 5–7; William Chapman, *Inside the Philippine Revolution* (New York: W.W. Norton, 1987), chaps. 2–3; Lawrence M. Greenberg, *The Hukbalahap Insurrection: A Case Study of a Successful Anti-Insurgency Operation in the Philippines, 1946–1955* (Washington, D.C.: U.S. Army Center of Military History, 1987); Richard J. Kessler, *Rebellion and Repression in the Philippines* (New Haven, Conn.: Yale University Press, 1989), chaps. 1–2; Richard J. Kessler, "The Philippines: The Making of a 'People Power' Revolution," in *Revolutions of the Late Twentieth Century*, ed. Jack A. Goldstone, Ted Robert Gurr, and Farrokh Moshiri, (Boulder, Colo.: Westview, 1991), pp. 196–97; Donald M. Seeskins, "Historical Setting," in *Philippines: A Country Study*, ed. Ronald E. Dolan, (Washington, D.C.: Library of Congress/U.S. Government Printing Office, 1993), pp. 1–63; and David Wurfel, *Filipino Politics: Development and Decay* (Ithaca, N.Y.: Cornell University Press, 1988), chaps. 1, 8.

2. On the origins and early activities of the CPP-NPA, see Chapman, *Inside the Philippine Revolution*, chaps. 1–2, 4–5; Greg R. Jones, *Red Revolution: Inside the Philippine Guerrilla Movement* (Boulder, Colo.: Westview, 1989), chaps. 3–5, 7; Kessler, *Rebellion and Repression*, chaps. 2–3; Larry A. Niksch, *Insurgency and Counterinsurgency in the Philippines*, prepared for the United States Senate Committee on Foreign Relations (Washington, D.C.: U.S. Government Printing Office, 1985), pp. 14–15, 26; and Wurfel, *Filipino Politics*, pp. 18–20, 226, 332.

3. Quoted in Chapman, *Inside the Philippine Revolution*, p. 111. See also, Jones, *Red Revolution*, pp. 6–7.

4. Niksch, *Insurgency and Counterinsurgency*, p. 49. See also Steve Lohr, "For Filipino Rebels, a 'New Deal' via the Gun," *New York Times*, 11 August 1985, Lexis-Nexis.

5. Stepen J. Solarz, "Last Chance for the Philippines," *New Republic*, 8 April 1985, Lexis-Nexis.

6. Chapman, *Inside the Philippine Revolution*, pp. 13–15, 104–11, 238; Jones, *Red Revolution*, pp. 107–12; Kessler, *Rebellion and Repression*, pp. 28–29, 42–44, 56–57; Steve Lohr, "Inside the Philippine Insurgency," *New York Times*, 3 November 1985, Lexis-Nexis; Niksch, *Insurgency and Counterinsurgency*, pp. 16–24; and Wurfel, *Filipino Politics*, p. 227.

7. For a discussion of the NDF and Bayan, see Chapman, *Inside the Philippine Revolution*, chap. 12; Jones, *Red Revolution*, chap. 14; Kessler, *Rebellion and Repression*, pp. 79–91; Lohr, "Inside the Philippine Insurgency"; and Wurfel, *Filipino Politics*, pp. 227–28, 293.

8. Quoted in Kessler, *Rebellion and Repression*, p. 82.

9. For an overview of the civil war, see Patrick Brogan, *The Fighting Never Stopped: A Comprehensive Guide to World Conflict since 1945* (New York: Vintage Books, 1990), pp. 214–26. The casualty figure of forty thousand deaths is a government estimate cited in Ruben Alabastro, " 'Dying' Philippine Insurgency Seeks Lost Lustre," *Reuters North American Wire*, 26 June 1995, Lexis-Nexis.

10. National Economic and Development Authority (NEDA), National Census and Statistics Office, Republic of the Philippines, *1980 Census of Population and Housing: Philippines, Vol. 2: National Summary* (Manila, Philippines: NEDA, 1980); and *Factbook Philippines* (Quezon City, Metro Manila, the Philippines: Active Research Center, 1994).

11. National Statistics Office [Republic of the Philippines] and Macro International, Inc. (NSO and MI), *National Demographic Survey, 1993* (Calverton, Md.: NSO and MI, 1994), p. 29.

12. Maria Concepcion Cruz et al., *Population Growth, Poverty, and Environmental Stress: Frontier Migration in the Philippines and Costa Rica* (Washington, D.C.: World Resources Institute, 1992), p. 15.

13. Alejandro Herrin, "Philippine Demographic Development and Public Policies: 1970–1985," in *Population, Human Resources, and Development*, ed. Alejandro N. Herrin (Diliman, Quezon City, the Philippines: University of the Philippines Press and the Center for Integrative and Development Studies, 1994), pp. 511–13; NSO and MI, *National Demographic Survey, 1993*, pp. 3–4; and World Bank, "Philippines: The Challenge of Poverty," Report No. 7144–PH (Washington, D.C.: World Bank, 17 October 1988), p. 58.

14. Wilfredo Cruz and Robert Repetto, *The Environmental Effects of Stabilization and Structural Adjustment Programs: The Philippines Case* (Washington, D.C.: World Resources Institute, 1992), pp. 37, 39, Table 4.1; Department of Environment and Natural Resources (DENR), Republic of the Philippines, *The Philippine Environment in the Eighties* (Diliman, Quezon City, the Philippines: DENR, 1990), p. 163; and Gareth Porter and Delfin J. Ganapin Jr., *Resources, Population, and the Philippines' Future* (Washington, D.C.: World Resources Institute, 1988),

pp. 2–3. It should be noted that the data on hectares of available arable land per person employed in agriculture dramatically understate the growing scarcity of good cropland available to poor farmers because these data are not adjusted for ownership. As I detail below, control over arable land was becoming increasingly concentrated during this period, meaning that the *actual* amount of available land was much lower than the data suggest.

15. Boyce, *The Philippines*, pp. 7–8, 70–71, 163; Kessler, *Rebellion and Repression*, pp. 7, 11; and Wurfel, *Filipino Politics*, pp. 4–6, 9–16.

16. Wurfel, *Filipino Politics*, p. 55.

17. Chapman, *Inside the Philippine Revolution*, p. 90; Cruz et al., *Population Growth, Poverty, and Environmental Stress*, pp. 27–28; Jones, *Red Revolution*, pp. 203–4; and Porter and Ganapin, *Resources, Population, and the Philippines' Future*, pp. 16–19.

18. Boyce, *The Philippines*, p. 127.

19. Cruz et al., Population Growth, Poverty, and Environmental Stress, p. 27 Table 10; and World Bank, "Philippines: Toward Sustaining the Economic Recovery: Country Economic Memorandum," pp. 54–55.

20. Porter and Ganapin, *Resources, Population, and the Philippines' Future*, p. 19.

21. Cruz et al., *Population Growth, Poverty, and Environmental Stress*, p. 25.

22. Boyce, *The Philippines*, p. 127. Until the 1970s most rice was produced by share tenants who turned over a percentage of the crop to the landlord at harvest time in exchange for the right to work the land.

23. See ibid., p. 135; Cruz and Repetto, *Environmental Effects*, p. 45; and Wurfel, *Filipino Politics*, pp. 165–70.

24. David Wurfel, "The Political Consequences of Population Growth in the Philippines," in *Population and Policies in the Philippines*, ed. Georges A. Fauriol (Washington, D.C.: the Center for Strategic and International Studies, Georgetown University, 1979), pp. 56–57.

25. Wurfel, *Filipino Politics*, p. 169. Moreover, between 1971 and 1981 the number of farms under tenancy arrangements actually increased from 289,418 to 581,456. See Cruz and Repetto, *Environmental Effects*, p. 45.

26. For a comprehensive discussion of the green revolution in the Philippines, see Boyce, *The Philippines*, chap. 3.

27. The sectoral distribution of GDP and employment show that the structure of the Philippine economy changed very little during the period under study. The share of agriculture as a percentage of GDP was 28.8 percent in 1970, 25.6 percent in 1980, and 26.1 percent in 1984; industry's share increased from 29.5 percent in 1970 to 36.1 percent in 1980 and then declined to 33.1 percent in 1984; and the service sector went from 41.6 percent in 1970 to 38.3 percent in 1980 and 40.1 percent in 1984. In terms of sectoral employment, agriculture made up 50.4 percent of employment in 1971, 51.4 percent in 1980, and 49.5 percent in 1984; industry made up 15.7 percent in 1971, 15.5 percent in 1980, and 14.7 percent in 1984; and services made up 33.9 percent in1971, 33.1 percent in 1980, and 35.8 percent in 1984 (Herrin, "Philippine Demographic Development and Public Policies," pp. 518–19, Tables 6 and 7). See also Cruz and Repetto, *Environmental Effects*, p. 4.

28. Boyce, *The Philippines*, pp. 67–72. See also, Wurfel, *Filipino Politics*, pp. 171–75.

29. As Wurfel concludes, "Population growth and the disappearance of free land on the frontier would have increased the landless class regardless of agrarian policy. But the net impact of policy was to contribute to the increase" (*Filipino Politics*, p. 175).

30. Cruz et al., *Population Growth, Poverty, and Environmental Stress*, p. 27.

31. Ibid., p. 39.

32. *Factbook Philippines*; and David M. Kummer, *Deforestation in the Postwar Philippines* (Chicago: University of Chicago Press, 1992), p. 77, Table 17.

33. World Bank, "Philippines: Environment and Natural Resources Management Survey," Report No. PJB-7388 (Washington, D.C.: World Bank, September 1989), p. 10.

34. Cruz et al., *Population Growth, Poverty, and Environmental Stress*, pp. 18–22, 33–42; and World Bank, "Philippines: Toward Sustaining the Economic Recovery: Country Economic Memorandum," Report No. 7438-PH (Washington, D.C.: World Bank, 30 January 1989), pp. 74–75.

35. Boyce, *The Philippines*, p. 226; Kummer, *Deforestation in the Postwar Philippines*, pp. 45–46; and Mark Poffenberger and Betsy McGean, "Upland Philippine Communities: Guardians of the Final Forest Frontiers," Southeast Asia Sustainable Forest Management Network Research Network Report No. 4 (Berkeley: Center for Southeast Asia Studies, International Area Studies, University of California, August 1993), pp. 1–12.

36. See Poffenberger and McGean. "Upland Philippine Communities," p. 1; and World Bank, "Philippines: Environment and Natural Resources Management Survey," pp. ix, 11. Historically tree species belonging to the family Dipterocarpacae have made up the major forest type in the Philippines and, in terms of economic value, have accounted for more than 90 percent of all commercial forest products. Thus "the history of deforestation in the Philippines is primarily the history of the decline of dipterocarp forest" (Kummer, *Deforestation in the Postwar Philippines*, p. 43).

37. Norman Myers, *Ultimate Security: The Environmental Basis of Political Stability* (New York: W.W. Norton, 1993), pp. 87–88; Porter and Ganapin, *Resources, Population, and the Philippines' Future*, p. 1; and World Bank, "Philippines: Environment and Natural Resources Management Survey," p. 25.

38. Fulgencio S. Factoran Jr., *Population, Resources, and the Philippine Future: An Ecological Perspective* (Diliman, Quezon City, the Philippines: DENR, 1989), p. 7.

39. Robin Broad and John Cavanagh, *Plundering Paradise: The Struggle for the Environment in the Philippines* (Berkeley: University of California Press, 1993), p. 35; DENR, *The Philippine Environment in the Eighties*, p. 169; and World Bank, "Philippines: Environment and Natural Resources Management Survey."

40. DENR, *The Philippine Environment in the Eighties*, pp. 90, 169; and Kirk Talbott, "The State of the Environment in the Philippines, February 1987," independent report (Washington, D.C., 15 April 1987), p. 36.

41. World Bank, "Philippines: Environment and Natural Resources Management Survey," p. 24.

42. United States Agency for International Development (USAID), *Sustainable Natural Resources Assessment—Philippines* (Washington, D.C.: USAID, 1989), p. B-8.

43. Boyce, *The Philippines*, pp. 230–31; Kummer, *Deforestation in the Postwar Philippines*, pp. 4, 41; and World Bank, "Philippines: Environment and Natural Resources Management Survey."

44. Porter and Ganapin, *Resources, Population, and the Philippines' Future*, pp. 24–25.

45. Kummer, *Deforestation in the Postwar Philippines*, pp. 44–45; and Poffenberger and McGean, "Upland Philippine Communities," pp. 7–8. For a discussion of Japan's role in deforestation in the Philippines, see Peter Dauvergne, *Shadows in the Forest: Japan and the Politics of Timber in Southeast Asia* (Cambridge, Mass.: MIT Press, 1997), chap. 5; and Rene E. Ofreneo, "Japan and the Environmental Degradation of the Philippines," in *Asia's Environmental Crisis*, ed. Michael C. Howard (Boulder, Colo.: Westview, 1993), pp. 201–19.

46. Factoran, *Population, Resources, and the Philippine Future*, p. 8.

47. Porter and Ganapin, *Resources, Population, and the Philippines' Future*, pp. 14–15.

48. Broad and Cavanagh, *Plundering Paradise*, p. 44.

49. Porter and Ganapin, *Resources, Population, and the Philippines' Future*, p. 15.

50. Boyce, *The Philippines*, p. 233; DENR, *The Philippine Environment in the Eighties*, p. 89; and Porter and Ganapin, *Resources, Population, and the Philippines' Future*, 28.

51. Boyce, *The Philippines*, p. 235; DENR, *The Philippine Environment in the Eighties*, p. 87; Factoran, *Population, Resources, and the Philippine Future*, pp. 8–9; Michael L Ross, *Timber Booms and Institutional Breakdown in Southeast Asia* (New York: Cambridge University Press, 2001), pp. 81–83.

52. The government agency in charge of Philippine forests has changed its name three times since 1945. In 1973 the Bureau of Forestry became the Bureau of Forest development, which then became the Forest Management Bureau in 1987. See Kummer, *Deforestation in the Postwar Philippines*, p. 39. For a general discussion of the weakening autonomy of forest bureaucracy in the Philippines, see Ross, *Timber Booms and Institutional Breakdown*, chap. 4.

53. In 1975, for example, the government imposed a ban on log exports only to see the logging lobby block its full implementation. Consequently, despite the ban, total log export volume dipped only 11 percent by 1980. Logging companies also flagrantly violated the government's selective logging system. Introduced in 1954 as a primary means of managing forest resources, this system required that only certain percentages of specified diameters of trees could be cut. The system was designed to allow a second-cycle cut of the forest after a few decades, thereby insuring the long-term viability of the industry. However, of the more than four hundred concessions in the 1970s, only two were able to harvest a residual forest by the late 1980s. See Boyce, *The Philippines*, p. 234; and Factoran, *Population, Resources, and the Philippine Future*, pp. 8–9. This corruption was embedded within the massive system of corruption that char-

acterized the Marcos regime more generally. Indeed, by the mid-1970s, 65 percent of government positions were political appointments, and between 1975 and 1980 the Commission on Audit's estimated that 10 percent of the total GNP went toward bribes. Thus it should come as little surprise that corruption in the forestry sector was tolerated. See Kummer, *Deforestation in the Postwar Philippines*, p. 71.

54. As Porter and Ganapin note: "The martial law regime's centralized, authoritarian political structure created both incentives and opportunities for military and civilian officials to take advantage of illegal exploitation of natural resources. Since mayors were, in effect, stripped of their political power and became mere distributors of largesse from the central government, they had little reason left for loyalty to that government except opportunities for corruption. Military officials acquired extraordinary power over all activities under their jurisdiction. . . . [T]hey helped protect the interests of wealthy businessmen in their regions in return for a percentage of profits. Both mayors and military officers watched over illegal logging, illegal fishing, and coral harvesting" (*Resources, Population, and the Philippines' Future*, p. 15). See also Boyce, *The Philippines*, p. 234; and DENR, *The Philippine Environment in the Eighties*, p. 87.

55. Boyce, *The Philippines*, p. 234.

56. Kummer, *Deforestation in the Postwar Philippines*, p. 72.

57. Factoran, *Population, Resources, and the Philippine Future*, pp. 8–9; USAID, *Sustainable Natural Resources Assessment—Philippines*, p. 33; and World Bank, "Philippines: Environment and Natural Resources Management Survey," pp. 17–20.

58. See Boyce, *The Philippines*, pp. 240–41; and Broad and Cavanagh, *Plundering Paradise*, pp. 143–45.

59. Myers, *Ultimate Security*, p. 89; and World Bank, "Philippines: Toward Sustaining the Economic Recovery: Country Economic Memorandum," p. vi.

60. Boyce, *The Philippines*, p. 236; Broad and Cavanagh, *Plundering Paradise*, p. 46; and Kummer, *Deforestation in the Postwar Philippines*, p. 63.

61. Cruz et al., *Population Growth, Poverty, and Environmental Stress*, pp. 28–29; Kummer, *Deforestation in the Postwar Philippines*, p. 86; and Poffenberger and McGean, "Upland Philippine Communities," p. 7.

62. Cruz et al., *Population Growth, Poverty, and Environmental Stress*, p. 23. The authors note that, because of the lack of available cropland in the lowlands, the remainder of this expansion was onto grasslands, shrublands, and abandoned areas unsuitable for agriculture.

63. *Kaingin* is an imprecise term often used to describe both sustainable techniques practiced by traditional forest dwellers and unsustainable techniques used by migrants from the lowlands (Boyce, *The Philippines*, p. 236; World Bank, "Philippines: Environment and Natural Resources Management Survey," p. 23). For the history of *kaingin*, see Porter and Ganapin, *Resources, Population, and the Philippines' Future*, p. 28; and Wurfel, *Filipino Politics*, p. 3.

64. Cruz et al., *Population Growth, Poverty, and Environmental Stress*, pp. 21–23; Porter and Ganapin, *Resources, Population, and the Philippines' Future*, p. 1;

and World Bank, "Philippines: Environment and Natural Resources Management Survey," p. 7.

65. Porter and Ganapin, *Resources, Population, and the Philippines' Future*, p. 29.

66. Cruz et al., *Population Growth, Poverty, and Environmental Stress*, chap. 2; DENR, *The Philippine Environment in the Eighties*, p. 89; Myers, *Ultimate Security*, p. 89; World Bank, "Philippines: Toward Sustaining the Economic Recovery: Country Economic Memorandum," pp. 30–31, 75; and World Bank, "Philippines: Environment and Natural Resources Management Survey," p. 21.

67. USAID, *Sustainable Natural Resources Assessment—Philippines*, pp. vii, B-5; and World Bank, "Philippines: Toward Sustaining the Economic Recovery: Country Economic Memorandum," p. 75.

68. For a summary discussion, see Boyce, *The Philippines*, pp. 240–41; and Kummer, *Deforestation in the Postwar Philippines*, pp. 62–75, 95–100, 143–149.

69. DENR, *The Philippine Environment in the Eighties*, p. 44; Porter and Ganapin, *Resources, Population, and the Philippines' Future*, p. 39; and World Bank, "Philippines: Toward Sustaining the Economic Recovery: Country Economic Memorandum," p. 75.

70. DENR, *The Philippine Environment in the Eighties*, pp. 39 Figures 9 and 10, 48–50; Porter and Ganapin, *Resources, Population, and the Philippines' Future*, pp. 41–43, esp. 43 Table 6; and World Bank, "Philippines: Toward Sustaining the Economic Recovery: Country Economic Memorandum," p. 75.

71. USAID, *Sustainable Natural Resources Assessment—Philippines*, p. E-24.

72. See DENR, *The Philippine Environment in the Eighties*, p. 50; Myers, *Ultimate Security*, pp. 90–91; and Porter and Ganapin, *Resources, Population, and the Philippines' Future*, pp. 36–38.

73. Factoran, *Population, Resources, and the Philippine Future*, p. 15. See also Broad and Cavanagh, *Plundering Paradise*, pp. 37–38; and DENR, *The Philippine Environment in the Eighties*, p. 52.

74. Cruz et al., *Population Growth, Poverty, and Environmental Stress*, p. 11.

75. World Bank, "Philippines: Toward Sustaining the Economic Recovery: Country Economic Memorandum," pp. 75–76.

76. Broad and Cavanagh, *Plundering Paradise*, pp. 37, 43; Porter and Ganapin, *Resources, Population, and the Philippines' Future*, p. 39; USAID, *Sustainable Natural Resources Assessment—Philippines*, p. 36; and World Bank, "Philippines: Toward Sustaining the Economic Recovery: Country Economic Memorandum," p. 75.

77. Boyce, *The Philippines*, pp. 14–15; see ibid., p. 15 Table 2.1 for GNP and per capita GNP data.

78. Ibid., p. 15; and Kummer, *Deforestation in the Postwar Philippines*, p. 79.

79. Boyce, *The Philippines*, pp. 25–29; and Porter and Ganapin, *Resources, Population, and the Philippines' Future*, p. 7.

80. Boyce, *The Philippines*, pp. 29–33. See also Herrin, "Philippine Demographic Development and Public Policies," p. 520; and World Bank, "Philippines: Toward Sustaining the Economic Recovery: Country Economic Memorandum," pp. 56–57, 106–7. This number combines open unemployment with underemployment data converted into a full-time unemployment equivalent. However, even with this combination, there are reasons to suspect that these

data underestimate the actual amount of unemployment. See Rosalinda Pineda-Ofreneo, *The Philippines: Debt and Poverty* (Oxford: Oxfam, 1991), p. 28.

81. Boyce, *The Philippines*, p. 46 Table 2.13. Herrin cites data that differ somewhat from those used by Boyce. Herrin notes a poverty rate of 49.3 percent for 1971 and 59.3 percent for 1985 based on Philippine government estimates. See Herrin, "Philippine Demographic Development and Public Policies," p. 515 Table 3.

82. World Bank, "Philippines: The Challenge of Poverty," p. 8; and World Bank, "Philippines: Toward Sustaining the Economic Recovery: Country Economic Memorandum," p. 54.

83. Boyce claims that the official survey data used to determine incomes in the Philippines must be corrected to account for three flaws. First, the data consistently understated the income of individuals, but the understatement by the rich increased over time whereas the understatement by the poor decreased. As incomes among the wealthy increased, and as martial law encouraged them to hide more of their income from the government, the propensity by the rich to understate their income increased. In contrast, as techniques improved for collecting data on non-cash incomes, which are relatively more important for poorer families, the understatement of income by poor families declined. The failure to correct for this creates the illusion that the income gap between rich and poor was decreasing.

Second, the use of a single consumer price index to determine real income for all income classes in the Philippines masked the distributional effects of changes in relative prices. In particular, food prices increased more rapidly than nonfood prices between 1962 and 1974, and thereafter more slowly. Since the poor devote a larger proportion of their income to food, the use of a single consumer price index underestimated the degree of income inequality prior to 1974, and overstated it thereafter.

Finally, the survey data are based on family income that is then translated into individual income. However, since poor families in the Philippines tend to be considerably larger than rich families, this also biased the data toward overestimating the individual income of the poor. All told, once the data are corrected for these shortcomings, it appears that inequality continued to increase in the 1980s. For a thorough discussion, see Boyce, *The Philippines*, pp. 33–44, 52–53. For the original data, see World Bank, "Philippines: The Challenge of Poverty."

84. Porter and Ganapin, *Resources, Population, and the Philippines' Future*, pp. 6–7.

85. According to the World Bank, there were 6.4 million families in the Philippines in 1971 and 9.5 million in 1985, and the average size of a poor family was 6.2 in 1971 and 5.99 in 1985. See World Bank, "Philippines: The Challenge of Poverty," pp. 1–2, esp. Table 1.1. If we use Boyce's data on the percentages of families living in poverty (43.8 percent of families in 1971 and 58.9 in 1985), then there were 2.8 million families living in poverty in 1971 and 5.6 million in 1985. See Boyce, *The Philippines*, p. 46, Table 2.13, for poverty estimates. Considering average family size, this means that there were 17.4 million Filipinos in poverty in 1971 and 33.5 million in 1985. The World Bank calculates a different number based on its finding that the percentage of families in poverty re-

mained constant at 52 percent in 1971 and 1985. The World Bank therefore calculates that the total number of impoverished people increased from 20.5 million in 1971 to 30.6 million in 1985. This produces an estimate of 10 million additional poor people compared to the 16 million calculated by using Boyce's figures on poverty. Herrin cites Philippine government estimates that differ from those cited by both Boyce and the World Bank. Government estimates suggest that 49.3 percent of families were impoverished in 1971 compared to 59.3 percent in 1985. This translates into 19.6 million poor Filipinos in 1971 and 33.7 million in 1985, representing a net increase of 14 million. See Herrin, "Philippine Demographic Development and Public Policies," p. 515 Table 3. For a discussion of the relative merits of the competing sets of data and reasons to doubt the viability of the World Bank's estimates, see Boyce, *The Philippines*, pp. 44–50.

86. Boyce, *The Philippines*, pp. 62, 146–54; Cruz and Repetto, *Environmental Effects*, pp. 40, 42–45; Porter and Ganapin, *Resources, Population, and the Philippines' Future*, pp. 18–19; World Bank, "Philippines: The Challenge of Poverty," pp. 13, 31, 46–49; World Bank, "Philippines: Toward Sustaining the Economic Recovery: Country Economic Memorandum," pp. vi, 55–57; and Wurfel, *Filipino Politics*, pp. 60–61.

87. Chapman, *Inside the Philippine Revolution*, p. 90

88. World Bank, "Philippines: The Challenge of Poverty," p. 13

89. Kessler, *Rebellion and Repression*, p. 19.

90. Factoran, *Population, Resources and the Philippine Future*, p. 4.

91. Broad and Cavanagh, *Plundering Paradise*, p. 24.

92. Cruz et al., *Population Growth, Poverty, and Environmental Stress*, p. 25; Jones, *Red Revolution*, p. 14; Porter and Ganapin, *Resources, Population, and the Philippines' Future*, pp. 6–7; and World Bank, "Philippines: The Challenge of Poverty," p. 10.

93. Cruz et al., *Population Growth, Poverty, and Environmental Stress*, p. 11; Factoran, *Population, Resources, and the Philippine Future*, p. 15; and USAID, *Sustainable Natural Resources Assessment—Philippines*, pp. 11–12, 34–35.

94. Porter and Ganapin, *Resources, Population, and the Philippines' Future*, p. 21. On the importance of fish to food supply, see ibid., p. 35.

95. Boyce, *The Philippines*, pp. 262 Table 9.3, 263–66; and USAID, *Sustainable Natural Resources Assessment—Philippines*, p. 7.

96. Boyce, *The Philippines*, pp. 39, 257–58; Cruz and Repetto, *Environmental Effects*, p. 52; Herrin, "Philippine Demographic Development and Public Policies," pp. 514–18; Bernardo Villegas, "The Economic Crisis," in *Crisis in the Philippines: The Marcos Era and Beyond*, ed. John Bresnan (Princeton, N.J.: Princeton University Press, 1986), pp. 168–71; World Bank, "Philippines: The Challenge of Poverty," pp. 17–22; and World Bank, "Philippines: Toward Sustaining the Economic Recovery: Country Economic Memorandum," p. 53.

97. Boyce, *The Philippines*, pp. 171–76, 254–57, 303–10; Cruz and Repetto, *Environmental Effects*, pp. 12–16; Cruz et al., *Population Growth, Poverty, and Environmental Stress*, pp. 29–31; Hal Hill and Sisira Jayasuriya, "The Philippines: Growth, Debt, and Crisis: Economic Performance during the Marcos Era," Working Paper No. 85/3 (Development Studies Centre, Australian National

University, 1985); Kummer, *Deforestation in the Postwar Philippines*, pp. 79–80; Porter and Ganapin, *Resources, Population, and the Philippines' Future*, pp. 15–16; USAID, *Sustainable Natural Resources Assessment—Philippines*, pp. 27–29; and Villegas, "The Economic Crisis."

98. Boyce, *The Philippines*, pp. 10–11, 328–30; Cruz and Repetto, *Environmental Effects*, pp. 3, 15, 51–52; and Villegas, "The Economic Crisis," pp. 161–62, 168–71.

99. Boyce, *The Philippines*, pp. 78–86; Cruz and Repetto, *Environmental Effects*, p. 25; DENR, *The Philippine Environment in the Eighties*, pp. 171–74; Kummer, *Deforestation in the Postwar Philippines*, p. 84; Pineda-Ofreneo, *The Philippines*, pp. 37–38; and Wurfel, *Filipino Politics*, pp. 171–73.

100. Pineda-Ofreneo, *The Philippines*, p. 37. Annual investments in irrigation, for example, climbed from less than P30 million a year in 1965–69 to more than P600 million in 1979 (valued in 1972 pesos) before declining in the 1980s, as the total area of irrigated land increased more than one-and-a-half times (Cruz and Repetto, *Environmental Effects*, p. 26 Table 2–11. The estimate on acreage under irrigation is from Boyce, *The Philippines*, p. 80, Table 3.5; and USAID *Sustainable Natural Resources Assessment—Philippines*, B-9 and Table 2.4–1. Meeting these demands served several interconnected interests. The Marcos government felt that investments were necessary to prevent rural unrest stemming from growing numbers of people competing for less land. Increases in production were also vital to provide inexpensive food to urban areas, with their burgeoning populations. Lastly, Marcos used the investments to build on his extensive patronage machine and to increase centralized control over rural elites. See Boyce, *The Philippines*, pp. 71–72, 329; and Wurfel, *Filipino Politics*, pp. 166–67.

101. Cruz and Repetto, *Environmental Effects*, p. 32; DENR, *The Philippine Environment in the Eighties*, pp. 233–38, 251–54; Factoran, *Population, Resources, and the Philippine Future*, pp. 16–17; Kessler, *Rebellion and Repression*, p. 140; NSO and MI, *National Demographic Survey, 1993*, p. 2; Pineda-Ofreneo, *The Philippines*, pp. 68–71; World Bank, "Philippines: The Challenge of Poverty," pp. 25–31; and Wurfel, "Political Consequences," pp. 57–60.

102. Dante B. Canlas, "Savings, Productivity, and Population: Notes on the Macroeconomics of Population Change," in *Population, Human Resources, and Development*, ed. Alejandro N. Herrin (Diliman, Quezon City, the Philippines: University of the Philippines Press and the Center for Integrative and Development Studies, 1994), pp. 751–62. See also Chita Tanchoco-Subido, "Rural Savings Behavior," Discussion Paper 8111 (University of the Philippines School of Economics, August 1981); and World Bank, "Philippines: Toward Sustaining the Economic Recovery: Country Economic Memorandum," pp. iii–iv. For a thorough discussion of savings rates in the Philippines during the period under investigation here, see William E. James, "Credit Rationing, Rural Savings, and Financial Policy in Developing Countries," Asian Development Bank Economic Staff Paper No. 13 (Manila, Philippines: Asian Development Bank, 1982); Wan-Soon Kim, "Financial Development and Household Savings: Issues in Domestic Resource Mobilization in Asian Developing Countries," Asian Development Bank Economic Staff Paper No. 10 (Manila, Philippines: Asian De-

velopment Bank, 1982); Basil J. Moore, "Domestic Savings in Selected Developing Asian Countries," Asian Development Bank Economic Staff Paper No. 2 (Manila, Philippines: Asian Development Bank, 1981); and Tanchoco-Subido, "Rural Savings Behavior." These studies conclude that rural households in the Philippines had substantial capacity to save but that their ability to do so was determined primarily by income. Low incomes for rural households thus had an important negative effect on domestic savings rates.

103. See Boyce, *The Philippines*, p. 308, Table 11.2; Cruz and Repetto, *Environmental Effects*, p. 16, Table 2.5; and Kim, "Financial Development and Household Savings," p. 15, Table 1.

104. Cruz and Repetto, *Environmental Effects*, p. 15. See also Boyce, *The Philippines*, pp. 307-8; Hill and Jayasuriya , "The Philippines: Growth, Debt and Crisis," pp. 16, 19; Kim, "Financial Development and Household Savings"; and Villegas, "The Economic Crisis," pp. 155-56.

105. Villegas, "The Economic Crisis," p. 168.

106. Herrin, "Philippine Demographic Development and Public Policies," p. 509. Normally a shift away from savings to consumption would lead us to expect an increase in demand. Yet in the context of declining incomes and a greater shift toward subsistence lifestyles, it is possible for savings and demand for industrially produced consumer goods to decline simultaneously. That appears to have been the case in the Philippines. As Boyce notes: "[The increase in rural poverty] had negative demand-side effects on both agriculture and industrial growth. The declining purchasing power of the rural poor . . . limited the home market for basic consumer good" (*The Philippines*, p. 155).

107. USAID, *Sustainable Natural Resources Assessment—Philippines*, p. 27 (emphasis mine).

108. Boyce, *The Philippines*, p. 228.

109. Ibid., pp. 171, 225-230; DENR, *A Report on Philippine Environment and Development: Issues and Strategies* (Diliman, Quezon City, the Philippines: DENR, 1991), pp. 2-3; Factoran, *Population, Resources, and the Philippine Future*, pp. 7-9; and Porter and Ganapin, *Resources, Population, and the Philippines' Future*, p. 19.

110. Cruz and Repetto, *Environmental Effects*, pp. 14-15; and USAID, *Sustainable Natural Resources Assessment—Philippines*, p. 28.

111. USAID, *Sustainable Natural Resources Assessment—Philippines*, pp. 31-32. See also, Boyce, *The Philippines*, pp. 234-35; and Factoran, *Population, Resources, and the Philippine Future*, pp. 9, 20-21.

112. USAID, *Sustainable Natural Resources Assessment—Philippines*, p. E-29 and Table 4.2-1.

113. Factoran, *Population, Resources, and the Philippine Future*, p. 9.

114. Porter and Ganapin, *Resources, Population, and the Philippines' Future*, pp. 23, 31-33.

115. Cruz et al., *Population Growth, Poverty, and Environmental Stress*, 1988. Because of inadequate data on agricultural yield losses and net farm income reductions as a result of erosion, the cost of soil erosion was measured as the cost of replacing lost nutrients with fertilizers. See also Wilfrido D. Cruz and Maria Concepcion J. Cruz, "Population Pressure and Deforestation in the Phil-

ippines," *ASEAN Economic Bulletin* 7, no. 2 (November 1991): 200–212; Cruz et al., *Population Growth, Poverty, and Environmental Stress,* p. 24; Cruz and Repetto, *Environmental Effects,* p. 19; and DENR, *The Philippine Environment in the Eighties,* pp. 93–100, 169–71.

116. World Bank, "Philippines: Environment and Natural Resources Management Survey," pp. xi–xii, 64–66.

117. Cruz and Repetto, *Environmental Effects,* pp. 23–24; and Cruz et al., *Population Growth, Poverty, and Environmental Stress,* p. 24.

118. Cruz and Repetto, *Environmental Effects,* pp. 11, 17. See also pp. 11–28.

119. Porter and Ganapin, *Resources, Population, and the Philippines' Future,* p. 45.

120. There was also a positive feedback loop between the economic crisis, the ensuing period of structural adjustment, and DES. The economic crisis and stabilization programs increased un- and underemployment, thereby encouraging further migration to the uplands and worsening population pressures and environmental degradation there. Even before the debt crisis, repayment obligations encouraged additional plundering of the country's forests and expanded the capitalization of commercial fishing, thereby contributing to overfishing, to generate foreign exchange. These pressures escalated during the 1980s. The increase in economic marginalization stemming from DES, in turn, made the poor more vulnerable to further economic dislocations. See Broad and Cavanagh, *Plundering Paradise,* pp. 53–54, 155; Cruz and Repetto, *Environmental Effects,* pp. 5–6, 47–48; Cruz et al., *Population Growth, Poverty, and Environmental Stress,* 5–6, 29–33; Kessler, "The Philippines," p. 200; and Porter and Ganapin, *Resources, Population, and the Philippines' Future,* pp. 15–21. On the effects of debt and structural adjustment on the poor, see Pineda-Ofreneo, *The Philippines;* and World Bank, "Philippines: The Challenge of Poverty."

121. Kessler, *Rebellion and Repression,* pp. 19–22; and Wurfel, *Filipino Politics,* p. 139.

122. Quoted in Niksch, *Insurgency and Counterinsurgency,* p. 11.

123. Ibid., pp. 8–9.

124. Pineda-Ofreneo, *The Philippines,* p. 15. See also Herrin, "Philippine Demographic Development and Public Policies," p. 509; and Pineda-Ofreneo, *The Philippines,* p. 3

125. Quoted in Kessler, *Rebellion and Repression,* p. 21.

126. Niksch, *Insurgency and Counterinsurgency,* p. 9.

127. See Jones, *Red Revolution,* chap. 11; Kessler, *Rebellion and Repression,* chap. 4; Niksch, *Insurgency and Counterinsurgency,* pp. 35–36; and Wurfel, *Filipino Politics,* pp. 140–46.

128. Quoted in Wurfel, *Filipino Politics,* p. 140.

129. See Chapman, *Inside the Philippine Revolution,* pp. 180–90; Jones, *Red Revolution,* pp. 123–25; Kessler, *Rebellion and Repression,* pp. 125–126; and Niksch, *Insurgency and Counterinsurgency,* pp. 39–40, 46–47.

130. Niksch, *Insurgency and Counterinsurgency,* pp. 41–46. See also Hill and Jayasuriya , "The Philippines: Growth, Debt and Crisis," pp. 52–53.

131. Quoted in Chapman, *Inside the Philippine Revolution,* p. 181.

132. Kessler, *Rebellion and Repression*, pp. 143–44, 145. See also Wurfel, *Filipino Politics*, pp. 315–16.

133. Kessler, *Rebellion and Repression*, p. 44. See also Steve Lohr, "Manila's Economy: Signs of Anguish Everywhere," *New York Times*, 20 August 1984, Lexis-Nexis; Kessler, *Rebellion and Repression*, pp. 44–45, 139–40; Kessler, "The Philippines," pp. 215–16; and Wurfel, "Political Consequences," p. 66; idem, *Filipino Politics*, pp. 37–40, 154, 165–10, 330–32.

134. Kessler, "The Philippines," p. 216. See also idem, *Rebellion and Repression*, pp. 44–45.

135. William Branigin, "Insurgency, Economic Crisis Threatens U.S. Ally," *Washington Post*, 12 August 1984, Lexis-Nexis; Solarz, "Last Chance"; Wurfel, *Filipino Politics*, pp. 237–40; and Paul D. Hutchcroft, "Oligarchs and Cronies in the Philippine State: The Politics of Patrimonial Plunder," *World Politics* 43, no. 3 (April 1991): 432.

136. On the nature and causes of growing factionalism in the military, see Kessler, *Rebellion and Repression*, chap. 4, esp. 128–35; Kessler, "The Philippines," p. 215; Mark R. Thompson, "Off the Endangered List: Philippine Democratization in Comparative Perspective," *Comparative Politics* 28, no. 2 (January 1996): 184–85; and Wurfel, *Filipino Politics*, pp. 150–51, 239–40, 289–91. See also William Branigin, "Police, Rebels Blamed for Killings," *Washington Post*, 15 August 1984, Lexis-Nexis; and Lindy Washburn, "Moving Toward Upheaval," *The Record*, 29 January 1985, Lexis-Nexis.

137. Quoted in Kessler, *Rebellion and Repression*, p. 131. See also Joel Rocamora, *Breaking Through: The Struggle within the Communist Party of the Philippines* (Manila, Philippines: Anvil, 1994), pp. 55–56.

138. Kessler, "The Philippines," pp. 211–12.

139. The vast majority of observers contend that economic need, not ideology, lay at the heart of initial support for the Communists. See William Branigin, "Guerillas Step Up Attacks in Philippines," *Washington Post*, 8 February 1983, Lexis-Nexis; Angus Deming and Melinda Liu, "The Philippines: Preparing for People's War," *Newsweek*, 16 April 1984, Lexis-Nexis; Branigin, "Insurgency, Economic Crisis Threatens U.S. Ally"; Lohr, "Manila's Economy"; Washburn, "Moving toward Upheaval"; Steve Lohr, "Rebels and Hunger Stalk Province in Philippines," *New York Times*, 6 May 1985, Lexis-Nexis; Steve Lohr, "Starting Over in Mindanao," *New York Times*, 28 July 1985, Lexis-Nexis; Lohr, "For Filipino Rebels, a 'New Deal' via the Gun"; and Lohr, "Inside the Philippine Insurgency." See also Guy Arnold, *Wars in the Third World since 1945*, 2nd ed. (London: Cassell, 1995), p. 549; Broad and Cavanagh, *Plundering Paradise*, pp. 103, 107–8; Kessler, *Rebellion and Repression*, p. 2; Myers, *Ultimate Security*, pp. 86, 92; Porter and Ganapin, *Resources, Population, and the Philippines' Future*, pp. 10–11; Talbott, "The State of the Environment," pp. 41–43; World Bank, "Philippines: The Challenge of Poverty," p. 31; Wurfel, "Political Consequences," pp. 56–57, and idem, *Filipino Politics*, p. 175.

140. Quoted in Jones, *Red Revolution*, p. 178.

141. José Maria Sison (with Rainer Werning), *The Philippine Revolution: The Leader's View* (New York: Crane Russak, 1989), pp. 25–27, 147.

142. Wurfel, *Filipino Politics*, p. 277. See also Lohr, "Rebels and Hunger"; idem, "For Filipino Rebels, a 'New Deal' via the Gun"; idem, "Inside the Philippine Insurgency"; Roy L. Prosterman, "Land Reform Is Essential to Democracy in the Philippines," *Los Angeles Times*, 7 February 1986, Lexis-Nexis; Fernando del Mundo, "Filipinos Search for Solutions to 17-year Insurgency," *United Press International*, 11 December 1986, Lexis-Nexis; Seth, Mydans, "In the Big Manila Land Plan, Steps Are Small," *New York Times*, 18 October 1987, Lexis-Nexis; Kessler, *Rebellion and Repression*, p. 151; and Wurfel, *Filipino Politics*, pp. 170, 266–67.

143. Jones, *Red Revolution*, chaps. 7, 8, 16. See also Sheilah Ocampo, " 'People's War' in the Philippines," *Christian Science Monitor*, 22 October 1981, Lexis-Nexis; Lohr, "For Filipino Rebels, a 'New Deal' via the Gun"; idem, "Inside the Philippine Insurgency"; and Clayton Jones, "Filipino Communists: Guns Mostly Silent, but Economic War Blazes," *Christian Science Monitor*, 21 January 1987, Lexis-Nexis.

144. Rocamora, *Breaking Through*, p. 16.

145. Fox Butterfield, "Bold, Growing Communists Drive," *New York Times*, 28 February 1986, Lexis-Nexis; Clayton Jones, "In the Philippines, Sugar Barons Seek Ways to Combat Insurgency," *Christian Science Monitor*, 24 September 1986, Lexis-Nexis; and Greg Hutchinson, "Aquino Announces Land Distribution to Poor Filipino Peasants," *Reuters*, 16 October 1986, Lexis-Nexis. See also Broad and Cavanagh, *Plundering Paradise*, p. 11; Chapman, *Inside the Philippine Revolution*, pp. 128–29; Jones, *Red Revolution*, pp. 90–93; Niksch, *Insurgency and Counterinsurgency*, pp. 11–13; and Wurfel, *Filipino Politics*, pp. 288–89.

146. Quoted in William Branigin, "Poverty on Negros Island Breeding Filipino Rebels," *Washington Post*, 21 September 1986, Lexis-Nexis.

147. Porter and Ganapin, *Resources, Population, and the Philippines' Future*, pp. 30–31.

148. Quoted in Jones, *Red Revolution*, p. 175.

149. Broad and Cavanagh, *Plundering Paradise*, pp. 61–63.

150. Niksch, *Insurgency and Counterinsurgency*, p. 12. See also, "Guerillas Gain in Mindanao," *Facts on File World News Digest*, 31 December 1981, Lexis-Nexis; and Wurfel, *Filipino Politics*, pp. 264–66.

151. Quoted in Branigin, "Insurgency, Economic Crisis Threatens U.S. Ally." At other times Marcos did concede that development problems were driving the insurgency. Still he insisted that "the basic conditions for a revolution just aren't there." See William Branigin, "Philippines Far Left Grows as Center Defers to Marcos," *Washington Post*, 22 November 1981, Lexis-Nexis.

152. Quoted in William Branigin, "Communist Insurgents Gaining Strength, Moving Into Cities," *Washington Post*, 14 August 1984, Lexis-Nexis.

153. Branigin, "Police, Rebels Blamed for Killings."

154. Jonathan Broder, "Red 'Robin Hoods' Take Aim at Marcos," *Chicago Tribune*, 20 November 1983, section 1, p. 3.

155. Quoted in "Guerillas Gain in Mindanao," *Facts on File World News Digest*, 31 December 1981, Lexis-Nexis.

156. Quoted in Branigin, "Insurgency, Economic Crisis Threatens U.S. Ally."

157. Niksch, *Insurgency and Counterinsurgency,* pp. 8, 11. See also Solarz, "Last Chance"; Edward L. Fike, "The Philippines: Communists Stalk a Troubled Land," *San Diego Union-Tribune,* 21 July 1985, Lexis-Nexis; Jones, *Red Revolution,* p. 12; and Kessler, *Rebellion and Repression,* pp. 19–22.

158. Lohr, "For Filipino Rebels, a 'New Deal' via the Gun."

159. Chapman, *Inside the Philippine Revolution,* p. 115; Jones, *Red Revolution,* pp. 245–46. This problem was magnified by the fact that the AFP was also bogged down fighting Muslim insurgents seeking independence in Mindanao. For a discussion of the Muslim insurgency, see Wurfel, *Filipino Politics,* pp. 28–31, 62–63, 154–65, 269–70. See also Solarz, "Last Chance."

160. See William Branigin, "Philippine Far Left Grows as Center Defers to Marcos," *Washington Post,* 22 November 1981, Lexis-Nexis; Branigin, "Police, Rebels Blamed for Killings"; Chapman, *Inside the Philippine Revolution,* pp. 118–121, 146; Kessler, *Rebellion and Repression,* pp. 120–21, 126–27; and Wurfel, *Filipino Politics,* p. 141.

161. See Thompson, "Off the Endangered List," p. 184.

162. The report was prepared by Frost and Sullivan, a New York–based international publisher of market analyses and forecasts for industry. The report is quoted in Manola B. Jara, "Philippines: Communist Takeover Not Far-Fetched," *Inter Press Service,* 13 November 1985, Lexis-Nexis. See also Branigin, "Police, Rebels Blamed for Killings"; Chapman, *Inside the Philippine Revolution,* pp. 180–82; Jones, *Red Revolution,* pp. 240–42; and Niksch, *Insurgency and Counterinsurgency,* pp. 3–4, 36–39.

163. Kessler, *Rebellion and Repression,* p. 147. See also Broder, "Red 'Robin Hoods,'" section 1, p. 3; and Rocamora, *Breaking Through,* p. 55.

164. Quoted in Ocampo, "'People's War.'" See also Solarz, "Last Chance"; Fike, "Communists Stalk a Troubled Land"; Dan Connell, "The 'Philippines Problem' is Far More Than Just Political," *Christian Science Monitor,* 7 January 1986, Lexis-Nexis; and Clyde Haberman, "Manila after Marcos," *New York Times,* 28 February 1986, Lexis-Nexis. Similar incentives increased support for the NPA in urban slums, especially in Davao city. See Washburn, "Moving toward Upheaval."

165. Quoted in Lohr, "Rebels and Hunger." See also Solarz, "Last Chance"; Lohr, "For Filipino Rebels, a 'New Deal' via the Gun"; idem, "Inside the Philippine Insurgency"; Chapman, *Inside the Philippine Revolution,* pp. 183–85; Kessler, *Rebellion and Repression,* pp. 78, 141–47, 150; and Wurfel, *Filipino Politics,* pp. 267–68, 294. When NPA killings became more indiscriminate in some areas, support declined. See Jones, *Red Revolution,* pp. 247–48; and Kessler, *Rebellion and Repression,* pp. 77–78.

166. Quoted in Branigin, "Communist Insurgents Gaining Strength."

167. Quoted in ibid.

168. Paul Quinn-Judge, "The Philippines Braces for a Power Vacuum," *Christian Science Monitor,* 26 February 1985, Lexis-Nexis; Peter Tarr, "Can Aquino Revive a Plundered Land?" *The Nation,* 19 April 1986, Lexis-Nexis; Jones, "Sugar Barons Seek Ways to Combat Insurgency"; Niksch, *Insurgency and Counterinsurgency,* p. 30; and Wurfel, *Filipino Politics,* p. 289.

169. Chapman, *Inside the Philippine Revolution,* p. 179.

170. See Branigin, "Insurgency, Economic Crisis Threatens U.S. Ally."

171. Quoted in Broder, "Red 'Robin Hoods,' " section 1, p. 3. Both government and communist sources came to agree that the rapid growth of the insurgency and the intensification of the civil war beginning in the late 1970s was the result of growing poverty, the lack of government services and programs in rural areas, growing lawlessness, and perceived abuses and injustices at the hands of government forces. See Branigin, "Communist Insurgents Gaining Strength." The combination of factors underlying the growth of the CPP-NPA was also recognized by the church. Bishop Federico Escaler, for example, observed that "the growing support for the dissidents [stems from] poverty, military abuses and unemployment. The situation is fodder to revolutionary groups." Quoted in Fernando del Mundo, "Bishops Warn of Growing Rebel Support," *United Press International*, 23 January 1983.

172. Quoted in Chapman, *Inside the Philippine Revolution*, p. 119. See also ibid., pp. 238–39; and Jones, *Red Revolution*, pp. 125, 128–29.

173. Quoted in Lohr, "For Filipino Rebels, a 'New Deal' via the Gun." See also Broder, "Red 'Robin Hoods,' " section 1, p. 3; Chapman, *Inside the Philippine Revolution*, p. 130; and Jones, *Red Revolution*, pp. 10–12, 60–61.

174. Niksch, *Insurgency and Counterinsurgency*, pp. 13–14; and Wurfel, *Filipino Politics*, p. 268.

175. Branigin, "Communist Insurgents Gaining Strength."

176. Myers, *Ultimate Security*, p. 92. See also Norman Myers, "Environment and Security," *Foreign Policy*, no. 74 (spring 1989): 25–27.

177. On the importance of exclusive institutions, see the discussion in chapter 5.

178. Thomas F. Homer-Dixon, *Environment, Scarcity, and Violence* (Princeton, N.J.: Princeton University Press, 1999), p. 77.

179. Ibid., p. 153.

180. See Ross, *Timber Booms and Institutional Breakdown*, pp. 71–84.

181. Betsy Hartmann, "Will the Circle Be Unbroken? A Critique of the Project on Environment, Population, and Security" in *Violent Environments*, ed. Nancy Lee Peluso and Michael Watts (Ithaca, N.Y.: Cornell University Press, 2001), pp. 51–52.

Chapter 4
Land and Lies: Ethnic Clashes in Kenya

1. This brief summary of Kenya's political history draws on D. Pal Ahluwalia, *Post-Colonialism and the Politics of Kenya* (New York: Nova Science, 1996); David Gordon, "A History of Kenya," in *Kenya: The Land, the People, the Nation*, ed. Mario Azevedo, pp. 35–60 (Durham, N.C.: Carolina Academic Press, 1993); Kenneth Ingham, *Politics in Modern Africa: The Uneven Tribal Dimension* (London: Routledge, 1990), chap. 5; and Jennifer A. Widner, *The Rise of a Party-State in Kenya: From "Harambee!" to "Nyayo!"* (Berkeley: University of California Press, 1992). See also chapter 5 of this volume for a more detailed discussion of the evolution of Kenya's political institutions.

2. For general discussions of the violence in and around the Rift Valley, see A.M. Akiwumi, *Report of the Judicial Commission Appointed to Inquire into Tribal Clashes in Kenya*, reproduced in a *Daily Nation* (Nairobi) *Special Report* (available online at http://www.nationaudio.com/News/DailyNation/23102002), part 1; Kenya Human Rights Commission (KHRC), *Killing the Vote: State Sponsored Violence and Flawed Elections in Kenya* (Nairobi, Kenya: KHRC, 1998), chaps. 2, 3; National Council of Churches of Kenya (NCCK), *The Cursed Arrow: A Report on Organized Violence against Democracy in Kenya* (Nairobi, Kenya: NCCK, 1992); National Election Monitoring Unit (NEMU), *Courting Disaster: A Report on the Continuing Terror, Violence and Destruction in the Rift Valley, Nyanza and Western Provinces of Kenya*, 29 April 1993; Binaifer Nowrojee, *Divide and Rule: State-Sponsored Ethnic Violence in Kenya*, An Africa Watch Report (New York: Human Rights Watch, 1993); John Oucho, *Undercurrents of Ethnic Conflict in Kenya* (Leiden: Brill, 2002), chap. 4; Republic of Kenya, National Assembly, *Report of the Parliamentary Select Committee to Investigate Ethnic Clashes in Western and Other Parts of Kenya, 1992*, September 1992.

3. Stephen N. Ndegwa, "Citizenship and Ethnicity: An Examination of Two Transition Moments in Kenyan Politics," *American Political Science Review* 91, no. 3 (September 1997): 612.

4. Nowrojee, *Divide and Rule*, chap. 3; Oucho, *Undercurrents of Ethnic Conflict*, pp. 91–92, Table 2.

5. "Some Significant Developments," *Weekly Review* (Nairobi), 19 March 1993, p. 7.

6. See Nowrojee, *Divide and Rule*, chap. 4; Human Rights Watch/Africa, "Kenya: Old Habits Die Hard," p. 5; and NEMU, *Courting Disaster*, p. 2.

7. Oucho, *Undercurrents of Ethnic Conflict*, pp. 94–95, Table 2.

8. "Ethnic Strife," *Weekly Review* (Nairobi), 20 March 1992, pp. 3–6; Republic of Kenya, *Report of the Parliamentary Select Committee*, p. 48; and Robert M. Press, "Tribal Clashes in Kenya Continue," *Christian Science Monitor*, 27 September 1993, Westlaw.

9. Nowrojee, *Divide and Rule*, p. 25.

10. Bakr Ogle, "Deal with Attackers, Midika Tells Luos," *The Standard* (Nairobi), 16 March 1992, p. 2.

11. "Neighbor Turns on Neighbor," *Daily Nation* (Nairobi), 10 May 1993, Part 5: "Life in the Clash Affected Areas." Quoted in Nowrojee, *Divide and Rule*, pp. 33–34.

12. Quoted in Nowrojee, *Divide and Rule*, 48. See also chap. 5.

13. "Ethnic Strife," p. 6. See also "New Spate of Ethnic Clashes," *Weekly Review* (Nairobi), 13 March 1992, p. 18; Ogle, "Deal with Attackers," pp. 1–2; "A Flood of Angry Reactions," *Weekly Review* (Nairobi), 5 March 1993, p. 14; and "Some Significant Developments," p. 7.

14. NEMU, *Courting Disaster*, pp. 18, 20, 22.

15. Nowrojee, *Divide and Rule*, pp. 1, 23, 70–71. The Kenyan government claimed that there were considerably fewer killed and displaced. There is every indication, however, that the government significantly underestimated the casualties involved. See "Clashes 'Claimed 365,' " *The Standard* (Nairobi),

6 May 1993, p. 1; and "Uproar over Clash Figures," *Weekly Review* (Nairobi), 14 May 1993, pp. 13–14.

16. NEMU, *Courting Disaster*, pp. 12–13.

17. Frank Holmquist and Michael Ford, "Stalling Political Change: Moi's Way in Kenya," *Current History* 94, no. 591 (April 1995): 178.

18. "Ethnic Strife," p. 9. See also "New Spate of Ethnic Clashes," p. 19; "FORD/Govt. on Collision Course," *Weekly Review* (Nairobi), 29 May 1992, pp. 12–14, 16; "A New Angle to the Strife," *Weekly Review* (Nairobi), 10 April 1992, p. 13; "Turmoil in Bungoma District," *Weekly Review* (Nairobi), 24 April 1992, p. 20; "A Report on Ethnic Violence," *Weekly Review* (Nairobi), 19 June 1992, p. 14; NCCK, *The Cursed Arrow*, pp. 23–34; "The Controversy Deepens," 26 February 1993, pp. 11–12; "Security Zones," *Weekly Review* (Nairobi), 10 September 1993, p. 4; and NEMU, *Courting Disaster*, p. 2.

19. The Inter-Parties Task Force was made up of representatives from the NCCK, all non-KANU political parties, the Kenya Section of the International Commission of Jurists, the Law Society of Kenya, and the University of Nairobi.

20. The Akiwumi Commission was appointed by Moi on 1 July 1998 and presented its report on the clashes on 31 July 1999. However, because of the nature of its findings, Moi delayed the release until 18 October 2002.

21. NCCK, *The Cursed Arrow*"; "A Report on Ethnic Violence," pp. 14–15; Republic of Kenya, *Report of the Parliamentary Select Committee*; and NEMU, *Courting Disaster*. See also Press, "Tribal Clashes in Kenya Continue."

22. Donatella Lorch, "New Round of Fighting Threatens Multiparty Democracy in Kenya," *Star-Tribune*, 19 September 1993, Westlaw.

23. NCCK, *The Cursed Arrow*, pp. 1, 4, 22; NEMU, *Courting Disaster*, pp. 5–6, 11; Oucho, *Undercurrents of Ethnic Conflict*, pp. 110–14; and Republic of Kenya, *Report of the Parliamentary Select Committee*, pp. 19, 30–31, 39, 45–46, 57–58, 68.

24. See, for example, "Clashes: Priests Speak Out," *The Standard* (Nairobi), 20 March 1992, p. 3.

25. Quoted in NEMU, *Courting Disaster*, p. 13.

26. "Security Zones," p. 7.

27. Republic of Kenya, *Report of the Parliamentary Select Committee*, pp. 14, 19, 76; Nowrojee, *Divide and Rule*, p. 19.

28. For a general discussion of government incitement of, and support for, attackers, see "Ethnic Strife," p. 13; "Getting to Grips with Tragedy," *Weekly Review* (Nairobi), 27 March 1992, p. 13; NCCK, *The Cursed Arrow*, pp. 17, 21–22; NEMU, *Courting Disaster*, pp. 6–15; Nowrojee, *Divide and Rule*, chaps. 1–4; and Republic of Kenya, *Report of the Parliamentary Select Committee*, pp. 15–19, 35, 37, 45, 49, 51, 68–71, 79–81.

29. See Nowrojee, *Divide and Rule*, chap. 5.

30. Quoted in Bill Berkeley, "An Encore for Chaos?" *Atlantic Monthly*, February 1996, p. 33.

31. Ng'ang'a Thiong'o, "This Violence Will Not Help Anybody," *The Standard* (Nairobi), 23 March 1992, p. 17.

32. "New Spate of Ethnic Clashes," p. 18.

33. "Security Zones," pp. 3–9; and Oucho, *Undercurrents of Ethnic Conflict*, pp. 93–94, Table 2.

34. William Brass and Carole L. Jolly, eds., *Population Dynamics of Kenya* (Washington D.C.: National Academy Press, 1993), pp. 14–16.

35. Robert A. Wortham, "Population Growth and the Demographic Transition in Kenya," *International Sociology* 8, no. 2 (June 1993): 114.

36. Norman Miller and Rodger Yeager, *Kenya: The Quest for Prosperity*, 2nd ed. (Boulder, Colo.: Westview, 1994), p. 64. TFR refers to the average number of children born to a woman over the course of her childbearing years.

37. Republic of Kenya, Ministry of Economic Planning and Development, *Kenya Population Census, 1979*, Vols. 1 and 2 (Nairobi, Kenya: Central Bureau of Statistics, 1981); Republic of Kenya, Office of the Vice President, Ministry of Planning and National Development, *Kenya Population Census, 1989*, Vols. 1 and 2 (Nairobi, Kenya: Central Bureau of Statistics, 1994). In recent years, Kenya's population growth rate has shown signs of decline. Two *Kenyan Demographic and Health Surveys*, conducted in 1989 and 1993, show a dramatic drop in the TFR, from the 1984 TFR of 7.7 to 6.7 in 1989 and 5.4 in 1993. See Mary Tiffen, "Population Density, Economic Growth and Societies in Transition: Boserup Reconsidered in a Kenyan Case-study," *Development and Change* 26, no. 1 (January 1995): 56. For a discussion of and competing explanations for Kenya's high rate of population growth, as well as the recent decline, see Brass and Jolly, *Population Dynamics*; Odile Frank and Geoffrey McNicoll, "An Interpretation of Fertility and Population Policy in Kenya," Working Paper, Center for Policy Studies (New York: Population Council, 1987); Allen C. Kelley and Charles E. Nobbe, "Kenya at the Demographic Turning Point? Hypotheses and a Proposed Research Agenda," World Bank Discussion Papers (Washington, D.C.: World Bank, 1990); Warren C. Robinson, "Kenya Enters the Fertility Transition," *Population Studies* 46, no. 3 (November 1992): 445–57; Tiffen, "Population Density"; Wortham, "Population Growth"; and Robert A. Wortham, "Prospects for Fertility Reduction and Projections for Future Population Growth in Kenya," *Population Research and Policy Review* 14, no. 1 (March 1995): 111–35. Notwithstanding this dramatic change, Kenya's population will continue to grow rapidly because of the demographic momentum generated by the large number of young people in Kenya's population (Brass and Jolly, *Population Dynamics*, p. 8).

38. Brass and Jolly, *Population Dynamics*, p. 9; S. H. Ominde, *Population and Development in Kenya* (Nairobi, Kenya: Heinemann Educational Books, 1984), chaps. 1–2; Republic of Kenya, Ministry of Environment and Natural Resources, *Kenya: National Report*, Prepared for the United Nations Conference on Environment and Development—1992 (Nairobi, Kenya: Ministry of Environment and Natural Resources, 1991), pp. 1–2.

39. See Republic of Kenya, *Kenya Population Census, 1979*; Republic of Kenya, *Kenya: National Report*, p. 17; and Republic of Kenya, *Kenya Population Census, 1989*.

40. Calestous Juma, "Sustainable Development and Economic Policy in Kenya," in *Gaining Ground: Institutional Innovations in Land-use Management in Kenya*, ed. Amos Kiriro and Calestous Juma, rev. ed. (Nairobi, Kenya: Acts

Press, 1991), p. 68. For slightly different figures, see Republic of Kenya, *Kenya: National Report*, p. 52.

41. Arne Tostensen and John G. Scott, *Kenya: Country Study and Norwegian Aid Review*, (Norway: The Chr. Michelsen Institute, Department of Social Science and Development, 1987), p. 329; Danida (Danish International Development Assistance), *Environmental Profile: Kenya* (Denmark: Danida Department of International Development Cooperation, 1989), p. 27; and Republic of Kenya, *Kenya: National Report*, p. 85.

42. Situma Mwichabe, *Environmental Problems in Kenya: Surviving a Spoiled Environment* (Nairobi: Konrad Adenauer Foundation, 2002), p. 42.

43. Quoted in Tostensen and Scott, *Kenya: Country Study and Norwegian Aid Review*, p. 289.

44. Republic of Kenya, *Kenya: National Report*, p. 85.

45. Danida, *Environmental Profile*, pp. 28–32; Juma, "Sustainable Development and Economic Policy," p. 71.

46. Danida, *Environmental Profile*, p. 8; Norman Myers, *Population, Resources and the Environment: The Critical Challenges* (New York: United Nations Population Fund, 1991), p. 96; and Tostensen and Scott, *Kenya: Country Study and Norwegian Aid Review*, p. 329.

47. Gloria Waggoner, "Economics and the Environment: What Is Kenya Doing?" in Watson, *Modern Kenya*, pp. 75–88.

48. One high-profile study of Machakos District in Eastern Province suggests that high population densities spurred technological adaptation, leading to enhanced conservation and agricultural production over the long term. See Mary Tiffen, Michael Mortimore, and Francis Gichuki, *More People, Less Erosion: Environmental Recovery in Kenya* (New York: Wiley, 1994); and Michael Mortimore and Mary Tiffen, "Population Growth and a Sustainable Environment," *Environment* 36, no. 1 (October 1994): 10–20, 28–32.

49. Mwichabe, *Environmental Problems in Kenya*, p. 66.

50. Myers, *Population, Resources and the Environment* *(New York: United Nations Population Fund, 1991), p. 96.*

51. Ian Livingston, *Rural Development, Employment and Incomes in Kenya* (Brooksfield, Vt.: Gower, 1986), p. 222; see also pp. 218–20.

52. Tostensen and Scott, *Kenya: Country Study and Norwegian Aid Review*, p. 105.

53. Miller and Yeager, *The Quest for Prosperity*, pp. 79–80.

54. Danida, *Environmental Profile*, pp. 20, 22.

55. Africa Watch, *Kenya: Taking Liberties* (London: Africa Watch, 1991), p. 26; and Michael F. Lofchie, "Kenya: Still an Economic Miracle?" *Current History* 89, no. 547 (May 1990): 211.

56. Republic of Kenya, *Kenya: National Report*, pp. 112–13.

57. Tostensen and Scott, *Country Study and Norwegian Aid Review*, pp. 59, 287. It should be noted that all landless are not poor; some are engaged in formal employment or trade.

58. Republic of Kenya, *Poverty Reduction Strategy Paper for the Period 2001–2004* (Nairobi, Kenya: Institute of Policy Analysis and Research, 2001), p. 21.

59. Tostensen and Scott, *Country Study and Norwegian Aid Review*, p. 54.

60. Republic of Kenya, *Kenya: National Report*, p. 105. One Kenyan pound (K£) is equivalent to 20 Kenyan shillings (Ksh).

61. Myers, *Population, Resources and the Environment*, p. 92.

62. Ibid., p. 95; Danida, *Environmental Profile*, p. 27.

63. Frank Holmquist and Michael Ford, "Kenyan Politics: Toward a Second Transition?" *Africa Today* 45, no. 2 (April–June 1998): 232.

64. Danida, *Environmental Profile*, pp. 19, 21; Republic of Kenya, *Kenya: National Report*, pp. 112–13. Migration to ASALs itself further increased land degradation and hence the prospects for further economic marginalization. By definition, ASALs have fragile ecosystems vulnerable to rapid desertification if used intensively by large numbers of farmers. New migrants from medium- and high-potential areas have tended to compound this natural vulnerability by using technologies and agricultural techniques ill-suited for their new environment (Republic of Kenya, *Kenya: National Report*, pp. 85–86).

65. Republic of Kenya, *Kenya Population Census, 1989*. See also Table 2.

66. Davider Lamba, *Nairobi's Environment: A Review of Conditions and Issues* (Nairobi, Kenya: Mazingira Institute, 1994), p. 4.

67. Miller and Yeager, *The Quest for Prosperity*, pp. 63–64.

68. Tostensen and Scott, *Country Study and Norwegian Aid Review*, pp. 59, 290.

69. Republic of Kenya, *Kenya: National Report*, pp. 113–14.

70. Danida, *Environmental Profile*, p. 49; Lamba, *Nairobi's Environment*, p. 6; and Tostensen and Scott, *Country Study and Norwegian Aid Review*, p. 291.

71. Republic of Kenya, *Kenya: National Report*, pp. 114–15. See also Lamba, *Nairobi's Environment*, pp. 7–8.

72. Tostensen and Scott, *Country Study and Norwegian Aid Review*, p. 288.

73. Republic of Kenya, *Kenya: National Report*, pp. 122–23.

74. Danida, *Environmental Profile*, p. 52.

75. Miller and Yeager, *The Quest for Prosperity*, p. 87.

76. Republic of Kenya, *Kenya: National Report*, p. 78.

77. Myers, *Population, Resources and the Environment*, p. 97; and Republic of Kenya, *Kenya: National Report*, pp. 105, 111.

78. Lamba, *Nairobi's Environment*, pp. 4–6.

79. Danida, *Environmental Profile*, p. 51.

80. Brass and Jolly, *Population Dynamics*, p. 12, Table 2–1, 13; and Wortham, "Prospects for Fertility Reduction," p. 112.

81. Tostensen and Scott, *Country Study and Norwegian Aid Review*, p. 54.

82. Kelley and Nobbe, "Kenya at the Demographic Turning Point?" pp. 10–11.

83. Ibid., p. 13.

84. Republic of Kenya, *Kenya: National Report*, p. 106.

85. David W. Throup and Charles Hornsby, *Multi-Party Politics in Kenya: The Kenyatta and Moi States and the Triumph of the System in the 1992 Elections* (Oxford: James Currey, 1998), pp. 22–23, 26, 45–50.

86. Holmquist and Ford, "Stalling Political Change," p. 177.

87. Africa Watch, *Taking Liberties*, p. 237.

88. Throup and Hornsby, *Multi-Party Politics in Kenya*, p. 47.

89. Republic of Kenya, *Kenya: National Report*, pp. 29–30.

90. Republic of Kenya, *Kenya Population Census, 1989*.

91. Ingham, *Politics in Modern Africa*, p. 113; Miller and Yeager, *The Quest for Prosperity*, p. 88.

92. Africa Watch, *Taking Liberties*, p. 73; and Throup and Hornsby, *Multi-Party Politics in Kenya*, pp. 26–27, 47–48.

93. Gilbert M. Khadiagala, "Kenya: Intractable Authoritarianism," *SAIS Review* 15, no. 2 (summer–fall 1995): 54.

94. Holmquist and Ford, "Stalling Political Change," p. 177; Ndegwa, "Citizenship and Ethnicity," p. 610.

95. Ahluwalia, *Post-Colonialism and the Politics of Kenya*, pp. 179–80; and Ndegwa, "Citizenship and Ethnicity," p. 609.

96. Ndegwa, "Citizenship and Ethnicity," p. 610; and Widner, *The Rise of a Party-State in Kenya*, pp. 195–97. For a general discussion of pressures to return to multipartyism, see Throup and Hornsby, *Multi-Party Politics in Kenya*, chap. 4.

97. For a detailed discussion, see Africa Watch, *Taking Liberties*, chap. 2.

98. Ibid., p. 56. See also Miller and Yeager, *The Quest for Prosperity*, pp. 107–8; and Widner, *The Rise of a Party-State in Kenya*, pp. 192–95.

99. Republic of Kenya, *Report of the Parliamentary Select Committee*, p. 7. These politicians made up the political portion of a growing coalition calling for political and economic reform. "Their quarrel with the government was primarily its failure to establish workable economic policies and the deterioration of education facilities and employment opportunities" (Africa Watch, *Taking Liberties*, p. 24).

100. Africa Watch, *Taking Liberties*, p. 73.

101. Economist Intelligence Unit, *Kenya: Country Profile, 1991–92* (London: The Economist Intelligence Unit, 1991), p. 4; and Widner, *The Rise of a Party-State in Kenya*, pp. 134, 138, 145.

102. Africa Watch, *Taking Liberties*, chaps. 3–4.

103. Holmquist and Ford, "Stalling Political Change," p. 177. See also Ahluwalia, *Post-Colonialism and the Politics of Kenya*, pp. 176–82; Miller and Yeager, *The Quest for Prosperity*, pp. 98, 108, 113, 122; and Widner, *The Rise of a Party-State in Kenya*, chap. 6.

104. Khadiagala, "Intractable Authoritarianism," p. 54.

105. NEMU, *Courting Disaster*, p. 5.

106. Quoted in Miller and Yeager, *The Quest for Prosperity*, p. 66; See also pp. 64–66, esp. p. 65, Table 3.2.

107. Ibid., pp. 95, 131.

108. Parts of the White Highlands cut across several contemporary provinces, including Nyanza, Eastern, Central, and Rift Valley Provinces. The bulk of the area, however, was located in what are now called Central and Rift Valley Provinces. See Ominde, *Population and Development*, p. 10.

109. Ibid., p. 18; Africa Watch, *Taking Liberties*, p. 1; and Miller and Yeager, *The Quest for Prosperity*, p. 5. For a firsthand account of life in the highlands, see Isak Dinesen, *Out of Africa* (New York: Random House, 1937).

110. Human Rights Watch/Africa, "Old Habits Die Hard," pp. 5–6 n. 13.

111. Ominde, *Population and Development*, p. 18; see also pp. 9–10; Gordon, "A History of Kenya," pp. 42–53; Livingston, *Rural Development*, pp. 218–19; and Miller and Yeager, *The Quest for Prosperity*, chap. 1.

112. NEMU, *Courting Disaster*, p. 4. See also Oucho, *Undercurrents of Ethnic Conflict*, p. 102.

113. African Watch, *Taking Liberties*, p. 2; and Republic of Kenya, *Report of the Parliamentary Select Committee*, p. 42.

114. Throup and Hornsby, *Multi-Party Politics in Kenya*, p. 7.

115. See Africa Watch, *Taking Liberties*, p. 4; Robert H. Bates, *Beyond the Miracle of the Market: The Political Economy of Agrarian Development in Kenya* (New York: Cambridge University Press, 1989), chap. 1; Miller and Yeager, *The Quest for Prosperity*, pp. 24–27; and Thomas P. Tomich, Peter Kilby, and Bruce F. Johnston, *Transforming Agrarian Economies: Opportunities Seized, Opportunities Missed* (Ithaca, N.Y.: Cornell University Press, 1995), p. 377.

116. Ahluwalia, *Post-Colonialism and the Politics of Kenya*, p. 40; York W. Bradshaw, "Perpetuating Underdevelopment in Kenya: The Link between Agriculture, Class, and State," *African Studies Review* 33, no. 1 (April 1990): 5–6; Colin Leys, *Underdevelopment in Kenya: The Political Economy of Neo-Colonialism, 1964–1971* (London: Heinemann, 1975); Oucho, *Undercurrents of Ethnic Conflict*, pp. 142–70; and Tomich, Kilby, and Johnston, *Transforming Agrarian Economies*, pp. 377–82.

117. Africa Watch, *Taking Liberties*, pp. 237–39.

118. Cheryl Jackson Hall, "Racial and Ethnic Antagonism in Kenya," in *Modern Kenya: Social Issues and Perspectives*, ed. Mary Ann Watson (Lanham, Md.: University Press of America, 2000), p. 292; Nowrojee, *Divide and Rule*, pp. 16–18; Oucho, *Undercurrents of Ethnic Conflict*, pp. 123–29.

119. NEMU, *Courting Disaster*, p. 4. See also "A Sense of Tribal Warfare," *Weekly Review* (Nairobi), 15 November 1991, p. 12.

120. "A Sense of Tribal Warfare," p. 18; "18 More Killed in Clashes," *The Standard* (Nairobi), 17 March 1992, p. 2; "The Main Cause of Ethnic Clashes," *The Standard* (Nairobi), 23 March 1993, pp. 16–17; "Security Zones," p. 9; and Press, "Tribal Clashes in Kenya Continue."

121. Republic of Kenya, *Report of the Parliamentary Select Committee*, pp. 47–48, 82.

122. Human Rights Watch/Africa, "Old Habits Die Hard," pp. 4–6. See also, Berkeley, "An Encore to Chaos," p. 33.

123. KHRC, *Killing the Vote*, p. 2.

124. See Ahluwalia, *Post-Colonialism and the Politics of Kenya*, chap. 2.

125. Throup and Hornsby, *Multi-Party Politics in Kenya*, p. 543.

126. "A Sense of Tribal Warfare," pp. 11, 13, 16; "'Warriors' Issue New Threat," *Weekly Review* (Nairobi), 29 November 1991, p. 18; "Ethnic Strife," pp. 6, 8, 10; "The Main Cause of the Ethnic Clashes," *The Standard* (Nairobi), 23 March 1992, pp. 16–17; "A Report on Ethnic Violence," p. 14; and NCCK, *The Cursed Arrow*, p. 22. See also the discussions in Republic of Kenya, *Report of the Parliamentary Select Committee*; and NEMU, *Courting Disaster*.

127. International Commission of Jurists (Kenya Section), *The Political Economy of Ethnic Clashes in Kenya* (Nairobi, Kenya: International Commission of Jurists (Kenya Section), 2000), p. 26; Ndegwa, "Citizenship and Ethnicity," p. 609; and Republic of Kenya, *Report of the Parliamentary Select Committee* pp. 8–9.

128. Throup and Hornsby, *Multi-Party Politics in Kenya*, pp. 29–30, 40, 49, 79–88, 174–75, 181–82.

129. Quoted in Akiwumi, *Report of the Judicial Commission*, part 1, p. 44.

130. Quoted in KHRC, *Killing the Vote*, pp. 11–12.

131. "A Sense of Tribal Warfare," p. 13.

132. Ndegwa, "Citizenship and Ethnicity," p. 610 (emphasis mine). See also NEMU, *Courting Disaster*, pp. 5–6.

133. Republic of Kenya, *Report of the Parliamentary Select Committee*, pp. 9, 36, 48.

134. Both quoted in Republic of Kenya, *Report of the Parliamentary Select Committee*, pp. 9, 10, respectively.

135. Human Rights Watch/Africa, "Kenya: Multi-partyism Betrayed in Kenya," *Human Rights Watch/Africa Report* 6, no. 5 (July 1994): 10.

136. Quoted in Throup and Hornsby, *Multi-Party Politics in Kenya*, p. 542.

137. Quoted in Nowrojee, *Divide and Rule*, p. 52.

138. See also Human Rights Watch/Africa, "Multi-partyism Betrayed in Kenya," pp. 11–12.

139. Republic of Kenya, *Report of the Parliamentary Select Committee*, pp. 38–39.

140. Ibid., pp. 22–39.

141. Ibid., p. 36.

142. Ibid., p. 28.

143. NEMU, *Courting Disaster*, p. 11. See also Republic of Kenya, *Report of the Parliamentary Select Committee*, pp. 55–60.

144. Republic of Kenya, *Report of the Parliamentary Select Committee*, p. 58.

145. Throup and Hornsby, *Multi-Party Politics in Kenya*, pp. 542–43.

146. Jacqueline M. Klopp, "Electoral Despotism in Kenya: Land, Patronage and Resistance in the Multi-Party Context," Ph.D. diss., Department of Political Science, McGill University, Montreal, Canada, 2001, p. 161.

147. Quoted in Klopp, "Electoral Despotism in Kenya," p. 165.

148. Quoted in Nowrojee, *Divide and Rule*, p. 42. See also "Eight More Killed in Kenyan Tribal Violence," *Agence France-Presse*, 16 October 1993, Westlaw; and "Kenya: Sinister," *Economist*, 4 February 1995, 36–37.

149. Quoted in Klopp, "Electoral Despotism in Kenya," p. 167. See also Throup and Hornsby, *Multi-Party Politics in Kenya*, pp. 554–55.

150. Throup and Hornsby, *Multi-Party Politics in Kenya*, pp. 198–99.

151. Quoted in Akiwumi, *Report of the Judicial Commission*, part 1, p. 18.

152. KHRC, *Killing the Vote*, p. 29. See also Throup and Hornsby, *Multi-Party Politics in Kenya*, pp. 542–43.

153. Nowrojee, *Divide and Rule*, p. 3.

154. "New Spate of Ethnic Clashes," p. 18; "Kenya: How Not to Seek Approval," *Economist*, 24 April 1993, p. 43; and NEMU, *Courting Disaster*, p. 21.

155. NCCK, *The Cursed Arrow*, p. 4. See also Robert M. Press, "Ethnic Violence Troubles Kenya," *Christian Science Monitor*, 2 April 1992, Lexis-Nexis.

156. Moi reportedly made this statement on 22 January 1992 (NEMU, *Courting Disaster*, p. 12). See also ibid., pp. 4–5; and Mark Huband, "Kenyan Politicians Stoke Flames in Tribal Clashes," *Guardian* (London), 24 July 1994, Westlaw.

157. Thobhani, "Political Developments during the 1990s," pp. 12–14.

158. Oucho, *Undercurrents of Ethnic Conflict*, p. 97.

159. Nowrojee, *Divide and Rule*, pp. 35–36. See also ibid., p. 48; and Human Rights Watch/Africa, "Multi-partyism Betrayed in Kenya," p. 13.

160. Mark Huband, "Death Toll Mounts in Tribal Wars," *Guardian* (London), 28 April 1993, Westlaw.

161. KHRC, *Killing the Vote*, p. 29.

162. Klopp, *Electoral Despotism in Kenya*, p. 171.

163. "Things Gradually Toning Down," *Weekly Review* (Nairobi), 2 April 1993, p. 10; Holmquist and Ford, "Stalling Political Change," p. 178; Human Rights Watch/Africa, "Old Habits Die Hard," pp. 4–8; Khadiagala, "Intractable Authoritarianism," pp. 55–57; NEMU, *Courting Disaster*, pp. 3, 8, 17, 21; and Nowrojee, *Divide and Rule*, pp. 2–3, 70, 76.

164. NEMU, *Courting Disaster*, p. 21. See also Horace Awori, "Kenya: Ethnic Violence Flares Up Again," *Inter Press Service Global Information Network*, 13 January 1993, Westlaw.

165. There was also sporadic violence in other parts of Kenya in the run-up to the 1997 election, including parts of both Nyanza and Rift Valley Provinces. Following a similar pattern, in each instance "KANU's leaders tactfully exploited genuine grievances and long-standing disputes relating to cattle rustling, border disputes, economic inequalities and religious differences to foment violence" (KHRC, *Killing the Vote*, p. 33).

166. Ibid., pp. 56–57. Likoni is, for all intents and purposes, an extension of Kwale District.

167. "Mijikenda" is Swahili for "nine communities" and the category includes several subgroups: the Chonyi, Digo, Duruma, Giriama, Jibana, Kambe, Kauma, Rabai, and Ribe. The Digo and the Duruma are the main groups in Kwale and the areas inhabited by the Digo were the most affected by the clashes (ibid., p. 57 n. 191).

168. Ibid., pp. 56–57.

169. The Kamba were largely farmers in the Shimba hills of Kwale District; the Kikuyu made up a disproportionate number of business owners in the area, with some owning land in Ukanda, Kwale Town, Mkongani, and Likoni, and the Luo were concentrated in local quarries and the stonecutting industry or employed on the island of Mombasa. See Akiwumi, *Report of the Judicial Commission*, part 2, p. 2; and KHRC, *Killing the Vote*, pp. 56–57, 68, Table 10.

170. Human Rights Watch, *Playing with Fire: Weapons Proliferation, Political Violence, and Human Rights in Kenya* (New York: Human Rights Watch, 2002), pp. 39, 58–61.

171. Ibid., pp. 61–64; KHRC, *Kayas of Deprivation, Kayas of Blood* (Nairobi, Kenya: KHRC, 1997), p. 1.

172. Human Rights Watch, *Playing with Fire*, p. 39; KHRC, *Killing the Vote*, pp. 2, 6, 68. Others put the figure of displaced at forty thousand. See Holmquist and Ford. "Kenyan Politics," p. 229.

173. KHRC, *Killing the Vote*, pp. 59–60; Sam Riley, "Kenya Victims Blame Leader," *The Australian*, 26 August 1997, Lexis-Nexis.

174. From *Daily Nation* (Nairobi), 24 August 1997; quoted in Human Rights Watch, *Playing with Fire*, p. 85.

175. Human Rights Watch, *Playing with Fire*, pp. 4, 78–83.

176. Ibid., p. 81.

177. Ibid., p. 79.

178. Akiwumi, *Report of the Judicial Commission*, part 2, pp. 39, 41; Human Rights Watch, *Playing with Fire*, pp. 45–46, 78–86; and KHRC, *Killing the Vote*, 58–59.

179. Quoted in KHRC, *Killing the Vote*, pp. 58–59. See also Akiwumi, *Report of the Judicial Commission*, part 2, pp. 20–21; and Human Rights Watch, *Playing with Fire*, p. 80.

180. Akiwumi, *Report of the Judicial Commission*, part 2, p. 4

181. KHRC, *Killing the Vote*, p. 59.

182. Ibid., p. 57.

183. Akiwumi, *Report of the Judicial Commission*, part 2, pp. 26–39; Human Rights Watch, *Playing with Fire*, pp. 5–6, 64–73, 83–93; KHRC, *Kayas of Deprivation, Kayas of Blood*, p. iv; and KHRC, *Killing the Vote*, pp. 62–63.

184. Republic of Kenya, Ministry of Finance and Planning, *The 1999 Population and Housing Census*, Vol. 1 (Nairobi, Kenya: Central Bureau of Statistics, 2001).

185. Brass and Jolly, *Population Dynamics*, p. 12, Table 2–1; and Republic of Kenya, *Poverty Reduction Strategy Paper*, p. 25.

186. International Commission of Jurists (Kenya Section), *Political Economy of Ethnic Clashes*, p. 44.

187. Holmquist and Ford. "Kenyan Politics," p. 232; Republic of Kenya, *Poverty Reduction Strategy Paper*, pp. 13–15.

188. Maina Kiai, "Commentary: A Last Chance for Peaceful Change in Kenya," *Africa Today* 45, no. 2 (April–June 1998): 188.

189. Ibid.

190. Ibid. p. 186.

191. Ibid., pp. 189–90; Thobhani, "Political Developments during the 1990s," p. 15.

192. Stephen N. Ndegwa, "The Incomplete Transition: The Constitutional and Electoral Context in Kenya," *Africa Today* 45, no. 2 (April–June 1998): 195.

193. Joel D. Barkan, "Toward a New Constitutional Framework in Kenya," *Africa Today* 45, no. 2 (April–June): 217; Joel D. Barkan and Njuguna Ng'ethe, "Kenya Tries Again," *Journal of Democracy* 9, no. 2 (April 1998): 36–37; Herman O. Kiriama, "Fundamental Constitutional Changes in Kenya," in *The Political Economy of Transition: A Study of Issues and Social Movements in Kenya since 1945*, ed. Eric Masinde Aseka et al. (Nairobi, Kenya: Eight Publishers, 1999), pp. 128–29; Ndegwa, "The Incomplete Transition," p. 196; Thobhani, "Political Developments during the 1990s," p. 16.

194. Kiai, "Commentary," pp. 185, 190.

195. Ibid., p. 190; Ndegwa, "The Incomplete Transition," pp. 195–96.

196. Throup and Hornsby, *Multi-Party Politics in Kenya*, p. 555.

197. Ibid.

198. KHRC, *Kayas of Deprivation, Kayas of Blood*, pp. 7–8. See also Human Rights Watch, *Playing with Fire*, p. 3; and KHRC, *Killing the Vote*, p. 33.

199. Quoted in Kiai, "Commentary," p. 190.

200. Barkan, "Toward a New Constitutional Framework," p. 217; Barkan and Ng'ethe, "Kenya Tries Again," 37; Holmquist and Ford, "Kenyan Politics," p. 239; Kiai, "Commentary," pp. 185, 191.

201. Akiwumi, *Report of the Judicial Commission*, part 2, p. 20.

202. Quoted in KHRC, *Killing the Vote*, p. 58. See also Human Rights Watch, *Playing with Fire*, p. 42; and Oucho, *Undercurrents of Ethnic Conflict*, p. 97.

203. Akiwumi, *Report of the Judicial Commission*, part 2, p. 3; see also pp. 20, 23.

204. Kenya Human Rights Commission (KHRC), *Kayas Revisited: A Post-Election Balance Sheet* (Nairobi, Kenya: KHRC, 1998), p. 41; and KHRC, *Killing the Vote*, pp. 67–73.

205. KHRC, *Kayas of Deprivation, Kayas of Blood*, p. iv. See also KHRC, *Killing the Vote*, p. 33.

206. KHRC, *Kayas of Deprivation, Kayas of Blood*, pp. 6–8, 50–53; KHRC, *Kayas Revisited*," pp. ii–iii; KHRC, *Killing the Vote*, pp. 33–34; "5 Killed as Violence Flares on Kenyan Coast," *Chicago Tribune*, 18 August 1997, Lexis-Nexis; "Government, Opposition Say Bloody Mombasa Violence 'Political,' " *Agence France Presse*, 18 August 1997, Lexis-Nexis; Moyiga Ndura, "Kenya-Politics: Violence Spreads in Tourism Belt," *Inter Press Service*, 20 August 1997, Lexis-Nexis; James C. McKinley Jr., "Ethnic Strife in Kenya Derails Talks on Reform," *New York Times*, 21 August 1997, Lexis-Nexis; and Gitau Warigi, "Was There a Political Link to the Violence in Mombasa?" *The East African* (Nairobi), 25 August 1997, Lexis-Nexis.

207. KHRC, *Kayas Revisited*," p. iii; see also the discussion in chap. 5.

208. Thobhani, "Political Developments during the 1990s," p. 16.

209. KHRC, *Killing the Vote*, p. 34.

210. KHRC, *Kayas of Deprivation, Kayas of Blood*, p. 14.

211. Holmquist and Ford. "Kenyan Politics," pp. 233–34; Human Rights Watch. *Kenya's Unfinished Democracy: A Human Rights Agenda for the Government* (New York: Human Rights Watch, 2002), pp. 7–8, 19–20; Jacqueline M. Klopp, "Pilfering the Public: The Problem of Land Grabbing in Contemporary Kenya," *Africa Today* 47, no. 1 (winter 2000): 8, 16–17; Klopp, "Electoral Despotism in Kenya," chap. 5; and Kiai, "Commentary," p. 187.

212. KHRC, *Kayas of Deprivation, Kayas of Blood*, p. 14.

213. Klopp, "Electoral Despotism in Kenya," pp. 129–32; for a general discussion of "patronage inflation," see also chap. 3.

214. Klopp, "Pilfering the Public," p. 17.

215. See Table 4.1 in this volume; and Republic of Kenya, *The 1999 Population and Housing Census*, Vol. 1.

216. Holmquist and Ford. "Kenyan Politics," p. 232; and Republic of Kenya, *Poverty Reduction Strategy Paper*, pp. 13–15.

217. Republic of Kenya, *Poverty Reduction Strategy Paper*, p. 17.

218. KHRC, *Kayas Revisited*," p. 51.

219. Akiwumi, *Report of the Judicial Commission*, part 2, p. 2; and KHRC, *Kayas of Deprivation, Kayas of Blood*, pp. 13–17.

220. Akiwumi, *Report of the Judicial Commission*, part 2, p. 3; and KHRC, *Kayas of Deprivation, Kayas of Blood*, pp. 13, 17.

221. As the Akiwumi Commission noted: "The Digo youth were[,] on the whole, unemployed, idle and hungry. This constituted a fertile ground which was waiting to be exploited to wreak havoc upon the perceived upcountry oppressors" (Akiwumi, *Report of the Judicial Commission*, part 2, p. 2). See also Human Rights Watch, *Playing with Fire*, p. 3; Prisca Mbura Kamungi, *The Current Situation of Internally Displaced Persons in Kenya*, Jesuit Refugee Service, 2001, p. 5; and Warigi, "Was There a Political Link to the Violence in Mombasa?"

222. Quoted in KHRC, *Kayas Revisited*, pp. 57–58.

223. Quoted in Human Rights Watch, *Kenya's Unfinished Democracy*, p. 20. It should be noted that one of the cruel ironies of the clashes at the Coast was that most of those targeted were poor up-country residents rather than the relatively small number of wealthy and politically connected individuals who were much more directly responsible for the significant inequalities in the area.

224. Human Rights Watch, *Playing with Fire*, pp. 44–48. Ultimately, most of these promises went unfulfilled by KANU. See *Playing with Fire*, pp. 105–6.

225. McKinley, "Ethnic Strife in Kenya Derails Talks on Reform." See also Lara Santoro, "After Unrest, Kenya Awash in Conspiracy Theories," *Christian Science Monitor*, 7 October 1997, Lexis-Nexis.

226. Both quotes are from Human Rights Watch, *Playing with Fire*, pp. 48–49 and 49, respectively; see also pp. 40–41.

227. KHRC, *Killing the Vote*, p. 64. See also "Kenya: War on the Coast," *The Economist*, August 23, 1997, Lexis-Nexis; and Warigi, "Was There a Political Link to the Violence in Mombasa?"

228. Lucy Oriang, "Drop This Simplistic Rhetoric on Land Issue," *The Daily Nation* (Nairobi), 8 May 2000, Lexis-Nexis. See also Carey F. Onyango, "Law Could Ease Land Rows," *East African Standard*, 23 November 2002, Lexis-Nexis.

229. Klopp, *Electoral Despotism in Kenya*, pp. 187–88.

230. Ibid., pp. 183–84.

231. Quoted in Awori, "Ethnic Violence Flares Up Again."

232. On the relationship between democratization and civil strife, see Jack Snyder, *From Voting to Violence: Democratization and Nationalist Conflict* (New York: W.W. Norton, 2000; and Fareed Zakaria, *The Future of Freedom: Illiberal Democracy at Home and Abroad* (New York: W.W. Norton, 2003).

233. International Commission of Jurists (Kenya Section), *Political Economy of Ethnic Clashes*, p. 55 (emphasis mine).

Chapter 5
From Chaos to Calm: Explaining Variations in
Violence in the Philippines and Kenya

1. David Wurfel, *Filipino Politics: Development and Decay* (Ithaca, N.Y.: Cornell University Press, 1988), p. 24.

2. The historical discussion to this point draws on Chester L. Hunt, "The Society and Its Environment," in *Philippines: A Country Study*, ed. Ronald E. Dolan (Washington, D.C.: Library of Congress/U.S. Government Printing Office, 1993), pp. 67, 75–81; Richard J. Kessler, "The Philippines: The Making of

a 'People Power' Revolution," in *Revolutions of the Late Twentieth Century*, ed. Jack A. Goldstone, Ted Robert Gurr, and Farrokh Moshiri (Boulder, Colo.: Westview, 1991), p. 194; and Wurfel, *Filipino Politics*, pp. 24–27.

3. See Hunt, "The Society and Its Environment," pp. 76, 81–84; Allen G. Miller, "National Security," in *Philippines: A Country Study*, ed. Ronald E. Doran, pp. 290–93 (Washington, D.C.: Library of Congress/U.S. Government Printing Office, 1993); and Wurfel, *Filipino Politics*, pp. 28–31.

4. Hunt, "The Society and Its Environment," pp. 76, 84–86.

5. James K. Boyce, *The Philippines: The Political Economy of Growth and Impoverishment in the Marcos Era* (London: MacMillan, 1993), pp. 127–29; Hunt, "The Society and Its Environment," pp. 89–90; Wurfel, *Filipino Politics*, pp. 33–36.

6. Hunt, "The Society and Its Environment," p. 88. On the importance and changing nature of patron-client ties, see Boyce, *The Philippines*, pp. 129–32, 141–45; Hunt, "The Society and Its Environment," pp. 92–93; Paul D. Hutchcroft, "Oligarchs and Cronies in the Philippine State: The Politics of Patrimonial Plunder," *World Politics* 43, no. 3 (April 1991): 422–23; Richard J. Kessler, *Rebellion and Repression in the Philippines* (New Haven, Conn.: Yale University Press, 1989), pp. 17–23, 139–40; and Wurfel, *Filipino Politics*, pp. 17, 35, 50–51, 61–64.

7. Wurfel, *Filipino Politics*, p. 335.

8. Boyce, *The Philippines*, pp. 132–34; Larry A. Niksch, *Insurgency and Counterinsurgency in the Philippines*, prepared for the United States Senate Committee on Foreign Relations (Washington, D.C.: U.S. Government Printing Office, 1985), pp. 11–12; and Gareth Porter and Delfin J. Ganapin Jr., *Resources, Population, and the Philippines' Future* (Washington, D.C.: World Resources Institute, 1988), p. 11.

9. Wurfel, *Filipino Politics*, pp. 326, 335, 71, respectively.

10. Porter and Ganapin, *Resources, Population, and the Philippines' Future*, p. 11. On the cooperation between the CPP-NPA and upland tribal groups, see Greg R. Jones, *Red Revolution: Inside the Philippine Guerrilla Movement* (Boulder, Colo.: Westview, 1989), p. 97; and Wurfel, *Filipino Politics*, pp. 27–28. Although there was occasional cooperation between the Communists and Moro insurgents in Mindanao, the conflicts were largely distinct, with fundamentally different causes and consequences.

11. Niksch, *Insurgency and Counterinsurgency*, p. 13.

12. William Chapman, *Inside the Philippine Revolution* (New York: W.W. Norton, 1987), pp. 134–35.

13. Jones, *Red Revolution*, p. 230.

14. Quoted in Kessler, *Rebellion and Repression*, p. 67.

15. Both quoted in Steve Lohr, "Inside the Philippine Insurgency," *New York Times*, 3 November 1985, Lexis-Nexis.

16. See Chapman, *Inside the Philippine Revolution*, 108–9, 125–28, 134–41; Jones, *Red Revolution*, pp. 93, 97, 229–30; Kessler, *Rebellion and Repression*, pp. 50–51, 67–68, 152–53, 156; and Wurfel, *Filipino Politics*, pp. 36–37.

17. Chapman, *Inside the Philippine Revolution*, chaps. 1, 5; Hutchcroft, "Oligarchs and Cronies in the Philippine State," pp. 420–27; Jones, *Red Revolution*, pp. 39–41; Mark R. Thompson, *The Anti-Marcos Struggle: Personalistic Rule and*

Democratic Transition in the Philippines (New Haven, Conn.: Yale University Press), chap. 1; Mark R. Thompson, "Off the Endangered List: Philippine Democratization in Comparative Perspective," *Comparative Politics* 28, no. 2 (January 1996): 185; and Wurfel, *Filipino Politics*, pp. 327–28. For a detailed discussion, see Wurfel, *Filipino Politics*, chap. 4.

18. Boyce, *The Philippines*, p. 8; Hutchcroft, "Oligarchs and Cronies in the Philippine State," pp. 415, 425, 439–46; Porter and Ganapin, *Resources, Population, and the Philippines' Future*, pp. 13–14; Thompson, *The Anti-Marcos Struggle*, chap. 3; Thompson, "Off the Endangered List," pp. 182–83; and Wurfel, *Filipino Politics*, chap. 5.

19. Wurfel, *Filipino Politics*, p. 248.

20. Kessler, "The Philippines," pp. 204–5; and Thompson, "Off the Endangered List," p. 183. See also Wurfel, *Filipino Politics*, chap. 9.

21. Boyce, *The Philippines*, pp. 10, 248, 329–31; David M. Kummer, *Deforestation in the Postwar Philippines* (Chicago: University of Chicago Press, 1992), pp. 139, 145; Mark Poffenberger and Betsy McGean, "Upland Philippine Communities," Southeast Asia Sustainable Forest Management Network Research Report No. 4 (Berkeley: Center for Southeast Asia Studies, University of California, 1993), pp. 8–11; and Porter and Ganapin, *Resources, Population, and the Philippines' Future*, pp. 13–15, 26–30.

22. Porter and Ganapin, *Resources, Population, and the Philippines' Future*, p. 15.

23. Wurfel, *Filipino Politics*, pp. 335–36. Kessler reached a similar conclusion: "Possibly no other act was as instrumental [as martial law] in legitimizing the CPP in the minds of the discontented" (*Rebellion and Repression*, p. 41).

24. Jones, *Red Revolution*, p. 94.

25. Quoted in William Branigin, "Philippine Far Left Grows as Center Defers to Marcos," *Washington Post*, 22 November 1981, Lexis-Nexis. See also Lohr, "Inside the Philippine Insurgency."

26. Quoted in William Branigin, "Guerrillas Step Up Attacks in Philippines," *Washington Post*, 8 February 1983, Lexis-Nexis.

27. Quoted in Kessler, *Rebellion and Repression*, p. 41.

28. William Branigin, "Communist Insurgents Gaining Strength, Moving Into Cities," *Washington Post*, 14 August 1984, Lexis-Nexis.

29. See Jones, *Red Revolution*, chap. 15; Kessler, "The Philippines," pp. 194–217; Donald M. Seeskins, "Historical Setting," in Dolan, *A Country Study*, pp. 56–63; Mark R. Thompson, *The Anti-Marcos Struggle: Personalistic Rule and Democratic Transition in the Philippines* (New Haven, Conn.: Yale University Press), chap. 8; and Wurfel, *Filipino Politics*, chap. 10. For a discussion of the U.S. relationship with Marcos, including the American role in his eventual removal, see Raymond Bonner, *Waltzing with a Dictator: The Marcoses and the Making of American Policy* (New York: Vintage Books, 1988).

30. Thompson, "Off the Endangered List," p. 180.

31. The number of coups is a matter of controversy. All agree that there were at least six attempts, but there may have been as many as eight. See Thompson, *The Anti-Marcos Struggle*, pp. 168–70; and Thompson, "Off the Endangered List," p. 198 n. 1. For a discussion of the threats posed by loyalists and the

military, see Thompson, *The Anti-Marcos Struggle*, chap. 9; and Thompson, "Off the Endangered List," pp. 186–89.

32. Jones, *Red Revolution*, pp. 182–83; Seth Mydans, "In the Big Manila Land Plan, Steps Are Small," *New York Times*, 18 October 1987, Lexis-Nexis; Joel Rocamora, *Breaking Through: The Struggle within the Communist Party of the Philippines* (Manila, Philippines: Anvil, 1994), pp. 62–65; Oliver Teves, "Communists Overshadow 1986 Revolution Celebration," *Japan Economic Newswire*, 24 February 1988, Lexis-Nexis; and Wurfel, *Filipino Politics*, pp. 321–23.

33. Kessler, "The Philippines," pp. 212–13; Thompson, "Off the Endangered List," pp. 190–91; and World Bank, "Philippines: Country Assistance Report," Vols. 1 and 2, Report No. 17417 (Washington, D.C.: World Bank, 1998), pp. 3–6.

34. See Jonathan Power, "Weighing Aquino's Failure," *San Diego Union-Tribune*, 15 November 1991, Lexis-Nexis; Teves, "Communists Overshadow 1986 Revolution Celebration"; Kessler, "The Philippines," p. 212; Thompson, *The Anti-Marcos Struggle*, chap. 5; Thompson, "Off the Endangered List," pp. 187–89, 195–96; and Wurfel, *Filipino Politics*, pp. 311–18. On the cease-fire negotiations, see also Jones, *Red Revolution*, chap. 15. On the formation of vigilante groups, see Joel Palacios, "Farmers Turn Soldiers in Philippine Anti-Rebel Drive," *Reuters Library Report*, 21 February 1988, Lexis-Nexis; Ramon Isberto, "Philippines Finds it Tough to Eradicate Vigilantes," *Inter Press Service*, 27 July 1988, Lexis-Nexis; Vyvyan Tenorio, "The Old Order Persists Despite Philippine Change," *Los Angeles Times*, 5 March 1989, Lexis-Nexis; "Philippines: Report Finds Govt. and NPA Both Violate Laws of War," *Inter Press Service*, 12 August 1990, Lexis-Nexis; and William Branigin, "Philippine Rebels Show Violent Signs of Life," *Washington Post*, 26 February 1992, Lexis-Nexis.

35. Kessler, "The Philippines," p. 213; and Thompson, "Off the Endangered List," p. 193.

36. Thompson, "Off the Endangered List," p. 189. See also Thompson, *The Anti-Marcos Struggle*, chap. 9.

37. Paul D. Hutchcroft, "Unraveling the Past in the Philippines," *Current History* 94, no. 596 (December 1995): 432; John McBeth, "The Final Test," *Far Eastern Economic Review*, 13 June 1991, 33; and Thompson, "Off the Endangered List," pp. 193–95.

38. See Jeremy Clift, "Magic Fades as Aquino Marks First 1,000 Days in Power," *Reuters Library Report*, 17 November 1988, Lexis-Nexis; Phil Bronstein, "Mirage: Philippine Prosperity Fades," *St. Louis Dispatch*, 8 December 1989, Lexis-Nexis; Tenorio, "The Old Order Persists"; Kunda Dixit, "Philippines: Guerrillas Predict Victory in Ten Years," *Inter Press Service*, 28 March 1989, Lexis-Nexis; Jeremy Clift, "Aquino Faces Daunting Problems in Battle for Development," *Reuters Library Report*, 28 March 1990, Lexis-Nexis; Jeremy Clift, "Philippine Communism Still Fueled by Deep-Rooted Poverty," *Reuters*, 29 March 1990, Lexis-Nexis; "Communist Threat Remains Real in the Philippines," *Reuters North American Wire*, 20 March 1991, Lexis-Nexis; Power, "Weighing Aquino's Failure"; Branigin, "Philippine Rebels Show Violent Signs of Life"; and Thompson, *The Anti-Marcos Struggle*, p. 172.

39. Department of Environment and Natural Resources (DENR), *A Report on Philippine Environment and Development: Issues and Strategies* (Diliman, Que-

zon City, the Philippines: DENR, 1991), section 2, pp. 2–6; and Rosalinda Pineda-Ofreneo, "Debt and Environment: The Philippine Experience," in *Asia's Environmental Crisis*, ed. Michael C. Howard (Boulder, Colo.: Westview), p. 225.

40. Pineda-Ofreneo, "Debt and Environment," p. 227. See also DENR, *A Report on Philippine Environment and Development*, p. ii.

41. Thompson, "Off the Endangered List," p. 196; and World Bank, "Country Assistance Report," pp. 4, 6.

42. Hutchcroft, "Unraveling the Past"; World Bank, "Philippines: Managing Global Integration," Vols. 1 and 2, Report No. 17024-PH (Washington, D.C.: World Bank, 1998), p. 2, Table 1; and World Bank, "Country Assistance Report," pp. 6–13, 42, Table 1.

43. Chapman, *Inside the Philippine Revolution*, pp. 218–22.

44. Quoted in William Branigin, "Insurgency, Economic Crisis Threatens U.S. Ally," *Washington Post*, 12 August 1984, Lexis-Nexis.

45. "U.S. Assistant Secretary of Defense Armitage Sees Philippines Insurgency on the Wane," *Japan Economic Newswire*, 3 March 1988, Lexis-Nexis.

46. "Rebels No Longer Grave Threat, Aquino Says," *Japan Economic Newswire*, 17 February 1991, Lexis-Nexis.

47. Jeremy Clift, "Ramos Says Philippines Gaining in Battle against Communists," *Reuters Library Report*, 27 November 1988, Lexis-Nexis; Richard D. Fisher, "A Strategy for Defeating Communist Insurgents in the Philippines," *Heritage Foundation Reports*, 19 December 1988, Lexis-Nexis; Jeremy Clift, "Philippines Sees Improving Economy Beating Communist Rebels," *Reuters Library Report*, 30 March 1989, Lexis-Nexis; "Communist Insurgency in the Philippines Declining," *Japan Economic Newswire*, 28 February 1991, Lexis-Nexis; "Communist Rebels End Ceasefire in Philippines," *Reuters Library Report*, 21 September 1991, Lexis-Nexis; "Philippine Guerrilla Strength Down to 16,350: Military Report," *Agence France Presse*, 22 December 1991, Lexis-Nexis; "Ramos Legalizes Philippine Communist Party," *U.P.I.*, 22 September 1992, Lexis-Nexis; Robert Karniol, "Philippine Army Prepares for a More Peaceful Future," *Jane's Defense Weekly*, 31 October 1992, Lexis-Nexis; William Branigan, "In Philippines, Communist Party Slowly Self-Destructs," *Washington Post*, 15 January 1993, Lexis-Nexis; "Communist Armed Strength Dips by 30 Percent," *U.P.I.*, 23 December 1993, Lexis-Nexis; and Rene Pastor, "Communist Chief Calls for a New War in Philippines," *Reuters World Service*, 29 March 1995, Lexis-Nexis.

48. Quoted in Rocamora, *Breaking Through*, p. 90.

49. Bob Drogin, "Philippine Rebels Down But Not Out," *Los Angeles Times*, 10 March 1992, Lexis-Nexis.

50. McBeth, "The Final Test," p. 33; and John McBeth, "Reds Down But Not Out," *Far Eastern Economic Review*, 13 June 1991, pp. 44, 47. See also Dan Thomas, "Philippine Government Says It Has Communists Rebels on the Run," *Reuters Library Report*, 27 December 1990, Lexis-Nexis.

51. "Communist Armed Strength Dips by 30 Percent"; Johanna Son, "Philippines-Politics: Left at the Crossroads," *Inter Press Service*, 21 July 1994, Lexis-Nexis; and Ruben Alabastro, " 'Dying' Philippine Insurgency Seeks Lost Lustre," *Reuters North American Wire*, 26 June 1995, Lexis-Nexis.

52. "Philippine Rebels Losing by Default," *St. Louis Post-Dispatch*, 22 October 1989, Lexis-Nexis; Bob Drogin, "Communist Insurgency in Philippines Weakens," *Los Angeles Times*, 5 November 1989, Lexis-Nexis; McBeth, "Reds Down But Not Out," pp. 44–48; and Thompson, "Off the Endangered List," p. 195. See also Rocamora, *Breaking Through*, p. 91.

53. This statement was made by Alex Magno, a political analyst in Manila familiar with the Philippine Left, in Branigan, "In Philippines, Communist Party Slowly Self-Destructs." See also William Branigan, "Communist Rebels in Philippines Show Strain over Doctrine," *Washington Post*, 2 March 1992, Lexis-Nexis; William Branigan, "Feud among Philippine Guerrillas Heating Up," *Washington Post*, 8 January 1994, Lexis-Nexis; "In Disarray, Communist Army Marks 25th Anniversary in Philippines," *U.P.I.*, 29 March 1994, Lexis-Nexis; "Philippines: Down from the Hills," *Economist*, 30 April 1994, Lexis-Nexis; Marites D. Vitug, "Between Pure Theory and Coarse Reality: The Left in the Philippines Now Has the Three Identities," *WorldPaper*, June 1994, Lexis-Nexis; and Hugh Filman, "Decades of Insurgency in the Philippines Nearing Their End," *Deutsche Presse-Agentur*, 27 June 1995, Lexis-Nexis. According to one joke making the rounds in diplomatic circles in 1994, "the only Communists left in Europe are Filipino Communists in the Netherlands" (Son, "Philippines-Politics").

54. Tenorio, "The Old Order Persists"; Kessler, *Rebellion and Repression*, pp. 94–95; and Thompson, "Off the Endangered List," p. 192.

55. This statement was made in 1989 during the NPA's twentieth anniversary celebration (Oliver Teves, "Twenty-Year-Old Philippine Rebel Movement Faces Some Tough Challenges," *Japan Economic Newswire*, 4 April 1989, Lexis-Nexis).

56. Quoted in Kessler, *Rebellion and Repression*, pp. 84, 93, respectively.

57. Quoted in Rocamora, *Breaking Through*, p. 69.

58. Chapman, *Inside the Philippine Revolution*, pp. 13–14, 258–59; and Jones, *Red Revolution*, pp. 150–53, 220.

59. Quoted in Chapman, *Inside the Philippine Revolution*, p. 246.

60. Jones, *Red Revolution*, pp. 159–63; and Kessler, *Rebellion and Repression*, pp. 92–97.

61. Chapman, *Inside the Philippine Revolution*, p. 251; and Jones, *Red Revolution*, p. 7.

62. Thompson, *The Anti-Marcos Struggle*, pp. 170–72; Thompson, "Off the Endangered List," pp. 192–95; and Wurfel, *Filipino Politics*, pp. 318–20.

63. Jones, *Red Revolution*, p. 163.

64. Quoted in Rocamora, *Breaking Through*, p. 80.

65. "Aquino's Policies May Be Fueling Communist Insurgency, EIU Says," *Reuters Library Report*, 31 October 1988, Lexis-Nexis. See also, Rocamora, *Breaking Through*, pp. 79–90.

66. "Communist Party of the Philippines and the New People's Army," *Department of State Dispatch*, 11 November 1991, Lexis-Nexis; and Rocamora, *Breaking Through*, pp. 91, 101–6, chap. 4.

67. Hutchcroft, "Unraveling the Past," p. 432. See also Seth Mydans, "With Aquino Popular, the Philippine Rebels Tread Tricky Political Waters," *New York*

Times, 15 January 1989, Lexis-Nexis; "Ramos Legalizes Philippine Communist Party," *U.P.I.*, 22 September 1992, Lexis-Nexis; Teresa Albor, "Manila's Bold Peace Initiative Starting to Win Over Rebels," *San Francisco Chronicle*, 21 January 1993, Lexis-Nexis; and Rocamora, *Breaking Through*, chap. 6.

68. See the polls cited in Thompson, "Off the Endangered List," p. 196.

69. Wurfel, *Filipino Politics*, p. 176.

70. Quoted in Kessler, *Rebellion and Repression*, p. 93.

71. Jones, "Filipino Communists."

72. Quoted in Jones, *Red Revolution*, p. 246; see also p. 299.

73. Both quoted in Clift, "Philippines Sees Improving Economy Beating Communist Rebels." See also "Communist Party of the Philippines and the New People's Army," *Department of State Dispatch*, 11 November 1991, Lexis-Nexis.

74. Jose Gerado A. Alampay, "Revisiting Environmental Security in the Philippines," *Journal of Environment and Development* 5, no. 3 (September 1996): 332.

75. Quoted in Colin Nickerson, "A Rebellion on the Wane: Filipino Communists Show Tenacity but They Are Hurt by Cuttoff of Marxist Aid," *Boston Globe*, 13 June 1992, Lexis-Nexis. See also Rocamora, *Breaking Through*, p. 93; Teves, "Twenty-Year-Old Philippine Rebel Movement Faces Some Tough Challenges"; Kathleen Callo, "Founder of Philippine Rebel Army Says Movement Falling Apart," *Reuters Library Report*, 3 August 1989, Lexis-Nexis; Filman, "Decades of Insurgency"; and Kessler, *Rebellion and Repression*, pp. 97–99.

76. McBeth, "Reds Down But Not Out," p. 44; and "Communist Party of the Philippines and the New People's Army," *Department of State Dispatch*, 11 November 1991, Lexis-Nexis.

77. Norman Miller and Rodger Yeager, *Kenya: The Quest for Prosperity*, 2nd ed. (Boulder, Colo.: Westview, 1994), p. 61.

78. Ibid., pp. 61, 72; and Vinston Burton and Roger Winsor, "Society, Culture, and the Kenyan Family," in *Kenya: the Land, the People, the Nation*, ed. Mario Azevedo (Durham, N.C.: Carolina Academic Press, 1993), pp. 5–34.

79. The Luhya (or Abaluhya) actually consists of sixteen ethnic groups, which include Bukusu, Dakho, Kabras, Khayo, Kisa, Marachi, Margoli, Marama, Nyala, Nyole, Samia, Tachoni, Tiriki, Tsotso, and Wanga. The umbrella term "Luhya" was a creation of the colonial period (Nowrojee, *Divide and Rule*, p. 5 n. 1).

80. "Kalenjin" is actually an umbrella term for a group consisting of several distinct Nilotic ethnic groups sharing a number of linguistic and cultural commonalties. Kalenjin groups include the Dorodo, Elgeyo, Keiyo, Kipsigis, Marakwet, Nandi, Pokot (or Suk), Sabaot, Sebei, Terik, and Tugen. In precolonial times the Kalenjin were largely pastoralists, and the various Kalenjin groups had few political links. The sense of common Kalenjin identity began during the colonial period when members of the community were officially referred to by the British colonial administration as Nandi-speaking or Mnandi. This common identity has been considerably strengthened in the postcolonial period. The term Kalenjin, which was first used in the late 1950s, means "I tell you" in all the Kalenjin languages (Nowrojee, *Divide and Rule*, p. 5 n. 2).

81. Miller and Yeager, *The Quest for Prosperity*, p. 72.

82. Africa Watch, *Taking Liberties*, p. 3; Cheryl Jackson Hall, "Racial and Ethnic Antagonism in Kenya," in *Modern Kenya: Social Issues and Perspectives*, ed. Mary Ann Watson (Lanham, Md.: University Press of America, 2000), pp. 275–301; Ndegwa, "Citizenship and Ethnicity," pp. 600–601; and Widner, *Rise of a Party-State*, pp. 23–24, 44–46.

83. Stephen N. Ndegwa, "Citizenship and Ethnicity: An Examination of Two Transition Moments in Kenyan Politics," *American Political Science Review* 91, no. 3 (September 1997): 609.

84. "A Report on Ethnic Violence," *Weekly Review* (Nairobi), 19 June 1992, p. 15.

85. Kenya Human Rights Commission (KHRC), *Kayas of Deprivation, Kayas of Blood* (Nairobi, Kenya: KHRC, 1997), p. 11.

86. Ibid., p. 12; and KHRC, *Kayas Revisited: A Post-Election Balance Sheet* (Nairobi, Kenya: KHRC, 1998), pp. iii–iv.

87. KHRC, *Kayas of Deprivation, Kayas of Blood*, pp. 17–18. See also Human Rights Watch, *Playing with Fire: Weapons Proliferation, Political Violence, and Human Rights in Kenya* (New York: Human Rights Watch, 2002), pp. 40–41.

88. NCCK, *The Cursed Arrow*, p. 7.

89. Ibid., p. 18. See also "Clashes: Priests Speak Out," *The Standard* (Nairobi), 20 March 1992, p. 3.

90. "Violence Shifts to Londiani," *Weekly Review* (Nairobi), 22 May 1992, p. 12. See also Alastair Matheson, "Kenyan Election Brings Only Violence," *Calgary Herald*, 27 November 1992, Westlaw.

91. NEMU, *Courting Disaster*, preamble, p. 2.

92. "Kenya: How Not to Seek Approval," *Economist*, 24 April 1993, p. 43.

93. Miller and Yeager, *The Quest for Prosperity*, p. 61.

94. "Situation Volatile in Some Parts," *Weekly Review* (Nairobi), 5 June 1992, pp. 21–22.

95. Holmquist and Ford, "Stalling Political Change," p. 177.

96. Ibid., p. 180; Joel D. Barkan, "Kenya after Moi," *Foreign Affairs* 83, no. 1 (January/February 2004): 93; Berkeley, "An Encore for Chaos?" p. 35; Jacqueline M. Klopp, "Electoral Despotism in Kenya: Land, Patronage and Resistance in the Multi-Party Context," Ph.D. diss., Department of Political Science, McGill University, Montreal, Canada, 2001, pp. 270–71; and Miller and Yeager, *The Quest for Prosperity*, pp. 78–79.

97. Frank Holmquist and Michael Ford, "Kenyan Politics: Toward a Second Transition?" *Africa Today* 45, no. 2 (April–June 1998): 242–45; and Widner, *Rise of a Party-State*, pp. 179–81.

98. David W. Throup and Charles Hornsby, *Multi-Party Politics in Kenya: The Kenyatta and Moi States and the Triumph of the System in the 1992 Elections* (Oxford: James Currey, 1998), p. 543.

99. Quoted in Berkeley, "An Encore for Chaos?" pp. 35–36.

100. Holmquist and Ford, "Stalling Political Change," p. 180.

101. Miller and Yeager, *The Quest for Prosperity*, p. 121. See also ibid, p. 62; and Berkeley, "An Encore for Chaos?" p. 36.

102. Berkeley, "An Encore for Chaos?" p. 36; and Widner, *Rise of a Party-State*, pp. 43, 181–82.

103. Throup and Hornsby, *Multi-Party Politics*, pp. 7–9.

104. Ibid., pp. 9–12.

105. Ibid., pp. 12–15.

106. As Miller and Yeager note: "In modern Kenya, wealth creates power, power generates wealth, and both are uncertainly grounded in the shifting sands of ethnic competition" (*The Quest for Prosperity*, p. 78). See also Widner, *Rise of a Party-State*, pp. 41–47.

107. Peter Gibbon, "Markets, Civil Society and Democracy in Kenya," in *Markets, Civil Society and Democracy in Kenya*, ed. Peter Gibbon (Sweden: Nordiska Afrikainstitutet, 1995), p. 10; Ingham, *Politics in Modern Africa*, pp. 105–6; and Throup and Hornsby, *Multi-Party Politics*, pp. 11–12, 19, 22–23.

108. Throup and Hornsby, *Multi-Party Politics*, p. 14.

109. Africa Watch, *Taking Liberties*, p. 25. For a detailed discussion of Moi's consolidation of power, see Throup and Hornsby, *Multi-Party Politics*, chap. 3.

110. Africa Watch, *Taking Liberties*, p. viii; Ingham, *Politics in Modern Africa*, pp. 111–12; and Miller and Yeager, *The Quest for Prosperity*, pp. 97, 105.

111. The attempted coup came as a response to several government policies: Moi's suppression of attempts to create a rival political party with a socialist platform; the 1982 constitutional amendment officially making Kenya a one-party state; the renewed resorting by the government to detention without trial; an agreement allowing the use of Kenyan air and naval bases for U.S. forces; and the onset of economic stagnation. For discussions of the coup attempt, see Ahluwalia, *Post-Colonialism and the Politics of Kenya*, pp. 138–45; Ingham, *Politics in Modern Africa*, p. 109; Miller and Yeager, *The Quest for Prosperity*, pp. 101–3; and Throup and Hornsby, *Multi-Party Politics*, pp. 31–32.

112. Prior to the Air Force coup attempt, rumors of another plot hatched by disgruntled Kikuyu politicians and officers were circulating in Nairobi; the majority of the Air Force coup plotters themselves had been Luo junior officers.

113. Throup and Hornsby, *Multi-Party Politics*, pp. 31–32.

114. Ibid., p. 17.

115. For a thorough discussion, see Ahluwalia, *Post-Colonialism and the Politics of Kenya*, chap. 7; and Widner, *Rise of a Party-State*, chaps. 5–6.

116. Africa Watch, *Taking Liberties*, pp. 12–14.

117. Ibid., pp. 15–17; and Widner, *Rise of a Party-State*, p.132.

118. Ingham, *Politics in Modern Africa*, pp. 110–11.

119. Widner, *Rise of a Party-State*, pp. 142–43.

120. Throup and Hornsby, *Multi-Party Politics*, p. 32.

121. Miller and Yeager, *The Quest for Prosperity*, pp. 104–5; and Widner, *Rise of a Party-State*, pp. 147–49.

122. Ndegwa, "Citizenship and Ethnicity," p. 609; and Widner, *Rise of a Party-State*, p. 165.

123. Widner, *Rise of a Party-State*, p. 162.

124. Throup and Hornsby, *Multi-Party Politics*, p. 40.

125. Ibid. pp. 38–45.

126. Ibid., p. 44.

127. Africa Watch, *Taking Liberties*, p. 21.

128. Quoted in ibid., pp. 17–18.

129. Herman O. Kiriama, "Fundamental Constitutional Changes in Kenya," in *The Political Economy of Transition: A Study of Issues and Social Movements in Kenya since 1945*, ed. Eric Masinde Aseka et al. (Nairobi, Kenya: Eight Publishers, 1999), p. 128.

130. Joel D. Barkan and Njuguna Ng'ethe, "Kenya Tries Again," *Journal of Democracy* 9, no. 2 (April 1998): 33; Klopp, "Electoral Despotism in Kenya," p. 121. In the short-term the 25 percent rule had precisely the effect Moi desired since he was the only presidential candidate to pass this threshold in the 1992 and 1997 multiparty elections. See Klopp, "Electoral Despotism in Kenya," p. 121; and Stephen N. Ndegwa, "Kenya: Third Time Lucky?" *Journal of Democracy* 14, no. 3 (July 2003): 147.

131. Kiriama, "Fundamental Constitutional Changes in Kenya," p. 128.

132. Holmquist and Ford, "Kenyan Politics," pp. 228–29.

133. Stephen N. Ndegwa, "The Incomplete Transition: The Constitutional and Electoral Context in Kenya," *Africa Today* 45, no. 2 (April–June 1998): 197.

134. Joel D. Barkan, "Toward a New Constitutional Framework in Kenya," *Africa Today* 45, no. 2 (April–June 1998): 216; and Ndegwa, "The Incomplete Transition," pp. 198–200.

135. Ndegwa, "The Incomplete Transition," pp. 200–201.

136. Ibid., p. 202.

137. Maina Kiai, "Commentary: A Last Chance for Peaceful Change in Kenya," *Africa Today* 45, no. 2 (April–June 1998): 186–87.

138. Barkan and Ng'ethe, "Kenya Tries Again," p. 35; Ndegwa, "The Incomplete Transition," pp. 207–8.

139. Barkan and Ng'ethe, "Kenya Tries Again," p. 35.

140. Kiai, "Commentary," p. 187.

141. Klopp, "Electoral Despotism in Kenya," p. 120.

142. Kiai, "Commentary," p. 186.

143. Ibid.; Barkan, "Toward a New Constitutional Framework," pp. 213–14; Barkan and Ng'ethe, "Kenya Tries Again," p. 33; Ndegwa, "The Incomplete Transition," pp. 201–2, 206; John Oucho, *Undercurrents of Ethnic Conflict in Kenya* (Leiden: Brill, 2002), pp. 67–69; and Akabarali Thobhani, "Political Developments during the 1990s," in Watson, *Modern Kenya*, pp. 10–11. For a thorough discussion of the rise and fall of the opposition during this period, see Throup and Hornsby, *Multi-Party Politics*, chap. 5.

144. Holmquist and Ford, "Kenyan Politics," pp. 234–35; Khadiagala, "Intractable Authoritarianism," p. 55; Miller and Yeager, *The Quest for Prosperity*, pp. 108–16; and Nowrojee, *Divide and Rule*, p. 1.

145. Barkan, "Toward a New Constitutional Framework," pp. 213, 223–24; and Barkan and Ng'ethe, "Kenya Tries Again," pp. 41–42.

146. Barkan, "Toward a New Constitutional Framework," p. 213.

147. Holmquist and Ford, "Stalling Political Change," p. 180

148. Jeffrey S. Steeves, "The Political Economy of Kenya: The 1997 Elections and Succession Politics," *Journal of Commonwealth and Comparative Politics* 37, no. 1 (March 1999), Lexis-Nexis; and Throup and Hornsby, *Multi-Party Politics*, pp. 533–35.

149. Throup and Hornsby, *Multi-Party Politics*, p. 554.

150. For a general discussion of the inability of victimized groups to influence the regime, see Throup and Hornsby, *Multi-Party Politics*, pp. 174–75, 190–92, 533–35.

151. Quoted in Miller and Yeager, *The Quest for Prosperity*, p. 111. See also "FORD/Govt. on Collision Course"; "It's FORD That Has Incited the Violence"; and "KANU Has Perpetuated Wanton Murder," all in *Weekly Review* (Nairobi), 29 May 1992, pp. 12–24.

152. Barkan, "Toward a New Constitutional Framework," p. 218.

153. In this scandal the Kenyan government paid the Goldenberg company perhaps as much as half a billion dollars in export compensation money for nonexistent exports. Several top Moi officials, including the vice president Saitoti and Moi's right-hand man Biwott, were allegedly involved.

154. Barkan, "Toward a New Constitutional Framework," p. 218; Barkan and Ng'ethe, "Kenya Tries Again," p. 37; Holmquist and Ford, "Kenyan Politics," pp. 231–32; and Throup and Hornsby, *Multi-Party Politics*, pp. 560–65.

155. Barkan and Ng'ethe, "Kenya Tries Again," p. 38. See also Barkan, "Toward a New Constitutional Framework," p. 219; and Thobhani, "Political Developments during the 1990s," p. 16.

156. Barkan, "Toward a New Constitutional Framework," pp. 219–20; Barkan and Ng'ethe, "Kenya Tries Again," p. 38; Holmquist and Ford, "Kenyan Politics," pp. 235–36; and Kiai, "Commentary," pp. 191–92. The quote is from Ndegwa, "The Incomplete Transition," p. 197.

157. Barkan, "Toward a New Constitutional Framework," p. 222; Barkan and Ng'ethe, "Kenya Tries Again," pp. 39, 41, 45; and Steeves, "The Political Economy of Kenya."

158. Institute for Education in Democracy, *Enhancing the Electoral Process in Kenya: A Report on the Transition General Elections 2002*, 27 December 2002, p. 19.

159. For a discussion of the IPPG reforms, see Barkan, "Toward a New Constitutional Framework," pp. 220–21; Barkan and Ng'ethe, "Kenya Tries Again," pp. 38–39; and Ndegwa, "The Incomplete Transition," pp. 193, 202–5.

160. Holmquist and Ford, "Kenyan Politics," pp. 246–47; and Ndegwa, "The Incomplete Transition," p. 205

161. Ndegwa, "Third Time Lucky?" pp. 150–51.

162. Joram Abuodha, "Election Fever: How Do We Vote in This Vital Transition?" *Daily Nation* (Nairobi), 15 September 2002, Lexis-Nexis. It should be noted that Moi's regime sought unsuccessfully to bring Kikuyus into the KANU fold at several points after the return to multipartyism. In 1994–95 the regime made a number of secret and public efforts to reach out to members of the Kikuyu upper class. But popular unease among the Kikuyu in the aftermath of the Rift Valley clashes, coupled with anxiety among KANU moderates of the prominent role played by the hard-liners Biwott and Saitoti, led to an end to the dialogue. See Holmquist and Ford, "Kenyan Politics," p. 233; and Steeves, "The Political Economy of Kenya." Nevertheless, the regime continued to court Kikuyu support, with only limited results. In the run-up to the 1997 election, for example, the government resettled some of those

who had been internally displaced by earlier clashes, especially the Kikuyu in Nakuru District. In November 1997 about seven hundred Kikuyu families displaced from Chapakundi, Olenguruone, in 1992 were resettled in Kapsita in Elburgon; Moi personally handed out the title deeds to victims. This effort, however, was widely viewed for what it was: a cynical ploy to attract Kikuyu voters rather than a true reconciliation with clash victims. Indeed, in the 1997 election, not a single parliamentary seat in Kikuyu-dominated areas went to KANU. See Kenya Human Rights Commission (KHRC), *Killing the Vote: State Sponsored Violence and Flawed Elections in Kenya* (Nairobi, Kenya: KHRC, 1998), p. 32; and Steeves, "The Political Economy of Kenya."

163. Frank Holmquist, "Kenya's Postelection Euphoria—and Reality," *Current History* 102, no. 664 (May 2003): 201; Alex P. Kellogg, "Electoral Showdown in Kenya: The Campaign: Ruling Party Faces Serious Challenge," *Atlanta Journal and Constitution*, 25 December 2002, Lexis-Nexis; "No More Moi," *Daily Telegraph* (London), 26 December 2002, Lexis-Nexis; and Marc Lacey, "Kenyan Is Poised Today to End Founding Party's Rule," *New York Times*, 27 December 2002, Lexis-Nexis.

164. In 1997 Kenyatta lost badly when he ran for Parliament.

165. Abuodha, "Election Fever"; "Democracy Has Never Been a One-Stop Event," *East African Standard*, 3 October 2002, Lexis-Nexis; Holmquist, "Kenya's Postelection Euphoria—and Reality," p. 201; and Human Rights Watch, *Kenya's Unfinished Democracy: A Human Rights Agenda for the Government* (New York: Human Rights Watch, 2002), p. 6.

166. Joel D. Barkan, "Kenya after Moi," *Foreign Affairs* 83, no. 1 (January/ February 2004): 90–92; Holmquist, "Kenya's Postelection Euphoria—and Reality," p. 201; Institute for Education in Democracy, *Enhancing the Electoral Process in Kenya*, pp. 23–25; and "Democracy Usually Wins, Eventually," *Daily Nation* (Nairobi), 26 October 2002, Lexis-Nexis.

167. Ndegwa, "Third Time Lucky?" pp. 147–48.

168. Holmquist, "Kenya's Postelection Euphoria—and Reality," p. 201.

169. Ibid.; and Ndegwa, "Third Time Lucky?" pp. 152–53.

170. Katy Salmon, "Politics-Kenya: Outgoing President Moi Urges Peaceful Transition," *Inter Press Service*, March 12, 2002, Lexis-Nexis.

171. KHRC, *Kayas Revisited*, p. 3.

172. Holmquist, "Kenya's Postelection Euphoria—and Reality," p. 201.

173. "Democracy Begins to Dawn in Kenya," *Daily Nation* (Nairobi) Web site, reproduced by BBC Worldwide Monitoring, 28 December 2002, Lexis-Nexis.

174. There were a total of twenty-eight thousand international observers during the election.

175. Quoted in John Nyaga, "Kenyan Opposition Demolishes Ruling Party in Landmark Kenyan Polls," *Agence France Presse*, 29 December 2002, Lexis-Nexis.

176. Quoted in Marc Lacy, "Kenya's Ruling Party Is Defeated after 39 Years," *New York Times*, 30 December 2002, pp. A1, A6.

177. The same KHRC report that warned of risks of violence in the lead-up to 2002 concluded that "genuine democratization at all levels of Kenyan society . . . [was necessary to minimize] the *exploitability* of ethnicity, regionalism and violence-prone situations, in general, by groups and alliances of self-interested politicians" (*Kayas Revisited*, p. iv).

178. As Stephen Ndegwa writes: "With Kenya's long-time leader a lame duck, there was little reason for officials and politicians to indulge in mischief or chicanery on KANU's or Kenyatta's behalf. Instead, everyone wanted to keep open as many options as possible, and reposition effectively in the face of whatever new reality was about to be born" ("Third Time Lucky?" pp. 153–54).

179. "I'll Hand Over Power, President Reiterated," *East African Standard*, 13 December 2002, Lexis-Nexis; and "Quite a Unique Moment for Kenya, This Is," *Daily Nation* (Nairobi), 15 December 2002, Lexis-Nexis. See also Holmquist, "Kenya's Postelection Euphoria—and Reality," p. 202.

180. Barkan, "Kenya after Moi," p. 90; Institute for Education in Democracy, *Enhancing the Electoral Process in Kenya*, pp. 51–53; Ndegwa, "Third Time Lucky?" p. 154; Njonjo Kihuria, "Electoral Violence Kills Democracy," *East African Standard*, 23 November 2002, Lexis-Nexis; Declan Walsh, "Corruption Destroys Cult of Moi as Kenya Goes to the Polls," *The Independent*, 27 December 2002, Lexis-Nexis; "Observer Teams Give Poll Clean Bill of Health," *Daily Nation* (Nairobi), 30 December 2002, Lexis-Nexis; and "Kibaki Wasn't the Real Winner of Kenya Polls So Who Was," *The Monitor* (Uganda), 31 December 2002, Lexis-Nexis.

181. Institute for Education in Democracy, *Enhancing the Electoral Process in Kenya*, p. 32.

182. "Adhere to Electoral Code, Says Kivuitu," *East African Standard* (Nairobi), 21 March 2002, Lexis-Nexis. See also "Political Fighting Is As Old as the Nation," *East African Standard* (Nairobi), 22 April 2002, Lexis-Nexis. These concerns were echoed by other members of the ECK as well. See "Electoral Commission Boss Warns over Poll Violence," *East African Standard*, 15 October 2002, Lexis-Nexis.

183. Quoted in Emily Wax, "Kenya Sets Date to Elect Moi Successor," *Washington Post*, 30 October 2002, Lexis-Nexis. See also "Kenyan Police, Election Commission, Warn against Violence," *Agence France Presse*, 27 November 2002, Lexis-Nexis.

184. Institute for Education in Democracy, *Enhancing the Electoral Process in Kenya*, pp. 32, 52–53, 62–63.

185. "Violence Mars Party Nominations," *UN Integrated Regional Information Network*, 25 November 2002, Lexis-Nexis; Marc Lacey, "Panel Tries Hard to Keep Kenya Vote Aboveboard," *New York Times*, 23 December 2003, Lexis-Nexis; "No More Moi," *Daily Telegraph* (London), 26 December 2002, Lexis-Nexis; and "Denounce Violence, Uhuru Told," *East African Standard* (Nairobi), 13 September 2002, Lexis-Nexis.

186. "Electoral Body to Sue Kenya's Broadcasting Corporation," *Panafrican New Agency*, 11 September 2002, Lexis-Nexis; and Human Rights Watch, *Kenya's Unfinished Democracy*, p. 18. The pro-KANU bias of government-controlled radio and TV was also circumscribed in other ways in the months leading up to the 2002 elections. As a consequence of the IPPG reforms, additional private operators were able to obtain broadcast licenses, lessening the state's media monopoly. See Holmquist, "Kenya's Postelection Euphoria—and Reality," pp. 201–2.

187. Institute for Education in Democracy, *Enhancing the Electoral Process in Kenya*, pp. 32, 52–53.

188. Holmquist, "Kenya's Postelection Euphoria—and Reality," p. 202. See also Njonjo Kihuria, "Electoral Violence Kills Democracy," *East African Standard*, 23 November 2002, Lexis-Nexis.

189. Michela Wrong, "Growing Political Maturity Erodes Tribalism," *Financial Times* (London), 28 December 2002, Lexis-Nexis.

190. Marc Lacey, "Kenya's Democracy Prepares for an Important Test," *New York Times*, 5 December 2002, Lexis-Nexis.

191. Holmquist, "Kenya's Postelection Euphoria—and Reality," p. 200; Institute for Education in Democracy, *Enhancing the Electoral Process in Kenya*, pp. 104–7; Ndegwa, "Third Time Lucky?" p. 148. For detailed results, consult the official election Web site http://www.kenyaelections.com.

192. " 'That's the Way Democracy Goes,' Moi Declares of Opposition Election Lead," allAfrica.com, reproduced by *Africa News*, 28 December 2002, Lexis-Nexis.

193. "He Was Fun while He Lasted," *Australian Magazine*, 22 February 2003, Lexis-Nexis; and Holmquist, "Kenya's Postelection Euphoria—and Reality," pp. 200–201.

194. Marc Lacey, "Kenya Joyful as Moi Yields Power to New Leader," *New York Times*, 31 December 2002, p. A8.

195. Holmquist, "Kenya's Postelection Euphoria—and Reality," p. 204.

196. Quoted in Michela Wrong, "Growing Political Maturity Erodes Tribalism," *Financial Times* (London), 28 December 2002, Lexis-Nexis.

Chapter 6
Conclusions and Implications

1. George A. Collier (with Elizabeth Lowery Quaratiello), *Basta! Land and the Zapatista Rebellion in Chiapas*, rev. ed. (Oakland, Calif.: Food First, 1999), chap. 1.

2. Ibid., pp. 41–45; Neil Harvey, *The Chiapas Rebellion: The Struggle for Land and Democracy* (Durham, N.C.: Duke University Press, 1998), pp. 190–92; Philip Howard and Thomas F. Homer-Dixon. "Environmental Scarcity and Violent Conflict: The Case of Chiapas, Mexico," Occasional Paper, Project on Environment, Population, and Security (Washington, D.C.: University of Toronto, the Academy of Arts and Sciences, 1996), pp. 7–18; Peter Rosset and Shea Cunningham, "Understanding the Chiapas Revolt in Mexico," Third World Network, Penang, Malaysia, 1998 (available online at http://www.independence.net/home/chiapas.htm; accessed 8 January 2005; and Philip L. Russell, *The Chiapas Rebellion* (Austin, Tex.: Mexico Resource Center, 1995), pp. 7, 17.

3. Thomas F. Homer-Dixon, *Environment, Scarcity, and Violence* (Princeton, N.J.: Princeton University Press, 1999), pp. 145–47.

4. Howard and Homer-Dixon, "The Case of Chiapas," pp. 18–19. For a general discussion of the negative consequences of liberalization for peasants in Chiapas, see Harvey, *The Chiapas Rebellion*, chap. 7.

5. Howard and Homer-Dixon, "The Case of Chiapas," pp. 19–20; and Andrew Reding, "Rebellion in Mexico," *Washington Post*, 11 January 1994, p. A19.

6. Collier, *Basta! Land and the Zapatista Rebellion in Chiapas*, pp. 31–32.

7. Ibid., p. 46.

8. See Renner, *Fighting for Survival: Environmental Decline, Social Conflict, and the New Age of Insecurity* (New York: W.W. Norton, 1996), pp. 122–31. For an argument challenging the importance of population growth and land scarcity to the rebellion in Chiapas, see Aaron Bobrow-Strain, "Between a Ranch and a Hard Place: Violence, Scarcity, and Meaning in Chiapas, Mexico," in *Violent Environments*, ed. Nancy Lee Peluso and Michael Watts, pp. 155–85 (Ithaca, N.Y.: Cornell University Press, 2001).

9. Quoted in Collier, *Basta! Land and the Zapatista Rebellion in Chiapas*, p. 87.

10. Quoted in Rosset and Cunningham, "Understanding the Chiapas Revolt in Mexico."

11. Ioan M. Lewis, *Blood and Bone: The Call of Kinship in Somali Society* (Lawrenceville, N.J.: Red Sea Press, 1994), pp. 225–28; and Marc Michaelson, "Somalia: The Painful Road to Reconciliation," *Africa Today* 40, no. 2 (2nd Quarter,1993): 55.

12. Lewis, *Blood and Bone*, p. 231.

13. David D. Laitin, "Somalia: Civil War and International Intervention," in *Civil Wars, Insecurity, and Intervention*, ed. Barbara F. Walter and Jack Snyder (New York: Columbia University Press, 1999), pp. 147–48; and Michaelson, "Somalia," pp. 55–56.

14. See Lee V. Cassanelli, "Explaining the Somali Crisis," in *The Struggle for Land in Southern Somalia: The War behind the War*, ed. Catherin Besteman and Lee V. Cassanelli (London: HAAN, 2000), pp. 13–26; Friends of the Earth, *Africa's Greenwars: The Ecological Roots of the Crisis in Somalia* (Washington, D.C.: Friends of the Earth, 1993); and Library of Congress, "Somalia: Country Study," http://countrystudies.us/somalia/.

15. Friends of the Earth, *Africa's Greenwars*, p. 11.

16. David D. Laitin, "Somalia—Civil War and International Intervention," unpublished manuscript, University of Chicago, 1997, p. 5. Laitin ultimately concludes that this explanation is not wholly satisfactory because it is not generalizable across cases (pp. 5–6). See also Laitin, "Somalia: Civil War and International Intervention," pp. 150–51. If the dynamics outlined in this book have merit, however, the explanation is more generalizable than Laitin assumes. Furthermore, the notion that DES exacerbated insecurities and conflicts of interest between Somali clans is perfectly compatible with Laitin's general model, which emphasizes inter-clan competition in the wake of state collapse. See also Abdisala M. Issa Salwe, *The Collapse of the Somali State* (London: HAAN, 1996), pp. 100–101.

17. Cassanelli, "Explaining the Somali Crisis," pp. 15, 23, respectively.

18. Catherin Besteman and Lee V. Cassanelli, "Preface to the Paperpack Edition," in Besteman and Cassanelli, *The Struggle for Land in Southern Somalia*, pp. x–xi.

19. Harm J. de Blij, "Geographic Factors in Ethnic Conflict in Africa," in *The Challenge of Ethnic Conflict to National and International Order in the 1990s: Geographic Perspectives*, Conference Report, Central Intelligence Agency (Washington D.C.: Central Intelligence Agency, RTT 95–11039, October 1995), p. 76; and

Christian Webersik, "Reinterpreting Environmental Scarcity and Conflict: Evidence from Somalia," paper presented at the Fourth Pan-European International Relations Conference, Canterbury, UK, 8–10 September 2001, pp. 2–3.

20. David Newbury, "Understanding Genocide," *African Studies Review* 41, no. 1 (April 1998): 88–91; Leif Ohlsson, "Environment, Scarcity, and Conflict: A Study of Malthusian Concerns," Ph.D. diss., Department of Peace and Development Research, Göteborg University, Sweden, 1999, pp. 93–96; Valerie Percival and Thomas F. Homer-Dixon "Environmental Scarcity and Violent Conflict: The Case of Rwanda," Occasional Paper, Project on Environment, Population, and Security (Washington, D.C.: University of Toronto, the Academy of Arts and Sciences, 1995), pp. 2–3; and Renner, *Fighting for Survival*, pp. 114–22.

21. Bruce D. Jones, "Military Intervention in Rwanda's 'Two Wars': Partnership and Indifference," in Walter and Snyder, *Civil Wars, Insecurity, and Intervention*, pp. 118–20.

22. For excellent discussions of the Rwandan genocide, see Philip Gourevitch, *We Wish to Inform You That Tomorrow We Will Be Killed with Our Families: Stories From Rwanda* (New York: Picador, 1998); and Gérard Prunier, *The Rwanda Crisis: History of a Genocide* (New York: Columbia University Press, 1995).

23. Percival and Homer-Dixon, "The Case of Rwanda," pp. 6–7.

24. Ohlsson, "Environment, Scarcity, and Conflict," pp. 107–8.

25. Catherine André and Jean-Philippe Platteau, "Land Relations under Unbearable Stress: Rwanda Caught in the Malthusian Trap," *Journal of Economic Behavior and Organization* 34, no. 1 (1998): 38.

26. Newbury, "Understanding Genocide," pp. 91–92.

27. Prunier, *The Rwanda Crisis*, p. 4. See also Gareth Austin, "The Effects of Government Policy on the Ethnic Distribution of Income and Wealth in Rwanda: A Review of Published Sources," Consultancy Report for the World Bank, 1996, p. 142.

28. André and Platteau, "Land Relations under Unbearable Stress," pp. 29–41; Ohlsson, "Environment, Scarcity, and Conflict," pp. 99–108; Renner, *Fighting for Survival*, pp. 117–18; and Michael Renner, "Transforming Security," in *State of the World 1997*, ed. Lester Brown (New York: W. W. Norton, 1997), p. 124.

29. Percival and Homer-Dixon, "The Case of Rwanda," pp. 9–10.

30. See Ohlsson, "Environment, Scarcity, and Conflict," pp. 112–18.

31. André and Platteau, "Land Relations under Unbearable Stress," p. 38; and Newbury, "Understanding Genocide," p. 93.

32. Howard and Homer-Dixon, "The Case of Chiapas," p. 6; and Rosset and Cunningham, "Understanding the Chiapas Revolt in Mexico."

33. Quoted in Collier, *Basta! Land and the Zapatista Rebellion in Chiapas*, p. 64; see also pp. 63–70.

34. Lewis, *Blood and Bone*, pp. 224–25; and Michaelson, "Somalia," pp. 53–54.

35. World Resources Institute, *World Resources 1987* (New York: Basic Books, 1987), p. 248; and World Resources Institute, *World Resources 1996–1997* (New York: Oxford University Press, 1996), p. 191.

36. Jean Carriere, "The Crisis in Costa Rica: An Ecological Perspective," in *Environment and Development in Latin America*, ed. David Goodman and Michael Redclift (Manchester, UK: Manchester University Press, 1991), pp. 187–88; and Lori Ann Thrupp, "Political Ecology of Sustainable Rural Development: Dynamics of Social and Natural Resource Degradation," in *Food for the Future: Conditions and Contradictions of Sustainability*, ed. Patricia Allen (New York: Wiley, 1993), p. 61, Table 2.

37. Maria Concepcion Cruz et al., *Population Growth, Poverty, and Environmental Stress: Frontier Migration in the Philippines and Costa Rica* (Washington, D.C.: World Resources Institute, 1992), p. 49.

38. Carriere, "The Crisis in Costa Rica," p. 190.

39. On the causes of land degradation in Costa Rica, see Carriere, "The Crisis in Costa Rica"; Cruz et al., *Population Growth, Poverty, and Environmental Stress*, chap. 3; Susan Harrison, "Population Growth, Land Use, and Deforestation in Costa Rica, 1950–1984," *InterCiencia* 16, no. 2 (March/April 1991): 83–93; and Thrupp, "Political Ecology of Sustainable Rural Development."

40. Carriere, "The Crisis in Costa Rica," pp. 190–91; and Thrupp, "Political Ecology of Sustainable Rural Development," pp. 56–57.

41. Cruz et al., *Population Growth, Poverty, and Environmental Stress*, pp. 46, 49.

42. Ibid., p. 51.

43. See John A. Booth, *Costa Rica: Quest for Democracy* (Boulder, Colo.: Westview, 1998), pp. 28, 51–52; and Cruz et al., *Population Growth, Poverty, and Environmental Stress*, pp. 3, 5–6, 54–59.

44. Fabrice Edouard Lehoucq, "The Institutional Foundations of Democratic Cooperation in Costa Rica," *Journal of Latin American Studies* 28, no. 2 (May 1996): 333. See also Booth, *Costa Rica*, pp. 17–19, 28, 86–89.

45. Booth, *Costa Rica*, p. 83; see also pp. 95–98.

46. Lehoucq, "Institutional Foundations," pp. 332–33.

47. Gourevitch, *We Wish to Inform You*, chap. 4; Jones, "Military Intervention in Rwanda's 'Two Wars,' " pp. 122–23; and Newbury, "Understanding Genocide," pp. 83–88.

48. Jones, "Military Intervention in Rwanda's 'Two Wars,' " pp. 125–28.

49. See Reding, "Rebellion in Mexico."

50. Collier, *Basta! Land and the Zapatista Rebellion in Chiapas*, p. 39, chap. 6.

51. Reding, "Rebellion in Mexico," p. A19.

52. Quoted in Collier, *Basta! Land and the Zapatista Rebellion in Chiapas*, p. 81.

53. Quoted in ibid., p. 82.

54. Cassanelli, "Explaining the Somali Crisis," pp. 16–22; Lewis, *Blood and Bone*, p. 223; Michaelson, "Somalia," p. 55.

55. Laitin, "Somalia: Civil War and International Intervention," p. 147.

56. Booth, *Costa Rica*, p. 57; see also chap. 4; Lehoucq, "Institutional Foundations"; Bruce Wilson, *Costa Rica: Politics, Economics, and Democracy* (Boulder, Colo.: Lynne Rienner, 1998).

57. Booth, *Costa Rica*, pp. 24, 50, 115–21.

58. Ibid., p. 99.

59. Ibid., pp. 121–22.

60. Ibid., pp. 123–26; and Jack Snyder, *From Voting to Violence: Democratization and Nationalist Conflict* (New York: W.W. Norton, 2000), pp. 300–304.

61. "Mali: Africa Review 1998," *Africa Review World of Information*, March 1998, Lexis-Nexis; World Resources Institute, *World Resources 1987*, p. 248; Central Intelligence Agency, *The World Factbook: 2003* (available online at http://www.cia.gov/publications/factbook/geos/ml.html); World Resources Institute, *World Resources 1992–1993* (New York: Oxford University Press, 1992), p. 246; and World Resources Institute, *World Resources 1998–1999* (New York: Oxford University Press, 1998), p. 244.

62. Kalifa Keita, *Conflict and Conflict Resolution in the Sahel: The Tuareg Insurgency in Mali* (Carlisle, Pa. Strategic Studies Institute, U.S. Army War College, 1998), p. 5; "Mali: Africa Review 1998," *Africa Review World of Information*, March 1998, Lexis-Nexis; "Mali: Country Profile," *Africa Review World of Information*, 26 September 2002, Lexis-Nexis; "Achieving Sustainability," *Forum for Applied Research and Public Policy*, 22 December 1999, Lexis-Nexis; and Central Intelligence Agency, *The World Factbook: 2003*.

63. Keita, *Conflict and Conflict Resolution in the Sahel*, pp. 5–9.

64. Sophi Boukhari, "Mali: A Flickering Flame," *UNESCO Courier*, January 2000, p. 27; and Keita, *Conflict and Conflict Resolution in the Sahel*, pp. 4, 9–12, 26–27.

65. Keita, *Conflict and Conflict Resolution in the Sahel*, pp. 4, 12–16, 20.

66. See ibid., pp. 16–27; Boukhari, "Mali," pp. 26–28; Howard W. French, "In Africa's Harsh Climate, Fruits of Democracy," *New York Times*, 4 January 1998, Lexis-Nexis; James Rupert, "African Democracy, Country-Style," *Washington Post*, 30 March 1999, Lexis-Nexis; and Zeric Kay Smith, "Mali's Decade of Democracy," *Journal of Democracy* 12, no. 3 (July 2001): 73–79.

67. See Keita, *Conflict and Conflict Resolution in the Sahel*, pp. 20–23, 27–28.

68. "Mali: Review," *Africa Review World of Information*, 26 September 2002, Lexis-Nexis; Abdoulaye Gandema and Brahima Ouedraogo, "Mali-Population: No Place Like Away from Home," *Inter Press Service*, 6 September 1996, Lexis-Nexis; and Johanna Mcgeary and Marguerite Michaels, "Africa Rising," *Time*, 30 March 1998, Lexis-Nexis.

69. Keita, *Conflict and Conflict Resolution in the Sahel*, p. 6.

70. See "Mali: Country Profile"; Howard W. French, "In One Poor African Nation, Democracy Thrives," *New York Times*, 16 October 1996, p. A3; idem, "Mali's Slips Reflect Stumbling African Democracy," *New York Times*, 7 September 1997, Lexis-Nexis; Nora Boustany, "Pondering Mali's 'Fragile' Democracy," *Washington Post*, 28 November 1997, Lexis-Nexis; French, "In Africa's Harsh Climate, Fruits of Democracy," *New York Times*, 4 January 1998, Lexis-Nexis; and Rachel L. Swarns and Norimitsu Onishi, "Africa Creeps along Path to Democracy," *New York Times*, 2 June 2002, Lexis-Nexis.

71. Michael T. Klare, *Resource Wars: The New Landscape of International Conflict* (New York: Metropolitan Books, 2001), pp. 191, 199–202; and Michael Renner, *The Anatomy of Resource Wars*, Worldwatch Paper 162, October 2002, pp. 22–26.

72. Renner, *The Anatomy of Resource Wars*, pp. 26–31; and Michael L. Ross, "How Do Natural Resources Influence Civil War? Evidence from Thirteen Cases," *International Organization* 58, no. 1 (winter 2004): 53–54, 56–57, 59.

73. See Renner, *The Anatomy of Resource Wars*, p. 10; Mohamed Suliman, "Civil War in Sudan: The Impact of Ecological Degradation," Occasional Paper No. 4, Environment and Conflicts Project (Berne and Zurich, Switzerland: Swiss Peace Foundation and Center for Security Studies and Conflict Research, December 1992); and idem, "Civil War in the Sudan: From Ethnic to Ecological Conflict," *The Ecologist* 23, no. 3 (May/June 1993): 104–9.

74. See Volker Böge, "Bougainville: A 'Classical' Environmental Conflict?" Occasional Paper, No. 3, Environment and Conflicts Project (Berne and Zurich, Switzerland: Swiss Peace Foundation and Center for Security Studies and Conflict Research, October 1992); Klare, *Resource Wars*, pp. 195–98; and Renner, *The Anatomy of Resource Wars*, pp. 9, 44–45.

75. Renner, *The Anatomy of Resource Wars*, pp. 45–47; and Michael Watts, "Petro-Violence: Community, Extraction, and Political Ecology of a Mythic Commodity," in Peluso and Watts, *Violent Environments*, pp. 189–212.

76. The population figures are taken from World Resources Institute, *World Resources 1996–1997* (New York: Oxford University Press, 1996), pp. 190, 192. For a discussion of the war, see Paul Richards, "Rebellion in Liberia and Sierra Leone: A Crisis of Youth?" in *Conflict in Africa*, ed. Oliver Furley (London: Tauris, 1995), pp. 134–70.

77. Jeffrey D. Sachs and Andrew M. Warner, *Natural Resource Abundance and Economic Growth*, Development Discussion Paper No. 517a (Cambridge, Mass.: Harvard Institute for International Development, 1995); and idem, "Natural Resources and Economic Development: The Curse of Natural Resources," *European Economic Review* 45 (2001): 827–38.

78. See, for example, Renner, *The Anatomy of Resource Wars*, pp. 32–35, 45–47; and Watts, "Petro-Violence."

79. John Tierney, "A Popular Idea: Give Oil Money to the People Rather Than the Despots," *New York Times*, 10 September 2003, p. A9.

80. Philippe Le Billon, "The Political Ecology of War: Natural Resources and Armed Conflicts," *Political Geography* 20 (2001): 561–84.

81. United Nations Population Division (UNPD), *World Population Prospects: The 2002 Revision* (New York: UNPD, 2003).

82. Ibid., pp. vi–viii, 1–9.

83. Over the past fifty years total fertility rates in developing countries have fallen from 6 to 3 children per woman. Assuming continued increases in family planning and public health services, the UN now predicts that future fertility levels in the majority of developing countries will fall below 2.1 children per women (the level ensuring long-term replacement of the population) at some point in the twenty-first century. All told, by 2050 three-quarters of all developing countries are expected to achieve below-replacement fertility. See ibid., pp. v–viii, 2.

84. Ibid., p. vi.

85. Overall the population of the countries most affected is projected to be lower by 479 million by 2050 than it would be in the absence of HIV/AIDS. This number is greater than the 278 million HIV/AIDS deaths because it also includes the deficit of births brought on by the early deaths of women in their childbearing years and the negative effects of HIV on the fertility of women living with the disease. See ibid., p. 10.

86. Ibid., pp. 11–14.

87. Richard P. Cincotta et al., *The Security Demographic: Population and Civil Conflict after the Cold War* (Washington, D.C.: Population Action International, 2003), chap. 6.

88. World Bank, *World Development Report 2003: Sustainable Development in a Dynamic World* (Washington, D.C.: World Bank, 2003), p. 4.

89. UNPD, *World Urbanization Prospects: The 2001 Revision* (New York: UNPD, 2002), p. 13.

90. Intergovernmental Panel on Climate Change, *Climate Change 2001: Impacts, Adaptation, and Vulnerability* (New York: Cambridge University Press, 2001).

91. World Wildlife Fund (WWF), *Living Planet Report 2002* (Gland, Switzerland: WWF, 2002), p. 20. See also Mathis Wackernagel et al., "Tracking the Ecological Overshoot of the Human Economy," *Proceedings of the National Academy of Sciences* 99, no. 14 (2002): 9266–71.

92. WWF, *Living Planet Report 2002*, p. 20.

93. Freedom House, *Freedom in the World 2004: Gains for Freedom amid Terror and Uncertainty*, 2004, p. 2. Available online at http://freedomhouse.org/research/survey2004.htm).

94. Jack A. Goldstone et al., *State Failure Task Force Report: Phase III Findings* (McLean, Va.: Science Applications International Corporation, 30 September 2000), pp. 14–16.

95. See Snyder, *From Voting to Violence*.

96. Marc A. Levy, "Is the Environment a National Security Issue?" *International Security* 20, no. 2 (fall 1995): 58 (emphasis mine).

97. This last point is also made by Thomas F. Homer-Dixon, "Correspondence: Environment and Security," *International Security* 20, no. 3 (winter 1995/96): 191.

Index